Learning and Development Practice in the Workplace

Fourth Edition

Learning and Development Practice in the Workplace

Kathy Beevers
Andrew Rea
David Hayden

Fourth edition published in Great Britain and the United States in 2020 by Kogan Page Limited

2nd Floor, 45 Gee Street
London EC1V 3RS
United Kingdom
www.koganpage.com

122 W 27th St, 10th Floor
New York, NY 10001
USA

4737/23 Ansari Road
Daryaganj
New Delhi 110002
India

ISBNs

Hardback 978 1 78966 044 9
Paperback 978 0 7494 9841 2
Ebook 978 0 7494 9842 9

British Library Cataloguing-in-Publication Data

A CIP record for this book is available from the British Library.

Library of Congress Cataloging-in-Publication Data

Names: Beevers, Kathy, author. | Rea, Andrew, author. | Hayden, David (Learning and development consultant), author.
Title: Learning and development practice in the workplace / Kathy Beevers, Andrew Rea, David Hayden.
Description: Fourth edition. | London, United Kingdom ; New York, NY : Kogan Page Inc, 2019. | Includes bibliographical references and index.
Identifiers: LCCN 2019035056 (print) | LCCN 2019035057 (ebook) | ISBN 9780749498412 (paperback) | ISBN 9781789660449 (hardback) | ISBN 9780749498429 (ebook)
Subjects: LCSH: Employees–Training of. | Employee training personnel.
Classification: LCC HF5549.5.T7 B4156 2019 (print) | LCC HF5549.5.T7 (ebook) | DDC 658.3/124–dc23
LC record available at https://lccn.loc.gov/2019035056
LC ebook record available at https://lccn.loc.gov/2019035057

Typeset by Integra Software Services, Pondicherry
Print production managed by Jellyfish
Printed and bound in Great Britain by Ashford Colour Press Ltd.

CONTENTS

Downloadable resources available here:

www.koganpage.com/ldpw/4

LIST OF FIGURES AND TABLES

Figures

Tables

ACKNOWLEDGEMENTS

We owe a big thank you to:

Andrea Young, Suzanne Copley, Wendy Strohm, Jill Nother and Michelle Simpson-Crew of Busec Ltd, Julie Cook and Bianca Winter of Acacia Learning, Barrie Hunt (Artist) and the many other brilliant people who contributed their thoughts and ideas to this book.

How to use this book

Welcome to *Learning and Development Practice in the Workplace,* 4th edition. Whatever your aim in reading this book, we hope you will find it an enjoyable and worthwhile investment of your time.

About the book

You may be reading the book because you work in learning and development (L&D) and want some guidance, or you may just be preparing for an L&D role. You might well be working towards a CIPD qualification in L&D, or maybe the L&D Apprenticeship or any other qualification for L&D professionals.

Whatever your reason, our aim is to give you a thorough and practical guide to learning and development in the workplace, along with some key thinking, research and further references.

The book includes lots of input and explanation as well as examples to illustrate how people are applying the ideas discussed. We are all practitioners and absolutely passionate about L&D and want the book to include real experiences and 'lessons learned' from practising trainers. We have therefore called on colleagues, students and people who have contacted us in response to previous editions, to share their comments and case studies, and have used these to 'bring the text to life'.

We have also included many suggested activities and questions throughout the text, to encourage you to think around the ideas and case studies and relate them to your own context. Some of these questions are just for you to reflect on whilst we hope others will inspire further discussion with your peers, colleagues and tutors. At the end of each chapter we have added some further ideas for consolidating learning, as well as some references to further information.

The book is designed to support the CIPD learning and development qualifications, particularly at foundation and intermediate levels, but will generally support most L&D professional qualifications.

Terminology

The L&D profession, as we will discuss in Chapter 1, uses a range of different words and titles to represent similar things, and organisations often use L&D terminology in different ways. We are quite general about this in the book, and may, for example, use the terms 'L&D professionals', 'L&D practitioners' or simply 'trainers' interchangeably. Equally, we might use terms such as 'L&D', 'L&D activity', 'learning session' or 'the training' in the same way. And there are other examples. Our recommendation is not to worry about this – if the term we are using is ever crucial to the point we are making, we will specifically define it.

Structure and content

The book is composed of 10 chapters encompassing the key and contemporary activities of L&D.

The first chapter explores what is required of an L&D professional, and how to meet these requirements. We discuss different L&D roles and the essential processes involved in developing and maintaining our own capabilities ('sharpening the saw').

Chapter 2 focuses on organisations and business – and the importance of aligning our work with organisational objectives and strategy. We look at how organisations work, and how we as L&D professionals contribute to their success.

Chapters 3 and 4 begin the essential technical skills which underpin our profession; identifying learning needs and designing effective L&D activities.

Chapters 5 to 8 explore different approaches to delivery, with each chapter focusing on a particular approach. We start with Chapter 5 (Face-to-face training and facilitation) and move through Chapter 6 (Delivery: Using technology), Chapter 7 (Delivery: Coaching and mentoring), and Chapter 8 (Delivery: Social and collaborative learning).

Chapter 9 looks at the fascinating subject of 'learner engagement' and the insights from psychology and neuroscience that are informing our L&D strategies in this area.

Finally, Chapter 10 completes the circle with an emphasis on the absolute importance of evaluating the impact of L&D. As well as considering the reasons for this, we take a very practical look at how to do it.

Each of the 10 chapters follows the same broad structure:

- Chapter introduction.
- Main body of text, divided into appropriate sections, in which we explain why the subject of the chapter is important, discuss the models, theories and ideas that underpin it, and provide lots of practical advice on how to carry it out. These main body sections also contain the case studies and reflective activities to help contextualise and consolidate your learning.
- A What Next? section giving suggestions for further consolidation activities.
- A section providing References, an Explore Further section with follow-up reading material, and a Useful Resources section of online sources.

Where to start?

This depends on you. You may be a logical reader – are you reading this section now because you naturally started at the beginning? Or are you more of a dipper – you've had a look around, read a few of the things that struck you as interesting and now have happened to find this page? Or maybe you are a focused reader – there are certain things you need from this book, and you are reading this page to find out how to meet those needs?

There is no requirement for you to work through the book 'chapter by chapter'. Each chapter stands alone as material about a particular area and, whilst the chapters are presented in a logical sequence, they can be read separately or in any order you choose.

If you are working towards a qualification, you might decide to read only the chapters that relate to that. However, if you can find time to read the whole book, you will find lots of useful content to inform your wider L&D practice.

In short – use the book in whatever way suits you best. The book is written to assist you and your learning. We hope it will inform your practice, assist your continuing development and, most of all, add to your enjoyment of being an L&D professional.

Kathy, Andrew and David

Note for CIPD students and tutors

If you are a tutor who has adopted this book as your core text or a CIPD student who has purchased this text, you can access the accompanying online resources:

- www.cipd.co.uk/tss : for tutor resources that will assist with course design and delivery, including a lecturer's guide, lecture slides and case studies;
- www.cipd.co.uk/sss : for student resources including self-test questions, annotated weblinks and activities.

01 The L&D professional

Introduction

The Learning and Development (L&D) profession is a wonderful profession to belong to and this era of social change and rapid technological development is one of the most interesting and exciting times to be a part of it! As a career, L&D can offer constant variety, creativity, travel, the chance to meet lots of interesting people, the satisfaction of seeing the results of your work, recognition in many different forms and endless opportunities for learning. Of course, the profession is not without its challenges, frustrations and occasional upsets, but in our experience, trainers love their work!

This first chapter explores three essential aspects of being an L&D professional: understanding what is required of us; fulfilling (or exceeding) requirements; and constantly developing ourselves so that we can handle the challenges, seize the opportunities and embrace the new developments.

Key areas of content covered in this chapter are:

- different L&D roles and titles;
- understanding what is required of L&D professionals;
- the CIPD and CIPD Profession Map;
- fulfilling requirements – managing the work and working collaboratively;
- CPD and reflective practice;
- selecting and recording CPD activities.

> 'The fire in my belly I've got for learning and development first came about when I discovered it would give me the opportunity to do something I've always enjoyed doing and that is sharing with others. I believe that 'you are what you share' and helping people find the knowledge they seek to achieve their potential is what excites me most about this profession. Since becoming a learning professional, I have helped and supported people learn and develop around the world in places ranging from Mexico to South Africa, from Dominican Republic to Peterborough. I enjoy the challenges the role brings and the rewarding feeling that you get from knowing you have made a positive impact.'
>
> *Adam Harwood, L&D Manager*

The L&D profession

Learning and development is rarely a first career. Often, we spend a few years developing expertise in a technical area or operational role and then move gradually towards helping others to gain the same expertise. This creates a sort of natural selection, in that it is the people who have a natural talent for helping others learn who move gradually into formal L&D roles.

There was a time when being competent in a technical role and having an interest in helping others learn was enough for someone to be deemed capable to pass their skills and knowledge on to others, and they became 'the trainer', with no further obligation to develop their training skills. But this is no longer the case; learning and development has now become a sophisticated and recognised profession, with its own standards and body of professional knowledge.

As well as being knowledgeable about our 'subject areas', we L&D professionals are now expected to be 'business savvy' with a good understanding of our organisations, and to have strong L&D skills, such as identifying learning needs, designing activities, delivering and supporting learning and evaluating impact. We connect with the wider L&D community and build our credibility through experience, effective work and external accreditation.

L&D professionals also commit to continuing professional development (CPD). Having built a sound base of knowledge and become skilled professionals we remain relevant and expert by always looking ahead, experimenting with new approaches and updating and extending our capabilities.

L&D roles

Our profession includes an unusually wide spectrum of job titles and roles – and varying terminology. For example, you may work in training, L&D or maybe HRD (human resource development). You may be a facilitator, L&D adviser, trainer, L&D partner, training officer, learning consultant, organisation development consultant, learning curator, coach, workplace assessor, curriculum designer, instructor, digital learning designer, learning champion or any other title considered to encapsulate your role.

L&D may be a part of your role or the whole of it. You might be directly employed in the L&D function of the organisation you provide training for, or you might be employed by a private training provider, delivering training services to a range of different organisations. You might equally be an independent L&D professional offering your services directly to organisations or working through an agency or training association who arranges the work for you. In a smaller organisation you may well be 'the L&D function'.

This variety of roles does not seem to be settling down; on the contrary new L&D roles are appearing all the time. An article in *People Management* (Finch, 2019) asked a number of L&D experts what they considered to be the L&D roles of the future. Their responses included: performance engineer, data analyst, technology specialist, community manager, marketing and communications expert, virtual facilitator, digital content creator/curator, and head of human intelligence.

Understanding what is required of us

We would suggest that there are at least two sets of requirements which specify, or at least indicate, what you should be doing at work and how you should do it:

- *organisational specifications*: specific job or role descriptions and internal competence frameworks, key performance indicators (KPIs) and objectives, possibly customer or service level agreements (SLAs) relating to the specific services you provide;
- *professional specifications*: sector- or profession-based frameworks and specifications, professional standards and membership criteria.

Organisational specifications

Most people working for an organisation will have some form of job description which sets out the essential requirements of their role. This may be supplemented by further information, about the skills, knowledge and experience required (for example in a person specification) or an internal competence framework which details the abilities and behaviours required of different roles within the organisation.

Your key activities might, for example, include:

- liaising with the business;
- monitoring and identifying learning needs;
- designing learning activities and materials;
- curating digital information for learners to access;
- delivering and evaluating learning activities;
- designing or supporting online learning;
- providing one-to-one coaching;
- assessing and reviewing learning;
- supporting managers to develop their teams;
- advising on L&D opportunities and requirements;
- maintaining learning management systems (LMS);

- organising learning programmes and events;
- monitoring training expenditure and budgets;
- researching and reporting on new developments in L&D.

Along with an overall description of the requirements of your job, it is likely that you will have specific objectives to meet – individual performance objectives or KPIs which extend aspects of your work role into measurable activities. For example, you may be responsible for delivering a certain suite of programmes or completing specific projects or supporting a specific improvement in staff performance.

In some organisations and contexts, L&D services may be specified as agreements with particular customers or customer groups. Such agreements, whether referred to as 'contracts', 'customer charters' or 'service level agreements' (SLAs) can be made with customers who are external to the organisation or internal. If you work within an L&D team in an organisation, then it is likely that your customers will be internal, ie the people who work within or for that organisation.

 Activity 1.1

1. What is your job title? How well does it reflect your work role?
2. How do you know what is required of you at work?
3. Where and how is the information stated?
4. Who are your customers (or customer groups) and how do you know what their specific requirements are of you?

Professional specifications – CIPD

The Chartered Institute of Personnel and Development (CIPD)

CIPD is the professional body for HR and L&D professionals. Operating across several continents, it is now a worldwide community of over 150,000 members, with a stated purpose of 'championing better work and working lives'.

Towards achieving its purpose and supporting members, CIPD has developed a comprehensive specification of the knowledge, behaviours and values required in different HR/L&D roles. This is known as *The CIPD Profession Map* (CIPD, 2018), which can be found on the CIPD website (www.cipd.co.uk/profession-map). There have been a number of different versions of the CIPD Profession Map, with the current 2018 version having replaced the former 2013 version.

The CIPD Profession Map (2018)

The map is initially presented in a layered half-circle (similar to half of an onion) but with the layers circling around the centre as the user interacts with them (see Figure 1.1).

At the centre of the circle is the CIPD's core purpose: 'to champion better work and working lives'. The layer surrounding the core purpose belongs to the three sets

Figure 1.1 The CIPD 2018 Profession Map

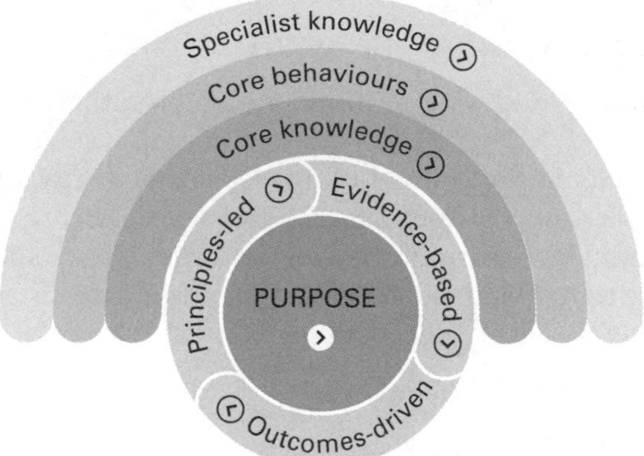

of values which CIPD believes underpin the people profession and which guide us to make better decisions. These three sets of values are:

- principles-led (seeing beyond the rules to do what's right by following three key principles: work matters, people matter, professionalism matters);
- evidence-based (adding weight to our professional judgement by supporting our case with strong evidence from diverse sources);
- outcomes-driven (championing better work and working lives by making a positive difference on every level – personal, professional and social).

The next layer in the map is 'core knowledge'. This layer divides into six segments or areas of knowledge that the CIPD believes all HR/L&D professionals need in order to be considered experts on people, work and change. The six areas of core knowledge are:

- people practice;
- culture and behaviour;
- business acumen;
- analytics and creating value;
- digital working;
- and change.

When accessing the map on the CIPD website, clicking on any of these areas takes the user into a more detailed breakdown of the knowledge within that area.

Next are the 'core behaviours' which CIPD says 'outline what it takes to be an effective people professional in our uncertain world of work'. They are:

- ethical practice;
- professional courage and influence;
- valuing people;
- working inclusively;
- passion for learning (obviously, our favourite);

- insights-focused;
- situational decision-making;
- and commercial drive.

Again, each behaviour can be viewed in more detail (on the website) by clicking on the relevant segment.

The outer layer contains the 'specialist knowledge': nine areas of specialist expertise within the people profession, of which learning and development is one. Each specialism has a high-level definition, which for L&D is 'ensuring workers have the knowledge, skills and experience to fulfil individual and organisational needs and ambitions'.

The specialist knowledge for L&D covers:

- continuing professional development;
- developing capability;
- adult learning theory and motivation;
- design and delivery of face-to-face learning;
- design and delivery of digital learning;
- content management, creation and curation;
- learning facilitation;
- social and collaborative learning;
- using coaching and mentoring;
- learner engagement, learning transfer and impact.

Within the detailed breakdown of L&D (or any of the other specialist knowledge sections) you will find the knowledge presented as 'standards', at four levels of impact. These reflect the typical knowledge expected at each level of CIPD membership, from Foundation through to the three professional levels: Associate, Chartered Member and Chartered Fellow.

You can use the map for many purposes, including:

- clarifying your own role and purpose;
- clarifying your professional and work requirements;
- benchmarking your knowledge, behaviours and values;
- planning your career;
- and identifying your professional development needs.

> 'The CIPD Profession Map (2018) is a great resource to work with. Aligned to the CIPD purpose, being principles-led, evidence-based and outcomes-driven leads L&D professionals to add value in a way that is right for the business or the climate in which they are operating. This is more about what is great L&D, what is "best-fit" rather than simply one size fits all in "best-practice". The shift with the 2018 updated map is that it doesn't tell you what to do, but looks at how you contribute and influence; about how our professional and personal values must underpin decision-making.'
>
> *Dr Frances McGregor, Senior Lecturer in Human Resource Management, University of Huddersfield*

Whilst we have explained the map in brief here, this is no substitute for you actually trying it out. The map is easily accessed from the CIPD website (www.cipd.co.uk) where there is more guidance about how to use it. As well as the general advice, there are guides, tools and downloads to help you understand and make best use of the map. The CIPD is also in the process of developing a range of supporting materials across each aspect of the map to further help members' professional development.

Case Example 1.1

Applying the CIPD Profession Map to reflective practice

Robert Labe, an experienced L&D Consultant, explains how he used the CIPD Profession Map to gain greater insights from his reflections on work performance and to enhance his CPD planning and recording.

Last year, instead of completing the usual CPD development record I mapped out my experiences and learning into key projects and work areas – eg training delivery, quality assurance, being a coach and mentor. Within each work area I reflected on what I had done and what the positives and negatives were of the experiences, what were the learning points, and what if anything I might do differently in the future.

I then linked my reflections to the components of the CIPD Map [2013 version] – the professional areas I had been working in, the bands I was working at, and the behaviours I had used, as well as the skills and knowledge I had used or acquired.

When I looked at my reflections on my work, in relation to the map, I recognised (and recorded) that I had used: knowledge of L&D practice, listening skills and questioning skills. In terms of my behaviours, I had demonstrated: being a role model, being personally credible and having the courage to challenge. The professional areas I had covered were: Learning and Development and Employee Engagement, and in this experience, I assessed that I was operating at Band 3.

Recognising my work in this way felt positive and confidence building and made me more aware of how I was performing. There were some other work projects that had not gone quite as well as they could, and exploring the map in relation to these helped me see how I could bring new skills and behaviours to similar work in future. The more I considered and plotted my reflections in this way, the more insights I was able to gain into how I had worked, what my key skills and behaviours are, and some areas I could usefully develop.

Robert Labe, FCIPD, HR/L&D Consultant

Case Example 1.2

Using the Profession Map to enhance understanding of the work

Rachel Mills, who works in the HR team at South Western Ambulance Service Trust (SWAST), and is a CIPD student, describes how the CIPD Profession Map (2018) helped her think more deeply about her work.

By personally conducting research using the CIPD's Profession Map, as well as my own experience and accessing other sources of information, I have been able to build my understanding of what it means to be an HR/L&D professional.

I explored a few different areas of the Map including two of the core behaviours: Valuing People and Professional Courage and Influence.

Valuing People re-enforced for me that HR/L&D always has a focus on the people in an organisation and an undertone of helping others, whether this be ensuring employees' health and well-being or ensuring that they have a voice, in order to keep the business honest and transparent.

Professional Courage and Influence is another behaviour I found particularly interesting. It can be hard to have the courage to communicate difficult messages to both managers and employees, particularly if they need different things from me. But HR/L&D has to deliver a fair and ethical service to all. Thinking about this I identified some useful material from the CIPD website about ethics and professionalism, including podcasts, articles and reports which I am working my way through.

Rachel Mills, SWAST

Other professional specifications

National Occupational Standards

Since the late 1980s there has been a movement in the UK and many other countries, to develop National Occupational Standards (NOS) which specify performance and knowledge requirements, across all occupations. Learning and Development NOS were the basis of National Vocational Qualifications (NVQs) in Learning and Development (no longer available in England and Wales, although SVQs remain available in Scotland) and still underpin various other L&D qualifications. The NOS standards relating to assessment and verification currently form the national units of assessment, sometimes referred to as the TAQA qualifications, for assessors, internal verifiers and external verifiers/quality assurers.

These include:

- Level 3
  - Award in Understanding the Principles and Practices of Assessment;
  - Award in Assessing Competence in the Work Environment;
  - Award in Assessing Vocationally Related Achievement.

- Level 4
  - Award in the Internal Quality Assurance of Assessment Processes and Practice;
  - Award in the External Quality assurance of Assessment processes and Practice.

The UK framework of learning and development, and other, national occupational standards can be accessed via a NOS database (https://www.ukstandards.org.uk).

Activity 1.2

1 Are you aware of other national frameworks of L&D standards?

2 If you are outside the UK, is there a national framework of L&D standards in your country?

UK FE and skills sector standards

Whilst CIPD tends to focus on L&D professionals within organisations, various government-led agencies – previously Lifelong Learning UK (LLUK), Institute for Learning (IFL), Learning and Skills Improvement Service (LSIS), Education and Training Foundation (ETF)) and currently the Society for Education and Training (SET) – have defined standards and acted as a professional body for *tutors, trainers and lecturers who work within the FE system.* The 'FE system' primarily refers to colleges and college staff, working in a further education setting, but also encompasses some trainers working within government-funded adult and work-based learning contexts. Consequently, the terms 'FE and skills' or 'FE and training' are also used, and there are some areas of overlap with the CIPD standards and qualifications.

In 2013, an updated suite of qualifications for FE system professionals was introduced, centred on three main qualifications:

- Level 3: Award in Education & Training;
- Level 4: Certificate in Education & Training;
- Level 5: Diploma in Education & Training.

Knowing our own requirements

Personal values

As well as knowing what others require of us, it is important to know what we require of ourselves – what is important to us and what are our personal values? Just as with the CIPD values, being clear about our own values can help us make better decisions and guide how we behave, both in work and life generally.

Table 1.1 Values

Recognition	Meeting people	Kindness
Equality	Animal welfare	Art
Risk-taking	Being creative	Self-development
Fairness	Environment	Sharing with others
Freedom	Fitness/Physical Challenge	Health
Wealth	Independence	Variety
Open-mindedness	Compassion	Professionalism
Honesty	Justice	Status

There are many exercises available for clarifying personal values, but if you are unsure of yours, you could try looking down the lists of words and phrases in Table 1.1 to see if any feel particularly relevant to you, and could form the basis of your own personal values.

Being professional

How do other people define 'being professional' or 'being a professional'? Here is what some experienced L&D professionals say:

DEFINING 'BEING PROFESSIONAL'

'You teach people who you are, by consistently showing up as trustworthy, respectful, truly knowing your business and seeking to understand theirs, and standing behind your work and your commitments to them'.

Karla Robertson, Executive NeuroCoach, Shifting Gears, New Jersey, USA

'An L&D professional works to elicit the very best of each individual's potential by applying their up-to-date skills and knowledge to deliver the highest standards of the industry'.

Helen Camilleri, Apprenticeships and Qualifications Manager

'Being professional means being able to stay at the top of your game by doing the following things well: 1) Recognise that we thrive by collaborating with others because aligned teams lead to more powerful business decisions; 2) Fostering a working environment where challenge and unlearning lead to continuous learning; 3) Have fun doing all of this'.

Adrian Nixon, Editor, Nixene Publishing Ltd, UK

'In the university context in which I work, and I'd argue, in any context, professionalism is about garnering information and evidence before making judgements, listening to and respecting others and honouring the commitment you make, both big and small, regardless of to whom you made them'.

Amanda Thompson, Head of Undergraduate Programmes, Nottingham Business School

Activity 1.3

1 Do you think of yourself as a 'professional trainer'?
2 Are any of the definitions above more meaningful to you than the others?
3 What does 'being a professional' or 'being professional' mean to you?

Fulfilling (and exceeding) requirements

Once we have a clear understanding of what is required, we can set about planning, managing and getting on with the work needed to meet our objectives.

Managing the work

Getting organised

Many of us find that keeping some form of simple 'to-do list' helps us to manage our handwritten workload most effectively. Some keep a separate to-do list for each work area (eg customer group or project or business area) whilst others prefer a single all-encompassing list. To-do lists might be daily or weekly, and those who particularly like to work with them recommend a 'master list', that everything goes onto, plus a specific daily or weekly list.

The term 'list' does not have to mean straightforward handwritten linear lists – try mind maps or spreadsheets – and if you need inspiration, check out some of the wide range of 'to-do-list apps' or detailed 'planning and organising stationery' available (getting organised appears to be a very healthy industry!)

Beware becoming a 'list addict'. We know people who put items they have already completed onto their to-do list, just for the immediate joy of ticking them off! But do check your lists regularly and keep updating them so that you don't forget any essential tasks. If you maintain a good overview of your work and make regular checks on how you are doing, you will be able to make any adjustments needed – and take early action to resolve any emerging problems.

Prioritising tasks

However, organised we are, things around us tend to change, and getting all our work done for required deadlines can be difficult. We often have to prioritise our work, taking into account key work objectives and project timelines, and a useful tool to help with this is the Time Management Matrix, which was popularised by Stephen Covey, in *The Seven Habits of Highly Effective People* (Covey, 1992).

To use the matrix, you first need to classify your tasks in terms of how important they are and how urgent they are:

- An *important task* is one that helps you achieve your main objectives, or moves you forward in an important direction. It is probably something you want to spend time on and do particularly well.
- An *urgent task* is one that has to be done to meet a deadline. The nearer you get to the deadline, the more urgent the job becomes.

You can then 'plot' your tasks on the two scales of the matrix – and in so doing, position your tasks within four quadrants or categories, which are further explained below (see Figure 1.2). How you approach your different tasks is then guided by which quadrant they sit in.

Quadrant 1 – Important and urgent: These are your top priorities and should be done first. However you should try to avoid tasks moving into this quadrant by planning important work ahead.

Quadrant 2 – Important but not urgent: You should start working on these as soon as you can. Plan in advance how you will address them and start 'chipping away' at them whenever you have some time. Because they are important, they should not be left to the last minute, when you may have to compromise your standards. Try to keep making small contributions to these tasks before the deadline so that you avoid the pressure and compromises of them becoming urgent.

Quadrant 3 – Urgent but not important: You will have to do these tasks quickly because there is a deadline, but do not spend too much time on them. Get them out

Figure 1.2 Time management matrix

	Not urgent	Urgent
Important	**Quadrant 2** Important but not urgent	**Quadrant 1** Important and urgent
Not important	**Quadrant 4** Not important and not urgent	**Quadrant 3** Urgent but not important

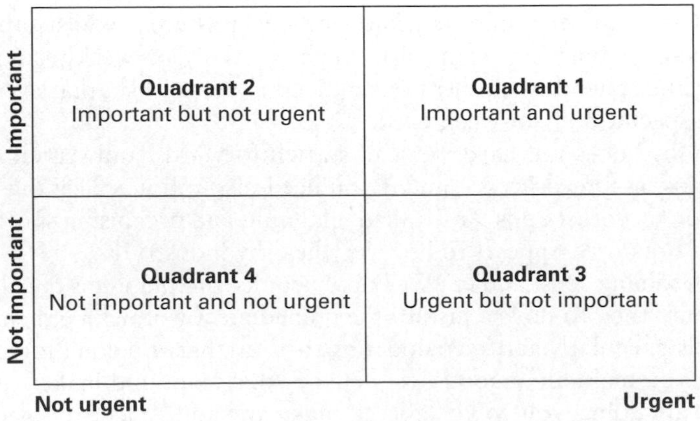

of your way quickly or if possible delegate them to someone who is capable and that you can trust.

Quadrant 4 – Neither important nor urgent: There are three ways to deal with these:

1 Do not do them at all if they are a waste of time.
2 Delegate them.
3 Forget about them until they are nearer to the deadline.

If you are managing your workload well, the majority of your time will be spent in Quadrant 2. If your time is taken up with Quadrant 1 activities then you are constantly fire-fighting and probably not achieving a great quality of work. If you are spending your time on Quadrant 3 and 4 tasks, then you may be neglecting important work for tasks that you find easier or more immediately interesting. If this is the case – it is probably a good time to review your priorities!

Improving organisation skills

If being organised is a weakness for you, the solution may partly be about learning new techniques, but is equally, and probably more, likely, to be about practice. Set yourself small improvement goals and take time to enjoy the feeling, or even reward yourself, when you meet them. You could also try working with a coach who will help you work out the best approach for you and identify the barriers you might need to overcome.

Collaborative working

One of the highlights of our profession is the amount of different people we often get to work with. This is a huge plus factor for most of us, but it also means we need to be able to build and maintain good positive working relationships. Good relationships make the work more enjoyable for everyone and make it easier to get our work done. They enable us to gain support or understanding from others when we need it most and can avoid or mitigate the adverse effects of any disagreements or problems. Poor working relationships, on the other hand, can be stressful, slow down the work, and make life a bit more difficult for everyone involved.

Being able to work effectively with others is an essential skill-set for L&D professionals, and this is captured in the CIPD Profession Map core behaviours Working Inclusively and Valuing People.

Activity 1.4

1 Tables 1.2 and 1.3 detail the standards expected for each of these two behaviours, presented at three levels of impact. Have a look at each standard below and 'self-assess', maybe out of 5, how your work behaviour matches the standards.
2 Which column best reflects the behaviour you demonstrate at work?
3 Do any of the standards generate ideas for your CPD?

Table 1.2 CIPD Profession Map behaviour – working inclusively

Foundation	Associate Member	Chartered Member
Show sensitivity and respect to others	Get to know people as individuals so you can work together more effectively	Role-model and advocate the value of including others and embracing difference
Demonstrate openness to diverse views and opinions	Actively seek and listen to diverse views and opinions	Explore and interpret a diverse range of perspectives and views
Build positive working relationships with immediate colleagues	Build purposeful working relationships with and collaborate with wider colleagues	Build collaborative relationships across organisation boundaries, cultures and other disciplines
N/A	N/A	Facilitate connections and joint-working across teams, disciplines and functions
Share data and information to inform work in your area	Readily share your knowledge and expertise with others to solve problems	Proactively share knowledge, experience and expertise to co-create solutions across boundaries
Handle difficult situations calmly and contribute to finding a way forward	Support others to resolve conflict and build trust before issues escalate	Coach and enable others to resolve conflict and build trust within teams and functions

Table 1.3 CIPD Profession Map behaviour – valuing people

Foundation	Associate Member	Chartered Member
Understand the purpose of your work	Build a sense of team spirit and purpose	Communicate the meaning and purpose of work to motivate and inspire people
Empathise with others	Treat people fairly and considerately in your work	Demonstrate compassion, humanity and fairness in your approach
Support others to develop and be their best	Enable others to develop skills and capabilities to be their best at work	Enable managers and leaders to support others to be their best at work

(continued)

Table 1.3 (Continued)

Foundation	Associate Member	Chartered Member
Ask a range of people for their opinion and listen carefully to responses	Enable people to have a voice when designing and delivering solutions which impact them	Enable people to have a meaningful voice by involving them in decisions that impact them, and bring a people perspective to organisation decision-making
Consider the well-being of others	Take into account the well-being of others in the design and delivery of your work	Promote the business and people benefits of well-being and integrate into your work

Improving collaborative working skills

If you want to develop your skills in collaborative working, you could try some of the following.

1. Seeking feedback on your current skills and behaviours There are many ways to do this – from psychometric tests to simple feedback questionnaires to full 360° reviews.

Psychometric tests have been around for many years now and are essentially intended to help you to understand aspects of your personality, behaviour or way of interacting with other people. There are a wide range available, from simple free online tests to highly specialised analysis instruments with expensive operator licensing requirements. Psychometrics can be an interesting way of analysing and gaining insights into your behaviour, but they are not always upheld by science – even some that may claim they are. We would always recommend that you do your research first to establish the validity of any test you undertake – and that you always consider any findings to be insights and ideas, rather than comprehensive judgements on you or your personality. Chapter 9 (Engaging learners) discusses in more depth some of the pros and cons of using analysis instruments.

A more meaningful way to gain feedback might be to ask a few people you trust for their impressions of particular aspects of your behaviour – or to ask a manager to include some specific areas in any performance review activities. If you are asking people for feedback, think carefully about this first and be clear about why you are asking, what you are asking, and how you will feel about, and deal with, any negative responses. Later chapters on Identifying L&D needs (Chapter 3) and Evaluating impact (Chapter 10) explore factors to consider when collecting different kinds of feedback and you might find it useful to refer to these.

Case Example 1.3

Making a small change after receiving feedback

As someone who is quite 'task focused' I recognised that my e-mails sometimes came over as a bit stern or unfriendly to recipients who are more 'people focused'. I tend to go straight into the main purpose of the communication, forgetting any of the 'opening words' that make an e-mail friendlier and more engaging for the reader.

Now, I still focus on writing the main purpose of the e-mail first (whilst it is clear in my thoughts), but before I send it I go back to the beginning and think about the recipient a bit more – and maybe add some more personal or sociable opening words. It doesn't take much – just a 'how are you doing' or 'I hope X project is going well' can make the e-mail more balanced and avoid it sounding too stern or impersonal.

Senior L&D Business Partner

2. Learning about human behaviour You could also read about and experiment with some of the research about human behaviour emerging from psychology and neuroscience. For example, David Rock's framework of human motivation, known as SCARF, is described by Rock as 'a brain-based model for collaborating with and influencing others' (Rock, 2009).

SCARF is based on two key concepts:

- Firstly, that human behaviour is essentially driven by two basic needs or desires, to *minimise threat* and to *maximise reward*. Rock points out how our natural response to threat, based on our basic survival need, is to cognitively label it as 'bad' and seek to avoid it (avoid response), whilst our natural response to something we perceive as reward is to label it as 'good' and seek to engage with it (approach response).
- Secondly, Rock explains that these responses can operate as much within a social context, where human beings interact and collaborate, as they would within a basic survival context. For the framework, he divides the social context into five 'domains of human social experience': Status, Certainty, Autonomy, Relatedness and Fairness (hence, S-C-A-R-F). Understanding how we might perceive threat and reward and react as a result, within each of these domains, can help us to both manage our own behaviour more effectively and understand a little more about how others behave.

SCARF may seem like a complex model at first, but with a little persistence you might find it helpful for managing your interactions with others.

Of course, there are lots of other approaches you could explore, such as assertive behaviour, emotional intelligence or positive intelligence – and many other useful writings on human behaviour. Ask people you trust and read book reviews to identify texts and resources that might be most helpful for you.

3. Going the 'extra mile' One approach that will always help build good working relationships is to 'go the extra mile' occasionally, such as:

- recognising when colleagues or managers are under pressure and doing something to help without being asked;
- collecting material and offering a quick update for someone who was unable to attend a meeting or event you attended;
- being courageous in telling someone when you think that what they are doing is not in their best interests or in the interests of their team;
- giving people your undivided attention sometimes, really listening to them, even though you are very busy.

> 'Twitter is a great way to connect with fellow practitioners and to share and tap into their knowledge. Many share blogs via Twitter and this is a fantastic source of CPD – and the forums on Twitter (such as @LnDConnect) allow for discussion around current and future professional practice. I also like how Twitter shows us to be more than just our job descriptions – you get to see those you are following as the "whole person", not just the L&D Practitioner!'
>
> *David Hayden, author*
> *@HaydenDavidhrd*

Continuing professional development (CPD)

Why?

As L&D professionals, our skills and knowledge are our tools and we have to keep these in tip-top condition. If we are not able to design, support and facilitate learning effectively, then how can we help others or contribute to our organisations? And how can we be confident that what we are doing is current and effective?

CPD is doubly important to us as L&D professionals, if we are to role-model the commitment to learning we expect from others. One of the best ways we can champion L&D is to show the benefits of learning through our own work and achievements. Learning and experimenting with new ideas makes our own work so much more interesting. And, of course, one of the key criteria for membership of any professional body or organisation is that we can evidence CPD.

> 'Organisations that develop the skills and knowledge of their L&D practitioners through planned continuing professional development see a significant positive impact on growth (21 per cent), productivity (12 per cent) and performance (15 per cent).'
>
> Professionalising Learning and Development,
> *CIPD/Towards Maturity, 2019*

Activity 1.5

1. What inspires you to learn?
2. What was the last learning activity you undertook?
3. How did this contribute to your abilities as an L&D practitioner?

Learning or CPD?

CPD is more than simply learning: it is the process of undertaking, reflecting on and applying learning within our professional role. It is about actively maintaining, updating and growing our knowledge and skills, *and applying these to our performance* – and is an ongoing commitment, for as long as we remain in our profession. Learning for the sake of learning – something that just interests us – is great, but it is not CPD unless we eventually do something with it, even if that is simply to 'think differently'. CPD means continually developing how we do things, as a result of our learning.

Figure 1.3 The training cycle

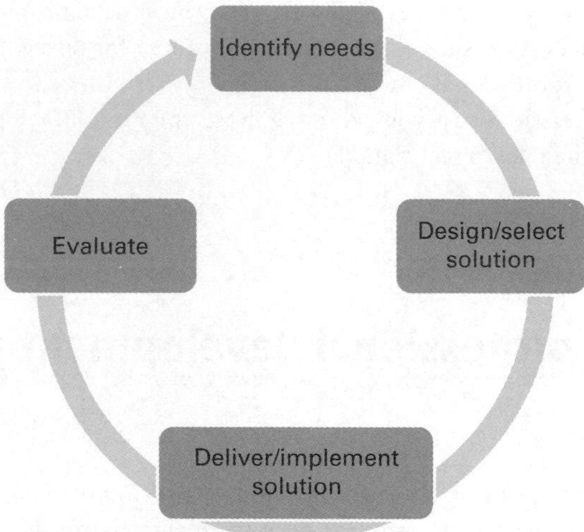

Figure 1.4 The Experiential Learning Cycle

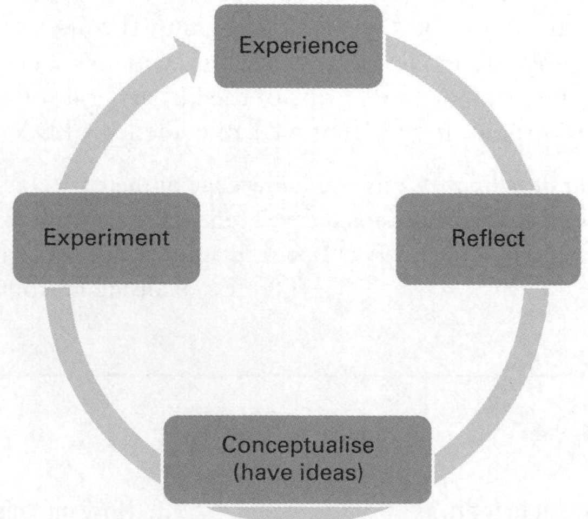

The concept of CPD reflects both the training cycle and David Kolb's Experiential Learning Cycle. It follows the training cycle in that we need to keep identifying our learning needs, selecting and undertaking learning to meet these, reviewing/evaluating the impact of our learning – and then starting all over again (Figure 1.3).

CPD also follows the Experiential Learning Cycle in that it requires us to reflect on our experiences, find new ideas and ways of doing things, experiment with our new ideas – and then again, reflect on our new experiences (Figure 1.4). (Chapters 4 and 9 of this book discuss the Experiential Learning Cycle in more detail.)

The benefits of continually developing ourselves, and our performance at work, are endless – not just for us but also for our learners, the organisations we work with, and the L&D team or function of which we are a part. Some of the potential benefits are shown in Table 1.4.

Table 1.4 Potential benefits of CPD

Benefits for you:	**Benefits for your learners:**
• improved skill-sets • increased confidence • improved professional status • improved career prospects • enhanced job variety and satisfaction • development is a transferable skill	• more creative and interesting L&D that employs new approaches and methods • better quality L&D services • up-to-date advice and information • greater confidence in the organisation • L&D provision
Benefits to your L&D function:	**Benefits to the organisation:**
• enhanced reputation • more likely to be seen as credible and reliable and to become a trusted partner in the business • more influence with key stakeholders • a more exciting learning environment • opportunities to learn from each other	• staff who are well trained using current and engaging approaches • more able to achieve evolving organisational goals • managers confident that staff skill levels are compliant and up to date • improved employee engagement • enhanced external reputation

Reflective practice

> 'It is so important that we take time to reflect upon learning, particularly from big L&D activities and conferences. How will things ever change if there isn't time to think? My advice is to block out specific time for reflection. Take some time out after an event to absorb, process and review what you've learned, or perhaps need to action to learn. Do what you need to do at work to get this time, build a business case, explain the benefits to management and what you'll do in return for this time. It will be time well spent.'
>
> *Blake Henegan, Optimus Sourcing Learning Solutions*

Reflective practice is much more than simply reflecting on a learning activity and deciding 'I enjoyed that and I learned some interesting things that might be useful'. It is also about the actions that come after the learning. It involves us in critically analysing our learning and the impact it might have on our ways of working and behaving, and determining the subsequent steps we will take to apply the learning. Reflective practice allows us to connect with our learning at a deep level and goes way beyond the learning event.

Karen Elliot from Bright Ideas HR shares her insights on CPD and how she has seen it evolve over the course of her experience and extensive research in this area:

> 'The world of continued professional development is changing. In days gone by, we would sit down at the start of the year with our CPD cycle to identify our development needs, often book on a course and afterwards reflect what we had learned and how we could apply it at work. Living in a VUCA (volatile, uncertain, complex and ambiguous) world and rapidly developing digital environment has changed the way we approach continued professional development, particularly with micro development. If we want to learn how to do something new, we are less likely to sit down and revise our CPD plan first; we simply google it. This, coupled with the shift towards experiential learning, means that more than ever, much of our development is learning in the flow of work. Within this context, the importance and value of reflection becomes increasingly central to professional development. Research shows that our ability to critically reflect on the value of learning and experiences can have a significantly positive impact on our professional practice. As we look to the future, the discipline of Reflective Practice is one which will become increasingly central to CPD in the people profession.'
>
> *Karen Elliot, Bright Ideas HR*

Selecting self-development activities

The fact that we are in this profession suggests that we are already enthusiastic learners and open to the many possibilities that exist for extending and developing our capabilities.There are a huge range of CPD options available. For example you could:

- create or join a Twitter, Facebook or LinkedIn group, where you can follow and contribute to debates or generate a new discussion by posing a question to the group;
- read books, articles or blogs (or write your own);
- job shadow someone in an area of work that interests you;
- attend a training session, seminar, conference or exhibition;
- experiment with new L&D technology – explore relevant new apps and software;
- pursue academic learning and qualifications;
- attend a real-time webinar or access some recorded ones;
- reflect on work events and discuss with someone who understands the work;

- find and contract with a coach or mentor;
- take part in a project, either at work or in a voluntary work context;
- set up or join an Action Learning Set with people in similar roles;
- attend networking events;
- find out what CPD means to other professions (for example, legal, medical, education or construction) and what lessons/ideas you can apply to your CPD.

In terms of *what* you choose to learn more about, there will be a number of factors influencing this, such as your job role, compliance or professional requirements, finance, availability and timescales. We also recommend that you consider some of the changes and developments currently 'shaking up' L&D.

The changing world of L&D

We are living and working in a rapidly changing world. It is amazing to think that the BBC's evening news bulletin on 18 April 1930 was actually that 'there is no news' and the 15-minute bulletin was filled with piano music instead. Can you imagine there being 'no news' today? Naturally, all the changes are impacting on our organisations and the people who work for them and in turn, the way we 'provide' L&D. Developments, particularly in technology, are changing the way people learn, and demanding new skill-sets from L&D practitioners. There are calls for L&D teams to develop more sophisticated digital skills, to be able to curate rather than create, work with organisational metrics and enhance their impact on organisation goals and targets. If we are to remain relevant and effective, we have to stay ahead.

A simple but effective way to assess how prepared we are for the changes around us is to undertake a personal PEST analysis, where PEST stands for political, economic, social and technological. These four categories can be used as filters to explore the specific changes that are happening in our world and impacting on our work. Our findings will then inform areas of professional development we may need to consider. (Chapter 2 includes an example of a completed PEST analysis.)

The 2019 research report, *The Transformation Journey* (Towards Maturity, 2019) compares the skills L&D practitioners believe to be a priority with the skills they actually have, and the resulting, very obvious skills gaps (see Figure 1.5).

The mapping provides a stark message to us all of the new skills we need to be developing, if we do not have them already. The asterisks show there is actually a decrease in some of these skills since they were previously reported, offering a challenge to L&D practitioners regarding how effectively we actually acquire new skills and apply them.

Activity 1.6

1. Try 'plotting' your own skills against the stated priorities. How do you match up?
2. Do you agree with the priority areas?
3. How does this research impact on your thoughts about your own CPD?

Figure 1.5 Infographic showing snapshot of L&D skills going into 2019

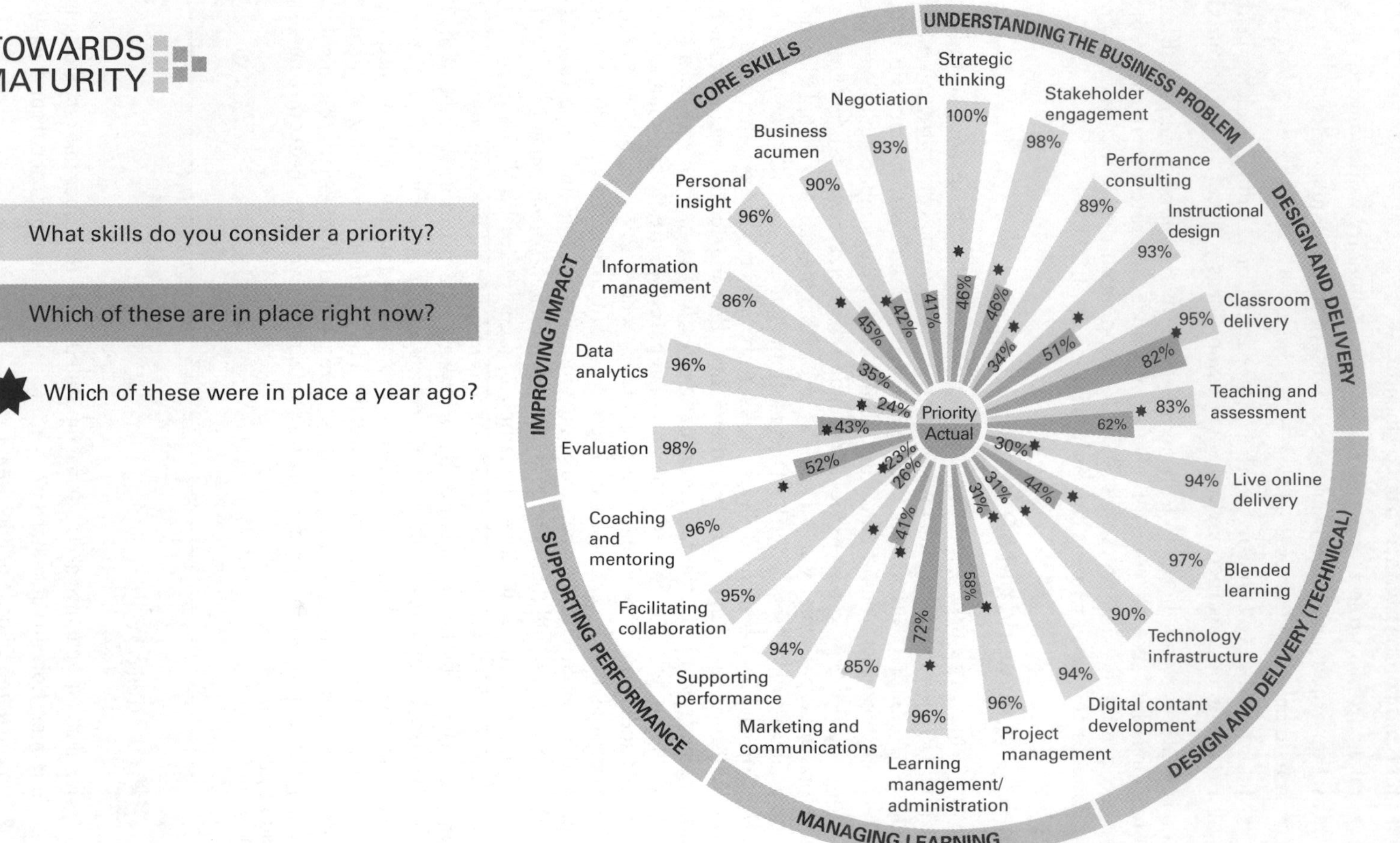

SOURCE: Reproduced with permission of Towards Maturity – towardsmaturity.org/TJ2019

Emerging neuroscience and technology

A huge amount of information is currently emerging from neuroscience which offers us all kinds of new insights, such as how gaming and augmented reality (AR) applications can enhance learning. We are also seeing the world of work change massively as artificial intelligence (AI) learns to perform tasks formerly performed by humans.

CIPD has been one of the organisations leading the way over the last few years, channelling this information for L&D professionals, and providing research reports, guidance material and related learning events (CIPD, 2014). Further chapters in this book also explore how neuroscience and technology are impacting on L&D, as these are key areas for L&D professionals to follow.

> 'Studying for a Masters in Digital Education online was, quite frankly, life-changing. We interacted using a variety of online mediums such as webinars, reflective blogs, live chats and even collaborating with others in Minecraft. All of this provided a rich learning experience that was shared with students from around the world and that we were in control of. I would definitely recommend it to others.'
>
> *Andy Jack, Digital Learning Consultant, Candle Digital*

Getting a good balance of activities

Along with the above considerations, and the many suggestions for CPD provided throughout this chapter, you might also take some of the following into account when planning your CPD.

Behaviours as well as skills and knowledge

We have discussed many behaviours in this chapter already. Along with the warnings that artificial intelligence will take over large percentages of our jobs are reassurances that the people who will be least affected will be those that have soft skills – these are the skills that are most difficult for robots to authentically adopt (Kai-Fu Lee, 2019). Soft skills and behaviours include the ability to think innovatively and offer creative solutions, the ability to empathise with others and respond appropriately, and the ability to inspire and influence other people. Developing yourself in these areas may add to your long-term professional value and employability as well as probably making you a nicer person to be around.

Specialist (technical) subjects as well as L&D skills

If you train in a particular subject area you will need to maintain your subject/technical abilities and knowledge, as well as developing your L&D skills. Make sure you are taking both into account in your CPD planning.

Short-term and long-term aspirations

Along with the learning you need to undertake for your current role, think about your longer-term career aspirations. Ask yourself questions such as: 'Where do I want to go in the profession?'; 'Do I want to be brilliant at the job I am doing, or do I want to gain a promotion to a head of L&D for a global company, or do I want to use the skills learned as an L&D practitioner in another role within the organisation?' It is important to think about your longer-term goals and ambitions, and the steps and sacrifices you are happy to make to reach your targets.

Different types of learning activities

If you tend to choose similar learning activities all the time, why not push your boundaries and try something new? For example, if you prefer online learning because it is easier to access, motivate yourself to attend a face-to-face networking event where you will meet new people and practise different skills. Or if you tend to rely on in-work learning sessions, register for some webinars as well so that your learning is two-fold, ie about the subject matter and an insight into how to lead webinars. If you usually get information from books or the Internet, try accessing Twitter and searching on a subject that interests you, instead. (Enter a one-word subject preceded by a hashtag (eg #neuroscience or #vuca) in the search bar to see recent tweets and their various attachments relating to that subject.)

Never forget the basics

Whilst exploring new areas is crucial, don't forget to keep honing your essential L&D skills. Learning about and enhancing your skills and knowledge in relation to identifying needs, designing learning, delivering learning, and evaluating and improving learning should always be part of your ongoing development. Take a different slant on them as well by learning about 'content curation' as well as 'content creation' or delivery skills in the context of a multigenerational workforce.

Planned and unplanned

Whilst formal development plans are important, don't ignore the opportunities that occur 'in the moment'. As organisations and their operating environments change and evolve, and new challenges appear every day, there are many sudden and powerful opportunities for personal and professional development. Whilst we are all for planning, we are equally for changing plans when good opportunities arise. Much of the learning in the 70 and 20 areas of Charles Jennings' 70:20:10 model of L&D is very much unplanned development. (More about this model in Chapter 9.)

Serious vs fun

Sometimes it does us good to do some light-hearted development that may appear to have little professional connection but could actually 'light a spark' of new thinking or creativity, or at least be a good stress reliever. Who knows what attending a magician-ship workshop, a science lecture or a stand-up comedy course could lead to – you won't know unless you try!

Activity 1.7

1 If you were suddenly given one month off all responsibilities and £3,000, which must be spent on your own development, what would you choose to do – and why?
2 What does this tell you about your passions and interests?
3 How might this development impact on your capability as an L&D practitioner?

Recording CPD

There are different ways of capturing and recording CPD, including: traditional CPD plans and reflective record formats; free-style text or personal blogs about our CPD activities; and digital platforms set up for us to store CPD information along with facilities to share and network with like-minded communities. The way you choose to manage and capture your CPD is a personal choice – experiment to find whatever system works best for you.

Traditional CPD plans and reflective CPD records

CPD records can be set up in word processing or spreadsheet applications, and if you don't want to design your own, you can access a number of templates on the CIPD website. Tables 1.5 and 1.6 give some examples of how you could structure your records.

Table 1.5 Example CPD plan layout

Outcome	What I want to achieve	How I will achieve it	Info/resources required	Review date

Table 1.6 Example CPD record (extract)

Key dates	What did you do and why?	What did you learn from this?	How have/will you use this? Any further action?
July	Researched adult learning theories – Reviewed CIPD's *Psychology and Neuroscience in Learning* and researched the 70:20:10 model. This to assist my knowledge and understanding of different adult learning techniques with a view to moving away from the more traditional four learning models.	I learned that the more traditional models – Active, Logical, Practical and Reflective – are more simplistic in nature (we cover these as part of our Induction course) and the move to link neuroscience with learning can lead to learners retaining more information based on different techniques including RAD, SCARF and AGES.	I will use this learning to enhance our current material. This will also prove useful when working with our management team as part of their ongoing learning and help me to understand how they can retain. Additionally, I will recommend to our Head of L&D that we start to incorporate the latest neuroscience theories into our material.
July	Completed a SWOT on myself based on how I approach work, what the downsides of my approach are and what opportunities exist. The purpose of this exercise was to understand what my strengths and development areas are in my current role – also to understand where my career will develop further.	In terms of strengths, I'm very methodical and process driven to deliver work – one of the key areas was to engage DMMs further to support their development as I'm still getting to grips with each department and their key KPIs so that I can best support them.	I will share this information with my line manager in our 121 – as it has enabled me to understand more about how I conduct my role and also what my weaknesses (development areas) are. In addition, what else I can learn to enhance my management training with those that I'm responsible for.
August	Created and launched a new Optimum Leadership Programme – The Art of Analysis – to replace current Report Writing. Researched alternative analysis models via Mindtools.com as part of my development with… [continued]	As part of the material creation, I utilised information from my CIPD course which has in turn enabled me to enhance our current analysis techniques. STEEPLE in particular has been very relevant when dealing with external challenges.	No further action – training session has been successfully launched. Will monitor effectiveness.

SOURCE: Provided by Tom Furber, L&D Executive at MarketMakers and student at Busec Ltd

Free-style text or blogs

Another option is to set aside regular time (every month, quarter or more frequently) to consider repeated questions such as:

- How have my skills and knowledge developed over the last three months?
- What have been the biggest contributors to my development and why?
- What do I want/need to do next?

As your writing/blogs build up you will have a very personal reflective record of your CPD. (Always remember that you may have to submit this to your employer or professional body.)

Digital platforms for managing CPD

Digital CPD tools are becoming an increasingly popular way of managing CPD. Free, or paid-for, software or apps such as Trello (which is free at low user levels) allow you to record your CPD online. Trello allows you to upload multimedia CPD materials, such as articles, notes, video or podcast links, for your own use and reflection and to share with a 'closed' group.

A main advantage of digital systems is that they get away from the regular 'logging' of your CPD activities, and give easy access to your CPD information. They also usually have other functions; for example, allowing easy networking and sharing with other people working in similar areas and with similar interests (thus vastly multiplying your access to resources).

Expert view on CPD

We posed some of our colleagues' questions to Karen Waite, who has developed and worked with online CPD systems.

1. Is there an easy way to record CPD or to get into the habit of recording CPD? I seem to leave it for ages and then can't remember everything.

There are a number of online portals and services that will assist you to capture and manage your CPD (try searching). Most work on the principle that your time is precious and if they can assist you with the mechanics of your plans and records and remind you about key events, this will give you more time to concentrate on your development and reflect on your learning. You could also use a smartphone to keep notes and voice messages and try out some of the CPD related apps and websites.

2. How do I decide which activities to record (there is so much learning happening all the time)?

Learning needs to be personalised and 'just in time, just enough and just for me'. The traditional way we think about and record CPD is changing significantly. CPD is so much more than attending a course or event. Learning includes making mistakes, getting feedback from our peers, social engagement and volunteering. The key is to be self-aware about your personal and professional development, reflect and record what is important to you.

3. I am so busy I never seem to have time for CPD – and I don't think my manager would want me to take much time off for this. Any tips?

Organisations are constantly looking for efficient ways to facilitate knowledge-sharing and speed up learning and we have seen significant growth in accessible online professional development. Content providers incorporate collaborative platforms such as discussion boards and wikis, which encourage interaction and optimize learning. Sharing and collaborating through online platforms and social media has created higher expectations, instant access, feedback and 24/7 availability. Be clear about your development plan and the reasons for your development so that you remain engaged and committed to your CPD.

Karen Waite, Founder and Director, Leap Like A Salmon

No matter how you choose to manage and record your CPD, remember that this in itself is a very valuable development activity. Defining your goals and planning how you will address them gives you a much greater chance of achieving them. Capturing or recording your development activities and reflecting on them consolidates and enhances the learning you get from them. Your CPD Record, whatever its format, is a symbol of your commitment to your own learning and something you can be very proud of.

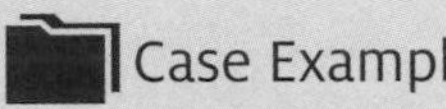

Case Example 1.4

Working in a busy L&D support role

I work within the Talent and Educational Development team of a university with around 1,400 staff in London and overseas. We are a subteam of the wider Human Resources team, and look after different areas of development: academic, online learning and professional development.

My key role is to manage all aspects of the administration, including: arranging the annual staff development programme (contracts, rooms, design); making sure our database and intranet site is updated; looking after the marketing and e-mail bulletins; and also the everyday details of making sure everything is ready to roll when the training commences and that everyone is happy whilst in training mode.

I also look after special projects, liaising with companies, colleagues, organising new initiatives and rolling them out for our staff members. As we have a large overseas staff base, we need to make sure everyone is being developed and has the relevant access, which can be tricky at times.

My average working day can be a walk in the park, or it can be hectic – which is the beauty of working in L&D. You or it do not sit still and no day is exactly the same. So, a day might consist of setting up a range of sessions, planning the upcoming week and also looking further ahead at sessions which need promoting. Also, looking back at evaluations and thinking what can be improved and transcribing that to the trainers. A quick cup of tea and a bite, then it could be meetings to discuss new processes and training which could enhance new systems within the School. Being one of the core support people, there is never a dull moment.

Working with different people, trainers and colleagues it sure has its perks and everyone has a different way to work, so it's dealing with all of that and also trying to check off items on my to-do list.

Working in Learning and Development is great; sometimes those that are in my position may not see the difference that they are actually making to the bigger picture, but good core support brings everything together, and enhances the true learning experience.

Yes, the trainer does a lot of hard work and that's where I am aiming to be, now that I have completed my CIPD qualification. But to those that are not there yet and are predominantly a support figure, I would say 'use this position to your advantage'. Not only are you exposed to trainers with vast amounts of experience, but also to learning materials and the knowledge needed to become a very good trainer – with options of face-to-face and online learning at your fingertips.

Hiren Vyas, Talent and Educational Development Coordinator (and former student at Acacia Learning)

Case study questions

1 What appeals to you most about Hiren's job?
2 What skills and behaviours would you say it involved?
3 What development areas/activities might be useful for Hiren?

 What next?

The activities below will help consolidate your knowledge from this chapter.

1 Have a look at the CIPD Profession Map at www.cipd.co.uk/learn/career/profession-map . Try looking at the specialist knowledge section for Learning and Development and review how it reflects your role and impact. You could also explore the related materials and resources.
2 Consider your CPD records (or set up new ones if you don't have any). Make sure that:
   - **a** you have a relevant development plan;
   - **b** it includes activities that inspire and excite you;
   - **c** you are putting your plan into action;
   - **d** you are reflecting on your learning;
   - **e** you are applying your learning to your performance;
   - **f** you are capturing your learning and how it is impacting on your performance.
3 Join our group. Share your answer to Activity 1.7 in this chapter on Twitter using the hashtag #LDPintheW and copy in the account @ LDPintheW.

References

CIPD (2014) *Neuroscience – Applying insight to L&D practice*, www.cipd.co.uk/knowledge/culture/behaviour/learning-report (archived at https://perma.cc/8XYT-JWKZ)

CIPD (2015) *Annual Survey Report – Learning & Development 2015*, www.cipd.co.uk/Images/learning-development_2015_tcm18-11298.pdf (archived at https://perma.cc/68J3-Z47J)

CIPD (2018) *Profession Map*, www.cipd.co.uk/learn/career/profession-map (archived at https://perma.cc/GV96-GEAT)

CIPD/Towards Maturity (2019) *Professionalising Learning and Development*, www.cipd.co.uk/knowledge/strategy/development/professionalising-learning-development-function (archived at https://perma.cc/3MWS-8ZMC)

Covey, SR (1994) *The Seven Habits of Highly Effective People: Powerful lessons in personal change*, Simon & Schuster, London

Finch, S (2019) The L&D Roles of The Future, *People Management*, March 2019 (pp 40–41)

Lee, K (2019) *AI Superpowers*, Houghton Mifflin Harcourt, Boston, MA

Rock, D (2009) *Your Brain at Work: Strategies for overcoming distraction, regaining focus, and working smarter all day long*, HarperBusiness, USA

Towards Maturity (2019) *The Transformation Journey – 2019 Annual Research Report*, https://towardsmaturity.org/2019/02/14/the-transformation-journey-2019-annual-research-report/?mc_cid=c18ffac425&mc_eid=4e32f5c66a (archived at https://perma.cc/3QRY-29HW)

Explore further

Dryden, W and Constantinou, D (2004) *Assertiveness Step By Step (Overcoming Problems)*, Sheldon Press, London

Goleman, D (1996) *Emotional Intelligence: Why it can matter more than IQ*, Bloomsbury Publishing PLC, London

Megginson, D and Whitaker, V (2007) *Continuing Professional Development*, 2nd edn, CIPD, London

Shaw, G (2014) *The Art of Business Communication: How to use pictures, charts and graphics to make your message stick*, Pearson, London

Useful resources

Websites

www.cipd.co.uk/profession-map
www.ukces.org.uk (archived at https://perma.cc/WZ8F-KD2A)
http://nos.ukces.org.uk (archived at https://perma.cc/464Z-Q35J)
www.towardsmaturity.org (archived at https://perma.cc/S7NQ-EZ3K)
www.alison.com (archived at https://perma.cc/7TRZ-8TJ5) [free online learning programmes]
www.joyandlife.wordpress.com (archived at https://perma.cc/FZ3B-U9FN) [blog by Gurrpriet Siingh]
www.cipd.co.uk/cpd (archived at https://perma.cc/AEJ6-7BXE)
www.cipd.co.uk/communities (archived at https://perma.cc/4MCM-ZHKF)
www.cipd.co.uk/podcasts (archived at https://perma.cc/6WDV-7CTL) [eg podcast 101 – CPD]
www.cipd.co.uk/news/blogs
www.linkedin.com/cipdmember
www.facebook.com/CIPDUK (archived at https://perma.cc/F44B-W3VK)

Twitter

@cipd.co.uk
@LnDConnect
@sahana2802 [Sahana Chattopadhyay, speaker and writer on coaching and facilitation]

02 The organisational context

Work is the next venue for human capital accumulation after school.

THE WORLD BANK, *WORLD DEVELOPMENT REPORT 2019: THE CHANGING NATURE OF WORK*

Introduction

In Chapter 1, we focused on the importance of managing our own development, as L&D professionals, so that we are effective in our work and can achieve our career and personal goals. From this chapter onwards the focus of the book shifts to how we can fulfil our professional purpose of *supporting other people's development*. However, before we explore the detail of this, ie identifying needs, designing activities, delivering L&D via various modes, supporting and engaging learners and evaluating activities, this chapter takes time to set the organisational and business context of L&D. This context differentiates us from other learning and education professionals and requires us to have a sound understanding of the organisations we work with and the impact we can (and must) have on their performance.

Key areas of content covered in this chapter are:

- why it is essential for L&D practitioners to understand organisations;
- different types and structures of organisations;
- factors which impact on organisations and how to analyse these;

- business strategy, goals and objectives;
- different ways L&D is arranged within organisations;
- how L&D contributes to the business and the achievement of organisational goals.

L&D, learners and the organisation

For some learning professionals, the overriding focus of their work is supporting the development of individual learners. This may be the case, for example, for lecturers and tutors, who operate within the further education system. However, for L&D professionals who are employed or contracted by an organisation for the purpose of supporting the development of the people who work for it, there should always be a double focus – the needs of the individual workers AND the needs of the organisation. Both areas are equally important and should be integrated in our design and provision of L&D.

The CIPD Profession Map (CIPD, 2018a) describes the purpose of the L&D specialist area as:

> 'Ensuring workers have the knowledge, skills and experience to fulfil individual and organisational needs and ambitions.'

If we base our L&D initiatives wholly on the stated requirements of individual learners, we may overlook business priorities and constraints and so, however successful initiatives might seem in terms of learner satisfaction, we may fail to address 'organisational needs and ambitions'.

Equally, if we provide L&D which doesn't encompass everyone and doesn't consider individual worker needs, contexts and preferences, we are unlikely to engage learners or 'fulfil individual needs and ambitions'. We are in a three-way partnership (see Figure 2.1), and if we are to be effective, we must understand our organisations and design L&D that meets individual needs and contexts, whilst being fully aligned to business strategy and goals.

Figure 2.1 A three-way partnership

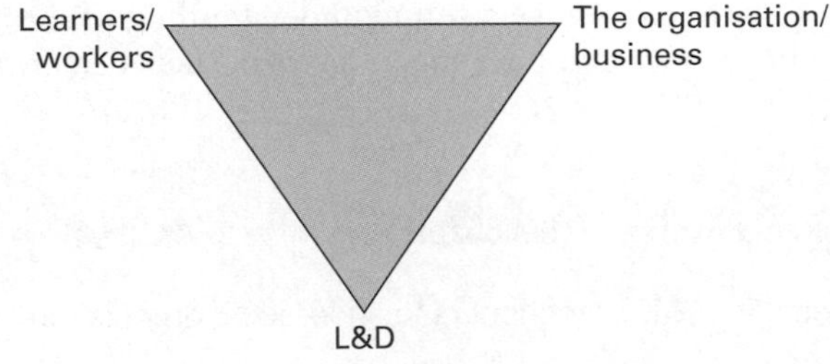

Most of the time there will be a natural overlap between the needs of individuals and the needs of the organisation but there may be different preferences and priorities, such as how learning is provided or the extent to which individual aspirations are accommodated.

When we began writing these textbooks, around 10 years ago, the idea of aligning L&D with 'the business' seemed like a relatively new concept. Promoting it was a main theme for us. We now find L&D professionals to be significantly more aware of their role in working with the business, and we have had several years of the 'business partner' model where L&D practitioners are paired with business areas and have a particular responsibility for the L&D requirements of that area. For many L&D professionals now, particularly those quite new to the profession, the idea of L&D activities not being aligned with business goals would just not make sense.

In the annual L&D *Global Sentiment Survey* respondents are asked to select three options reflecting what they think will be 'hot in L&D' for the coming year (Taylor, 2018). The surveys for 2016, 2017 and 2018 place the option 'consulting more deeply with the business' in overall 3rd, 5th and 4th place, respectively. In 2019 the option fell to 9th place but remained a hot topic, although the report does mention that very few respondents actually choose to put this option in first place.

The LinkedIn Learning's 2019 *Workplace Learning Report* identifies that L&D is working more closely with business than in 2018 and reports, for example, that '61 per cent of talent developers attend meetings with executives or senior partners to help them identify which are the most important skills to train for' (LinkedIn, 2019).

The CIPD report *Professionalising Learning and Development* highlights that 90 per cent of L&D practitioners consider business acumen to be a priority development area, reflecting L&D's recognition of the need for integration with the business (CIPD, 2019). However, it also states that 'only 42 per cent of practitioners think their teams (currently) possess sufficient business knowledge'. So, whilst we have made significant progress, it seems we still have some way to go in building and applying our understanding of organisations and their business.

This requirement for L&D professionals to understand organisations and how they operate is reinforced in the CIPD Profession Map (CIPD, 2018) Core Knowledge and Core Behaviour areas, which include:

- Business Acumen: understanding your organisation, the commercial context and the wider world of work.
- Culture and Behaviour: understanding people's behaviour and creating the right organisation culture.
- Commercial Drive: using a commercial mindset, demonstrating drive and enabling change to create value.

And so, in the next sections of this chapter we will step back from L&D to explore how organisations are established and how they operate.

Understanding organisations

DEFINING 'ORGANISATION'

The definition of an organisation provided by Oxforddictionaries.com is:

> 'An organised group of people with a particular purpose such as a business or government'.

And by Cambridge Dictionaries Online:

> 'A group of people who work together in an organised way for a shared purpose'.

The organisation as a system

One way to understand organisations is to view them as simple systems, with *inputs*, *transformation processes* and *outputs*:

Inputs: might be raw materials, money, labour, knowledge, information.

Processes: might be manufacturing, teaching, cooking, healing, caring, constructing.

Outputs: could be particular goods or services, profits, knowledge, waste products.

For example, the main elements of a food processing factory might be as in Table 2.1 and for a small training consultancy company, Table 2.2.

Table 2.1 Inputs→processes→outputs: food processing factory

Inputs	Processes	Outputs
Raw ingredients Labour Capital equipment Energy	Measuring Mixing Cooking Refrigeration Packing Selling	Chilled ready meals Profit Wages Waste products

Table 2.2 Inputs→processes→outputs: small training company

Inputs	Processes	Outputs
Information Labour/time Technology and equipment Money	Research Design Writing	L&D courses Articles/blogs Online learning materials

We can take this idea a stage further by looking at what happens around the organisation, whether this is local or global or anywhere in-between, and we can refer to this as the organisation's 'operating environment'. For example, we can consider an organisation's suppliers, advisers, financiers, investors, service or delivery partners, regulators, competitors and, perhaps most importantly of all, its customers (Figure 2.2).

Figure 2.2 The operating environment

Partners

Suppliers

Inputs	*Processes*	*Outputs*

Customers

Government Competitors

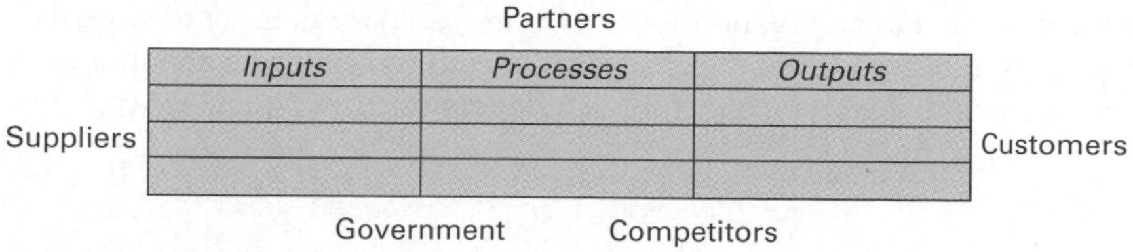

Activity 2.1

Consider the key inputs, processes and outputs of your own organisation, and the other 'players' in their operating environment.

Can you represent this as a basic systems diagram, as in Figure 2.2?

Why are organisations established?

Often, when we think about an organisation we think of a commercial enterprise, but there are many different types of organisations and different reasons for establishing them. For example, organisations may be established for a business, social, educational or religious purpose: to provide a particular service, to make a profit, to change society or any combination of these reasons.

Vision, mission, values and stories

Organisations typically express their purpose through various vision, mission and value statements, and increasingly, in 'about us' types of stories which explain their purpose and values. These company statements and explanations serve the organisation in a number of ways, including:

- creating the 'start point' for the organisation's strategic objectives;
- demonstrating organisational transparency and openness – 'who we are, what we do, what we stand for';
- positioning the organisation in the marketplace and emphasising its 'uniqueness' amongst the competition;
- enabling others to quickly understand the organisation and gauge how far it aligns with their own values;
- attracting and engaging customers and building brand loyalty;
- attracting and engaging staff who are likely to be aligned with the organisation's values.

Let us have a look at some examples of these statements.

Vision statements

The vision statement of an organisation is a future-based ideal, either of what the organisation intends to become or of the changes it intends to help bring about. It is intended to be motivational by painting a picture of a desired state for people to work towards.

VISION STATEMENT

An aspirational description of what an organisation would like to achieve or accomplish in the mid-term or long-term future. It is intended to serve as a clear guide for choosing current and future courses of action.

BusinessDictionary.com

Our Vision – CIPD

'We want to create a world of work that's more human. By changing hearts and minds about the purpose of work, the value of people and the role of people professionals, we'll help ensure that work creates value for everyone.'

Our Vision – Lightbulb Learning Ltd

'A world where farm animals are treated with compassion and respect.'

Mission/Purpose statements

The word 'mission' typically means purpose, vocation or intended task and so a mission statement is a formal written statement of an organisation's key purpose and aim.

MISSION STATEMENT

A written declaration of a firm's core purpose and focus which normally remains unchanged, whereas business strategy and practices may frequently be altered to adapt to changing circumstances.

BusinessDictionary.com

CIPD

'The CIPD's purpose is to champion better work and working lives by improving practices in people and organisation development for the benefit of individuals, the economy and society'.

Calderdale SmartMove

'To inspire local disadvantaged people on their journey to independence by providing housing support and education tailored to their specific needs.'

Value statements

Value statements are usually a declaration of the main principles which reflect the 'character' of the organisation and which underpin and guide the way it undertakes its activities. Here are two examples.

CIPD – our values

- Customer first.
- Collaborative.
- Expert.
- Impactful.
- Innovative

Lightbulb Learned Ltd – our core values

1. To deliver a high-quality customer-focused service.
2. To value and respect the rights and views of all stakeholders.
3. To ensure equal opportunities are key to all our activities.
4. To act with tolerance, integrity and consideration at all times.
5. To encourage innovation and creativity within the organisation.

Increasingly, organisations are finding more creative and appealing ways of expressing who they are and what they stand for. The straightforward statement of mission and values is being replaced or extended with stories and videos which say more about what the organisation believes and wants to achieve, and which are likely to have a greater engaging effect on potential customers.

Activity 2.2

Look at the vision/mission/value/'about us' statements of a couple of organisations you are aware of.

1. What do you think about the way they have chosen to present this information?
2. To what extent do you think these statements are reflected in the actual work of the organisations?

Different types of organisation

Along with purpose, there are several other factors which differentiate and define different organisations. For example:

- **Legal status:** in legal terms, organisations might be categorised as sole-traders, partnerships, cooperatives, limited companies or public limited companies (for more detailed information see www.companieshouse.gov.uk).

- **Financial factors**: organisations can be defined by how they are funded and how they use their funds. For example:
  - whether they sit within the public (government funded) or private sector;
  - whether they seek to make a profit or simply cover their operational costs (not-for-profit organisations);
  - whether profits raised are for shareholders or for all workers (cooperatives) or for social purposes (social enterprises);
  - whether workers are paid or not (voluntary organisations).
- **Organisation size**: organisations which employ fewer than 10 people are often referred to as 'micro', with those which employ 10–49 employees as 'small', 50–249 employees as 'medium' and over 249 as 'large'. The term 'small to medium enterprise' therefore relates to an organisation which employs between 10 and 249 employees.
- **Geographical reach**: larger organisations with bases in several countries may be referred to as multinationals or global organisations, depending on their spread. However, as smaller and virtual organisations extend their reach of operations across the globe these titles have become more blurred.
- **Sector:** of course, organisations can also be classified by the sector in which they sit, for example, construction or health and social care, and by the nature of their business, such as manufacturer, retailer, service provider, regulator, etc.

PAUSE FOR THOUGHT

Can you think of two different examples of organisations for each category above?

Organisation structure

Another key way in which organisations differ is in their structure.

Most organisations tend to be structured in some form of hierarchy (and are therefore referred to as having a hierarchical structure) with a CEO or senior management team at the top, and various layers of management and teams below, as in Figure 2.3.

The lower the number of layers of management, the flatter the organisation structure is said to be (Figure 2.4). Flatter structures are often considered to be more desirable as fewer levels of management can simplify lines of responsibility and decision-making, empower team members and give them more responsibility and significantly reduce the wage bill!

How the different areas or teams are arranged in an organisation can also differ, for example teams may be *functionally based* as in Figures 2.3 and 2.4, ie divided into functions such as sales, operations, customer service and so on.

However, a functional structure like this does not work for all organisations. Smaller organisations are unlikely to have the resources, or need, to operate highly separated functions and are more likely to have cross-over between functions and roles. Someone who is responsible for product sales, for example, may also

Figure 2.3 Example hierarchical structure

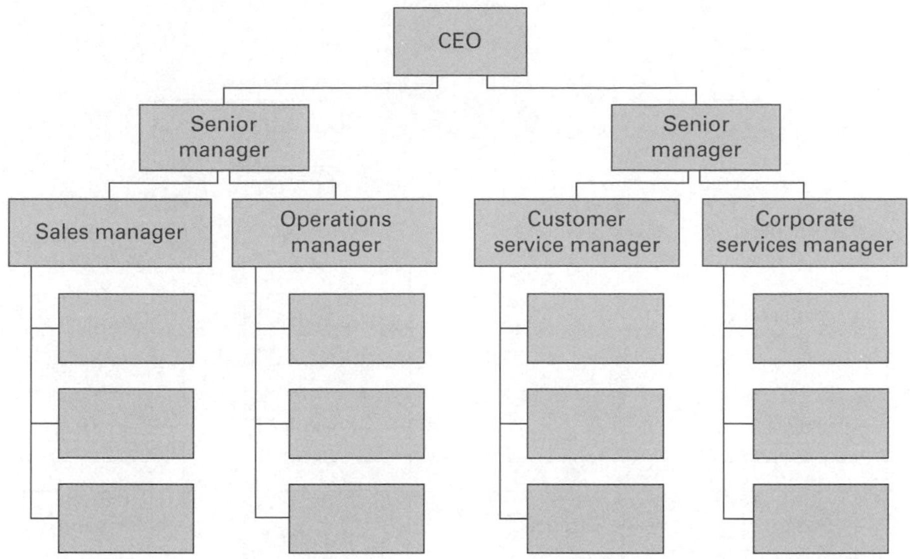

Figure 2.4 Example flatter hierarchical structure

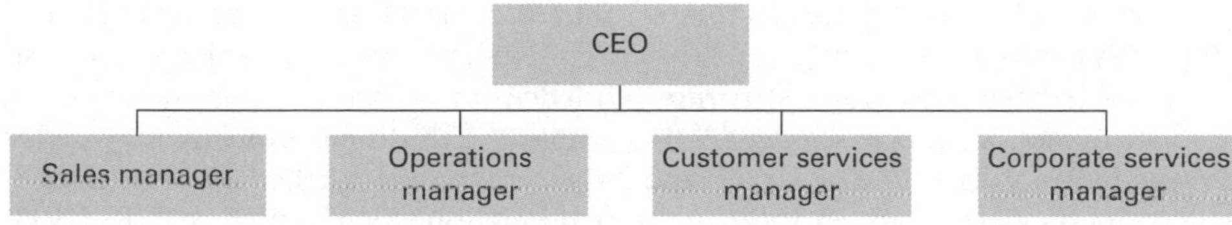

Figure 2.5 Example divisional structure

Figure 2.6 Example matrix structure

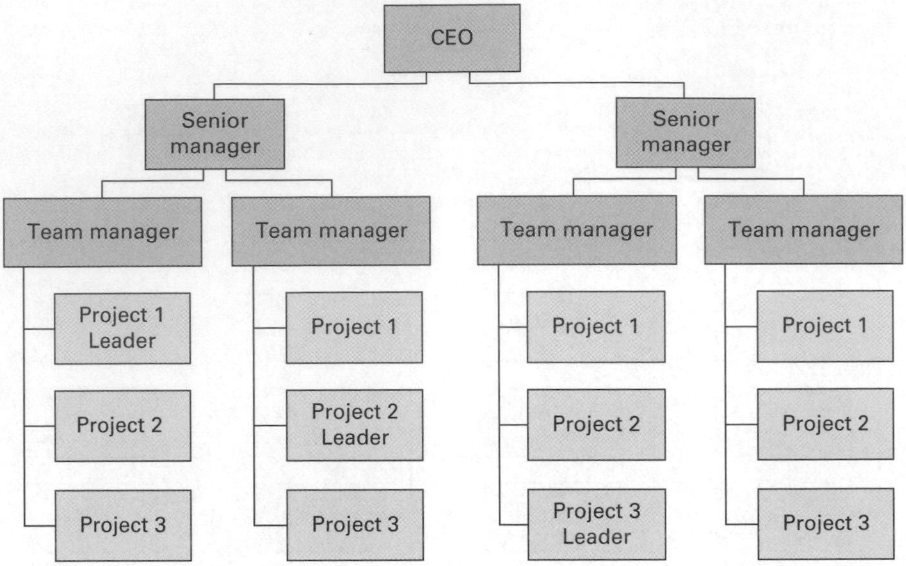

CEO

Senior manager | Senior manager

Team manager | Team manager | Team manager | Team manager

Project 1 Leader | Project 1 | Project 1 | Project 1

Project 2 | Project 2 Leader | Project 2 | Project 2

Project 3 | Project 3 | Project 3 Leader | Project 3

be responsible for the distribution of the goods they sell and the related ongoing customer service.

There are also good business reasons why organisations may be structured in other ways than a simple functional basis. For example, it might make better business sense to have a 'divisional structure', with divisions based on geographical areas, product ranges or market segment (for example, a publishing company may divide itself in terms of its 'schools market' and its 'general public market'), with each division containing aspects of each organisational function (such as finance, HR, L&D) so that it can operate semi-independently (Figure 2.5).

Over the last few decades, we have seen more organisations move towards a 'matrix structure', where teams are arranged (vertically) in functions, but also come together across the functions in (horizontal) project teams. So, a worker could be a team member in one team whilst also leading another team (Figure 2.6).

Charles Handy in *Understanding Organisations* (1985), developing Roger Harrison's work, shows how organisational structure is often closely tied in with organisational maturity and culture (Figure 2.7).

Activity 2.3

1 Thinking about any organisation you know, how would you describe its structure?

2 In what ways does its structure support the organisation's purpose?

3 How do you think the organisation's structure affects its culture – eg how people interact and work together in the organisation?

Figure 2.7 Organisational structure and culture (Charles Handy)

Power culture – a spider's web 	**Power culture** – frequently found in small owner managed organisations where there is a central figure, or figures, controlling the organisation. Handy pictures this culture as a spider's web, with the controlling figure (the spider) in the centre. Organisations with this culture are unlikely to have very formal roles and procedures and are shaped by the day-to-day choices of the central power. As these organisations get bigger and extend away from the power source there is a danger that they will start to 'break up' in the same way an overly large spider's web will also break up.
Role culture – a Greek temple 	**Role culture** – refers to a more formal organisational culture where the organisation is arranged in a rational and logical structure and employees have clearly defined roles and procedures. Handy pictures this structure as a Greek temple, with pillars (departments) and an overarching pediment or roof (head office). In a role culture, fulfilling the role is more important than showing special or extra initiative, which could be disruptive, and power comes from the particular role and position held. Such organisations are strong as long as their environment is stable but may be unable to adapt quickly to a changing environment, which could ultimately cause their downfall.
Task culture – a matrix or net 	**Task culture** – is job or project orientated and its accompanying structure is pictured as a net or matrix. In this culture, team structure is not entrenched but involves different people coming together, in different arrangements, to meet the requirements of different tasks and projects. Power and influence is more widely dispersed than in other cultures and employees generally have a high degree of control over their work. Handy describes task cultures as highly flexible and adaptable to the changing environment but less capable of producing economies of scale or great depths of expertise.
Person culture – a cluster 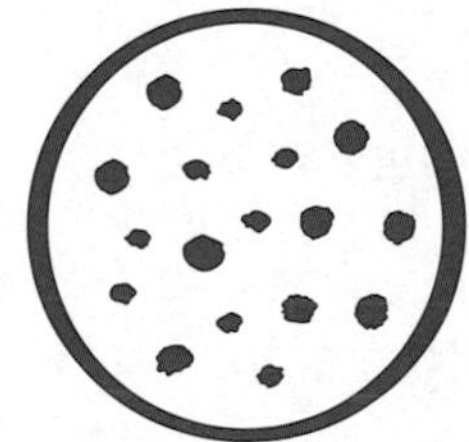	**Person culture** – Handy describes this culture as 'an unusual one' where the organisation exists to serve the individuals who work within it. Its structure, if there is a structure, is a 'cluster' or galaxy of stars. This type of organisation is most likely to exist where a number of individuals have decided to 'band together' in order to better fulfil their individual purpose, for example: an architect's partnership, a small consultancy firm or doctors in a group practice.

Business strategy and objectives

STRATEGY

A particular long-term plan for success.

Collins Concise Dictionary

Earlier in the chapter we discussed different purposes of organisations and their vison, mission and values. In order to achieve their purpose and mission, organisations need to take specific action in a specific direction. Business strategy is about determining these actions and direction. Whilst some organisations may declare an overarching strategy (eg to grow the business), detailed strategy is time-bound and determined in relation to particular circumstances.

The term 'strategy', originally a military term, is derived from the ancient Greek *strategos* and *strategia* meaning 'generalship' or the command of an army.

H Igor Ansoff is generally credited with bringing the term into the business arena in his book *Corporate Strategy* (Ansoff, 1965).

Organisational strategy can involve a whole range of projected activities, for example:

- developing new products and services;
- discontinuing certain products and services;
- developing or moving into new markets or client groups;
- implementing new technologies;
- changing supply chain arrangements;
- transforming of image or market position;
- changing ethical, environmental or customer relations approaches;
- changing financial or funding approaches;
- organisation restructuring, expansion or reduction;
- addressing specific current issues or failures;
- acquisitions, mergers and partnerships.

When broad strategic aims have been determined, these can be broken down into more specific strategic objectives, and ultimately much more detailed business plans. Many examples of strategy statements, strategic objectives and plans can be found on corporate websites.

Activity 2.4

Think about a specific national or global organisation you know through being a regular customer of that organisation.

1 In very general terms, what do you think the organisation's current strategic objectives might be?

2 Have a look at any corporate information on the organisation's website to see how close your ideas are to the reality.

Using analysis models

Strategy is about how an organisation will achieve its purpose – and to be successful, strategic plans have to take account of all the factors that might impact on activities. These might be internal or external. Internal factors might be: the organisation's stage of life cycle (a new organisation is likely to require different strategies to a more established one); organisational type, size or structure; the workforce; and, importantly, business performance. External factors might include: competitor activity; political context; technological, demographic and social trends; and legal changes. To survive and thrive, business leaders must be aware of their operating environment and how they will negotiate the challenges and maximise the opportunities around them.

There are a number of analysis models to help organisations with this, including PEST or PESTLE Analysis, SWOT Analysis, Mendelow's Matrix (Mendelow, 1991), Michael Porter's Five Forces Model (Porter, 2004), Igor Ansoff's Product–Market Matrix and Boston Consulting Group's Boston Matrix (BCG). We will consider the first three of these below.

PEST/PESTLE analysis

PESTLE is a popular framework for identifying factors which impact on an organisation and so help determine appropriate strategic directions. Originally known as PEST which stands for Political, Economic, Social and Technological, it has evolved to become PESTLE where L = Legal and E = Environmental or sometimes as PESTLEE or STEEPLE which adds an additional 'E' to cover the Ethical dimension (such as governance and levels of corruption). However, some feel that these areas are already covered in political, economic and social considerations.

Political factors to consider might include:

- election activity/potential changes of national or local government;
- current and predicted legislation at a national, regional and global level;
- regulatory bodies;
- pressure groups;

- funding policies;
- political unrest.

Economic factors might include:

- the economy (international, national and local);
- global trends;
- current and predicted inflation rates;
- current and predicted growth rates;
- labour supply and wage rates;
- income levels/disposable income/tax rates.

Social factors might include:

- demographics;
- labour supply/skills shortages;
- lifestyle trends and fashions;
- ethical issues;
- major events;
- religious and cultural influences.

Technological factors might include:

- information and communications systems;
- service delivery developments;
- competitor IT advantages;
- new and emerging technologies, such as artificial intelligence (AI);
- automation of labour processes;
- buying and lifestyle behaviour as impacted by technology.

Case Example 2.1

PEST analysis for Aristotle Education

Aristotle Education is a small but well-established provider of education and training, including CIPD and ACCA programmes. They deliver programmes in the UK, Singapore, Hong Kong and Dubai. Most of their learners are working professionals.

A PEST analysis undertaken by Brian O'Donoghue identified the following factors:

Political

- Some political unrest/instability around certain delivery sites creating risk to further expansion in those markets (do we invest in offices?).
- Government funding being made available to students in international markets to study professional programmes.
- Good support from the British government for overseas expansion.

Economic

- Increasing strength of local currencies.
- Rising levels of disposable income.
- Solid economic growth in foreign markets.
- Moderate levels of inflation across all markets.
- Favourable tax regimes in foreign markets.

Social

- Significant expat populations in some international delivery sites – already aware of the CIPD and ACCA brands.
- Increasingly positive attitudes to (and demand for) professional education.
- Changing working patterns require highly flexible programmes.
- Learners highlighting desire for social learning opportunities/sharing and learning from peers (ie group learning sessions) as well as online learning.

Technological

- High Internet and smartphone penetration in all markets enabling wider marketing of programmes – and reaching new markets.
- Availability of better quality online learning platforms (better programmes).
- Increased learner acceptance of (and demand for) online learning.
- Generally higher levels of IT skills enabling wider access of programmes.
- Need to manage staff capabilities in relation to technology developments.

It can often be particularly useful to undertake a PEST analysis before a SWOT analysis as the PEST analysis will bring out factors which can then be considered as potential threats or opportunities.

SWOT analysis

Another very popular and easy to use analysis model, SWOT stands for: Strengths, Weaknesses, Opportunities and Threats. Strengths and weaknesses are generally factors that are existing and *internal* to the organisation. Strengths are the things that an organisation is good at and which help it to achieve its goals. Weaknesses are the things that are less good and may get in the way of the organisation's success.

Opportunities and threats are generally factors that are *external* to the organisation and may not yet have come about. Opportunities are situations an organisation could take advantage of, which are likely to enhance organisational success. Threats are factors which may require action to avoid them, or to prepare for them, in order to limit any adverse impact on the business.

A SWOT analysis can be applied to the whole organisation or to a specific part of it, such as a department or business function.

Case Example 2.2

A SWOT analysis

The following is an example of a SWOT carried out by a small family-owned independent department store in a UK town centre:

Table 2.3 Example SWOT

Strengths	**Weaknesses**
Good local reputation. Loyal customers. Long-serving/well-trained staff. Only local supplier of key fashion brands. Excellent relationships with suppliers. Buyers and managers understand the customer base. Recently refurbished ground floor.	Limited product range. Lack of a 'budget range'. No online selling function. Poor range of menswear. Seen by non-customers as a store for 'older' women. Buyers not skilled at negotiating discounts with suppliers and tend to stick to familiar suppliers.
Opportunities	**Threats**
Pedestrianisation and regeneration of town centre. Potential to use ground floor for something new. Also space available to enhance café. Some shops in town centre closing down – could expand product range to fill gaps. Increased consumer interest in quality clothing. Some new fashion brands looking for in-store concessions.	Competition from out of town developments. Staff leaving to work at new out of town store. Disruption caused by pedestrianisation of town centre. Budget stores and supermarkets selling low price clothing and schoolwear. Competitors online shopping facilities. Town regeneration could attract new stores.

Case study question

From the information here, what might be the store's key strategic priorities?

Activity 2.5

Complete a PEST and a SWOT analysis for your organisation, or one you know well.

1. What factors are likely to have the biggest impact?
2. How can L&D contribute to these?

Stakeholder analysis

An organisational analysis would not be complete without a consideration of the organisation's stakeholders. Stakeholders, as the name indicates, are people who have some kind of interest in the organisation or business and how it is run. Sources disagree as to whether the name derives from the act of placing a stake in a particular area of land, particularly during the times of the gold-rush, or from the act of being the third-party holder of a betting stake until the outcome of the bet was known.

Stakeholders might, for example, be owners, directors, managers, staff, customers, suppliers, donors, neighbours or the local community. It is important for organisations to consider the needs and requirements of each stakeholder group when determining strategic objectives. These are likely to differ for the different groups. Whilst some may have a main focus on profits, others may be more interested in sustainability or environmental approach.

There are a number of useful models to help us analyse stakeholders and how we should respond to their requirements. One of the most widely used is Mendelow's Matrix, sometimes referred to as the Stakeholder Interest–Influence Grid (see Figures 2.8 and 2.9).

The first step in using the grid is to plot two key factors about each stakeholder or stakeholder group. These are: the amount of influence (eg power, financial leverage) they have in relation to the organisation; and the level or depth of the stakeholder's interest in the organisation (eg a shareholder's interest in an organisation may be greater than that of a particular customer group – of course this may be the reverse in a different context). These values are then plotted on the Influence and Interest axes, as in Figure 2.8.

In plotting the stakeholders against these two axes, they are loosely divided into four boxes, and the model gives an indication of how we should respond to stakeholders in each of the boxes (summarised in Figure 2.9).

Large organisations often use stakeholder analysis to manage how they interact with their stakeholders. The analysis informs sophisticated 'communication plans' which ensure that different groups receive the information they need, in a relevant and appropriate format, and remain fully engaged with the organisation.

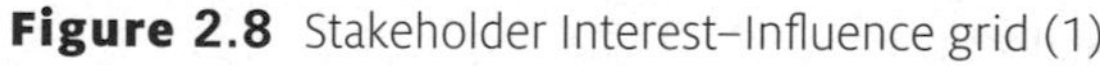

Figure 2.8 Stakeholder Interest–Influence grid (1)

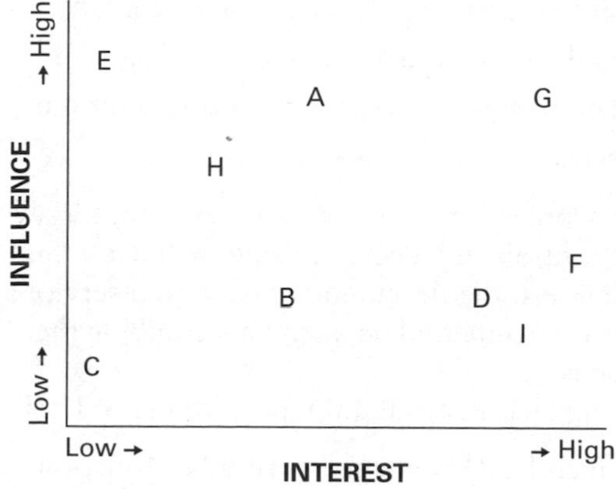

NOTE: Letters represent different stakeholders

Figure 2.9 Stakeholder Interest–Influence grid (2)

INFLUENCE	Low → Interest	→ High
→ High	Keep satisfied	Manage closely
Low →	Monitor (minimum effort)	Keep informed

Activity 2.6

1 Who are the stakeholders of your organisation (either the organisation where you work or the organisation where you study)?

2 How are they kept engaged in the organisation?

L&D's position within the organisation

Different arrangements of L&D

As with so many aspects of L&D, the way the function is arranged and positioned within an organisation varies enormously – and is dependent on several key factors:

- the size and structure of the organisation;
- the organisation's purpose, products and services;
- the organisational culture and attitude to learning;
- the learning technologies in use within the organisation;
- manager preferences.

There have also been prevailing, largely economic, trends which have influenced arrangements, either centralising, decentralising or outsourcing the L&D (and HR) function. We have also seen the development of shared service arrangements, where organisations such as governmental departments combine their L&D resources into a single centralised service.

Other differentiating factors around the positioning of L&D are:

- the extent to which L&D is merged with other functions, particularly HR or organisation development (OD);
- how L&D is structurally linked to, and aligned with, the business;

- the amount of direct contact L&D has with learners, as opposed to being curators of online learning resources;
- the balance between internal and external provision of L&D.

L&D and HR

In some organisations the L&D team is part of an integrated HR function whilst in others L&D stands alone as a separate function within the organisation. There are advantages and disadvantages of both positions (see Table 2.4).

Recent data is hard to come by on the actual positioning of HR & L&D (perhaps we are no longer as bothered by this debate?) but in the 2015 CIPD Annual L&D Survey the following metrics were presented (Figure 2.10).

L&D and the business

As discussed in the initial sections of this chapter, one of the biggest, and most welcome, changes we have seen in L&D over the last decade or so has been the greater integration and alignment of L&D with the business. Once relatively isolated functions which undertook aspects of people management not usually required of managers, L&D (and HR) have slowly moved closer to the business, and in many organisations at least, have become effective partners with business managers.

Table 2.4 Positioning of L&D and HR – advantages and disadvantages

L&D integrated with, or subteam of, central HR	Standalone L&D (positioned in the business)
Advantages 'Strength in numbers' – HR and L&D are a unified force on 'people issues'. Can offer a one-stop-shop for all people needs – a more streamlined service. Can build a combined professional reputation and work in partnership across the business. Could be financial savings in working together and sharing systems. Better sharing of knowledge and skills. More integrated metrics to inform business development.	**Advantages** L&D can be tailored to the individual functions that it supports. Can allow for more specialist interventions. L&D can build a deeper understanding of the parts of the business it supports. Allows L&D to be regarded as a profession in its own right, 'specialists' rather than a subset of HR. Stronger direct relationships with the business.
Disadvantages Can become a 'generalist' function and lack specialist knowledge. L&D function may feel like 'poor relation'. Could be slow to respond to needs of some smaller departments. Might be seen by some workers as 'too corporate'.	**Disadvantages** Could be a disjointed approach with a lack of corporate focus. May result in inconsistency of coverage. May be disproportionately affected by budget cuts.

Figure 2.10 Position of L&D – 2015 CIPD Annual L&D Survey

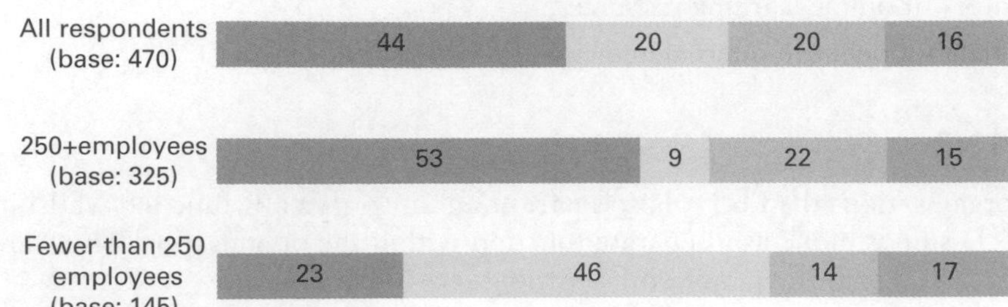

L&D practitioners may actually be positioned within the business where their work is fully focused on the needs of that business area or they may be in a central L&D team with an allocated client relationship with one or more business units or projects. Typically, the title 'business partner' or 'business consultant' is used in this context to reflect how the L&D professional works alongside the business area, providing advice and services to support the achievement of business goals.

The statistics in this chapter and in recent surveys confirm that we still have some way to go in aligning L&D with the business. For example, the *Workplace Learning Report* (LinkedIn, 2018) highlighted a mismatch between the importance placed by managers and that placed by talent developers (L&D) on identifying future skills gaps. Whilst managers considered this to be the second most important focus for L&D (after developing employee's soft skills), talent developers only rated it as the sixth most important area of their work. However, there is no doubt that alignment with the business is an established and very unstoppable direction of travel for L&D. (And in the 2019 LinkedIn report talent developers place 'identify and assess skills gaps' as their no. 1 focus.)

L&D as curators

Another unstoppable trend has been the shift to technology-based L&D with all the flexibility this brings. Depending on the organisation's learning culture and level of adaptation to learning technologies, L&D professionals will have differing levels of direct contact with the workforce. Technology-based L&D means that individuals can self-select and access development activities from learning management systems and databases, without an obvious need for contact with L&D – and the rapid development of artificial intelligence and chat-bots may well accelerate this shift! Consequently L&D's new role as a curator of learning content and materials is changing how they may be positioned within the organisation, for some, possibly, more closely connected to IT departments than to HR.

L&D as brokers of external provision

Whilst some organisations have a wholly internal L&D team managing all employee development internally, and some have no internal training function at all allowing line managers to buy in training as needed, it is perhaps more typical for organisations to have a combination of internal and external provision. This mixed approach allows the use of learning specialists for particular areas of L&D, whilst still having the benefits of an internal function which knows the business in some depth and can coordinate learning across the organisation to best meet organisational needs. However, this approach can require L&D professionals to undertake wider roles. As well as being competent L&D professionals, they may also need to be expert in determining and negotiating best solutions across a very wide remit, and coordinating the activities of different suppliers and contributors.

Taking all of the above into consideration, here are some possible arrangements of L&D:

L&D Arrangement 1: A central L&D team which is a subteam of the central HR function and provides L&D services to the whole organisation/business.

L&D Arrangement 2: A central L&D team which is independent of central HR and provides L&D services for the whole organisation/business.

L&D Arrangement 3: A central L&D team in which each team member is allocated areas of the business and acts as a business partner/L&D consultant to those particular business areas.

L&D Arrangement 4: No central L&D team, but small L&D teams situated within each business unit and responsible to the business unit managers.

L&D Arrangement 5: A small central L&D team who provide some key L&D activities but who procure the majority of the organisation's L&D services from external providers, as required.

L&D Arrangement 6: A small central L&D team who provide some key L&D activities whilst business unit managers independently procure any other L&D services they require from external providers.

L&D Arrangement 7: A shared service arrangement where all organisations in the arrangement agree to procure all their L&D services from a semi-independent 'shared' provider (possibly made up of elements of each of the organisation's original L&D teams).

L&D Arrangement 8: No internal L&D function; business unit managers independently procure all the L&D services they require for their team members from external providers.

L&D Arrangement 9: An internal L&D function whose role is to manage an internal LMS system based on business needs cascaded to them from the L&D director, who liaises with business leaders. Any other employee learning/CPD needs, and related solutions, are self-identified by employees who then request financial support from their manager. Support is only given if the manager agrees the validity of the chosen activity.

L&D Arrangement 10: No internal L&D function. Individual team members have an individual L&D budget, provided by the organisation, and are able to spend it externally as they consider most appropriate, without any checks.

Activity 2.7

For each of the 10 arrangements of L&D provision above:

1. What do you think might be the advantages and disadvantages?
2. What arrangement of L&D do you prefer (one of the above or a different one again) – and why?

Case Example 2.3

Providing L&D services in a small organisation

As HR/Training Manager for a small recruitment agency I work with our MD to support a range of learning and development activities for our recruitment and compliance associates. We have an Employee Development Plan which is fully aligned to our business goals and which was developed in association with the Recruitment Manager and Senior Recruitment Consultant.

We take a two-path approach to L&D, whereby our employees are firstly trained and mentored by line managers and later receive training from external providers. This allows us to have a strong internal emphasis on the recruitment and compliance processes that set us apart from our competitors, but also at a later stage, to give our consultants the opportunity to broaden their horizons, bring in external knowledge and develop new ideas for their and our success.

As a small enterprise, this mix of L&D works well for us, allowing us to use internal expertise, but also saving (expensive) time on developing a wide range of programmes. We also like the fresh approaches external training can bring to our existing processes.

Noemi Kirschbaum, HR/Training Manager

The L&D contribution

HOW L&D SUPPORTS THE BUSINESS

'Considering the talent war, the ageing population and the world of work shifts, it is increasingly important for workers to level up their capability, to be able to shift from being passive staffers to dynamic and engaging enablers in their organisations. L&D is a crucial tool for individuals and employers to unlock potential and create competitive advantage.'

May Leng Kwok, Regional Head, CIPD Asia-Pacific

> 'In the context of the workplace, learning needs to be specifically designed to support the organisation's strategy. Accelerating and facilitating learning for individuals or groups to achieve organisational goals is seen as critical for an organisation's productivity and performance.'
>
> CIPD *Factsheet: Learning in the Workplace* (CIPD, 2018b)
>
> 'The only sustainable competitive advantage is an organisation's ability to learn faster than the competition.'
>
> *The Fifth Discipline: The art and practice of the learning organisation,* Peter M Senge (2006)

As technology and communication processes have developed it has been increasingly difficult for organisations to offer unique products and services. Instead it has often been more about *how* they deliver their products and services that has enabled them to gain any competitive advantage. More than ever, therefore, the skills and performance of the people delivering the products and services has been crucial to gaining and sustaining organisational success. This factor has heightened the profile of L&D over the last few decades and increased the contribution we can make to the achievement of organisational goals and objectives.

The *2019 Workplace Learning Report* (LinkedIn Learning, 2019) identifies the seven most important areas of focus for L&D in 2019, as:

1. identify and assess skills gaps;
2. increase engagement with learning programmes;
3. develop career frameworks;
4. provide consistent and valuable learning to employees globally;
5. train for soft skills;
6. deliver company specific insights to close organizational skills gaps;
7. understand the impact of technology and automation on skills.

Technology is not the only area of change and our modern world is often referred to as being volatile, uncertain, complex and ambiguous (VUCA). This makes it more difficult for organisations to predict the future and increases the need for L&D to be business aware and responsive. To be successful in this VUCA world, organisations need L&D to support the development of new capabilities, such as agility, flexibility, adaptability, creativity and innovation. They also need L&D to be provided in ways which allow for fast learning where, when and how it is required.

CIPD's Head of L&D Content, Andy Lancaster, has highlighted 10 shifts that are taking place, or need to take place, in order for L&D to continue to support organisations effectively. These are:

1. **A shift from L&D priorities to business needs:** the need to continue building alignment with business objectives. Working with different stakeholders to provide learning that drives organisational performance. Building a

deeper understanding of the challenges of the organisation and providing creative solutions rather than relying on people attending courses. Working collaboratively with colleagues from across the organisation to provide a range of business led solutions. (This shift echoes the content of this chapter.)

2 **Metrics, not guesses:** the need for L&D to 'mine' and make use of (often existing) metrics and big data to inform our approaches. Understanding business measures and metrics so that we can talk the same language as the metrics owners. Connecting with the owners and linking L&D provision to relevant measures. For example, if L&D delivers a recruitment course, how do the relevant business measures (number of days a role is vacant, cost of hire or time to hire, etc) inform the course? And is the impact of the course evaluated against these measures? We consider different metrics in Chapter 3 (Identifying L&D needs) and Chapter 10 (Evaluating impact.)

3 **Ensure that L&D is underpinned by science:** this shift requires L&D practitioners to embrace the science behind how people learn. This might be new insights from neuroscience about how the brain works, or aspects of learning psychology and motivation theory. We explore these concepts in Chapter 4 (Designing L&D activities) and Chapter 9 (Engaging learners).

4 **Curating as well as creating:** this means L&D finding great (existing) content, some of which may be free and online, and making it easily accessible to learners. For example, collecting together the best videos on how to create pivot tables for workers who need to use spreadsheets for a new task. Another example could be curating a regular monthly set of resources linked to specific development goals. It can be time-consuming, and sometimes technically challenging, to select the best resources and make them easily available to learners, but good curation skills allow L&D to be pro-active and to respond quickly to learner/business needs. Well-curated resources also encourage learners to self-direct learning and to take responsibility for their own development – and maybe develop their own curation skills. Curating is discussed in Chapter 4 (Designing L&D activities) and Chapter 8 (Social and collaborative learning).

5 **Learner choice:** building learner choice into L&D systems and activities rather than being overly prescriptive. Whilst this might be problematic in contexts such as compliance training, our challenge is to weave in creative approaches to all kinds of training activities and to build in as many opportunities for choice as we can. We look at how learner choice can be woven into the design process in Chapter 4 (Designing L&D activities).

6 **Value social learning:** social learning is, and always has been, a huge part of most learning processes and something we should not underestimate. Social media is a great enabler of social learning – for ourselves as well as others – and something we could make more use of within, and alongside, our L&D activities. This is a main focus of Chapter 8 (Delivering L&D: Social and collaborative learning).

7 **Just-in-time and in the flow of work:** sometimes it is more important for things to get done, rather than for them to be perfect or to follow long-established timetables. For example, we can provide L&D activities as and when they are needed, rather than on a protracted annual schedule. Or we

can sometimes forego complex planning and piloting processes in order to make a (maybe less than perfect) L&D product available more quickly. Chapter 6 offers some insight into how we can deliver more just-in-time learning by embracing technology solutions.

8 **Bite-size learning resources not feasts:** several bite-size chunks of learning are often more manageable for learners than a one-off event. The challenge for us here is to think creatively about how the content of a several-day face-to-face programme (an example of the *feast* of this shift) can be spaced out, without incurring additional costs or travel. For example, could some activities be designed so that they are undertaken prior to a face-to-face workshop (webinars or videos are good examples here) and some further learning activities signposted after the workshop? Delivering learning in bite-size chunks reflects neuroscience findings and is discussed in Chapter 4 (Designing L&D) and Chapter 9 (Engaging learners).

9 **Digital and mobile, not just face-to-face:** this shift encourages L&D to embrace relevant technology to get learning out to people globally and to those 'on the road'. This approach allows learners to access learning at their own time and pace – which is a benefit for many – although there are a number of related ethical issues to consider. For example, people may feel pressure to access learning out of work time, impacting negatively on their personal time, or there may be confidentiality issues to consider. Chapters 6 and 8 explore digital approaches further.

10 **Measure value not volume:** keep measuring the impact of what you're doing – not the quantity! The challenge here is whether L&D is spending time evaluating the right things, at the right time, and doing something with the data being collected. Metrics like 'average percentage spend on training per employee' simply tells the organisation how much money is being spent on training – something the finance team already know. Of much more use to almost all stakeholders is the *value* of the training spend, ie the impact the training has had on the organisation. Are L&D approaches effective? Are they enabling the organisation to meet its goals and objectives? We explore the importance of measuring impact in Chapter 10 (Evaluating impact).

So, there is much to do and these are exciting times for L&D, when we need to hone our expertise in everyday L&D skills whilst also embracing new thinking, techniques and developments. The more capable we are, the better we can contribute to our organisation's objectives and the more options we have for doing this. L&D teams all over the globe are making major contributions to organisational success every day, through activities such as:

- establishing organisational requirements and priorities;
- identifying capability/skills gaps and learning needs;
- designing and delivering effective, engaging and resource-efficient learning activities that drive organisation and individual performance;
- curating and managing learning systems and facilities for social learning;
- coordinating coaching and mentoring programmes;
- monitoring and assessing learning and supporting transfer to the workplace;

- developing manager capabilities;
- supporting managers in delivering L&D activities;
- measuring the impact and effectiveness of L&D and continuously improving;
- ensuring the capability of the L&D team through continued professional development;
- promoting and championing L&D…

… and by effectively ensuring that organisations have all the capabilities they need to respond to customer demands, remain sustainable and grow their business.

The three case studies at the end of this chapter illustrate how three L&D professionals, in different parts of the world, are contributing to the success of their organisations.

> 'The single biggest change I have seen in the role of L&D in recent years has been the recognition that we don't exist in a self-righteous exclusion zone, embattled, unloved and misunderstood. Instead, we are now moving towards seeing ourselves – and being seen – as trusted business contributors, adding value to and contributing to the business aims, objectives and bottom line.'
>
> *Niall Gavin, How to Future-proof L&D, Training Zone, March 2019*

All of the activities above, and the skills and knowledge which underpin them are explored in more depth in further chapters of this book.

Activity 2.8

Thinking of a particular L&D team or practitioner (yourself maybe?), can you identify three different ways they support the achievement of organisational objectives?

Case Example 2.4

Supporting the business (European car dealer network)

Emmanuel Tsochas, L&D Assistant Manager at Kia Motors Europe (KME) Customer Quality (CQ), explains how his team supports the business.

The core purpose of L&D at KME is to create knowledge within our European dealer network and effectively make our dealers' lives easier, more productive and efficient.

The automotive industry is not just a car's world – it is a people job. Certainly, our main business is based on producing and selling cars to customers, however these cars are being sold and serviced by people (dealers) for people (customers). So, in order to consistently provide the best possible customer experience, KME L&D

focuses on developing capabilities, sharpening our dealers' skills and creating L&D options which respect different learning preferences.

In KME L&D we believe that our work is 'not about training, but about learning' and we offer a range of online and offline programmes, which can be blended to meet specific learning needs. These programmes are based on:

Online learning

- Virtual classroom training (VCT): synchronous online group training designed for sales consultants & service advisers;
- Web-based training (WBT): asynchronous online self-paced training designed for sales consultants & service advisers;
- Micro-learning/small private online videos (Kia Fast Facts): asynchronous online self-paced training designed for sales consultants, service advisers, Kia colleagues and end customers.

Offline learning

- Train the Master Trainer (TTMT): synchronous offline group training (IBT/instructor-based training) designed for our master trainers. After the delivery (in English), the content is translated, localised and delivered by the master trainer to sales consultants and service advisers (car dealers) in market level.

How we work

1. New product launch

Every time a new product launch (new Kia vehicle) occurs, KME L&D designs and develops courses in English Master. To make sure all relevant product and technology info is offered to our dealers, I work closely with KME Marketing (product managers). These people are the subject-matter experts and their input (product information, market and business data, insights and content such as images, videos, CAD, product guides, etc) is fundamental to our training courses.

When all the essential product and marketing info has been identified, KME L&D designs the learning objectives, breaks content into clear and structured chunks, selects training methods: (IBT/instructor-based training), (WBT/web-based training) or a blend of both (IBT and WBT). We include all different sort of didactics and make sure the info is relevant, easy to follow, properly explained and that nothing more than necessary is included in the training content.

2. Soft skills training

Whenever a new vehicle is launched, our role is not just about training our master trainers on the product – that would not provide the best value to our dealers (and customers). We also train our people on: a) how to promote the product by translating features and functions into benefits; b) how to assist customers during the purchase process; c) how to provide service to customers during the ownership period; and d) how to improve the financial performance of the dealership overall in the long term.

Therefore, KME L&D also design, develop and deploy soft skills training. As with product launches, we analyse our specific training needs, set up learning objectives and select training methods (IBT/instructor-based training or just WBT/web-based training or IBT together with WBT). Then we select a training agency, review the course storyboard/wireframes, propose changes, involve stakeholders within Kia (top management), proceed to sign off and finally deliver the content via a master training in English (all master trainers across Europe).

Impact

KME L&D facilitates business and learning excellence. What we do is aligned with our organization priorities, shapes mindsets and develops skills across our dealer network. We do what we do to support the brand's growth.

From 2014 to 2018, along with other dealer network projects of course, we have achieved an increase in both dealer satisfaction and dealer recommendation. Specifically, Kia has been ranked as a second best (no.2) in dealer satisfaction (no.7 in 2014), and second best (no.2) in dealer recommendation (no.9 in 2014). The explanation of features/controls (this KPI is an assessment question within an internal dealer study) has also been significantly increased. (The views expressed here are personal views and do not necessarily represent the views of Kia Motors Europe GmbH. Emmanuel Tsochas, Frankfurt am Main.)

Case study question

Looking in detail at the above, what contribution or benefits are the L&D team providing for:

1 Kia (the organisation)?

2 The Kia dealers?

3 Kia customers?

Case Example 2.5

Supporting business objectives in a manufacturing organisation

When we were first established, as a two-person HR/L&D team in a large manufacturing/retail organisation (1,000 employees), the main organisational need was for operational and health and safety training, along with employment relations. However, it quickly became apparent to us that if we could enhance leadership capability, this would enable the organisation to operate, and achieve its objectives, much more effectively.

With this in mind, we developed, launched and delivered a management Academy within a four-month time frame. The Academy is essentially a suite of training activities designed to address the bigger people issues we face. Key stakeholders were engaged to help us understand their views, along with possible end users to understand the daily problems they face. From the research we saw there were two distinct groups – line managers and their supervisors and so the Academy was split into two suites, to meet the needs of each user group.

The Academy activities included training in: influencing and delegation; coaching skills; situational leadership; recruiting the right people; leading great performance reviews; managing attendance; discipline and grievance; and our payroll system. All the subjects were wrapped up in engaging and creatively named training sessions.

After the first four months of roll-out, we took feedback that showed:

- a reduction in payroll errors;
- a reduction in the instances of grievances and appeal;
- an increase in the autonomy of our line managers (fewer e-mails and phone calls regarding various issues);
- feedback from both supervisors and managers that they felt their development was being taken seriously and that their confidence had improved.

Mel Morehouse, HR/L&D Partner, UK

Case study question

What other benefits, as well as those mentioned, might Mel's training have for the organisation in the longer term?

 Case Example 2.6

Developing a learning organisation

I am a member of the L&D team within a fast-paced global ICT organisation which needs staff to be capable and responsive but does not have much time available for learning. To enhance and develop the performance of our workforce and build a learning culture which will benefit both the organisation and individual employees, we have undertaken several innovative L&D initiatives, including:

- An Employee Mentorship Programme – employees (supported by their line manager) can access a mentor to help them to improve a certain aspect of their lives be it personal or professional. As well as helping individual employees, this is helping to shift management culture from simply managing a team's performance to playing a key role in coaching and mentoring them and providing development support.
- Pink Potential – a women in leadership forum that encourages women to take on more leadership responsibility. Women already in leadership (We Lead) mentor those aspiring (We Aspire to Lead). We also held the first ever sub-Saharan IT Women Event at our workplace which was attended by women of all walks working in the IT and STEM industries.
- A range of support and development forums for other groups, for example: working mums, young people and male employees.
- Making use of different platforms to stimulate the appetite for learning, such as group mailers, campaigns such as 'Each One Teach One' and 'It's my Responsibility'.
- Engaging those managers and employees who are supportive of learning as departmental Learning Champions.

Adding to these initiatives, we speak out about the importance of learning in every opportunity we get. In recent years our key achievement has been stimulating a culture of, and appetite for, learning amongst the employees and showing the executive the link between learning, skills and capability development, and performance improvement.

José María Ngacha, Group Learning & Development Executive, Techno Brain Group, Kenya

Case study question

How does the work of José María and his L&D colleagues contribute to the organisation – both now and in the longer term?

What next?

The activities below will help consolidate your knowledge from this chapter.

1 Consider your organisation's size, type and structure. Also consider how L&D is positioned within the organisation and how it serves the business. If you were employed as an organisation design consultant to your organisation, what changes to the structure of the organisation or to the positioning of L&D would you recommend? Why?

2 Analyse the key factors likely to impact on your (or another) organisation in the next year and in the next five years. Consider how L&D will need to support these changes and the implications this might have for the development of the L&D function (including the size and skill-set of the L&D team, the systems and approaches they use, and the resources they might need)?

3 Search on Twitter to see if there is a professional group for any aspect of your organisation section (eg health, education, finance, marketing, procurement, logistics, etc) and retweet some links you think might be useful to other L&D practitioners in your industry. Use the hashtag #LDPintheW and copy in the account @LDPintheW.

References

Ansoff, I (1965) *Corporate Strategy: An analytic approach to business policy for growth and expansion* (updated 1988), Penguin, London

BCG (1968) The Growth Share Matrix, Boston Consulting Group, www.bcg.com/about/our-history/default.aspex (archived at https://perma.cc/JZ23-KA6N)

CIPD (2015) *Learning and Development Survey*, www.cipd.co.uk/knowledge/strategy/development/surveys (archived at https://perma.cc/83NF-8K9A)

CIPD (2018a) *Profession Map*, www.cipd.co.uk/learn/career/profession-map (archived at https://perma.cc/GV96-GEAT)

CIPD (2018b) *Factsheet: Learning in the Workplace*, https://www.cipd.co.uk/knowledge/strategy/development/learning-factsheet (archived at https://perma.cc/3KGC-F3GR)

(continued)

(Continued)

CIPD/Towards Maturity (2019) *Professionalising Learning and Development*, www.cipd.co.uk/Images/professionalising-learning-development-report19_tcm18-53783.pdf (archived at https://perma.cc/3X66-K5VZ)

Gavin, N (2019) *How to future-proof L&D*, Training Zone, https://www.trainingzone.co.uk/develop/cpd/how-to-future-proof-ld (archived at https://perma.cc/3ADM-AWJ3)

Handy, C (1985) *Understanding Organisations*, 4th edn, Penguin, London

LinkedIn Learning (2018) *Workplace Learning Report: The rise and responsibility of talent development in the new labor market,* https://learning.linkedin.com/resources/workplace-learning-report-2018 (archived at https://perma.cc/XBT2-PXXR)

LinkedIn Learning (2019) *Workplace Learning Report: Why 2019 is the breakout year for the talent developer,* https://learning.linkedin.com/resources/workplace-learning-report-2019

Mendelow, AL (1991) Environmental Scanning: The impact of the stakeholder concept, in *Proceedings from the Second International Conference on Information Systems*, Cambridge, MA

Porter, M (2004) *Competitive Advantage,* new edn, Free Press, New York

Senge, P (2006) *The Fifth Discipline: The art and practice of the learning organization*, Random House, London

Taylor, DH (2018) *The Learning and Development Global Sentiment Survey*, http://donaldhtaylor.co.uk/wp-content/uploads/10_GSS-2018-mail.pdf (archived at https://perma.cc/X3B7-R78A)

World Bank (2019) *World Development Report 2019: The changing nature of work*, The World Bank, http://www.worldbank.org/en/publication/wdr2019 (archived at https://perma.cc/MBC8-QUVX)

Explore further

CIPD (2018) *Factsheet: Learning and development strategy and policy,*

CIPD (2018) *The People Profession in 2018: Asia-Pacific*, CIPD, www.cipd.asia/knowledge/reports/people-profession-survey-asia-pacific (archived at https://perma.cc/55S6-LZPV)

CIPD (2018) *Learning and Development Strategy and Policy,* www.cipd.co.uk/knowledge/strategy/development/factsheet (archived at https://perma.cc/U5D9-HZPV)

CIPD/Towards Maturity (2015) *Evolving Roles, Enhancing Skills,* www.cipd.co.uk/knowledge/strategy/development/roles-skills-report (archived at https://perma.cc/MU7J-22ZJ)

Big Ideas (2014) *The Business Book: Big ideas simply explained,* Dorling Kindersley, London

Matthews, P (2014) *Capability at Work: How to solve the performance puzzle*, Three Faces Publishing, Milton Keynes, UK

McKeown, M (2015) *The Strategy Book*, 2nd edn, FT Publishing International, London

Towards Maturity (2016, 2017) *Making an Impact: How L&D Leaders can demonstrate value,* https://towardsmaturity.org/2016/06/13/focus-making-impact-demonstrate-value (archived at https://perma.cc/J7C3-CKXS)

Useful resources

Websites

www.businessballs.com (archived at https://perma.cc/UW7U-5HS8)

www.mindtools.com (archived at https://perma.cc/KU9K-TBA5) [some free online access to analysis models]

www.gov.uk/browse/business (archived at https://perma.cc/SJE8-3PW3) [UK government advisory site]

www.iccwbo.org (archived at https://perma.cc/UU5S-6KPW) [International Chamber of Commerce]

www.cipd.co.uk/hr-resources/factsheets (archived at https://perma.cc/6ZH5-U2B8) [CIPD Factsheets eg Business Partnering]

http://2020workplace.com/blog/ (archived at https://perma.cc/VJ4B-969N) [2020 Workplace blog]

03 Identifying learning and development needs

Introduction

In this chapter, we begin to explore the technical knowledge and skills required to support other people's learning and development. Identifying needs is the first stage of the basic training cycle and is the foundation for what comes after it, in terms of design, delivery, assessment and evaluation. However quickly we may need to provide an L&D solution, we should always know what we are trying to achieve before we set off on the design and delivery journey. Being able to accurately identify needs, and to effectively engage learners and other stakeholders in the process, is a highly valuable skill-set for any L&D professional.

Key areas of content covered in this chapter are:

- what learning needs are (and are not) and why they arise;
- the importance and benefits of identifying learning needs;
- how to involve learners and other stakeholders in the process;
- the information required for identifying learning needs;
- methods for collecting and analysing information;
- factors that affect the prioritisation of learning needs;
- how to specify learning needs.

'This is the year that L&D hones its ability to identify, assess and close skills gaps.'
Workplace Learning Report, LinkedIn Learning, 2019

Learning needs

In the simplest terms, a learning need usually exists where there is a gap between current capability and desired or required capability.

In this context, we are using the term 'capability' to refer to a combination of knowledge, skills and behaviours (Table 3.1).

Table 3.1 Capability

Knowledge	What someone needs to know, eg facts, processes, causes and effects, technical knowledge
Skills	What someone needs to be able to do, eg operate specific equipment, apply a first-aid dressing or listen actively
Behaviours	How someone needs to do things, personal and interpersonal approaches taken, eg being pro-active or considerate of others feelings

Different levels of learning need

Many organisations operate on some kind of team-based structure, where the organisation's strategic goals and plans cascade down to form the basis of team objectives. Team objectives in turn underpin the job descriptions, targets and work activities of each individual in the team. This is represented in Figure 3.1.

Learning needs can exist at any of these levels. For example, learning needs at an *organisational level* are about whether an organisation has the capability it needs to meet its overall current and emerging objectives.

At the next level, there may be *team learning needs*, relating to the combined capability of a particular work or project team to fulfil its objectives. Learning needs can also be common to other groups of individuals who are not necessarily a team, for example: all managers on a particular site, everyone who accesses a particular IT system, everyone who is to be involved with a new product or service, or a group of new recruits.

Figure 3.1 A team-based organisational structure

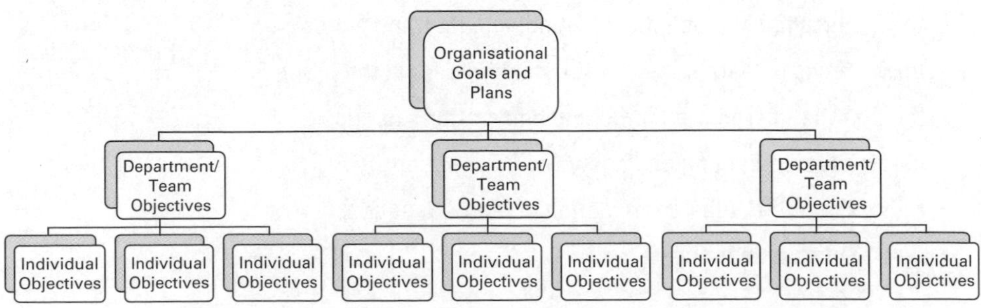

 Case Example 3.1

'Key user group' learning needs

When a medical practice wanted to implement a new online translation facility, the L&D manager recognised that all staff would require a short briefing on the new system, probably at a practice meeting, but that a group of staff, across different teams, would be particularly affected by this change and would need more in-depth training. This group included three reception staff, one of the outreach health advisers, two assessment nurses and a specialist doctor. This group was labelled the Main Access Group and their learning needs in relation to the system were identified to inform the design of the L&D solution.

Finally, we have *individual* learning needs where there are gaps between the desired or required level of capability and the individual's actual level of knowledge, skills and behaviours.

Maintenance or developmental learning needs?

Learning needs can be about maintaining current capability or about looking ahead at the learning needed to meet emerging or future changes and developments.

Learning needs which focus on current capabilities are sometimes referred to as *maintenance learning needs*. For example:

- At an organisational level, ensuring that there are sufficient staff with the skill-sets required to fulfil the organisation's key current purpose.
- At an individual or team level, maintaining skills and keeping knowledge up to date, in order to remain competent in a set job role. This may just be necessary to remain effective in role or it may be an essential aspect of having work-related licences or approvals renewed.

Learning needs which are about developing readiness for emerging and future changes can be referred to as *future learning needs* or *developmental learning needs*. For example:

- At an organisational level, preparing for the introduction of a new product or service or a move into new markets.
- At an individual level, preparing for a significant change to job role or to take on an additional responsibility.

As the incidence and rate of change in all our work roles has increased, the difference between these two types of needs has lessened, with most of us having to learn completely new aspects of knowledge and skills just to remain competent in our current role. Whilst it is still useful to consider both categories of needs, it is very likely that you will find considerable cross-over and merger between the two.

Not learning needs

Activity 3.1

Consider a sales team in which one person is not performing as well as the others in the team.

What factors, *other than* capability factors, could be affecting the person's performance?

It is important to remember that performance problems do not always signify a learning need – and that not every performance problem can be 'solved' by training. When we defined capability earlier in this chapter, we accurately included behaviours in that definition and said that a learning need 'usually occurs where there is a gap in current capability and required or desired capability'. However, a gap between current behaviours and desired or required behaviours may not always represent a learning need. There are several reasons why someone may not behave in a desired way, such as interpersonal issues or lack of motivation. For example, someone may be highly capable, but because of personal problems may not be motivated to perform well at work.

This concept is neatly illustrated in the Skill–Will Matrix, a version of which was first introduced by Max Landsberg in his book *The Tao of Coaching* (2003, updated 2015). The Skill–Will Matrix shows how capability (ability) is just one dimension of good performance (Figure 3.2).

There are also several non-personal factors which can be mistaken for learning needs. For example, if a team consistently fails to meet required outcomes, there may be a recruitment need (not enough people to do the job) or a system problem (insufficient or inappropriate equipment, cumbersome procedures) or something external to the organisation, which is impacting on the team.

Figure 3.2 The Skill–Will matrix

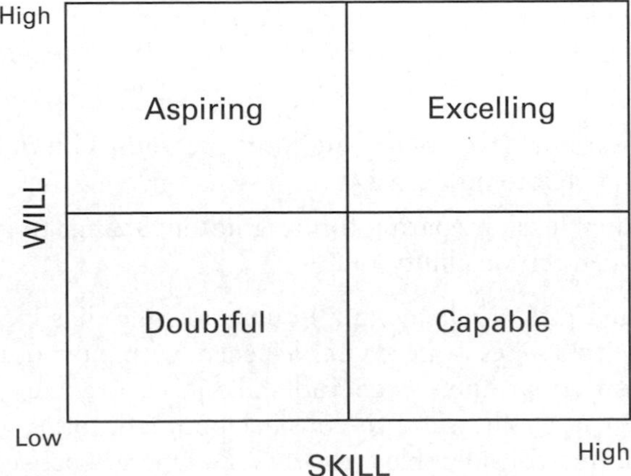

Case Example 3.2

Training needs or other needs?

An equipment hire company commissioned software training for staff whose job involved booking out hired equipment in a computerised control system. The system required staff to input an item code for the item being hired, using either a code scanner or manually inputting the code if necessary. Frequent mistakes inputting these codes meant that the system rarely gave an accurate picture of stock in and out – hence the decision to commission the training.

The staff attended the training and performed competently. The code scanners mostly worked well on the demonstration equipment and manual input was easy enough in the training environment where staff were not under time or other work pressures. However, the training had no impact on the level of mistakes in the workplace and just angered some staff who felt their valid complaints about the system were being ignored.

In the workplace, item codes had often faded or been rubbed off equipment which meant more manual input was required. To do this, staff had to refer to item lists, where it was easy to misread a code or inadvertently select the one above or below the code required. When the system was eventually adapted, so that code labels were more durable and items could be manually inputted by simply using the item name as a keyword, the level of mistakes immediately fell to almost zero.

Providing an L&D solution to address non-L&D factors is likely to be a big waste of time and money, both for the L&D team and for the business as a whole. No one gains. If we carry out an effective learning needs analysis, we can identify the real issues behind a performance gap and ensure that we are very clear that learning is the correct solution.

Case Example 3.3

Homecare provider

The MD of a small organisation, providing private homecare in two neighbouring towns, was frustrated by the different strengths and weaknesses of the two location teams (each of around 25 team members, including a team manager and divided into two or three subteams, where senior team members play an informal team leader role within the subteams). One team had very good relationships with service users, received excellent feedback and had very few customer complaints but the customer list remained static, whilst the other team had much higher customer numbers, seemed to be far better at selling and building the service, but also had a higher customer turnover and feedback was not always good.

The MD wanted the teams to learn from each other and for both to become stronger as a result of this. She organized monthly meetings for staff representatives of both teams to share good practice, but saw little change as a result of this. If anything, staff seemed a bit unwilling to share how they worked and the meetings were generally unproductive. Having read about the benefits of team-building activities, she decided to send everyone on a one-day team-build event at a local outdoor centre. The aim of the event was to 'enable teams to learn more about each other and build trust through undertaking various physical activities in which they are reliant on each other for their safety'.

Feedback from the event was mixed – some team members thought it had been 'good fun', others hated it. Two months later, the MD felt that the team-build had had little impact on the team's performance or how they interacted with each other. She was now considering sending the team members on an 'effective meetings' training day.

Case study questions

1. What advice would you give the MD?
2. What learning needs might exist here – for whom?
3. What other factors may be causing/affecting team performance and sharing of good practice?
4. How would you go about identifying the teams' learning needs?

Key causes of learning needs

Before we move on from defining and explaining learning needs, let's consider some of the typical factors which cause them. Above we have discussed how learning needs can be caused by current or future issues, and that they exist at different levels. As you will see in the lists below, factors can also be internal or external to the organisation.

Typical drivers of learning needs at an *organisational level*:

- succession planning;
- regulation and compliance requirements;
- changes in organisational strategy;
- development of new products and services;
- mergers and acquisitions;
- downsizing and rightsizing of the business operations;
- changes in the workforce demographics or working patterns;
- changing trends in customer needs;
- organisational performance issues and challenges;

- availability of technology and technological developments;
- changes in the organisation's operating environment;
- changes in legislation and government policy.

At a *team (department or function) level*:

- a need to improve team effectiveness or work results;
- team reorganisation or changes to team make-up;
- new products or services affecting the team;
- new technology or changes to specific teamwork practices;
- factors external to the organisation which affect one area of the business more than others.

And at an *individual level*:

- induction;
- the need to develop and maintain the skills required to fulfil job requirements;
- individual compliance requirements, such as licences or certificates;
- individual performance issues and challenges;
- promotion or temporary additional responsibilities;
- changes or potential changes to job role;
- continuous professional development;
- qualification requirements;
- aspirations and career planning.

Activity 3.2

1. What have been your own main learning needs over the last year or two?
2. What caused them to arise?
3. Were they about maintaining existing abilities or developing new ones?
4. Did they just apply to you or to your whole team or organisation?

Why and when to identify learning needs

A story sometimes recounted in the L&D world is of a discussion between two managers. The first, concerned about wasting money on providing training says to the other:

> 'What if we train them and they leave?'

The other, rather astutely, replies:

> 'Hmmm – but what if we don't train them and they stay?'

Of course, we support the latter viewpoint here, but the first manager's nervousness about spending on training is also understandable – few, if any, organisations have unlimited training budgets. Time spent clarifying learning needs and priorities not only ensures that a business maintains the skills it needs, but also that limited L&D budgets are used effectively – and helps gain everyone's buy-in to the L&D solution.

Different organisations take a whole range of approaches to analysing their learning needs, as in Figure 3.3.

Figure 3.3 Approaches to identifying learning needs

Inactive (ignore)	⟶	Reactive (respond to crises)	⟶	Active (regular planned)	⟶	Pro-active (constant monitoring)

Organisations that are inactive or reactive about their analysis will do nothing until something goes wrong or stops being effective, at which point, of course, it may be too late. They will always be following the pack when it comes to learning and development.

From the middle of the continuum are organisations which are active in identifying learning needs, on a planned basis, maybe via their appraisal system. In some ways this reflects good practice, but because analysis only takes place at certain times and in certain ways, it can be retrospective and also dependent on the effectiveness of particular line managers. The focus here is on ensuring that individual skills gaps are addressed and that staff maintain the main skills and knowledge required for their role.

At the pro-active end of the scale are the organisations that know the benefits of analysing and acting upon their learning needs as they arise. As well as 'maintenance needs', ie learning required to maintain current capabilities, high attention is paid to emerging and future needs. The L&D staff in these organisations will be working with line managers and maybe with organisational development (OD) colleagues to monitor organisational talent and capability and ensure that needs are addressed as the business evolves and new challenges emerge. These organisations use a range of activities to research and analyse learning needs and draw a number of benefits from doing so.

> 'I have learned over the years that a business area's learning needs are never quite met by a particular project, and that needs keep evolving, even between LNA and design/delivery. So, you never really follow a perfect process of analysis, design, delivery – or achieve the perfect solution. If we accept that development is a journey, each project or initiative is just a step along the way, never an end in itself.'
>
> *Jill MacLean, former Head of Learning (Group), Standard Life Assurance Limited*

The potential benefits of good learning needs analysis include:

- a more agile organisation, able to anticipate and respond to change – and gain the competitive advantage of being able to respond quickly;
- a well-trained and responsive workforce, who have the knowledge, skills and confidence to be high-performers in their roles, even as those roles evolve and change;

- a more satisfied and motivated workforce, as workers feel that their learning needs are being addressed and that they have opportunities for development – an increasingly cited factor in staff satisfaction and engagement surveys, particularly for new generations of workers;
- greater customer and stakeholder satisfaction as changing needs and expectations are anticipated and catered for as, or before, they arise;
- improved overall knowledge management within the organisation, as evolving knowledge gaps are identified and rectified, and organisational knowledge is continually updated;
- accurate targeting of the L&D budget on learning activities that are most relevant, useful and likely to have the greatest impact.

Activity 3.3

1 Where does your organisation fit on the learning needs continuum above?
2 What are the positive and negative effects of that?
3 What could you do, within your role, to change this situation?

Learning needs analysis

Learning needs analysis is the process of monitoring an organisation's (or individual's) capability, in terms of having the required skills, knowledge and behaviours, to fulfil required current or future objectives.

The main objectives of a learning needs analysis are therefore to:

- determine current capability;
- determine required (or desired) capability;
- identify any gaps between the two;
- identify factors about how these gaps might best be filled.

In practice this might mean determining and comparing either, or both, of the current and required capabilities shown in Figure 3.4.

Figure 3.4 Identifying gaps

Capabilities Current position	Gaps	Capabilities Required position
ACTUAL capability to meet current work objectives	←←→→	Capability required to meet ALL current work objectives
Capabilities required to meet CURRENT work demands	←←→→	Capabilities required to meet NEW and EMERGING demands

Learning needs information

Current capabilities information

To establish *current capability*, we need to collect a range of information that fairly and consistently identifies levels of knowledge or performance and the factors affecting this. This information might include individual worker feedback, manager feedback, observation and assessment outcomes, customer/other feedback and a range of individual, team or organisational metrics.

Required capabilities information

Establishing the required position or the *required capability* may involve some of the same information sources mentioned above, but is particularly likely to be found in job and role descriptions, competence frameworks and current or projected work plans. Other sources of information re the required position could be individuals themselves (regarding their own desired performance levels and aspirations), line managers (regarding work expectations of individuals), expert practitioners (regarding how effective performance should be defined) and industry- or sector-based quality standards. For L&D professionals, for example, one source of information could be the CIPD Profession Map.

PAUSE FOR THOUGHT

What information could you use to measure yourself against in order to identify any current or future learning needs?

Other factors

Along with collecting information about specific learning needs, an effective analysis will also identify a range of other factors which will assist in identifying the best solution later on. For example, we should establish:

- how urgent are the different learning needs and any required timescales;
- the scale of the learning need and number of people involved;
- the work situations and locations of people involved (eg one site, remote, international?)
- any non-learning needs identified to be addressed by other solutions;
- (individual) learner factors and preferences, where appropriate.

Data protection

As with any information we collect about people, we should always remember that this might be sensitive and, in some cases very personal information, and that we have a responsibility to use and store it responsibly. In most countries/territories there are specific laws and guidance on how to handle data. For example, in the

UK, the use of data is governed by the Data Protection Act 2018. This Act requires organisations to use data fairly and responsibly and allows individuals appropriate access to any information held about them. There is a wealth of up-to-date information about the requirements of the 2018 UK Data Protection Act and related codes of practice on the UK government's website (www.gov.uk/data-protection) as well as on the CIPD website (www.cipd.co.uk).

Collecting and analysing learning needs information

> 'An L&D professional should never be afraid to ask their client or manager for an opportunity to spend time with, or even work in, an area of the business before getting involved with their training. Expanding awareness of roles, tasks and challenges is the best way of understanding learning requirements.'
>
> *Heather Neilson-Cox, Neilson-Cox Training Ltd*

In many organisations, it is L&D specialists who take primary responsibility for collecting and analysing learning needs information – although this usually involves working in partnership with line managers. Below are some of the methods they are using:

1. interviews and discussions;
2. questionnaires and surveys;
3. organisation information and metrics;
4. analysis models;
5. performance review;
6. assessments and tests;
7. skills matrices;
8. LMS system data.

1. Interviews and discussions

Probably the most important factor in identifying any learning needs is to communicate with the people or individual involved. They are likely to understand the issues more than anyone.

Where the analysis is in relation to *team or business area* learning needs, discussions are likely to be held between the L&D professional and a manager or representative(s) from the area. Where the analysis is in relation to an *individual*, there might be an informal performance conversation between the individual and their line manager or between the individual and an L&D practitioner.

These discussions might be pre-planned and structured or may be immediate and informal, in response to a work need or performance issue. Discussions will focus on:

- reasons for learning needs;
- required capabilities;
- current capabilities;
- perceived gaps;

- preferences re how gaps are filled;
- logistics and constraints such as timing or resource issues.

Remember that discussions about learning needs can be very sensitive, particularly where there is a performance gap. Individuals are likely to feel nervous and may be defensive about admitting to learning needs. It is therefore important to be sensitive to these feelings and to emphasise, and of course maintain, appropriate confidentiality throughout.

USEFUL STAGES IN AN INDIVIDUAL LEARNING NEEDS INTERVIEW

- (Prior to) Ensure both parties are aware of what is to be discussed and have had the chance to prepare for the discussion, and if relevant gather any useful 'documentation' or evidence.
- (Beginning) Re-establish the purpose of the meeting and take a little time to establish a relaxed environment.
- Establish 'required capability'. Ask the job-holder about their current role (or job aspiration). What is important about the role? What is its key purpose? What knowledge, skills and behaviours are needed in order for the job to be carried out well? (At this stage, the job-holder is not assessing their own skills, but describing the skills of people who do the job well. A good question here is: 'If I wanted to be good at your job (or future role), what would I need to know or do?') Refer to any required capability information here as appropriate.
- Establish 'actual capability'. Ask about the knowledge, skills and behaviours the job-holder actually has, possibly reviewing any evidence of this with them.
- Discuss and identify where there are gaps and check with the job-holder how filling that gap would improve their performance.
- Discuss possible and preferred ways in which the performance gaps could be overcome.
- Agree and record. (Including agreement of who will have access to the recorded information and what the next steps will be.)

Focus groups

For bigger initiatives, affecting several teams or functions, it can be useful to establish a focus group for exploring, identifying (and addressing) learning needs.

 Case Example 3.4

Introducing a new financial product

When a national bank launches a new product – such as a different type of investment account – this is likely to create learning needs for a range of teams and individuals across the organisation. For example, a new product could affect the work of call centre staff, branch staff, customer relations staff, back office/processing teams, marketing teams and general managers.

To ensure everyone's learning needs are recognised and addressed, the central training team holds focus groups for one or two representatives from each affected area (ideally 10 to 12 people). The group then explores the training implications of the product launch from everyone's angle. The kinds of issues discussed include:

- How will the new product impact on different areas?
- How will the new product impact on how areas work together?
- How will this change current ways of working?
- What will different areas need to know about the product?
- What other learning needs might the launch generate for different areas (eg in relation to new systems involved or new customer groups)?
- How many people are affected in each area?
- What are the best ways of up-skilling different areas?
- How will this fit with other training initiatives in the area?
- What logistical issues might get in the way of training?

Having collected this information, the central team has a full picture of requirements to help them design an appropriate overall learning solution. A second focus group is likely to be held to review the proposed solution and check that all needs are being fully addressed before the training is implemented.

Case study questions

1. How could focus groups (face-to-face or online) help your organisation to analyse learning needs?
2. Who would you want to include in your focus groups?

2. *Questionnaires and surveys*

Questionnaires and surveys can be used to help individuals prepare for a learning needs discussion or as the basis of larger-scale (group) learning needs surveys.

Questions will usually focus on assessing capabilities, performance requirements and outcomes, and issues for potential improvement and development. For example, Figure 3.5 is an extract from a survey, devised by Haithamyaseen Alawi, to gauge the current effectiveness of teams and team learning within an organisation.

Questionnaires can be designed to capture whatever type of information is required, including quantitative data and qualitative information.

Figure 3.5 Team working and learning survey (extract)

Teams in organisations can learn in a number of ways. Please tick the appropriate box to show how far you agree or disagree with the 12 statements in this section.

	1 Strongly Agree	2 Agree	3 Neither Agree Nor Disagree	4 Disagree	5 Strongly Disagree
1. In my organisation teams/groups have the freedom to adapt their goals of learning as needed.	☐	☐	☐	☐	☐
2. In my organisation teams/groups treat members as equals, regardless of rank or other differences.	☐	☐	☐	☐	☐
3. In my organisation teams/groups focus both on the group's task and on how well the group is working.	☐	☐	☐	☐	☐
4. In my organisation teams/groups revise their thinking as a result of group discussions or information collected.	☐	☐	☐	☐	☐
5. In my organisation teams/groups are confident that the organisation will act on their recommendations.	☐	☐	☐	☐	☐
6. Team learning increases the level of learning and promotion of knowledge.	☐	☐	☐	☐	☐
7. The opportunities for formal and informal learning fosters work perfomance.	☐	☐	☐	☐	☐
8. Team learning is important for teams to learn how to work with each other and for organisations to adapt to continuously changing environment.	☐	☐	☐	☐	☐
9. Collaboration and interaction among team members improves the work outcomes.	☐	☐	☐	☐	☐

Table 3.2 Quantitative and qualitative information

Quantitative information	Qualitative information
Quantitative information is about facts, things that can be measured,ie quantities.	Qualitative information is less 'absolute' and more about qualities than quantities.
For example, it could be about percentage improvements in a skill area or the number of years' experience in a work role.	It might be opinion-based, for example what someone thinks about their own or someone else's performance.
An example of quantitative information is that '10 new team members need to undertake compulsory safeguarding training'.	An example of qualitative information is a team member's feedback that 'manager X doesn't communicate enough with her team'.

Although questionnaires can be issued as documents, it is so easy to convert them to online surveys, accessible via PC or mobile devices, with the benefits of impressive analytics and professional presentation of findings, that this is usually a preferable option. Most survey software allows you to work through pre-set design steps and access 'templates' which make the creation of online questionnaires easy. Responses are automatically collated and analysed and the 'survey owner' can browse through individual responses or access a range of collated and analysed summary information.

As a word of warning, when putting together a questionnaire/survey, think about the possible bias, assumptions or ambiguities that may be within your questions. Equally, consider the potential for subjectivity in responses, which may invalidate some of the information collected.

For example, the question *Do you agree with statement A or statement B?* may reflect the questioner's underlying belief (bias) that there are only two possibilities (A or B), whereas respondents may not fully agree with either of these options, whilst feeling 'forced' to choose one. This may be OK if it is your intention, but be aware that the response may not fully reflect the respondents' thinking.

The question *Are your English language skills sufficient to fulfil your job role?* could be seen as a little intimidating with respondents not wanting to say 'no' to this as it may affect their employment status. Equally the response is bound to be subjective, depending very much on a respondent's concept of 'sufficient' in this context and also their tendency to inflate or under-sell their abilities.

Check your questionnaire/survey design before issuing it and ask others to check it too ('a fresh pair of eyes'). Using a good range of questions and ensuring you involve different sources of information and respondent groups will help you gain a more accurate and balanced picture.

> 'Questionnaire design is a skilled task that rewards experience.'
>
> R Horn (2009) *Researching and Writing Dissertations: A complete guide for business and management students*

Activity 3.4

1 How could you use a survey to identify learning needs – of a team or individual?
2 What questions would you want to ask?
3 When you have time, try out some of the free survey tools and apps, to create your own questionnaire and send it to your chosen target group (one you can guarantee will respond!).

3. Organisation information and metrics

> Clear and systematic identification of learning and development needs is a key aspect of ensuring effective learning provision across an organisation. However, the process can be seen as a rigid, box-ticking one-time exercise unless it's aligned with organisational requirements. The need for organisational agility means people professionals must act quickly to deliver a learning needs analysis when required.
>
> **SOURCE:** CIPD (2018) Factsheet

There is likely to be a vast range of information already available in most organisations which can hugely inform learning needs analysis. For example:

Organisation vision, mission, strategic goals and business objectives: the key basis of information about current and future required capabilities.

Business results and outcomes/key performance indicators (KPIs): KPIs are measures of how an organisation is performing in areas considered most vital to its success, eg sales, costs, productivity. Looking at actual performance against targets can give a clear indication of a learning need – although, of course, there may be other factors to blame for this.

Customer feedback: satisfaction surveys, comments, complaints and even compliments can all give an indicator of specific areas where there may be a gap in some aspect of capability and therefore, a possible learning need.

Critical incident information: investigating major problems and issues that have occurred will usually expose potential areas of learning needs.

External information: industry and sector publications will highlight emerging trends which may form the basis of future learning needs. Information about oncoming changes to legislation and work practices, provided by professional bodies such as CIPD, will also help organisations identify future learning needs in good time.

L&D data: as trainers/facilitators we are privy to a whole range of information about the organisation and workplace which can highlight further learning needs. This may be our L&D evaluation data – one of our best sources of information about further learning needs – or simply from us seeing patterns in more informal learner comments.

> 'One of the privileges of being in L&D is that when you deliver a workshop, people will share their stories with you, often some of the more challenging aspects of work, sometimes deep organisational insights, process bottlenecks and system peculiarities. I believe L&D has a duty to act on this information and partner with the organisation to work on solutions to drive performance forward. I am not advocating going back to line managers and saying "Oh, your staff member X told me this" but about sharing themes and insights. It is rich powerful data that will build on the L&D practitioner's credibility.'
>
> *L&D Consultant*

When looking for answers, it can be tempting to take information at 'face value' rather than digging deeper to get to the root cause of an issue. When looking for learning needs it is also essential to distinguish between whether the problem is caused by a learning gap or by something else. One of the simplest ways of digging deep and uncovering root cause is to keep asking the question 'why?'

This is recognised as a questioning technique, often referred to as 'The Five Whys' (and you might recognise it as a technique that young children seem to naturally excel at).

The Five Whys

With this technique, you identify an issue and then ask yourself, or the people most likely to know... *Why is this (A) happening?*

When that question is answered (say the answer is B) the question... *So why is this (B) happening?* is asked.

When an answer is given (say the answer is C), the question is again repeated... *So why is this (C) happening?* and so on.

The same line of questioning is repeated until the issue has been taken apart and examined at the most basic level. Five is not necessarily a magic number. The key is to keep asking 'why?' until the most basic cause has been uncovered.

4. Analysis models

SWOT analysis is a great way of engaging teams and individuals in identifying their own learning needs and starting the identification process. It can be used in relation to a whole organisation, a work team, project team, group or individual. In Chapter 2 we used the SWOT model as a means of getting to know and better understand an organisation, and as the model leads us to explore both current performance and potential future performance it is also a useful indicator of learning needs.

SWOT stands for: Strengths, Weaknesses, Opportunities, Threats. In an organisational context, strengths and weaknesses are usually 'internal factors', things that are happening within the organisation:

- *Strengths* are the things that an organisation is good at and which it may be able to build upon, to help it to achieve its goals.

- *Weaknesses* are the things that can let the organisation down and may get in the way of success, if they are not somehow addressed or compensated for.

Opportunities and threats are usually 'external factors', things in the wider world that may impact on the organisation:

- *Opportunities* are those things that an organisation could take advantage of if they prepare ahead.
- *Threats* are factors which could have an adverse effect on the business, and may require some avoidant action or damage limitation.

It is useful to get as many views and contributions to the SWOT analysis as possible to bring out lots of ideas. An organisational SWOT will be more accurate and informative if different people within, and possibly external to, the organisation are involved. A team SWOT analysis will be most useful and meaningful if all team members are involved and able to contribute (see Table 3.3).

Table 3.3 SWOT analysis for a new customer relations team

Strengths	**Weaknesses**
Team get on well. All qualified in technical aspect of role. High technical expertise. Lots of contacts in the organisation. Good at building relationships across the organisation. Established procedures, based on goodcustomer service practice.	Team admin resource not yet recruited – will be external recruit. Team newly formed – still some uncertainty around specific roles. Not much experience in dealing with difficult or complex customer issues. Remote working limits team communication and 'bonding'.
Opportunities	**Threats**
New team, new start. New IT system could lead to better ways of communicating across team. Chance to develop new skills in customer service. Team and individual roles could expand and develop if successful. Good customer records available for follow-up contact. New loyalty products available to offer customers. Chance to contribute in a very obvious way to the organisation.	High-performance targets to be met. New system could prove difficult to operate. Lack of customer relations skills could lead to wrong decisions or wrong advice (could be legal issues to tackle). Lack of communication could mean essential details are not passed on. Customers might feel hassled. Technical skills could become outdated as no longer in technical roles. Risk of team not being successful and being discontinued.

This analysis suggests potential learning needs for everyone in general customer relations skills, related legal issues and the operation of the new IT systems. There may also be a need for the team manager to undertake some training in remote team management and for the whole team to consider how to improve team communications. The manager may also consider undertaking some whole-team development activities and thought needs to be given to the induction of the new admin person. Finally, to ensure team members remain technically competent, there is a need for ongoing CPD or refresher activities in relation to each team member's technical areas.

It could also be useful to carry out a PESTLE analysis, in which the impact of political, economic, social, technological, legal and environmental changes is explored. (For more detail about PESTLE, and an example, see Chapter 2.)

5. Performance review

Performance review or appraisal is one of the most commonly used processes for identifying learning and development needs. As appraisal is generally about reviewing current performance and agreeing objectives for future performance; it is also often a timely occasion to discuss learning needs.

However, whilst integration of these two processes is fairly typical, some organisations actively seek to separate performance review from identification of learning needs. This is to avoid development being seen only as a (corrective) response to performance issues, and any negativity implied by this. Certainly, as L&D professionals, we should be wary of L&D being perceived in this way, and of appraisal being seen as the only time when learning needs are considered.

Most performance reviews are carried out by line managers, supported by the L&D function.

They are often a culmination of a number of assessment activities, including self-reflection, manager observation, feedback from colleagues and customers, and examination of work results. In some cases, they may involve a full 360° feedback exercise managed internally or externally by specialist providers. Information from all these activities forms the basis of a discussion where any gaps in current or future capability can be explored and agreed and consideration given to how gaps can best be filled.

Depending on organisational policy, identification of learning needs might focus directly on improving work performance or, in more generous cases, may include consideration of some wider continuous professional development (CPD) options. However, most organisations would expect a clear alignment between individual development activity and organisational objectives.

Case Example 3.5

Aligning individual and business development needs

JOHN Willis (L&D Manager at The Insolvency Service) explains how the process works in his organisation.

Learning/CPD needs, and relevant solutions to meet these, are identified and agreed between a team member and their manager. Any funding or support implications for the solution are then referred to the budget-holder with an application for the required funding.

The application requires team members to respond to a number of questions, including: How does this (activity) link into your performance objectives?

In order for a considered decision to be made about if and how to support the request, the team member and their manager must also give the activity a priority rating from the three options listed below:

Priority 1 – Business Critical: The objectives of the individual and/or team/office/section/organisation will not be met if this development need is not addressed.

Priority 2 – Important: The objectives of the individual and/or team/office/section/organisation will be met if this development need is not addressed, but there will be significant and tangible improvements in performance and/or professionalism and/or level of service provided if this development need is met.

Priority 3 – Nice to have: The intended improvements in the performance of the individual and/or team/office/section/organisation will be relatively small, or the development need is one that has been identified and agreed to aid future career development.

Case study questions

1 How does your organisation (or any you know) manage requests for funding for L&D activities?

2 To what extent do you think an organisation should support activities that fall into Priority 3 above?

Performance review can be implemented and recorded in all kinds of ways, from a simple discussion captured in an internally devised review form through to extensive commercially available or custom-built performance review systems. (Several of the latter can be explored via a simple Internet search.) Organisations with more sophisticated systems will be able to draw down summary information about skill levels and gaps across the organisation. In other contexts, it may be a matter of L&D practitioners monitoring individual performance review records – or a representative sample of them – to identify key information. The kind of pointers performance review information can provide includes:

- specific individual or team learning needs;
- general training needs which apply across the organisation, a team or particular role;
- systems or procedures that may be causing problems;
- management behaviours or approaches which could be improved;
- emerging trends and work developments which indicate future learning needs.

 Activity 3.5

'I got an e-mail from my manager to say that he needed to tell me my learning needs for this year. Apparently, it is a safeguarding course. This is the first I had heard about my learning needs.'

This is a shortened version of a genuine quote. We have included it as we think it reflects some bad practice and mistakes relating to learning needs. What do you think these are?

6. Assessments and tests

A very precise way of identifying learning needs is to undertake direct assessment activities – such as observation or testing.

Observation is particularly useful for practical skills such as interviewing a client or repairing a heating system. Typically, an observation would be done against specific standards or requirements, such as internal or external performance standards, quality standards or specific qualification criteria.

Tests can take various forms, from simple knowledge tests through to formal professional exams. They may focus on technical knowledge, basic skills – literacy, language and numeracy – or practical work skills. Many organisations are now using online programmes for maintaining and updating professional knowledge and most of these programmes have embedded knowledge checks and end-tests. Monitoring these can provide the organisation with very accurate information about areas of specific knowledge weaknesses and learning needs.

It is crucial that tests and assessments are operated within clear and fair guidelines using methods that are valid for the type of assessment being undertaken. For example, it would usually be inappropriate to ask someone to write an essay to prove their basic plumbing skills! A more appropriate way would be to observe them actually demonstrating these skills. Some formal tests and assessments require that the assessors are specifically trained or licensed – and as a minimum, assessors should be competent in what they are assessing and have a good understanding of the criteria they are assessing against. Before operating a formal test or assessment make sure you check guidelines and requirements with the test provider.

A particular benefit of assessments and tests is that if we have assessed or tested knowledge and skills before learning, it enables us to better measure the impact of learning activities later on. The same tests or assessments can be repeated, giving a measure of how knowledge and skills have improved.

7. Skills matrices

Developing a skills matrix can be a really useful way of exploring learning needs within a team.

With this technique, you begin by listing all of the separate skill areas or activities involved in the team's work. This could come from job descriptions, team objectives, or by getting team members to analyse the skills or activities involved in their roles.

Each team member's abilities, based on direct assessment, qualifications or self-rating, are then marked against each of the activities on the matrix. The resulting pattern gives a very visual indication of where there may be gaps.

For example, Figure 3.6 is a skills matrix for a catering team within a large leisure centre.

In this version, the matrix just shows who is deemed competent or not competent within each activity. A more sophisticated version might give more information about the level of competence of each team member, say on a scale of 0–3, where 0 = no training or experience, 1 = trained but no experience, 2 = trained and some experience, 3 = fully competent.

Knowing which team members are fully competent also helps identify who could coach or role-model the skills for the other team members.

Figure 3.6 Skills matrix – Example 1

	Food Hygiene	Ordering and Stock	Receive Delivery	Menu	Cold food prep	Hot food prep	Bakery	Service	Cash till	Wash up	Supervise	Assess
AJ	✓	✓	✓	✓	✓	✓	✓	✓	✓	✓	✓	
BM	✓	✓	✓	✓	✓	✓		✓	✓	✓	✓	✓
CJ	✓	✓	✓	✓	✓	✓		✓	✓	✓		
DG	✓		✓		✓	✓	✓	✓		✓		
EL	✓				✓					✓		
FR	✓				✓			✓				
GA	✓				✓							

Of course, not all of the gaps in the 'boxes' need to be filled. It may only be necessary for some team members to have some of the skills. Again, the matrix can be adapted to reflect this, as in Figure 3.7.

Figure 3.7 Skills matrix – Example 2

	Food Hygiene	Ordering and Stock	Receive Delivery	Menu	Cold food prep	Hot food prep	Bakery	Service	Cash till	Wash up	Supervise	Assess
AJ	3	3	3	3	3	3	3	3	3	3	3	1
BM	3	3	3	3	3	3		3	3	3	2	3
CJ	3	1	2	2	3	3		3	1	3		
DG	3	0	2		3	2	3	3	0	2		
EL	3				3	2		0		2		
FR	3				3	1		1		1		
GA	3				1	1				1		

Here, the shaded boxes reflect where the skill area is a requirement of a team member's job, and the rating indicates the level of competence reached by that team member.

An advantage of skills matrices is that they can be as simple or sophisticated as context and resources allow. Some commercial performance management systems can create a range of skills matrix-type documents automatically, and dedicated skills matrix software is also available, but matrices produced on a simple spreadsheet can be just as useful and visually engaging. Another advantage of skills matrices is that users report them to be motivational, as team members like to see themselves well represented in the visual matrix.

Activity 3.6

How could you set up a skills matrix to capture useful information about the abilities and learning needs of a team you are involved in?

8. LMS system data

Organisations with some form of learning management system (LMS) or organisational intranet have a ready source of learning need information. Monitoring key search terms or popular discussion themes will reveal areas of knowledge that are most required by, or are of most interest to, users.

Relying on this method alone might only give a limited picture of requirements, but it can be a quick and easy way of gauging immediate, as well as emerging, areas of learning need. As well as informing ongoing L&D strategy, this approach can enable an almost immediate response to some learning needs, as they arise.

Determining priorities

Once you have collected and analysed information about learning needs, and the needs have been identified, it will usually be necessary for you to prioritise these needs. In order to do this effectively and ensure the most effective spend on follow-up L&D, there are a number of important factors to consider:

- What learning is most urgent? For example, do any of the identified needs concern risks to health and safety or to legal compliance?
- Commercial urgency – what is needed, and by when, to prepare for oncoming changes?
- Which learning needs are having the most negative impact on performance?
- Which needs, if addressed, would have the most positive impact on performance?
- Which needs could be addressed most easily, quickly, cost-effectively?
- Who are key stakeholders in the learning needs and what is their influence?

'One of the problems with learning needs analysis (LNA) is that not a lot of analysis is done. Often what is done is the generation of 'good ideas' with little analytical foundation.'

B Johnson (2017) Learning needs analyses often feature too little analysis, *People Management*

Presenting a recommendation for learning

Finally, having collected and analysed learning need information and identified and prioritised learning needs, you will need to present your conclusions back to key stakeholders.

Depending on the nature of the analysis, a straightforward listing of needs and related factors may be sufficient, but if a formally written learning needs analysis report is required, it should include:

- an introduction and reasons for the learning needs analysis;
- a summary of the methods used and information collected;
- an overview of existing capabilities;
- details of required capabilities;
- needs identified and prioritised;
- details of any other factors which need to be taken into account when determining the L&D solution.

Moving onto the next stage in the training cycle you might also want to include your initial recommendations for meeting learning needs within your report. This could be anything from an internal solution, designed specifically to meet the identified needs, to an externally sourced solution. Either way, your recommendations should be an accurate response to the needs identified and should clearly reflect your organisation's (or the individual's) priorities.

When presenting your recommendations, think about the particular stakeholders involved and the information they will need, such as benefits and indicative costings, in order for them to make a decision about what happens next.

If, having completed your identification of learning needs, your next step is to design an L&D activity to meet these needs, you will find that this is fully covered in Chapter 4 (Designing learning and development activities).

Case Example 3.6

Identifying needs for a management development programme

An interview with Kieleigh Dixon, an L&D Manager, regarding an in-depth identification of learning needs for middle managers in a medium-sized UK organisation.

What was the aim of the learning needs initiative?

The ultimate aim was to create a new management development programme that would enhance the skill-set of our middle managers so that they could lead and support their departments and people more effectively. We already had development programmes in place for this group but we had a growing sense that these were not meeting current needs as effectively as they could. We therefore wanted to go back to basics, and establish what the real current learning needs were.

What information did you decide to collect?

We needed to establish:

- what the business needed from our middle managers;
- what the role was, or should be, now (how had it changed over the years);
- the skills, knowledge and behaviours needed to fulfil the role effectively;
- where we were now in terms of middle manager capability, both as individuals and as a group.

How did you collect this information?

First of all we spent time with senior managers, looking at how the business had changed and how this impacted on the role of the middle managers. Then we interviewed the learner group's line managers to get a really good idea of what they wanted the middle managers to achieve as a result of the programme, ie what they expected middle managers to know and be able to do.

We held some group sessions with the middle managers to get them involved and bought-in from the start. We asked about how the role had changed for them, what would help them in the role and what they wanted from a programme. This helped when it came to analysing their working practice. They were more open to being observed in the role, understanding that this would help us identify strengths and areas for development. We were also able to get some good data and trends from the group sessions, eg areas that affected everyone as well as individual needs. It also provided a good way for us to measure their progress throughout the programme.

We also held one-to-one discussion and self-assessment sessions with middle managers looking at 'where they were now' in relation to the requirements, and carried out some observations of their working practices to help us identify strengths and weaknesses.

Other information we reviewed included:

- were job descriptions up to date to accurately reflect the requirements for the role?
- how were individuals currently measured?
- how long had they been doing the role?
- when had they last been on training or completed any personal or professional development?

How did you analyse the information?

Based on what we'd observed, assessed and discussed, there were various things we had to consider here, ie:

- What were the gaps, from where they were to where they needed to be? This pulled out key areas of focus for the programme.
- What were the trends? There were clear areas that they all needed support with and there were other areas that would need to be developed in smaller groups and in one-to-one coaching.
- What were the areas where they worked together well as a team and where did they need to work more effectively as a team – and how could they do this?

What were the key findings and recommendations?

The recommendation was for a year-long programme to be implemented that would provide key areas of focus for them all, to bring them to a consistent standard (again based on our findings and their suggestions). This would be achieved through training and workshops, led by us, their line manager and other heads of the organisation. As part of the programme they would also spend time working through their own development needs which would be addressed through coaching, buddying up with each other, mentoring and self-led learning.

How did you confirm/agree these recommendations?

We got everyone very involved from the start. We did presentations to the senior and middle managers, including a 'facts and fiction' quiz about the findings and recommendations to stimulate discussion. We did a lot of asking questions and a lot of listening so that the individuals could see from the start that it was their programme – we were just there to help them create it. We also provided a full report for the senior manager who had initially requested the programme, summarising the analysis (methods, needs, findings, recommendations) so that she could share it with other function heads and the executive team.

What factors did you have to take account of (organisational or individual) in making your recommendations?

The main factors for us are always cost and time constraints. Getting people involved from the start really helped with this. We set the learners tasks of pulling together information which helped with time constraints and their own development.

Rather than spend lots of money on external coaches and mentors we gave them coaching skills and got them coaching one another. We got them buddying up and mentoring one another based on each other's strengths. Through this they developed all sorts of skills including: emotional intelligence such as self-awareness and self-regulation, their own and others' personal preferences through MBTI, working more effectively as a team, where their strengths lay as a team, and areas they needed to work on.

You really don't need a big budget to create a successful programme. Ours was fairly minimal. We built all the courses in-house to keep cost to a minimum and we utilised department specialists and heads of department to give overviews in workshops. We also volunteered to do charity work with external organisations which was a very cost-effective way of doing some really effective teamwork and developing leadership skills with next-to-no cost.

What next?

The activities below will help consolidate your knowledge from this chapter:

1 Look into your own (or a familiar) organisation's methods for identifying learning needs. How is it carried out in your organisation and by whom? How quickly does the organisation recognise and respond to learning needs? Is there room for improvement in this approach? What improvements would you recommend?

2 Find an individual who would benefit from clarifying their learning needs and undertake a learning needs analysis with them, following the guidance in the chapter. Finish by helping them identify how they could fill their learning and development gaps and goals.

3 Imagine you have been asked to contribute your three Top Tips to an online article entitled 'Making learning needs analysis effective and engaging – A guide for practitioners'. What would your three top tips be? Share on Twitter using the hashtag #LDPintheW and copy in the account @LDPintheW.

References

CIPD (2018) *Factsheet: Identifying Learning and Development Needs*, www.cipd.co.uk/knowledge/fundamentals/people/development/learning-needs-factsheet (archived at https://perma.cc/6ZNX-ZZDR)

Horn, R (2009) *Researching and Writing Dissertations: A complete guide for business and management students*, CIPD, London

Johnson, B (2017) Learning needs analyses often feature too little analysis, *People Management*, 8 April 2017, www.peoplemanagement.co.uk/voices/comment/learning-needs-analyses (archived at https://perma.cc/QP8V-YEGS)

Landsberg, M (2015) *The Tao of Coaching: Boost your effectiveness at work by inspiring and developing those around you*, Profile Books, London

LinkedIn Learning (2019) *Workplace Learning Report: Why 2019 is the breakout year for the talent developer*, https://learning.linkedin.com/resources/workplace-learning-report (archived at https://perma.cc/CE6K-WST7)

Explore further

Boydell, T and Leary, M (1996) *Identifying Training Needs*, CIPD, London

Donovan, P and Townsend, J (2015) *Learning Needs Analysis Pocketbook*, Management Pocketbooks, London

Shepherd, C (2015) Twenty questions to ask when taking a brief, www.cliveonlearning.com/2015/06/twenty-questions-to-ask-when-taking.html?m=1 (archived at https://perma.cc/M2PN-A35J)

Useful resources

Websites

www.cipd.co.uk/subjects/lrnanddev/trainingneeds/idtlneeds.htm (archived at https://perma.cc/WH97-SV3L)

www.cipd.co.uk/subjects/emplaw/dataprot/dataprotec.htm (archived at https://perma.cc/Z867-R9FU)

www.cipd.co.uk/hr-resources/research/l-and-d-roles-skills.aspx (archived at https://perma.cc/8VN2-XNUH)

www.cipd.co.uk/hr-resources/survey-reports/learning-development-2015.aspx (archived at https://perma.cc/6E67-NNEM)

www.acas.org.uk (archived at https://perma.cc/G9YN-WUF8)

www.businessballs.com (archived at https://perma.cc/UW7U-5HS8)

www.freeonlinesurveys.com (archived at https://perma.cc/4FTN-ZHPP)

www.surveymonkey.com (archived at https://perma.cc/5H4T-TKWS)

www.smart-survey.co.uk (archived at https://perma.cc/BRS6-7CUS)

www.hse.gov.uk (archived at https://perma.cc/6ZUS-VMFJ)

04 Designing learning and development activities

Introduction

In this chapter, we move to another core L&D skill – the design of L&D activities. The best training design, however simple it may appear on the surface, is underpinned by a breadth of theory, technical knowledge and development skills. The chapter considers each of the different design stages and explains the essential knowledge and skills required at each. Putting this knowledge into practice will enable L&D practitioners to provide activities that engage learners whilst effectively meeting learning needs and supporting the transfer of learning to the workplace.

Key areas of content covered in this chapter are:

- the importance of confirming L&D requirements;
- the key stages in designing L&D activities;
- how to devise meaningful objectives;
- how adult learning theory, psychology and neuroscience can inform design;
- different L&D methods, activities and resources;
- how to select, sequence and combine methods and resources;
- professional formats for presenting a session or programme design.

Designing L&D

'People do not wander around and then find themselves at the top of Mount Everest.'
Zig Ziglar, author and motivational speaker

In the previous chapter we discussed the benefits of accurately identifying learning needs and priorities. This is crucial because it means that we can focus resources on the areas of learning that will have the most impact on individual and organisational performance.

But, just knowing what we want or need to achieve is not enough. To ensure learning needs are met effectively, and in the available timescale, we need a carefully planned route to achievement. This is our 'training design'.

The terms 'designing training', 'designing L&D' and 'designing learning and development activities' are generally interchangeable and can refer to a range of different design tasks. For example, a trainer may be involved in the design of a particular *learning material,* perhaps a work-related case study or an online learning module, to be used as a standalone activity or within a wider training session or programme.

Equally, a trainer may be involved in designing a single face-to-face learning *session* to be delivered separately or within a bigger programme of learning. Designing a learning session is about bringing together a range of training methods and learner activities to meet specific learning needs. This is often for a group of learners, but could be for an individual, and could be delivered in a classroom or online.

Finally, a trainer may be involved in designing a wider training or learning *programme*, which blends a range of different learning sessions and learner activities into a bigger learning experience. For example, a learning programme for retail staff, aimed at developing new selling skills, might consist of a number of linked activities over a specific period of time (Table 4.1).

Table 4.1 Learning programme

Introduction – 'New Approaches to Selling' (group session)	Application in the workplace, using video guides and supported by 'sales coaches'	'Review of Practice' (webinar)	Further application in workplace with an online discussion forum for peer support	Observation assessment in the workplace	'Review of Practice and Next Steps' (group session)

Whatever the context, good training design is crucial if we are to fulfil learning objectives and engage learners. Carefully selecting, sequencing and spacing learning content and methods will maximise the impact of L&D and support the transfer of learning to the workplace. Fortunately, there is a lot of information available to help us do all these things.

Key stages in the design process

We have referred to the steps below as 'stages', suggesting that you will move through them in a linear way. However, as in most design tasks, it is more likely that you will move backwards and forwards through these steps as your programme or activity takes shape.

Key stages

1. Clarify requirements and other factors which affect design.
2. Convert requirements into aims and learning outcomes.
3. Determine and sequence learning content.
4. Select methods for delivery of learning content.
5. Select and include review and assessment methods.
6. Determine evaluation methods.
7. Select (or develop) training/learning resources.
8. Present the design as a comprehensive session or programme plan.
9. Agree the final plan with stakeholders.

Clarifying requirements and factors which affect design

For the L&D activity to be a success, we need to know who the key stakeholders are, and their specific requirements and expectations. If there has been a thorough learning needs analysis (see Chapter 3) then much of this information will be available, but there will still be a need to clarify final requirements and liaise re ongoing design issues. Time spent on this will pay off several times over, not just in terms of involving and engaging stakeholders, but also when it comes to reviewing and evaluating the activity.

Key stakeholders might be the learner(s), a team manager, a function or product manager, a project manager, the chief executive – whoever is the main owner of the need, and the more we can involve them the more we will build their engagement and ownership.

Some stakeholders will have a very clear idea of their requirements whilst others may need some assistance to check these out more deeply. If this is the case, ask questions such as:

- How will this L&D activity support current business objectives?
- What do you expect (learners) to be able to do differently as a result of this training?
- What specific outcome/result/situation do you want to be brought about by this training?
- What would the best outcome of this activity be (or look like) for you?

As well as clarifying expectations, you will also need to confirm 'logistical' information such as:

- Who are the target group(s) – explore all – profile and numbers?
- What is their starting point in relation to the learning topic? And to any related skills required, such as IT or language skills? (Refer to previous needs assessments or question/assess thoroughly to ensure the correct starting point.)

- What constraints are there in relation to time, access, location, working hours and release for training arrangements?

Once you have gained all this information, it is good practice to confirm it in writing – either within an overall training or project agreement or, for smaller or less formal initiatives, an e-mail detailing your discussions and agreeing requirements. (More of this later in the chapter.)

Other factors that might affect design

As well as essential information about requirements and logistics, there will be other factors to consider when putting together your design. Depending on how well you know the organisation and/or individuals involved, you may already have some of this information or you may need to extend your initial discussions to ensure that you are familiar with the context and potential constraints that might impact on your programme. Some of the areas that may need consideration are listed below.

Factors about the organisation and its L&D processes

- What resources – space, technology, existing learning content – are available?
- How is the learning activity to be funded? Is there a specific budget?
- What timescales are involved? Time available for design? Timings for delivery?
- Who else in the organisation may be affected by this initiative?
- What are the organisation's preferred training approaches – blended, face-to-face, online learning, on-job training? How open is the organisation to different methods?
- What other L&D is happening in the organisation that might affect or align with this initiative?
- Is external accreditation important to the organisation? Does this L&D initiative link to any external accreditation or qualification process?
- Has anything similar been done before in the organisation and are there lessons to be learned from this?

Legislative factors

- What health, safety and welfare issues need to be considered?
- Does the L&D activity link to any professional licensing and/or compliance requirements (eg for gas engineers or drivers)?
- Are there any aspects of different country legislation to be considered?

Individual factors

At an individual level, consideration needs to be given not only to learning needs, but also to factors which may affect how needs should be met. The kind of information we may want to clarify could include:

- What do they want to achieve from the learning? What are their priorities?
- What is their preferred way of learning at this point in time?
- What is their previous experience of learning? Any concerns or barriers to overcome?
- How may levels of related knowledge and skills affect access to learning (eg literacy, IT skills, language skills, numeracy)?
- What may be the impact of personal circumstances (eg time, funding, other responsibilities and priorities)?
- What support may be available beyond the specific learning activity?

Agreeing requirements

As suggested earlier, once essential information is collected about the learners and the required learning activity, it is good practice to capture this information in a summary document – such as a training project plan or training agreement – and seek confirmation from key stakeholders. Smaller initiatives or less formal contexts may be equally served by an e-mail detailing discussions and agreeing requirements.

Creating some form of agreement documentation, and even the agreement process itself, will not only support your design and evaluation work; it has the added benefit of helping to engage stakeholders in the L&D activity.

A simple agreement might follow the format in the box below:

TRAINING AGREEMENT

Title (of *your* training/L&D project)

General requirements/aims/objectives: What is required of the training – key outcomes – learning needs to be met and preferences for how learning is delivered?

Scope: Numbers and profiles of learners and any different levels of training required for different groups.

Deliverables: The specific activities, learning programme, materials, etc that will be provided by L&D, including any pre- and post-training activity.

Resources: The available people, space, equipment, funding, expertise, agreed for the activities – and who will provide it (eg different stakeholders may contribute).

Timescales: When the activities have to be complete, duration of training, milestones (for bigger initiatives) and follow-up timetable.

Risks: Anything likely to throw activities 'off track', eg if there is a dependence on the availability of a new system or there is a particularly busy work period coming up, and what has been agreed to address these circumstances.

CASE EXAMPLE 4.1

Knowing requirements

Michael Privett explains how his organisation ensures that requirements are fully clarified prior to any L&D activity.

As a small L&D team of four, we wanted to increase our footprint in the company by training managers and team leads on how to become effective face-to-face trainers. To achieve this, I designed and wrote a five-module online course called Train the Trainer, which is distributed through our LMS. The five modules are:

- creating a learning objective;
- designing a training plan;
- determining logistics of training;
- facilitating training;
- observing results in action.

The Determining Logistics of Training module emphasises the importance of being clear about what is required before the training is delivered. In the module, we share an analogy of how we plan for a party with date and time, invitation list, venue etc. Participants are asked to consider similar questions such as who, what, where, how and when for their training plans. We introduce the importance of the learning environment and share tips for how they can optimise it for learning.

Participants clarify and add all this to their training plan, using the headings below and then submit their plan to us for review:

- learning objective;
- relevance (to business goals);
- knowledge, skills and abilities to be developed (to meet the learning objective);
- participation (how learners will participate in the training);
- validation (how the effectiveness of the training will be demonstrated);
- expectation of use (how the learning will be used back in the workplace);
- audience (who the training is for);
- logistics (learning environment, training dates, length of training);
- tools and resources;
- advance preparation required;
- detailed training material.

We find that this process makes the Train the Trainer participants really think through what they are going to do and how best to do it, and leads to very comprehensive and effective training plans.

Michael Privett, Training Specialist, Lightspeed POS (London)

Aims, objectives and learning outcomes

Having thoroughly clarified and agreed the requirements of the learning activity, the next stage is to convert requirements into specific aims and objectives or learning outcomes. As this is a subject with a range of differing approaches, let's begin by considering some definitions and differences.

Aims

Aims tend to be fairly general statements, broad ranging and possibly combining a number of intentions into a 'bigger' statement. For example:

- The programme aims to develop the skills and knowledge required to operate the Cashtime Accounting system.

Aims can be long-term or indefinite and, for all the reasons mentioned above, are generally quite difficult to measure. They are, nonetheless, important as they give an overall perspective to the proposed activity.

Objectives

Objectives are often considered to be a 'subdivision' of aims – a means of breaking down an aim into measurable chunks. Objectives are more precise and specific than aims and are intended to be measurable. For example:

- List the Cashtime System data input commands.
- State the categories of information held within sales ledger.
- Create an invoice template.

There are a number of recommended approaches and guiding principles to assist our specification of objectives, listed below.

1. Objectives as outcomes

As far back as the 1960s Robert Mager proposed that objectives should be positioned as outcomes and be composed of three elements:

1. a behaviour – what should be done;
2. a condition – the context or conditions in which it should be done;
3. a standard – the standard to which the outcome should be performed.

For example:

- Trainees will be able to undertake an outbound sales call, in a real work situation, to the standard set out in XCo's 'Quality Calls' checklist.

Mager's approach has been widely accepted in the world of learning and development and underpins the way most L&D objectives are written (Mager, 1998).

2. Objectives linked to evaluation

John Rodwell, trainer and author, suggests a further approach to setting objectives, linked to Donald Kirkpatrick's model of Levels of Evaluation (Kirkpatrick, 1994 – for more information about Kirkpatrick's work see Chapter 10, Evaluating impact). Rodwell emphasises the benefits of making clear and close links between L&D objectives and later evaluation activity. So, in determining our L&D objectives he suggests we think about what we are trying to achieve at each of Kirkpatrick's evaluation levels and then word our objectives accordingly – giving us four 'subcategories' of objectives, as below.

Level 1:

- *Evaluation:* Immediate reaction to the training.
- *Objectives:* Statements of what you want learners to rate or comment positively on regarding the training (eg content, methods, trainer's knowledge, overall 'experience', etc).

Level 2:

- *Evaluation:* Actual learning and development – knowledge and skills acquired.
- *Objectives:* Statements of what participants will actually learn and how they will demonstrate this during the training (through tests, questions, exercises, case studies, etc).

Level 3:

- *Evaluation*: Impact on individual performance.
- *Objectives:* Statements of what learners should be able to do as a result of the training (after a period of application and consolidation in the workplace).

Level 4:

- *Evaluation*: Impact on the organisation.
- *Objectives*: Statements of what the training should achieve for the organisation (where applicable).

In this model, objectives at Level 3 (and 4 if appropriate) would be established first, during the learning needs analysis stage, and would form the evaluation criteria to be used some time after the training; objectives at Levels 1 and 2 would be determined during the design stage, and achievement of them would be determined within the L&D activity.

3. SMART objectives

Another popular guiding principle relating to objective setting is SMART (Table 4.2). Although more closely linked to the setting of performance objectives (and opinion is divided on whether SMART can always be applied to learning objectives), SMART provides a useful reminder that objectives should seek to be concise and measurable.

Learning outcomes

One slight problem with setting objectives is that, because they are so useful, they have a range of different applications – for example, we often have performance objectives at work, as trainers we have objectives for our training activity, and many of the books we refer to have chapter objectives – and the wording of objectives can vary slightly depending on how they are being used.

In a learning context, objectives are most useful when they are written from the point of view of the learner, not the trainer. They should also focus on outcomes, ie what learners will be able to do as a result of the learning, rather than inputs, ie

Table 4.2 SMART objectives

Specific	Objectives should be clearly and simply defined, usually, with a single focus.
Measurable	Objectives should be written in a way that will make it possible to assess/observe/measure whether or not the objective has been met.
Achievable	Objectives should be achievable within the context they are set. Can they realistically be achieved in the time and with the resources available?
Relevant	Objectives should be relevant to the context they are set in. In an L&D context, they should be relevant to the overall aim of the L&D activity.
Timebound	Objectives should have a related time period, partly to increase motivation, but also to aid accurate measurement of achievement.

NOTE: Some models of SMART are extended to SMART**ER**, where **E** represents Exciting or Ethical, and **R** represents Recorded, Rewarded or Re-visited.

what they will spend time doing during the training. See the difference in the two perspectives below.

Trainer (and inputs) point of view:

- to teach learners how to apply a dressing to an open wound;
- to provide an opportunity to practise applying dressings.

Learner (and outcomes) point of view:

- learners will be able to select appropriate dressings for different wounds;
- learners will be able to apply the dressings in a safe and correct manner.

To help ensure objectives are always positioned from the learner point of view and always focus on outcomes, it can be helpful to think of 'learning outcomes', rather than objectives. Learning outcomes would then always be written with the starting sentence:

> 'As a result of the learning, learners will… (or learners will be able to…)'

followed by the specific outcomes, eg:

- …select appropriate dressings for different wounds;
- …apply the dressings in a safe and correct manner.

Objective verbs

A final aspect of setting objectives or learning outcomes to consider is the choice of verb used, as this will impact considerably on how measurable or assessable objectives are – probably the most important factor about objectives. On the other hand, the desire to keep things wholly measurable can lead to an overuse of lower level outcomes, such as 'state', 'demonstrate' or 'describe' and we need to think more creatively about this.

There are many verbs to choose from (as in Figure 4.1).

Figure 4.1 Choosing verbs for objectives

identify design
write contrast describe
state discuss connect repair open
classify recognise select explain
compare determine
manipulate replace operate
assemble solve name adjust develop
create list accept listen
appreciate judge distinguish rationalise
justify associate carry out derive make
receive perceive decide influence
define construct measure
align critique

In some cases, and particularly if you choose verbs such as 'understand' or 'be aware of', it may be appropriate to provide more information about how your learning outcome will be assessed. This is the approach taken by awarding bodies when specifying the learning requirements for some qualifications – including many of the CIPD's L&D qualifications. The qualifications are specified in terms of learning outcomes, but each learning outcome has extra information in the form of 'assessment criteria' to qualify how it should be assessed, as in the example in Table 4.3.

In most learning situations, however, it is sufficient to capture the intended learning in a number of simple and clearly written learning outcomes.

Table 4.3 Learning outcomes and assessment criteria

Learning outcome	Assessment criteria
The learner will:	**The learner can:**
1 Understand different ways L&D is positioned within organisations.	1.1 Describe different ways L&D services are arranged within, or accessed externally, by organisations.
	1.2 Explain the factors which affect how organisations arrange or access L&D services.

Activity 4.1

1 Considering the information about objectives above, which of the following do you consider to be effective objectives (or learning outcomes) for a learning activity – and why/why not?

- Learners will improve their communication skills.
- Learners will understand the challenges faced by lone workers.
- Learners will be able to justify the selection of different food groups within a lunchtime menu for 5- to 7-year-olds.
- Learners will be able to use their mobile phone to record their daily activities in the company time log system.
- To build confidence in making loan recovery calls.
- Learners will have a go at replacing a heat exchanger.
- During the training, learners will select and apply appropriate dressings for a range of surface wounds.
- Key points of the 2018 UK Data Protection Act and 2018 General Data Protection Regulation (GDPR) and how they impact on our work.
- Learners will be able to compare the advantages and disadvantages of two different homecare approaches.
- To demonstrate the stages in soufflé preparation and cooking.

2 Can you improve any that are not effective?

Determining and sequencing learning content

Determining content

Outline learning content will be determined by the learning needs analysis or by a particular stimulus for the training, such as a product launch. However, you might still need to undertake some further analysis, perhaps of a specific task, process, product or subject area, to ensure that all the relevant content areas are included.

There are a number of ways of doing this: for example, a task, job or process might be analysed through observation, examination of documentation or discussion with experts. Analysis of a general subject area can be undertaken by starting at the highest level (topic or job title) and asking:

- What does someone need to know/do to understand/be capable in this area?

Then for each answer to the above question, ask again:

- What does someone need to know/do to understand/be capable in this area?

And so on.

This kind of analysis is similar to the Five Whys technique described in Chapter 3 and is sometimes referred to as 'pyramid analysis', because of the resulting shape

Figure 4.2 Analysing a subject area

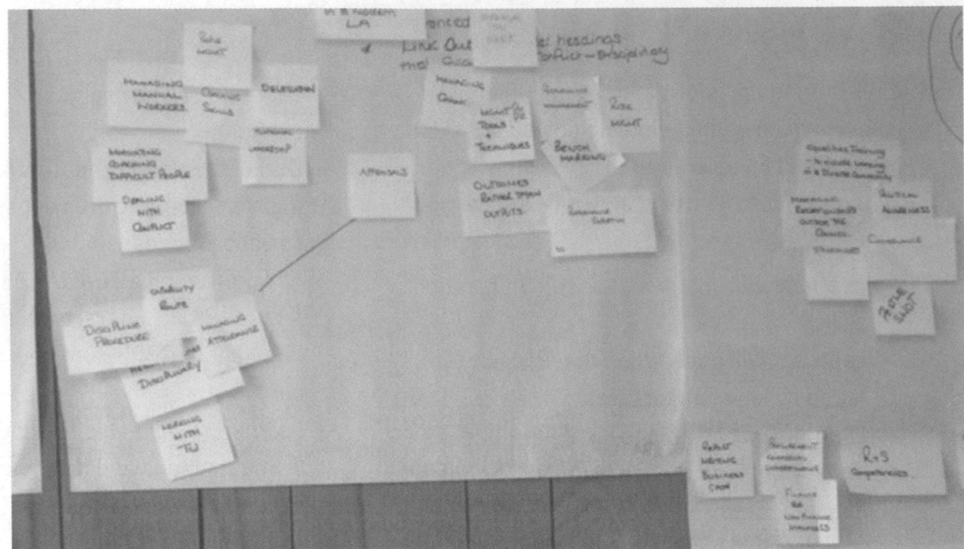

of information. To encourage creativity and open thinking, analysis is often best done on big pieces of flipchart paper or on a wall using sticky notelets which can be moved around until the final content and subdivision is complete (see Figure 4.2). If you are more comfortable using technology for this process, you could try a simple spreadsheet or if you have access, specialist design software.

Having identified the *possible* content, consider whether you need to include all of this in your activity or just some key parts. Depending on the stage of the learning and the learners' starting point, you may just want to focus on some essential areas, leaving other areas for later on. It can be tempting to cram every bit of content into an activity and 'overfill' the time available, but it is more important to adjust the depth and breadth of information to suit the learner group. Allowing plenty of time for learners to explore a topic will enable more effective internalisation of the detail.

Another important point to emphasise here is that it is not always necessary to devise new content. Once you know what content areas you need, think about the various sources of existing content available to you both inside and 'outside' the organisation. We have video channels, social media feeds and articles, online talks and specialist TV channels, MOOCs (massive open online courses), sector body resources and professional body resources, to list just a few. One thing our world is not short of is information.

Sequencing

Sequencing learning requires us to consider how learners will be best able to 'take in' the learning topic. The more effective we make the learning process the more likely learners will be to retain and be able to make use of their new learning after the learning activity. For example, it may be necessary for learners to have grasped one concept before they can think productively about another. Neuroscientists are increasingly telling us that our brains work best when they focus on one thing at once, rather than multitasking.

Case Example 4.2

Design and delivery colleagues working together

Claire Hughes, L&D Portfolio Manager at HMRC explained the importance of involving her delivery colleagues in the L&D design stage.

Collaboration with delivery colleagues is critical when scoping and designing L&D activities. Where possible, we like to include our trainers in the LNA stage as they can identify if any face-to-face (F2F) learning already exists and they are able to draw on their knowledge of the business areas and their working practices. When scoping and designing the activity, delivery colleagues can offer insight into the best media for delivery and the activities to be included. They will know the practicalities of delivering the L&D products and so need to work closely with the designers when planning them.

Allyson Beardmore, also an L&D Portfolio Manager at HMRC, added how involving designers in the delivery stages can also enhance design.

Within HMRC our F2F events tend to be a consolidation event for prerequisite learning. Giving designers the opportunity to observe delivery of products has provided really useful feedback that informs design. For example, that invaluable time in delivery has been spent revisiting knowledge that should have been known from prerequisite learning.

Following this feedback, we worked collaboratively to reshape the content of a product, ensuring that F2F time could focus on the areas originally intended. This made the product better for everyone. Bringing delivery into the design area can have much more far reaching benefits than you'd think!

Case study question

If your role was to design L&D activities for others to deliver – what questions would you want to ask of your delivery colleagues?

It can be helpful to think about learning as 'blocks', which build on top of each other until the desired level and scope of learning has been covered. To be most accessible, learning content should be delivered in a logical flow, allowing learners to build up through simple to more complex areas of learning:

Simple → Complex → Increasing Complexity

However, there may be other logical approaches to sequencing, perhaps:

- following the natural sequence of a task, process or activity;
- following any related timelines, eg activities on each day of the working week or seasonal considerations for outdoor work;
- natural groupings, eg age groups or categories of products;
- the structure and sequence of a related qualification;
- logically considering what can be done prior to the learning event (eg in pre-reading or listening), what is best done during the event and what can be signposted after the event (eg by watching a useful video).

Selecting training and learning methods

Some ideas and theories

Having identified the learning content to be included in your session, you will then want to find appropriate methods for delivering this, and there are some useful ideas and theories around which can help with this.

> 'Applying learning theory into practice impacts the wider success of the organisation. Those that do were found to be twice as likely to leverage networks and collaboration to drive transformation and nearly four times more likely to improve leadership capabilities based on approaches that are proven to drive learning impact.'
>
> *Professionalising Learning and Development,* CIPD/Towards Maturity, February 2019

Adult learning theory

Malcolm Knowles, in his 'theory of andragogy' (Knowles, 1980) discusses how adult learners need to feel responsible for their own decisions and directions, and the negative impact of imposing learning on adults in the way it might be done more typically for children. Knowles put forward six key assumptions or principles about adult learners:

1. Adults are self-directing and capable of making their own decisions about learning (Self-Concept).
2. Adults bring a range of prior learning and experience to learning which forms a basis for, and affects, new learning (Foundation).
3. Adults are most interested in learning which has immediate relevance to their work or personal life (Readiness).
4. Adults are most interested in learning which helps them perform tasks or solve problems (Orientation).
5. Intrinsic (internal) motivation may play a bigger part in motivating adult learners than extrinsic (external) motivators (Motivation).
6. Adults need to know and understand the reason for learning something (Need to Know).

The more involvement we can give learners in determining the nature and format of their learning, the more ownership they are likely to feel, and the greater commitment to the learning activities they are likely to have. If we are working with small numbers of individuals, it is relatively easy to involve them in the design of the L&D activity – we can just ask them and co-design. If we are working with larger groups of individuals, this gets more challenging, but there are still plenty of ways of ensuring their involvement. For example, we can ask them to identify representatives from the learner group who can put forward their needs and views, and be involved in the design process. We can ensure that the design allows plenty of opportunities for individuals to make their own decisions, maybe choosing from optional activities or determining their own approach to learning tasks. We can also benefit everyone by building in a facility for learners to curate their own bank of programme related materials and video clips.

Hase and Kenyon (2013) have built on Knowles' approach and discuss the concept of 'heutagogy' or fully self-determined learning, whereby the learner decides on the route they will take to learn. As a very simple example, this will work in a blended approach where a mix of resources are available and the learner chooses their own learning path through the material.

PAUSE FOR THOUGHT

How have you, or could you, involve learners in designing L&D activities within your work or subject area?

Domains of learning

Another concept which can inform how we design L&D, primarily attributed to Dr Benjamin Bloom, is Domains of Learning. In Bloom's model or 'taxonomy', learning is divided into three main domains or categories (Bloom, 1956):

- cognitive: about knowledge and facts and understanding;
- psychomotor: about physical dexterity, practical skills and doing;
- affective: about attitude and beliefs and the basis of some of our behaviours.

For learning to be effective, learning methods should be appropriate to the type of learning required. For example, appropriate methods to develop knowledge might include reading, listening to presentations or questioning experts. Physical skills, however, will be more effectively developed through the use of demonstration, supported practice or coaching. Finally, if we want to influence peoples' opinions or beliefs, then training methods may need to include discussion, real examples or coaching which challenges their current thinking.

> '...taking in information is only distantly related to real learning. It would be nonsensical to say, "I just read a great book about bicycle riding – I've now learned that".'
>
> *Peter M Senge*, The Fifth Discipline: The art and practice of the learning organisation

If we use the wrong methods in relation to what we want to achieve, it is likely that we will not achieve our objective. For example, change-related programmes may well fail if they concentrate too much on the facts and logistics of the change (*cognitive and psychomotor*), but underplay the emotional effects that change can have on individuals (*affective*).

Case Example 4.3

Affective learning methods

When a large public organisation wanted to introduce a new staff performance review system, the L&D team knew it would not be enough for people to just understand how to use the system. The previous system had been unpopular and the team knew that for the new system to be implemented effectively, they would have to convince staff of its merits.

The session they developed to introduce the new system therefore included:

- factual information about how the system worked;

plus:

- a comparison with the previous system showing the need for the change and how unpopular aspects of the previous system had been addressed;
- opportunities for staff to discuss the new system and air their concerns.

Although the discussion sessions made the delivery of the training more demanding and challenging for the L&D teams, approaching the subject at a cognitive level only (ie how the system worked) would not have met the required need.

In reality, most work-related learning will involve more than one domain or type of learning, and therefore a mix of approaches will be required within most learning programmes.

Case study questions

Think of a programme that you have designed recently:

1. What were its objectives?
2. How well did the methods align with the objectives?
3. How (if at all) would you enhance that programme if you were to design it again?

The Experiential Learning Cycle

The Experiential Learning Cycle (Kolb, 1984) can give us a structure for learning design. The cycle presents four stages of learning: concrete experience (having experiences); reflective observation (reflecting on experiences); abstract conceptualisation (thinking, having new ideas); and active experimentation (experimenting with the new ideas). Each of these, Kolb suggests, should take place for learning to be most effective (see Figure 4.3).

To enable learners to move around each stage of the learning cycle, we can design training activities which include all of the following:

- activities/experiences or learners can 'bring' their prior experiences to the activity;
- opportunities to reflect on these experiences, maybe through reviewing and discussing them with other learners;

Figure 4.3 The Experiential Learning Cycle

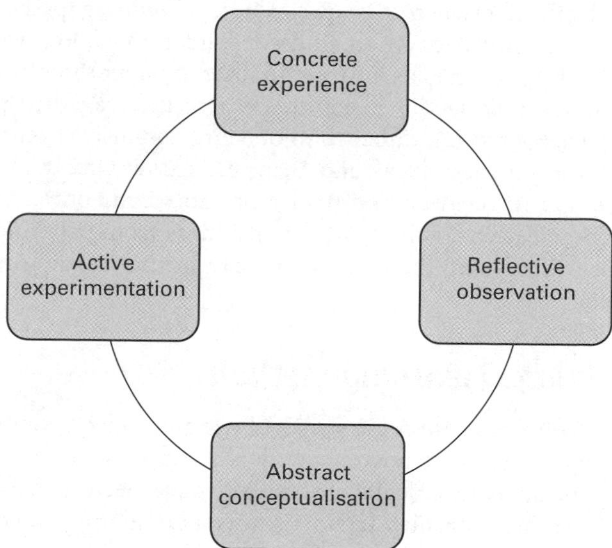

- new thinking and ideas to inform how things could be done differently, perhaps through tutor input, video, expert speakers or the sharing of good practice and information amongst learners;
- and, finally, safe opportunities to experiment with the new ideas, maybe through role play, skills practice or application in the workplace.

Neuroscience

There is a huge amount of research information emerging from neuroscience which is starting to inform how we design learning and development. Whilst the findings are not all new, they are increasingly giving us a scientific basis for many things that we have long suspected.

For example, we are now seeing evidence that learning is most effective when learners have just the right amount of challenge. If learners are interested in the subject, recognise its relevance and want to learn, they are likely to give the learning more focused attention. But if the learning is too challenging or causing anxiety, this will impact on learning and memory processes reducing the effectiveness of the L&D activity. Knowing this makes it even more important for us to make clear links between accurately identified learning needs and the L&D activity so that we gain the learners' 'buy-in', and for us to be aware of existing knowledge levels so that we can pitch learning content accordingly.

We are also learning that, as important as it is to help learners assimilate new information and learning, it is equally important to help them to be able to retrieve that information when they need it. Therefore, as well as providing opportunities for gaining new knowledge, L&D activities need to include lots of opportunities for applying new learning so that learners strengthen the brain pathways involved in them retrieving information and using it in different contexts.

Neuroscience is also telling us about 'spacing' learning and that learning has been found to be most effective when it is spread out, allowing gaps between learning activities. This allows for reflection on, and consolidation of, knowledge as well as strengthening memory processes as information has to be repeatedly recalled at each stage of the learning. Bearing this in mind, we are encouraged to provide several short and well-spaced activities, rather than one large intensive event.

More information on these ideas and theories is now widely available and we would encourage you to research and read more about the ones that interest you. Chapter 9, Engaging learners, delves further into ideas from psychology and neuroscience that inform L&D and there are also some further reading resources at the end of this chapter.

Different training & learning methods

The days when a training session consisted of a trainer giving out information to learners for the whole session, possibly with the information also on slides, are hopefully long gone (and technically this would have been a presentation rather than training). Designing a learning session is now a fascinating and creative activity involving the selection and combination of different L&D approaches.

> 'The change in emphasis from classroom trainer to learning facilitator that has taken place over the past 15 years has proved incredibly valuable, both for us as trainers and for our learners. As trainers, it has encouraged us to develop new skills and imaginative approaches to the design of learning opportunities. For our learners it has encouraged a real shift in approach, from passive recipients of whatever the trainer decided they needed to know, to active partners in the learning process.'
>
> *Jane Church, Learning Facilitator, Novus Professional Development Ltd*

The best L&D sessions will involve a good range of methods and activities that engage learners and allow them to relate content to their own context. We know that, as in any aspect of life, different learners will enjoy some activities more than others and find some more useful. We also know that some methods are better suited to developing certain types of learning than others. And we know that to maintain learners' interest and provide a stimulating learning environment we need to keep changing things around a little. Taking all this into account, it is really important that our learning sessions use a rich and varied mix of training approaches and learner activities – for example, we might include some trainer input (presentation or demonstration) followed by some small group sharing activities, and then some individual practical activities, and finish with a full group discussion.

Several training and learning methods that could be included in a learning session are discussed below in Table 4.4.

Table 4.4 Training and learning methods

	Reasons for selecting	Challenges
Trainer input (presentation, with or without presentation software)	• an effective and quick way of passing on information • allows for learners to hear a 'common message' • provides an opportunity for learners to check own knowledge against input, ask questions and clarify • provides initial learning/ information for use within further activities • takes pressure and attention off learners when they might be feeling uncertain, eg at the beginning of a session and allows time to settle in	• can be boring if it goes on for too long • little learner involvement • does not encourage learner ownership of learning • learner retention of information may not be great • dependent on quality of presentation skills
Demonstration	• quick way of passing on information • crucial first step in skills development • allows learners to see activity done 'properly'	• demonstrator might pass on bad habits • task might be over-simplified to make demonstration possible • in-course demonstration might not reflect actual pressures of the workplace
Group discussion	• learners are a huge source of learning for each other • learners' 'agendas' can be aired • hearing others' views can help challenge learners' limiting beliefs or resistance to change • enables learning to be learner-led and engage learners in the topic – providing the subject has meaning from them	• learners might not participate • discussion could be dominated by a few • discussion may stray into areas where the trainer lacks knowledge or feels uncomfortable • discussion may stray away from learning focus • requires good facilitation skills

(*continued*)

Table 4.4 (Continued)

	Reasons for selecting	Challenges
Videos/video clips and the use of actors	• adds variety to the input of information • makes learning more interesting • video clips are accessible, wide ranging and can be very current (or can be produced to meet a particular need) • smartphones mean video clips can be easily created and uploaded by learners (building ownership of learning) • use of actors allows customisation of presented scenarios and can make practice more 'real' than relying on role-play within a learner group.	• commercial videos can be too generic or not wholly applicable to the audience, and can soon become out of date • need to be aware of copyright issues • learner video clips may not always reflect correct approaches or good practice – difficult to quality assure • actors can be expensive
Expert speakers	• adds variety to the input of information • learners tend to respect info from 'experts' • expert will be able to talk about and answers questions on the real situation • experts can enthuse listeners if passionate about their subject and proficient speakers	• dependent on availability of speakers • could be a speaker bias to information • expert could be technically brilliant, but a poor speaker
Learner activities: ice-breakers/ warm-ups and games not directly related to the learning topic	• can help put learners at ease and act as a 'warm-up' (the term 'warm-up' is replacing 'ice-breaker') • can introduce a fun, light-hearted atmosphere to the learning • high-energy activities can lift group energy levels • can leave learners in a relaxed state for learning to take place	• need to be used with care • should be appropriate to age group, type of learning, organisational culture • can embarrass learners if inappropriate • can be considered childish or irrelevant by learners unless carefully selected

(*continued*)

Table 4.4 (Continued)

	Reasons for selecting	Challenges
Learner activities: written exercises, case studies, real work examples	• allows learners to work together in an in-depth way and learn from each other • can help learners shift into deeper level of learning and concentration • opportunity to apply knowledge and skills • begins transition of knowledge to workplace activity • can provide assessment opportunities	• activities need to be well constructed to be valid and have credibility • may be dependent on access to real work examples from workplace • confidentiality and data protection issues may have to be addressed • can be 'low-energy' activities
Learner activities: brainstorming, preparing and delivering presentations, knowledge tests and quizzes	• allows learners to work together and share knowledge and experience • moderate energy activities – can lift energy levels, whilst still focusing on learning topic • can be a useful activity to end a session – end on a high • opportunity for learners to check knowledge and fill gaps • provides assessment opportunities	• tend to be about knowledge retention rather than application • brainstorming can be stilted if wrongly focused on getting the 'right answer' rather than on bringing out creative thinking and ideas • can create competition and division
Learner activities: role-play/try-outs and skills practice	• allows learners to work together to share knowledge and experience • moderate energy activities – can lift energy levels, whilst still focusing on learning topic • opportunity to act out procedures and skills in safe environment • begins transition of knowledge and skills to real work activities	• can be considered artificial and not representative of real work • response from learners is usually more positive if asked to do 'skills practice' or 'try-outs' rather than 'role-play'! • requires good feedback skills
Learner activities: individual analysis, self-reflection, and action-planning	• helps to identify needs • reviews where learning is in relation to desired goals • informs further learning • can be motivational • action-planning helps in the transfer of learning to the workplace • action-planning provides a vehicle for later evaluation	• learners can find concentration for self-assessment difficult within, or just after, a high-energy group session • learners may feel uncomfortable about self-reflection or analysis • learners may 'skew' analysis results to make them more favourable

Case Example 4.4

Converting trainer input to an activity

One of the objectives of a coaching programme was for learners to understand the difference between directive and non-directive approaches and how different coaching techniques fitted into this.

Rather than just having some trainer input about this (as originally intended), an activity was designed instead whereby:

- lots of different coaching techniques, such as questioning, active listening, paraphrasing, etc were written on small sticky notelets;
- learners were divided into teams and each team given a set of the notelets, plus some blank ones to add some further techniques;
- each team was allocated a wall of the training room;
- each wall was labelled with 'directive' at one end and 'non-directive' at the other;
- teams were then given a set amount of time to discuss and arrange the techniques (notelets) in order of directive to non-directive.

When it came to feeding back the team's 'arrangement' to the whole group (which could be 'marked' by the trainer), teams were asked to give an example of each technique and to explain why they had positioned it as they had.

The aim of this design approach was to build learner energy and engagement and to help ensure that everyone remembered the learning points.

Management trainer and coach, public sector

Combining methods

If time is an issue, or to space out the L&D activity, you might consider breaking your session down into 'bite-size' chunks and delivering these at different times, maybe added to staff or team meetings (if everyone is on one site) or in short virtual meetings at the beginning of the working day.

You could also consider delivering your session as a 'flipped classroom' (see box below).

THE FLIPPED CLASSROOM

An increasingly popular trend, particularly in education, is for the 'flipped classroom', in which learners are provided with the main factual or theoretical information of the learning session, prior to the session taking place. The session then assumes a level of learner knowledge and is spent discussing the topic, answering more complex questions and undertaking related activities, with the tutor available to support and assist with these. This is a 'flip' of the traditional classroom which is traditionally centred on the delivery of knowledge (a lecture or presentation) followed up by 'homework' in which learners are asked to apply their knowledge to various questions and activities, often in a context where there is no immediate support.

The initial factual information is provided in the form of reading material, video, podcast, etc and learners can have access to the tutor at this stage to clarify any uncertainties and check their understanding. Tutor contact might be via e-mail, a messaging platform or within a learning management system where the whole flipped classroom can be managed. Learners are able to spend as much time as they need (prior to the learning session) revisiting the information, contacting the tutor, as needed, and building their understanding – thus allowing for individual differences and speed of learning.

When the time comes for the classroom or group learning session, learners are all able to participate fully in the more complex questions and activities and reach a greater depth of learning.

For a larger L&D initiative, you might choose to blend a trainer-led session with some other L&D approaches. As well as allowing for better retention and transfer, through carefully building and spacing out the activities, this will provide a more varied and engaging programme for learners. For example, you could combine a face-to-face learning session with:

- on-job training or practice;
- one-to-one coaching;
- one-to-one mentoring;
- peer learning/Action Learning Sets;
- online learning modules;
- learner-generated 'curated' content;
- online or social media-based discussion forums;
- webinars or virtual classrooms.

These are considered in more detail in Table 4.5.

When combining activities to create your session or bigger programme of learning, remember to give some thought to how the activities 'flow' from one to the other, and to ensure that each builds on the former and leads into the next. You will also need to think about the overall timing of the programme and the gaps needed between different programme elements for learners to apply the content in their own context and to internalise their learning.

Table 4.5 Some more approaches to L&D

Method	**On-job training**
Overview	Learning in the workplace through real work activities
Good for	Learning and practising essential job skills
Pros	Very timely – training as it is needed Learner learns the 'realities of the job' Learner tends to learn informally, from expert colleagues or manager May help engage learner's manager in the training No major reduction in work time
Cons (if used in isolation)	Might lose out on the bigger picture Might not be time to reflect on learning or ask questions Pressures of workplace might detract from quality of training Learner might feel uneasy about admitting weaknesses
Method	**One-to-one coaching** (see Chapter 7)
Overview	(Mostly) non-directive support from a coach, to help learner develop and apply skills and knowledge in the workplace
Good for	Developing skills Improving behaviours Developing confidence and self-management skills
Pros	Tailored to individual needs Develops learner responsibility for own development
Cons	Coach needs to have good coaching skills Coach style may clash with learner style
Solution	**One-to-one mentoring** (see Chapter 7)
Overview	General support from a more experienced person who can advise and help learner to apply skills and knowledge
Good for	Building confidence Improving behaviours Establishing networks
Pros	Attention focused on individual needs Can cover a wide range of areas
Cons	Mentor role may conflict with line manager role Dependent on availability of mentors
Method	**Peer learning/Action Learning Sets**
Overview	Groups meet together to support each other through work projects and share learning and ideas
Good for	Getting new ideas Different perspectives Sharing good practice Building team/group support
Pros	Learn from others' experiences Saves time in learning Outlet for discussing and resolving workplace frustrations Encourages ownership of learning and action

(*continued*)

Table 4.5 (Continued)

Cons	Dependent on others wanting the same format Takes time away from the workplace Can be difficult to sustain a group – requires discipline and commitment
Method	**Online learning modules (e-learning)**
Overview	Learner manages own learning working through online learning modules
Good for	Acquiring knowledge Re-capping knowledge Working at own pace
Pros	Flexible in terms of access – as and when required Online modules are inexpensive if used for large number of learners Learner can work at own pace and re-cap as required Learning access can often be measured and useful statistics collected
Cons	E-learning has suffered from some bad design in the past (but is improving with increased availability of augmented reality and learning functions) Learners miss the stimulation of learning with others May require extra equipment or IT skills to access some information
Method	**Learner-generated content**
Overview	Learners finding and uploading relevant resources on a theme, usually into a messaging platform or LMS, that can be accessed by the learner group
Good for	Enhancing learner involvement and engagement Finding wider resources
Pros	Learners have an active role in the content and delivery Not all of the resourcing is down to a single trainer Learners can often come up with novel resources Results in a unique group-curated collection of resources which can be added to and used long after the learning event
Cons	Quality of learning resources can be variable Resources need validating and curating, although this can be done by the group
Method	**Online or social media-based discussion forums**
Overview	Chat rooms, messaging hubs, forums or social media platforms such as Twitter or Slack, where learners can communicate and connect
Good for	Sharing perceptions and perspectives Clarifying areas of uncertainty with peers Reflecting and reviewing an activity
Pros	Enables real-time discussion about a common theme Opens up the range of contributors and can bring in experts and others not involved in the actual learning event Learners can participate as and when they choose Learning is social and collaborative
Cons	Some learners may be alienated by or lack the skills to access discussions Discussions may need moderation

(continued)

Table 4.5 (Continued)

Method	**Webinars or virtual classrooms**
Overview	Facilitated training delivered online ('virtual face-to-face')
Good for	Gaining knowledge where some level of interaction is also needed
Pros	Can cater for large numbers of participants Relatively inexpensive Greener option as it reduces travel and paper Can easily reach a geographically spread or global audience
Cons	Risks of technology not working or not being compatible Can be difficult to control contributions from learners Learners may 'switch off' and not be paying attention Some learners find online learning less engaging than face-to-face

Supporting learning transfer

Many of the methods and principles we have discussed in this chapter have a role to play in supporting the transfer of learning to the workplace. As far back as 1885, German psychologist Hermann Ebbinghaus (1885) presented the concept of a Learning Curve; however, he also identified an accompanying Forgetting Curve which showed us how quickly the things we learn can be forgotten.

If we are to enable retention of learning, and further than this, transfer of learning to the workplace, we must bear this need in mind throughout our design and take active steps to support it. Firstly, we need to design relevant activities that engage learners and, secondly, we need to sequence and space the activities in a way that builds and consolidates their learning.

However, transfer is not all about learning retention. It is also, as Malcolm Knowles highlighted, about learners understanding and owning the need for the learning so that they are motivated to learn and put their new skills and knowledge into practice. This requires us to involve learners in analysis and design as much as possible and to ensure that the reasons for any learning activity, and the projected outcomes and benefits, are clearly communicated.

Finally, we can make use of a range of techniques that will help learners apply their learning, such as meaningful action-planning, ongoing access to curated information such as guides and video clips, structured line management support or follow-up access to workplace coaches or peer support groups.

Case Example 4.5

Customer returns and complaints programme

A 'Handling Customer Returns and Complaints' programme, for staff at a chain of fashion retailers, was designed as follows:

- issue of the new organisational policy on complaint handling for staff to read;
- a short online learning module about the theory of positive behaviour;

- a video clip of a simulated complaint interview being handled badly and then handled well – with follow-up questions;
- a half-day group session in which learners discussed their responses to the questions and put the theory into practice with role-play sessions;
- a workplace assessment by the store manager, within three months of the group session (format to be agreed between the manager and the staff member), followed by a 1:1 coaching session on any remaining areas of uncertainty, if needed.

The timing of the first three activities was completely flexible, as long as everything was completed in time for the group session. The workplace assessment took place by agreement between staff member and store manager, (within three months) when the staff member had had the opportunity to apply the new procedure in real work a few times and felt ready to be assessed.

Case study questions

1 What do you like or dislike about this programme?
2 Would you do anything differently if you were designing it?
3 How would you suggest spacing the different components?
4 What approach would you take to the workplace assessment?

Methods for monitoring, assessing and evaluating learning

Deciding on the monitoring and assessment methods we will use within a learning session or programme of learning is a key part of the initial learning design and cannot be left until the learning is taking place.

Assessment can be divided into three main phases or types: initial assessment (testing suitability for learning); formative assessment (assessment of how learners are progressing in their learning); and summative assessment (judgements about learning achievement, usually at the end of a period of learning). In this context we are primarily concerned with formative and summative assessment.

Most learner activities within a learning programme can also form the basis of formative and/or summative assessment – case studies, quizzes, tests, learner presentations and demonstrations, performance in discussions and activities – all reflect how well a learner is progressing towards learning objectives.

Selecting assessment activities will depend on the context and nature of the learning; for example, learning undertaken as part of a qualification course is likely to require formal assessment activities, such as tests or assignments, whilst less formal learning may be assessed by general performance in a learning activity or through a question and answer exercise during, or at the end of, a session.

 Activity 4.2

Identify two methods for monitoring each of the following *within* a related learning programme:

1 How well learners have understood the stages involved in a disciplinary interview.
2 How well learners have understood the process of making beef wellington.
3 If learners understand how to replace an engine in a motor vehicle.
4 If learners recognise the risks in lone working.
5 The extent to which learners support and will comply with a change in working practices.
6 The extent to which learners are engaged in the learning process.

Evaluation methods

Any session design is incomplete without consideration of how it will be evaluated. If this thinking is left until after the session, vital pre- or during-session opportunities to evaluate will be missed. When designing your learning activity, think about what should be evaluated, how this can best be done, and when it needs to be done – and make sure this is embedded in your training design. All of these factors are thoroughly covered in Chapter 10 (Evaluating impact) and we strongly recommend that you read this chapter before completing your L&D design.

Selecting and developing learning resources

We can think of the different learning resources needed for an L&D session in terms of the trainer/training resources (to be used primarily by us) such as a slide deck, presentation equipment and props; and learner/learning resources (to be used primarily by the learner) such as handouts and activity materials. In practice, however, these items all tend to be grouped together under any one of the headings.

In Table 4.4 we considered the uses and challenges of a number of resources. If you are considering designing and developing some of these yourself, here are some factors to consider, including some tips from the experts.

Curated content (curated by L&D team or by learners)

- There is so much information and media around, a better option than developing more might be to review and make use of some of the excellent materials already available.
- Information, including video clips, blogs, articles, podcasts, etc can be used within learning sessions and uploaded to a dedicated site to create a unique collection of information relevant to the learning.
- L&D curated: materials can be uploaded and curated by L&D as a central source.

- Learner curated: learners can upload their own choice of materials for sharing with peers. This enhances the learners' ownership of the learning and leads to a much wider and richer collection of resources than could probably be provided by the trainer alone. (You may need to agree some 'rules' for how this facility operates.)

Handouts/notes/guides

- If handouts are to be provided electronically after the event, avoid just sending out your full slide deck – a concise version of key slides is likely to be much more useful.
- If handouts are to be provided at the beginning of the session, format them using the Handout or Notes facility so that learners have space to add their own thoughts.
- Consider whether handouts are really needed – maybe the information is already available with learners or within work systems (see 'curated content' above).
- Ensure language does not discriminate or offend – check for indirect discrimination, eg shorthand, acronyms or language that only certain learners will understand.
- Include diagrams and illustrations, if relevant, to make information more interesting.
- Use different colours (font or background) to make text more visible and also to classify handouts or slides into different topic areas.

Slide decks

- Use an easy-to-read font and big letters – never less than 22 point and ideally bigger.
- Use bullets rather than sentences (no more than around six words per bullet and six bullets per slide).
- BUT… better still… use pictures, sounds, film and images (making sure that they are culturally sensitive and from an appropriate source) rather than, or between, bullets.
- Don't use too many slides (some say no more than 20 in one session) but don't balance this by cramming too much information on a smaller number of slides!

Presentation software is an excellent tool – as long as it is used as a visual aid and not a crutch (ie something to remind the trainer what to read out!) Slides should support what you are saying, whilst you remain the main focus. Using colour, images and effects makes slides more interesting and helps learners remember the key learning points. Personally, I prefer to use images instead of bullet point lists. Consider the two slides below – they both say the same things but one is much more visually interesting and pleasant for the audience:

Figure 4.4a Slide using a bullet point list

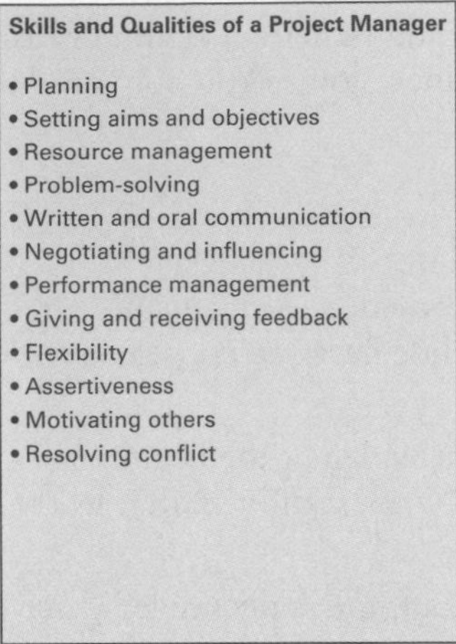

Skills and Qualities of a Project Manager
• Planning
• Setting aims and objectives
• Resource management
• Problem-solving
• Written and oral communication
• Negotiating and influencing
• Performance management
• Giving and receiving feedback
• Flexibility
• Assertiveness
• Motivating others
• Resolving conflict

Figure 4.4b Slide using a visual

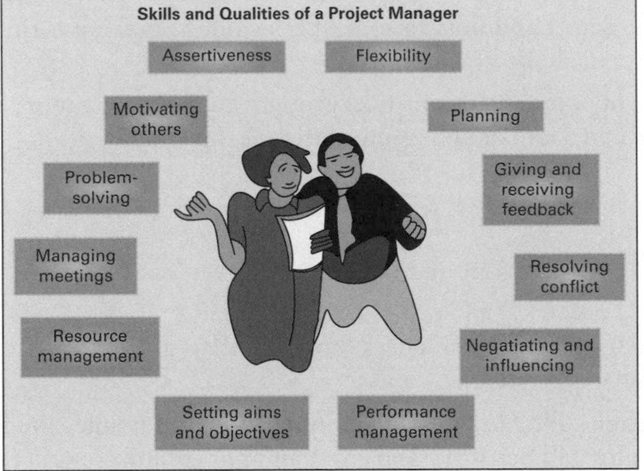

You could even consider using your spoken words alone with just a strong visual to support your message, and virtually no words on the screen at all! This allows the audience to *listen* to what the presenter is saying but still have the visual link to help recall the message later.

John Rodwell, Training Consultant and Author

Activity 4.3

1 Make a note to explore some different presentation software that you are not already familiar with.
2 Try downloading one of the free trials and explore the features available, such as embedding videos, interfacing with aspects of social media, and adding your own oral narrative to presentations.

Currently available packages you could explore include: Sway, Prezzi, Adobe Captivate, Slidebean, Slidedog and Canva – and an internet search will identify many more.

Exercises and activity materials

- Be clear about the purpose of the activity – is it fun or a serious part of the learning? If the latter make sure it fully reflects the knowledge and skills development needed, and that the activity is credible to learners.
- Include clear instructions and timings.
- Make sure that the knowledge level and skill or physical requirements of the activity do not exclude any learners or are likely to cause embarrassment or offence.
- Have a range of activities available which learners can select from or you can distribute according to learner needs.
- Remember to include extra or optional questions to accommodate the quicker learners.
- Ensure that you can also provide the resources learners will need to complete the activity.

Case studies

- Make case studies as real and related to the learners' work roles or situation as possible.
- Have a look at case studies in textbooks, such as this one, to get some ideas.
- If taken from real work, be careful about data protection and confidentiality issues.
- If developing your own case studies, think carefully about how your examples may be received and be careful to avoid stereotyping or offending. Get someone else to read through case studies before you use them – both for accuracy and sensitivity purposes.

Case Example 4.6

Using case studies

When asked to deliver a health and safety course for a group of women's refuge organisations, I felt that the standard course they had requested would not be the most relevant solution for them. As the course was linked to a qualification, I did not have much room to adapt the content and so I decided to use case studies as a means of making the material relate more closely to them. I spent time with a representative of one of the organisations to increase my awareness of health and safety issues in a refuge context, and then researched a number of court cases relating to refuges which could be used as the basis of case studies.

Although the case studies took some time to develop, they really made the training. What was potentially a dry subject was brought to life by the discussion around each case study – with different refuge representatives sharing how they had addressed the issues concerned and everyone sharing good practice. The case studies helped generate lots of ideas and new thinking as well as engaging everyone in the subject matter. The feedback from the learners was excellent, and more courses have now been requested. For me, the course turned out to be one of the most fulfilling and enjoyable I have ever designed or delivered.

Gordon Linford, Risk Manager, D E Ford Insurance Brokers

Specifying the L&D session

When all factors have been considered and your learning session has been designed, the information can be captured and presented in a number of formats. This will depend to some extent on the software you are using, but the guiding principle is that a programme plan or session design should be presented in a way that another trainer, with the same technical expertise as you, could follow.

> 'In the face-to-face activity pack we also include a 'read me first' document which gives the trainer foresight into anything that they need to be aware of ahead of the session. Also, a product information form is issued to the business areas to prepare them ahead of the delivery of the session so that they can ensure that adequate resources are sourced and available and that learners are prepared and ready to receive the learning.'
>
> *Claire Hughes, L&D Portfolio Manager, HMRC*

A simple but effective format to use for session notes is provided in Figure 4.5.

Figure 4.5 Session plan example format (extract)

Delivering Induction for New Team Members (1-day Session for Team Leaders)

Session Aim
To equip delegates with the knowledge and skills to deliver induction at local sites.

Learning Outcomes
By the end of the workshop, delegates will be able to:

- describe the six areas of new staff induction;
- explain the support information required for each area;
- complete the online induction checklist and induction record;
- explain the purpose of weekly review meetings for inductees;
- demonstrate active listening and effective questioning within a review scenario.

Planned Evaluation: Post-event survey, L&D team review with new starters
Links: Part of overall Induction Programme for New Starters

Sessions:	Mins:	Resources:
Welcome and introductions	30	• AV equip, Induction clip,
The Induction experience	30	• Flip chart
The six areas of Induction	120	• Hard copies of Induction checklists and records
Completing the records	30	
Successful reviews	90	• Active listening materials
Summary review and evaluation	30	• Access to intranet

Timing	Activity	Content	Resources / Notes
		Introductions, Welcomes and Admin	
10mins	Tutor input	**Welcome** delegates to the session and introduce self. Ask delegates to introduce selves. **Housekeeping** – fire exits, toilets, mobiles, breaks, additional needs, etc **Overview** of the session – explain what is included in the session (Slide 1).	Flip chart with welcome message Session outline Slide 1
20mins	Pairs activity	Share the **aim and learning outcomes** for the session. Anything learners want to add? **Delegate Introduction presentations**	

(continued)

Figure 4.5 (Continued)

Timing	Activity	Content	Resources / Notes
		Session 1: The Induction Experience	
40 mins	Individual activity	Ask each delegate to reflect on and say a little about their own experiences of starting new job(s) in the past, and the induction (or lack of) they received. Ideally, each delegate to think of a positive and a negative aspect of this.	Flip chart
	Group discussion	Take feedback from each person, creating two lists on flip chart – 'factors that made induction good' and 'factors that made induction bad'. For any negative experiences ask 'what could have improved the experience' and, if not already listed, add these improvement ideas to the 'good factors' list. **Show video scenario** – ask delegates to identify the 'good and the bad' aspects. Add to lists.	
		Session 2: The Six Areas of Induction	
120	6 x small groups activity	Introduce the six areas – and allocate an area to each group. Groups to research and create an outline of essential content for their area.	Access to Intranet Policies and Procedures
		AND SO ON...	

And Table 4.6 is a simple example of a 'high-level' specification, or overview, of a bigger L&D programme.

Table 4.6 L&D programme high-level overview (extract)

NEW STARTERS (APPRENTICES) – Programme Overview					
When	**Where**	**People**	**Activity**	**Resources**	**Notes**
10th May	Head Office	Managers	Training day – Managing Your Apprentice	See session plan	Facilitator – L&D
May to July	Own Settings	Managers and Apprentices	Managers deliver inductions on-site Followed by weekly 1:1 Reviews	L&D support LMS	All forms on LMS
12th July	External Provider	Apprentices	Apprentices attend Week 1 qualification workshop	LMS	Facilitated by L&D and externalprovider
July to March	Own Settings	Managers and Apprentices	Apprentices complete framework with line manager support and 8 weekly review visits from external provider	Apprentice tablets	L&D support as required
	Head Office		Monthly breakfast meetings, with L&D support, for managers		Facilitator – L&D

Case Example 4.7

Designing an L&D activity for extending home-working

A medium-sized organisation has business objectives to increase flexible working and reduce the use of office space costs. In connection with this, the L&D team has been asked to support the organisation's plans to:

- significantly increase the number of employees working mainly from their home base, to around 100;
- extend 'hot-desking' across the organisation.

From an earlier 'pilot' initiative, the organisation already has 20 staff who work at home for most of their working week. These people had originally been managed by one line manager, but had gradually been deployed across the organisation and moved to working under different managers, who had not necessarily been trained in the relevant procedures and practices. Over time, this has resulted in inconsistency – a mix of some very good and some 'not so good' practice in the way the home-working is managed.

The L&D team identified that, along with updating the home-working procedures, they needed to address three main areas of learning need:

1 For managers (approximately 20):
   - how home-working and hot-desking should be implemented;
   - the supporting documentation for home-working;
   - how to select people for home-working;
   - how to manage home-workers (this could be quite a 'culture change' for some managers who still had reservations about how levels and quality of work could be ensured from a distance).
2 For staff, before selection (up to 200):
   - what is involved in home-working?
   - how to decide if home-working is for them or not;
   - how to apply for home-working.
3 For staff, after selection (up to 80):
   - more detailed information about what is involved in home-working;
   - their responsibilities as home-workers;
   - procedures and supporting documentation;
   - strategies, tips and techniques for managing themselves as home-workers.

Case study questions

1 How would you approach designing a learning solution to meet these needs?
2 What overall programme might you suggest?
3 Take any one of the three areas of need above and design a detailed training session or workshop (content areas, sequencing, methods, activities, pre- and post-activities, etc) to address the requirement.

What next?

The activities below will help consolidate your knowledge from this chapter:

1 Have a look at some of the different learning activities that take place within your organisation:
   - What range of methods and activities are there?
   - Which ones seem to be used the most?
   - Which ones are missing or underused?
   - Why do you think this is?
2 Reflect on a training session or other learning activity that you have been involved in as a learner:
   - In terms of the sequencing of the learning content and the methods used – was it an effective activity?
   - How might you have designed it differently?
3 Imagine you have been asked to contribute your three Top Tips to an online article entitled 'Designing effective and engaging L&D activities – A guide for practitioners':
   - What would your three top tips be? Share on twitter using the hashtag #LDPintheW and copy in the account @LDPintheW.

References

Bloom, BS (1956, ed) *Taxonomy of Educational Objectives Handbook 1: Cognitive domain,* Longman, New York

CIPD/Towards Maturity (2019) *Professionalising Learning and Development,* www.cipd.co.uk/knowledge/strategy/development/professionalising-learning-development-function (archived at https://perma.cc/3MWS-8ZMC)

Ebbinghaus, H (1885) *Memory: A contribution to experimental psychology,* Columbia University, New York

Hase, S and Kenyon, C (2013) *Self-Determined Learning: Heutagogy in action,* eds S Hase and C Kenyon, Bloomsbury, London

Kirkpatrick, D (1994) *Evaluating Training Programmes: The four levels,* Berrett-Koehler, San Francisco, CA

Knowles, MS (1980) *The Modern Practice of Adult Education: From pedagogy to andragogy,* Cambridge Adult Education, New Jersey, NJ

Kolb, D (1984) *Experiential Learning: Experience as the source of learning and development,* Prentice Hall, New Jersey

Mager, RF (1998, updated 2012) *Preparing Instructional Objectives,* Mager Associates Inc, USA

Senge, P (2006) *The Fifth Discipline: The art and practice of the learning organization,* 2nd edn, Random House, London

Explore further

Anderson, L W, Krathwohl, D R, Airasian, P W, Cruikshank, K A, Mayer, R E, Pintrich, P R, Raths, J, and Wittrock, M C (2013) *A Taxonomy for Learning, Teaching and Assessing: A revision of Bloom's taxonomy of educational objectives,* Pearson, London

Bergmann, J and Sams, A (2014) *Flipped Learning: Gateway to student engagement,* International Society for Technology in Education, USA

Casebourne, I (2015) *Spaced Learning: An approach to minimize the forgetting curve,* www.td.org/insights/spaced-learning-an-approach-to-minimize-the-forgetting-curve (archived at https://perma.cc/387N-GRKR)

CIPD (2014) *Research Insight: Fresh thinking in learning and development (Part 1 of 3), neuroscience and learning,* www.cipd.co.uk/Images/fresh-thinking-in-learning-and-development_2014-part-1-neuroscience-learning_tcm18-15114.pdf (archived at https://perma.cc/9ZVG-SUEW)

CIPD (2014) *Neuroscience in Action: Applying insight to L&D practice,* www.cipd.co.uk/Images/neuroscience-action_2014-applying-insight-LD-practice_tcm18-9714.pdf (archived at https://perma.cc/S3BT-Q4RY)

Davis, J, Balda, M, Rock, D, Mcginniss, P and Davachi, L (2014) The Science of Making Learning Stick: An update to the AGES model, *5, Neuroleadership Institute,* https://davidrock.net/portfolio-items/the-science-of-making-learning-stick-an-update-to-the-ages-model-vol-5/ (archived at https://perma.cc/3F6A-7WWJ)

Downs, S (2008) *Making Learning Happen,* Downs Publications, London

Hackett, P (2003) *Training practice,* CIPD, London

Horton, W (2011) *E-Learning by Design,* 2nd edn, Pfeiffer, San Francisco, CA

Kolb, D (2014) *Experiential Learning: Experience as the source of learning and development,* 2nd edn, Pearson FT Press, London

Lehmann-Willenbrock, N and Kauffeld, S (2010) Sales Training: Effects of spaced practice on training transfer, *Journal of European Industrial Training,* www.emeraldinsight.com/doi/abs/10.1108/03090591011010299 (archived at https://perma.cc/K4DR-CUYG)

Phillips, D J P (2014) *How to avoid death by PowerPoint,* TEDxStockholmSalon, www.youtube.com/watch?v=lwpi1Lm6dFo (archived at https://perma.cc/8PDP-756U)

Rodwell, J (2007) *Activity-Based Training Design: Transforming the learning of knowledge,* Gower, London

Stewart, J and Cureton, P (2014) *Designing, Delivering and Evaluating L&D: Essentials for practice,* CIPD, London

Willis, J (2007) The Neuroscience of Joyful Education, *Psychology Today,* www.psychologytoday.com/files/attachments/4141/the-neuroscience-joyful-education-judy-willis-md.pdf (archived at https://perma.cc/BYU6-LAB4)

Useful resources

Websites

www.cipd.co.uk/subjects/lrnanddev/designdelivery

www.cipd.co.uk/subjects/lrnanddev/selfdev

www.cipd.co.uk/subjects/lrnanddev/elearning/elearnprog.htm (archived at https://perma.cc/4NMP-GA53)

www.cipd.co.uk/subjects/lrnanddev/designdelivery/creatmthds.htm

www.mindtools.com (archived at https://perma.cc/KU9K-TBA5)

www.trainingzone.co.uk (archived at https://perma.cc/PQQ4-K6N5)

www.brainboxx.co.uk

www.teachertrainingvideos.com (archived at https://perma.cc/2AVP-2SAT)

www.cipd.co.uk/onlineinfodocuments/atozresources.htm (archived at https://perma.cc/RX35-684P)

05 Delivery

Face-to-face training and facilitation

Introduction

Having designed engaging and effective L&D activities, our next stage is to deliver them, whether that is in a training room, the workplace or via a learning platform. This chapter is primarily focused on the face-to-face delivery of L&D, where a trainer works directly with, and mostly in the same room as, a group of learners, leading or facilitating learning activities. In practice, many of the delivery skills and approaches we discuss here are equally relevant to delivery in a virtual learning environment. However, there are differences and these are explored in more detail in Chapter 6 (Delivery: Using technology) and Chapter 8 (Delivery: Social and collaborative learning).

Key areas of content covered in this chapter are:

- characteristics of good face-to-face L&D delivery;
- preparing to be great;
- how to open and close learning sessions;
- using different delivery styles, methods and techniques;
- working with training and learning resources;
- facilitating learning in a group;
- monitoring learning and making adjustments;
- assisting transfer of learning to the workplace.

Delivery of L&D activities

Face-to-face (F2F) learning

Technology has helped shift L&D into a new dimension and presents all kinds of further opportunities for us, but sometimes the emphasis on using technology can make us feel that we are failing as L&D professionals if we choose F2F training methods. In fact, we may well have 'failed' if our choice is just based on F2F being our *easiest* option ('we have always done it this way'), but if we have opted for F2F because it is the best and most appropriate method for the identified need, even allowing for the constraints of cost or geography, then we should be extremely proud of our choice. Face-to-face learning still provides some of the most engaging experiences for learners and can still be the most effective method for achieving organisational and individual development objectives.

From an organisational point of view, well-designed and -delivered F2F L&D sessions can enable a common and consistent understanding of complex work requirements or organisational change projects and have a quick and high impact on learning. For individual learners face-to-face group sessions can provide a chance to focus on learning away from the demands of the workplace, test out new knowledge and skills in a safe environment, and learn with, and from, others who share the same learning goals. Face-to-face can also be one of the most enjoyable, rich and stimulating ways to learn.

> If asked, trainers and HR departments will readily concede that if the objective is to convey information and develop skills, and ensure the objectives of the course have been met, then if possible, face-to-face is the preferred delivery method.
>
> Trainers will also patiently explain that this is not a pedagogical issue; they are, many of them, at the forefront of developing e-learning materials and are well versed in the intricacies of Learning Management Systems.
>
> Face-to-face learning: Old hat or the future?
> Julian Roche, Opinion, *Trainingjournal.com,* 2018

Of course, along with the benefits, there are also costs – F2F training can be expensive. It takes people away from their workplace, it can be costly in terms of venue and travel costs, and it also costs time and money to prepare and deliver. It might also not suit everyone's learning preferences. All of these factors place a big responsibility on L&D professionals to ensure that F2F activities are delivered effectively and that the valuable resources spent on them are not wasted.

> 'Training is a big investment and not one to be made lightly... but as a manager there is nothing better than seeing staff who have previously struggled with aspects of their job flourish after they have had the benefit of appropriate and good-quality training.'
>
> *Janet Medcalf, Manager*

The good – and not so good – learning experience

Just because it is face-to face, doesn't mean it is good quality – as evaluation responses world-wide testify. Think about your own experiences. Have you attended an L&D event where the content was not what you had expected, or at a level you could not relate to? Or where the content was generally good but the trainer did not inspire you? What about a session where the learner group didn't work together well or was dominated by one or two of the more extrovert delegates?

When learners describe their 'best training experiences', the descriptions usually include a combination of the following:

- the content was just what I needed to meet my learning objectives;
- the learning activities were relevant and engaging;
- useful learning resources were provided/available;
- the trainer had great training skills and was knowledgeable in the subject area;
- the group worked well together, sharing ideas and learning from each other;
- the whole activity (before, during, after) was well organised.

A further aspect sometimes mentioned is where the learning provides something very new to the learner or presents a different way of thinking about something, leading to one of those 'lightbulb moments' when something suddenly falls into place or the solution to a long-held problem comes to mind. These are the learning sessions that learners never forget.

Of course, learning is never all about the trainer and, however well we play our part in providing great opportunities, the responsibility for learning is not all ours. The success of any adult learning intervention is also dependent on adults choosing to access and participate in learning and to undertake the activities required to meet their learning needs.

But, this understanding of adult learners should not lead us to underestimate the huge impact we can have as trainers. We can help to provide ALL of the 'best training experience' aspects listed above. All we have to do is carefully plan learning activities so that they are effective and address learning needs, deliver them in a way that is relevant and engaging, and create learning environments in which learners feel safe, confident and motivated to participate. Not a simple task perhaps – but the rest of this chapter will explore and help build the knowledge and skills we need for this.

Activity 5.1

1 What are your best experiences of being a learner?
2 What made them so positive for you?
3 How could you use this awareness in your training delivery?

Preparing for learning and development activities

Providing effective L&D activities and creating the best environment for learning starts long before the actual day of the session. Here are some main considerations before the activities start.

Preparing the session

Before we embark on any training activity, we need to be very sure about what we are trying to achieve and how we intend to get there. This means being clear about learning needs (see Chapter 3) and having a carefully designed plan for how to address these (Chapter 4).

A good L&D plan will include the following:

- agreed and clearly specified learning objectives based on identified learning needs;
- relevant, accurate and up-to-date training content, sequenced and spaced to assist learning;
- a good mix of training activities, methods and resources that will enable learning and support transfer of learning to the workplace;
- a range of relevant monitoring and evaluation activities.

If your prime role is to deliver learning activities, you may not be responsible for the earlier stages of identifying needs and designing activities and session plans, but you still have a responsibility to ensure that any pre-designed session plan is appropriate for the needs of the learners you are to provide it to, and that you can deliver the material effectively. If at all possible, you might visit learners in their workplace to check on the relevance of activities to their context, and if the plan requires any updates or additions make sure that these are undertaken in conjunction with main stakeholders and content owners.

Having checked the quality of the training plan and made any adjustments to suit context and audience, you will also need to ensure that whatever resources are required for the session will be available on the day. Main areas to consider here are rooms, presentation equipment (eg AV equipment, whiteboard, laptop, mobile devices, slide-decks, videos) and learning materials (eg practical equipment, exercises, games, simulation items).

Preparing ourselves

When we asked a number of learners what makes a good trainer, one of the main areas of response we received was 'someone who knows what they are talking about and can make it interesting'. We think this is a quick way of saying that a trainer needs to be fully conversant with the content and how it applies to the learners' context, knows how best to deliver it and has the skills to engage learners and motivate them to learn. Ideally, they should also be passionate and excited about the material themselves if they are to have a chance of transferring those same emotions. One of the most negative experiences learners have of trainers is when a trainer just stands at the front, passively reading out a series of slides. This is not training: it is simply reading aloud in front of a (probably very bored) group of people!

Naturally we can't be complete experts on every subject, but if we are to be credible, we have to know our material, and this means spending time before delivery going through any areas of content we are less familiar with, maybe observing it being delivered by someone else if possible, and practising how we personally will bring it to life. If we didn't design the session ourselves it may not reflect our delivery style and so practising using the material, and adapting it to our style and timing is important if it is to flow well on the day.

> 'If you can't explain it simply, you don't understand it well enough.'
>
> *Albert Einstein*

As well as thinking about our competence as a deliverer of L&D, we may also need to pay attention to how we present ourselves to learners. This includes our emotional state as well as the image we project. If you are tired and unprepared on the day, you are unlikely to project as confident and credible or have the energy to manage the session effectively. Give yourself every chance of success by following the usual good advice about eating well and trying to get a good night's sleep before the learning activities.

It is quite normal to feel nervous. Try to balance this by being well prepared – this is probably the biggest anxiety-reducing factor and the one most likely to make you feel more confident. You can also reassure yourself that feeling some level of stress is positive. Some stress will help you focus on the day and can make you seem more lively, animated and passionate about your subject. According to psychologist Kelly McGonigal, the author of *The Upside of Stress: Why stress is good for you (and how to get good at it)*, the more positively you can view the stress you are feeling, the better you will cope with it.

It can also help to 'look the part', so think about the image you want to present. Try to dress in a way that is congruent with your message and context – wearing jeans and a T-shirt could affect your credibility with one learner group, but equally, a 'power suit' could work against you in another context. If this is an area of interest for you, there is lots of opinion and advice available on how what you wear affects how you feel and how you are perceived by others. For example, some experts advise that wearing bold colours (reds and oranges) and heavier accessories (watch, jewellery) can make us feel more confident, as they add to our overall 'weight' and gravitas, and we support this view to some extent. But probably the best advice is the simplest: wear whatever you feel most comfortable and confident in, as long as it is appropriate for your context and audience.

Case Example 5.1

Getting in the zone (one trainer's approach)

No matter what has happened before a session I am facilitating (be it online or face-to-face) I always try to be professional, knowledgeable, focused and engaging. As an L&D practitioner you are on display – many in the profession have particular questions on evaluation sheets that score or rate the facilitator, so getting 'in the zone' is really important. However, it can be a challenge. It may have been a stressful journey to the venue or a difficult meeting before a web session. The morning commute may have been challenging or someone else might be having a crisis and calling on me to help. I might have had a restless night wanting to nail the facilitation. Lots of things can conspire against us actually being in the zone on the day.

I now have a number of methods that I employ to help with overcoming some of these challenges. They include:

- Getting to the venue or online early, sometimes really early. Ensuring I can access the room to work out how activities will pan out or to test the online technology and get the slide deck or polls uploaded.
- Using comedy podcasts or radio shows to help alter my mood if I have had a difficult morning.
- Listening to professional podcasts which build on my existing knowledge. The Good Practice podcasts, for example, involve some good humour between the presenters and the guests in them too so make me laugh as well as learn.
- Listening to music that brings back great memories for me, that makes me smile and sing along.

These are all tools that work well for me, allowing me to become engaged, focused and present, in a state that is receptive to the needs of the learners and ready for the facilitation challenge ahead.

L&D Consultant (Global remit)

Case study question

What helps you to 'get in the zone' for delivering an L&D activity?

Preparing learners

Learners are unlikely to feel comfortable in a learning situation if they are worried about logistical, personal or domestic factors – and often need information well in advance of learning so that they can ensure any necessary arrangements are made. It is worth noting that one of the most common negative comments on evaluation sheets is 'the joining instructions' – either because they arrived too late, causing stress in making personal or travel arrangements, or because they provided inaccurate information.

Make sure that learners have all the information they need in advance, such as venue details, timings, session objectives and key content areas, so that they can also prepare and be in an appropriate emotional state to get the best from the learning activity. It may also be relevant to provide links to related reading or preparatory activities.

The use of imagery can make joining instructions more engaging, for example, an image or hyperlink to something relating to your content or a welcome video from you as the facilitator. You could even use the joining instructions creatively to begin the learning, by presenting them in a way that relates to and will get learners thinking about the learning subject area – for example present the instructions as a 'to-do' list for a time-management session.

Establishing the physical environment for learning

The physical environment can be a major factor in the success of any session. An excellent presentation or demonstration is pointless if people cannot hear/see it very well. Equally, cramming learners into a small room where they are unable to move about or claim any personal space is likely to make them irritated and distracted. If we want learners to relax and focus on learning, you will need to think about the environment in which learning will take place and pay particular attention to some key factors: accessibility and safety, room layout and learner comfort.

Accessibility and safety

Learners can only take up learning if the physical environment is accessible to them. Any barriers created by the location of a building or the particular design of a room need to be addressed, particularly where learners have special equipment needs or are wheelchair users. Give careful consideration to access issues, and to the particular needs of individual learners.

Along with ensuring that everyone can access the training area, we must also ensure that learners are safe. Learning environments should be risk assessed and any risks addressed before the session. If this is not already fully addressed in your organisation you should be able to find guidance on your government's Health & Safety website. In the UK this is the Health & Safety Executive website (www.hse.gov.uk), where you will find a range of risk checklists and templates for this purpose.

As well as the dangers inherent in specialist technical or demonstration equipment, most training areas are vulnerable to some potential hazards, such as:

- fire exits made less accessible by changed room layout;
- trailing wires;
- unsafe positioning of learning equipment, flipchart stands, screens, projectors, laptops;
- too many electrical items plugged into an extension lead.

It is up to you to make sure that these have been checked and addressed. Remember also that as the facilitator of a session, you need to inform your learners of key safety information including the location of fire exits, frequency of alarm tests and the assembly point in the event of an evacuation. Make sure that you include these at the beginning of your session notes so that you do not forget.

Activity 5.2

1. Do you always check health and safety factors before a session?
2. And cover these with learners at the beginning of the session?
3. If not – how will you make sure that you always do this in future?

Room layout

The layout of a room can have a huge influence on how the occupants of the room behave – and this can be a powerful tool for trainers. Levels of participation, interaction between group members, and individual learning and enjoyment can all be significantly affected by how a room, and particularly seating, is arranged.

> 'I am dismayed when trainers turn up at the training room five minutes before delivering a session having not given any thought to the room layout or assuming that it will have been laid out satisfactorily by someone else. By this time, learners have already arrived and sat down and, even if the trainer recognises that the arrangement is not good, it is too late to move it around. Ironically, the trainer might later complain that groups "never join in very much", oblivious to how the cramped and poor layout of the room made learners uncomfortable and inhibited group interaction.'
>
> *Training Practice Assessor*

Activity 5.3

Consider how some different types of 'room' are arranged, for example: restaurants, cinemas, libraries, classrooms, classrooms set out for exams.

1 How do these different layouts affect the way people behave?

2 What can you learn from this for your delivery of training?

3 What do you consider to be an appropriate time before a session starts for the trainer to arrive?

As well as choosing a layout that suits the learning activities being delivered – and remember that you can rearrange the room for different sessions as the event progresses – your choice of room layout will also depend on the size of the group and the type of activity. An event which requires individual IT equipment, for example, would be set up differently to an event which was mainly based on group activities or discussion.

You might also consider whether or not to use tables – some people see them as a barrier to interaction, while others believe that learners are more comfortable when they have tables around them to put things on and can comfortably make notes or carry out activities. The key is to give the matter some consideration and select a layout suitable for the size of the group and most conducive to the type of learning activities to be undertaken. If possible, build in some flexibility so you can use the room in different ways during the day. Some example seating arrangements are shown in Figure 5.1.

As well as seating arrangements, do not forget to consider how training equipment is arranged. If using slides, for example, consider where the AV equipment is – will the audience be able to see all they need to? Many training rooms have the screen in the prominent central position, pushing the trainer off to the side of the room and giving the impression that the screen is more important than the explanation of the

Figure 5.1 Room arrangements

Cabaret Style

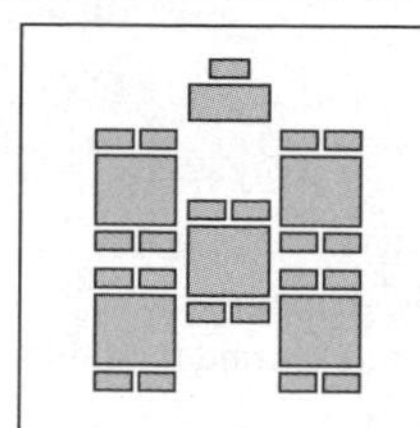

Good for:

- informal groups
- facilitator style
- promoting discussions

Potential drawbacks:

- can be difficult for the trainer to keep focus of attention
- learners may stick to their own table and miss the opportunity of working with others
- some learners will have backs to others so seeing and listening may be uncomfortable

Theatre Style

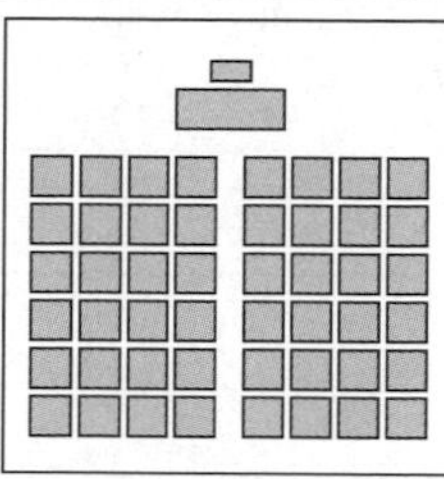

Good for:

- large groups for certain activities
- lecture style of delivery
- short presentations

Potential drawbacks:

- limits interaction between learners
- uncomfortable for long periods
- no tables for learners to write or lean on

Horseshoe Style

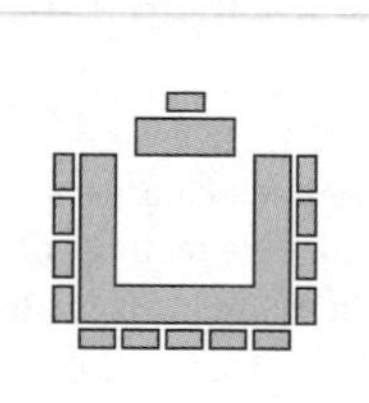

Good for:

- encouraging some interaction between learners
- training style of delivery
- interaction between trainer and learners
- trainer can use the middle space

Potential drawbacks:

- some learners will be side on, making it uncomfortable to see the front
- takes up a lot of room
- discussions are limited when people are in a line

(*continued*)

Figure 5.1 (Continued)

Boardroom Style

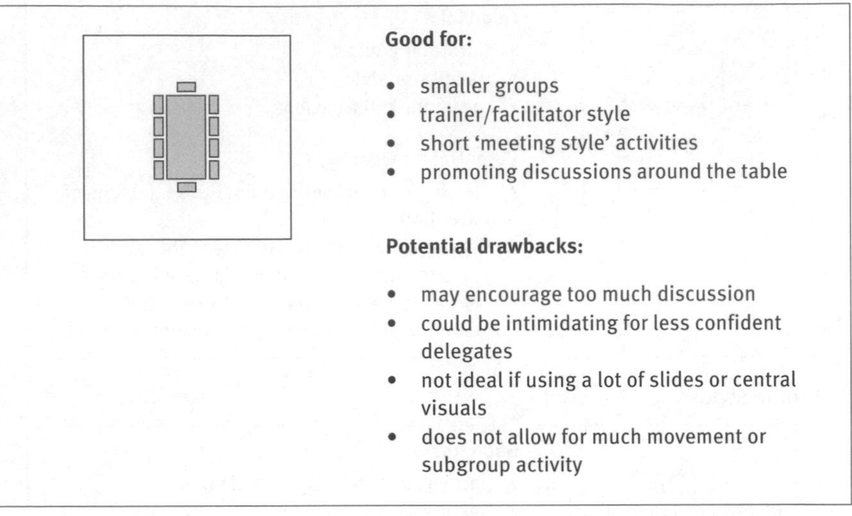

Good for:

- smaller groups
- trainer/facilitator style
- short 'meeting style' activities
- promoting discussions around the table

Potential drawbacks:

- may encourage too much discussion
- could be intimidating for less confident delegates
- not ideal if using a lot of slides or central visuals
- does not allow for much movement or subgroup activity

Schoolroom Style

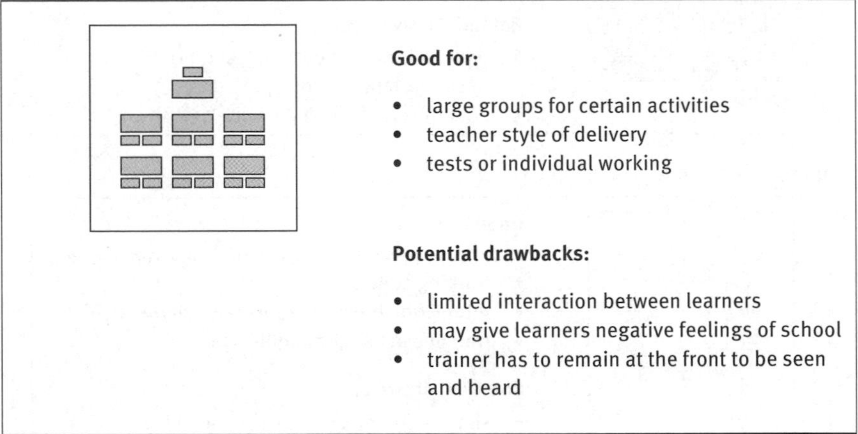

Good for:

- large groups for certain activities
- teacher style of delivery
- tests or individual working

Potential drawbacks:

- limited interaction between learners
- may give learners negative feelings of school
- trainer has to remain at the front to be seen and heard

trainer or the group discussion. A better arrangement, if possible, might be to have the screen to one side and, if you're using one, a flipchart at the other for capturing learner comments.

Comfort factors

Heating and ventilation Make sure that the temperature is at a comfortable average to suit most people (likely to be somewhere between 18°C and 25°C) but there are no specific legal limits. (The UK government does issue some guidelines, however, including a recommended minimum temperature of 16°C, www.gov.uk/workplace-temperatures.) Remember that overly warm temperatures can make people feel drowsy, particularly after lunch, and try to have a good flow of fresh air to keep people well energised. If people are cold you could try getting them to move around a bit more, as part of an activity, rather than simply turning up the heat.

Lighting If lights are too bright it can cause tiredness and headaches; too dim may lead to eyestrain and lethargy. Some venues provide different lighting options which can add to the delivery dynamics with a slightly darker room for presentations or a bright room for group work. Check comfort levels with the group throughout the day or hand over responsibility for maintaining appropriate light and heat settings to the group.

Distractions Relevant posters, pictures or interesting quotes on the walls can all help set the tone of an event, add interest for learners and contribute to the overall learning experience. But remember to remove things that are not relevant and which will be distracting. A whiteboard that still has the details from another training session or old flipchart pages left stuck on the walls indicates that you have not paid much attention to preparing the training room and can devalue your session for the learners – not to mention your credibility as a professional trainer.

Refreshments If your session is running for more than an hour or two, it is appropriate to provide refreshments. Your budget might not allow for anything too lavish, but, as a minimum, provide water and access to hot drinks or a vending machine. This is not just about comfort – one of the strong messages coming from neuroscience is the importance of hydration to efficient brain functioning, and therefore to learning. You might also consider healthier alternatives to sweets and biscuits, such as pieces of fruit.

Movement If learners are to be in a room for longer than an hour or two, they will need to move around. The requirements for a training space are quite different to those for a meeting room, for example, where people might sit closely around one table. Ensure there is space for activities that involve learners moving around. Physical movement gets the blood circulation going and refreshes both body and brain – and scientists are increasingly telling us that we are not designed to sit down for long periods. If room space is limited, make sure there is alternative 'break-out' space outside the room and have frequent breaks.

Opening learning sessions

Arrivals and welcome

When learners arrive for a learning session, they may be experiencing a number of different feelings or emotions. Some may feel confident and positive, while others may be thinking 'I wish I didn't have to be here', or 'I am worried about what is going to be expected of me'. Anxiety is a natural response to doing something new or joining a new group of people – and something we can probably all relate to. Happily, there are a number of things we can do to reassure anxious learners.

It is usually better to let learners come into the learning environment as they arrive (or once the room is set up) so that they can prepare themselves for the activities ahead. Keeping everyone waiting outside the room can build up tension and frustrate those who like to arrive early and settle themselves in.

Greet people individually when they arrive – think of it as like welcoming guests to a party at your home! Names are important and create an immediate emotional engagement so be aware of who is coming and find out who is who. Even if you are busy organising things, you can still take a few minutes to welcome learners and point out essentials such as toilets and drink machines, especially if learners are unfamiliar with the venue. A friendly 'just make yourself comfortable and let me know if you need anything' gives them the freedom to do whatever they need to do to prepare themselves, knowing you are there if needed. A welcoming message can also be written on a whiteboard or AV screen for people to see as they come in.

Some trainers like to play music as learners arrive and this can be selected for the relevance of the lyrics to a topic or just for a relaxing effect. Baroque music such as Vivaldi's *Four Seasons* and Handel's *Water Music*, for example, have been said to have a positive calming effect on the brain. Conversely you may want to select music that is energising. Using music of any relevant type can be a great approach to welcoming learners, but always listen to any lyrics in full before you play something and ensure appropriateness. You should also check and comply with any music copyright issues, which can vary across venues and regions.

Unless there is a very good reason to delay, start the session at the agreed time. This is respectful and fair to those that did arrive on time. Not starting on time is likely to irritate some learners or make them anxious that the session may over-run the agreed finish time.

Introductions and session outline

To begin the session, a good starting point is to introduce yourself to the group. This may be as simple as telling everyone your name, or you may think it appropriate to give a little more information – your background, your experience – to help establish your credentials in the subject area. Find the right balance here, if you over-self-promote you risk turning people off and may struggle to get them back. Show enthusiasm, humility and respect for learners' experience by highlighting that you are looking forward to the session and to gaining new insights from the group.

The next area of introduction might be to 'the domestics' and the learning session. This is a chance to ensure learners are aware of:

- health and safety requirements and fire procedures;
- domestic arrangements, eg refreshments, toilets;
- the overall aim of the session;
- the planned learning outcomes;
- the overall structure and general timing of the session.

Adult learners often like to have an overview or 'big picture' of the learning activity so that they can see how it all fits together and what will be expected of them. It can help to have a visual overview or 'road map' of the session on a flipchart, slide or on the wall, showing the learning route, key stages, stopping points and breaks.

Learners also need to know what the intended aims and outcomes are so that they can check this against their own expectations and, if appropriate, add anything they feel has been overlooked. Convey the programme aims confidently so that learners also have confidence in them and the training they are about to access. A strong 'today we are going to explore X and learn how to Y' will inspire much more confidence than a rather weak 'I hope you might learn Y today'.

Finally, it is important to give learners a chance to introduce themselves – except perhaps in a short formal session, such as a presentation, where there is no real need for whole group introductions. Introductions are the first step in getting the group to work together and people will generally feel more at ease if they know who the other people in the room are.

Learner introductions could equally be made before the introduction to the session. We prefer to position them afterwards, partly because this gives learners a little more time to settle in before they are asked to contribute, but also because it can be useful to use some programme information within the learner introductions. For example, as well as introducing themselves, learners could say a little about:

- Their own learning objectives and reasons for attending the learning – this will help you to pitch the event at the right level (or to manage expectations about personal objectives that may not be met). Make a note of learner's objectives on a flipchart so that you can revisit them during the session, and at the end, to ensure they have been addressed.
- Their existing knowledge or experience of the subject – again useful for getting the level right, or for allowing delegates to reflect on how much they already know, and so build their confidence. You might also identify particular knowledge and experience that learners could share in more detail with the group, later on in the session.
- Any questions they would like covering during the day – allowing you to add these into the content if not in already and so meet learning needs more fully. Again, note these down for reference and if you are unable to answer everything you can consider following up with learners after the session.

Learners will need some time to collect their thoughts before giving this information and, rather than asking them to give it one by one, going around the room in an anxiety-creating 'creeping death' style, it can work better to ask people to volunteer until everyone has been included.

To help you remember names, create a rough diagram of the room layout for yourself and then add learners' names and a few key details about them as they are given. This will help you quickly match and remember names and faces and will also be useful later on, when working out ways to organise learners into pairs or small groups for activities.

Ice-breakers (warm-ups) – for and against

An ice-breaker or warm-up is an activity at the start of an event which is intended to lessen formality and break down people's reserve, and can help the process of group members getting to know each other a little.

An easy and 'low risk' ice-breaker is to make the learner introductions (as above) the basis of the activity. Ask people to form pairs or small groups to introduce themselves to each other and then to feed back a summary of their learning objectives, prior experience, further questions, etc as a pair or group. As well as covering the introductory information, this gets learners talking to one another and working in smaller groups, where some may feel more comfortable. It also gives everyone a bit of time to move about and relax a little before returning to the whole group session.

Another effective way of using an ice-breaker is to choose an activity which sets the scene for the event or whets the appetite for the learning that is to come. A short activity which draws on the skills that are going to be learned during the event will give the trainer and the learners some reference points which can be drawn upon later. For example, at the start of a training session about 'influencing skills' you could have an ice-breaker in which participants have to persuade a partner to do a simple but random task, such as swap seats or leave the room. The variety of tactics learners employ to do this, both ethical and manipulative, will provide a wealth of examples throughout the event about the skills to use and those to avoid!

Ice-breakers can be very effective in relaxing or energising the group; however, they can also embarrass or alienate group members or reduce the credibility of the training session if used inappropriately – so always use with care!

> 'Shortly after we arrived at the event, we were each given a card with the name of an animal on it – mine said "horse". Then we were asked to walk around the room introducing ourselves to each other by making the noise of the animal on our card! When we found someone making the same noise (there were two of each animal) we had found our partner for the introductory exercise. It may have worked for some people – but most of us were just very embarrassed.'
>
> *Delegate on a 'Managing Conflict' programme*

There are whole books devoted to ice-breakers (some references at the end of this chapter) and here are just a few more ideas:

- Everyone states a couple of words about how they are feeling – or you provide a sheet with plenty of examples (eg excited, curious, stressed, motivated) for them to select from. This is a great way of gauging feeling in the room and honesty can help build the learning environment. Negatives can be turned into positives; if Joe feels 'hassled' after a tough journey, you can show the group you are looking to support his needs.
- Similarly, people draw a picture or a diagram to represent themselves or how they feel (lack of drawing skills is no obstacle and should add a humorous element).
- Learners work in pairs or small groups and try to identify at least three things they all have in common (not including obvious physical things, like a nose!)
- The trainer provides a selection of random objects, learners select one each and explain some kind of link, however tenuous, between them and the object (eg an orange may relate back to a favourite holiday in Spain). You could also try asking them to link the object to a work context or to the subject of the training session.

- Word association: learners think of a single word that reflects the subject of the training session for them – and then share their words in pairs or small groups and discuss until they all agree on one single word (this can bring out lots of information, concerns or questions that might be useful later on in the session).
- The group is presented with a list of personal characteristics or facts (eg 'has an unusual hobby', 'can speak another language', 'has appeared on TV or radio') and tries to identify a group member who can fit (or nearly fit) each of the descriptions. The facts may be known characteristics or just random ideas, and can be general or work related. This ice-breaker is often known as 'learner bingo'.

Different L&D delivery styles

Trainers may become used to always delivering material in a similar style. This might be a style that comes naturally to them, or one they have learned over time. The best trainers, however, choose from a range of different styles – basing that choice, not on their personal preference, but on the needs of their learners.

One way to think of this is to imagine a continuum of delivery styles, from the primarily 'tell' style of the lecture, through to the learner-led style of facilitation:

Figure 5.2 Continuum of delivery styles

Lecturer/presenter	Trainer	Facilitator

→→→--------------------→→→--------------------→→→

Lecturer style

- Primarily a one-way method of delivery in which the presenter imparts information to the learners.
- As a 'tutor-led' style, learners are mostly passive receivers of learning.
- Good as a short activity, where the audience know little about the subject or where the presenter is recognised as an expert in the field.
- A good style for providing initial knowledge to the learners, but will do little to enhance their practical skills.

Trainer style

- More of a two-way, 'partnership' method of delivery, which employs a number of different tools and techniques.
- The trainer still imparts information to the learners, but also provides opportunities for them to experience and experiment with the topic. Learners make some decisions about how they participate in the session.

- The learners are therefore active receivers of the learning, with some of their learning coming directly from the input of the trainer, and some of it being the result of their participation in the activities and experiences the trainer planned for them.
- This style is ideal to develop both skills and knowledge as it combines a mixture of knowledge input, demonstration and skills practice all in a safe environment that has been created and controlled by the trainer.

Facilitator style

- This style focuses on supporting learners to find and follow their own route to learning.
- The style creates an environment in which the learners explore a subject for themselves, and gives very little input or direction.
- The facilitator does not need to be an expert in the subject matter – the skill here is one of enabling people to learn for themselves.
- This style works best where learners already have a knowledge of the subject and some experience or existing skills.

Activity 5.4

1. Do you tend towards any particular style when delivering learning activities?
2. Where would you place yourself on the continuum above?
3. Where would others place you on the continuum above?
4. How can you identify which delivery style would most suit your learners?
5. Would you like to develop your style at all? How?

Case Example 5.2

A trainer's development

Looking back on my training work, I can see that I have moved through different phases.

For example, when I first started training, I was so nervous my main focus was just on remembering everything. I was terrified that I would forget what I was supposed to be saying or doing and that I would look like an idiot! I suspect that my training style seemed a bit stilted and not very relaxed at the time.

As I got more confident, I think I became a bit of a show-off. Not in a bad way really, but I was probably a bit too keen to show learners how much I knew about the subject and give them the 'right answers'. I suppose, having done so much work to learn the material myself, I really wanted the group to be impressed about 'how knowledgeable I was'.

Luckily that phase didn't last long, and I realized that learners would learn and gain so much more if I stopped trying to impress them and let them come up with things for themselves. I became much better at creating opportunities for learning and thinking about how my interaction with the group impacted on them – and my need to impress eased off! My focus had now mostly switched from 'me' to 'them'.

Business trainer (retail sector)

Case study questions

1 Can you relate to any of the stages described above?
2 Are you in any of these phases now?
3 Can you recognise any of these behaviours in other trainers?

Delivery methods and techniques

Giving presentations

Structuring the presentation

Whether we are delivering a standalone presentation or including some presentation of learning input within a training session, there are lots of guidelines, tips and techniques to help.

Winston Churchill, a former British prime minister, who was considered to be a great speaker (whether or not people agreed with his content), described his technique as:

'Tell them what you are going to tell them.'
'Tell them.'
'Tell them what you have told them.'

Many have followed this approach and adopted this simple structure, which helps to keep the speaker on track while reinforcing the message and learning points for the audience.

The first sentence or two of any presentation is probably the most important, as that is when we grab learners' attention and set their expectations of what is to come. Try to find something with high impact – a quote or anecdote, a current film, book or TV reference, an unusual object or impactful visual – that will hook people in and make them want to hear more, and use this as your opener.

A great source of some excellent presentations and presentation skills to inspire you is TED talks (www.ted.com/talks). Similar sites include Ignite (www.ignitetalks.io) and the Do Lectures (www.thedolectures.com). You could also try watching anything presented by the late Steve Jobs (Apple), who was often considered to be a master of giving presentations.

Don't be fooled by how easy good presenters can make presenting seem, the so-called natural presenters are usually just the people who have planned best and practised most. YouTube can also be a good source, although it perhaps contains as many very bad presentations as very good ones! A humorous but still insightful look at presentation skills is Will Stephen's video, coincidentally about TED talks, (www.youtube.com/watch?v=8S0FDjFBj8o).

TED talks are intentionally short as presentation is a method which suits short inputs of expert information. If you have lots of information to input, it might be worth picking out the key details you want to present and capturing the remainder in some pre-reading or a follow-up activity. A little input followed by a related activity often works well.

Activity 5.5

The technique of having an impactful first sentence can be seen in many contexts: books, films and all kinds of presentations (eg the TED talks).

1 Explore a few of these and see if you can identify some good examples of first sentences that grab attention and pull the audience in.
2 When you have explored, consider some of your past or future presentations and see if you can think of some good openers for your session(s).

Presenting with confidence

While you are presenting, try and project a confident, relaxed image to give credibility to your message and help learners feel at ease. Adopt confident body language (a steady open stance and relaxed but direct eye contact) even if you do not feel as confident as you would like. Psychologists (eg Cuddy, 2015) tell us that our physical posture can significantly affect our emotional state, and that 'acting as if' we feel emotions such as confidence or happiness can actually make us feel more of that particular emotion. If you want to see this concept illustrated, a quick Internet search will reveal various pictures of 'politicians adopting power postures', to increase their gravitas and probably to make them feel more confident in difficult situations.

Make use of any 'trainer tricks' that will help when presenting some content. For example, you could create a simple one-page summary diagram, with the key points listed in sequence, in a very big font, that you can refer to quickly and easily if your mind goes blank. Or, if you are going to be writing or drawing something complex on a flipchart during the session, prepare the chart in advance with a pencil outline (pencil won't show to the group) and then amaze learners on the day with the quick and accurate diagram you produce as you copy the pencil lines.

Case Example 5.3

Using a variety of media in L&D design

I like to use Prezi to create an eye-catching presentation. Unlike traditional presentation authoring tools that are based around slides, Prezi zooms around one big canvas on a journey and I can embed YouTube and audio files to bring the session to life. In one session I embedded audio examples of role-plays which caught everyone's attention and made the session really memorable.

Prezi is a really useful tool when used effectively. However, I wouldn't use it all the time as it may become stale and lose its impact. Variety is the key; if something is different from the norm it enables learners to remember key messages much more effectively.

Scott Fellows, Learning and Development Officer

Appealing to all the senses

If we want to ensure we have learners' attention and give them every chance of 'receiving' the information being given, we need to embrace the different ways learners might take in information. Even a formal one-way presentation can be brought to life and made more effective by appealing to different senses. Rather than just hearing what is said, we can provide learners with opportunities to see, feel, imagine and maybe even smell or taste aspects of information. Consider:

- visuals: images, pictures, video clips, animations, colours and patterns;
- imagined visuals: invite learners to envision how something would look for them or tell stories to stimulate their imagination;
- objects: pass objects around so that learners can feel them;
- music: perhaps a relevant background tune while you pass something around;
- scents and tastes: can have high impact if relevant, but be very careful as learners might react badly to these – always make these an option!

Activity 5.6

1. What examples of appealing to all senses have you experienced?
2. What could you use?
3. Will these help with the content and context of learning?

Learner questions

Because learners may have experienced some presentations with a 'save questions until the end' policy, less extrovert learners may feel uncomfortable about interrupting a trainer while they are presenting information, unless this has been clarified with them. This can mean opportunities to clarify and resolve learner questions and uncertainties get missed.

Unless it is a very formal presentation, it is often more engaging to invite and encourage learners to 'chip in' and ask questions as things go along. This can be made clear at the beginning of some input and reinforced by checking for questions throughout the input. If answering a question at the point it is asked will detract from the overall logic of the presentation, then it is usually enough to thank the questioner for raising the point and reassure them that the question will be answered later on or, if not done so to their satisfaction, that you will revisit the point at the end.

Giving demonstrations

Demonstration is an essential method for helping learners to develop new skills, understand processes and even develop new behaviours. Imagine how long it would take to teach someone to drive, for example, or operate a computer if you could not demonstrate the skills and processes to them.

Demonstration can be useful for many topics, from how to manipulate a spreadsheet to how to deal with an angry customer. A good thorough structure to follow when demonstrating is:

1. Demonstrate the whole process first – this gives the 'big picture'.
2. Break down the process into manageable chunks and demonstrate them step by step – this helps people to understand the detail and sequence of the process.
3. Repeat the step-by-step demonstration, this time encouraging questions from the audience – this helps people to make sense of the process in their own way.
4. Demonstrate the whole process again – to pull it all together and embed the understanding.

The next step would be for learners to try the skill or process for themselves and to be given feedback on their efforts. Depending on the complexity of the activity, this might be done in one single move or in the series of broken-down steps, each being further demonstrated and checked by the trainer. Finally, learners will need time to repeat and practise the skill. An old proverb states: 'I hear and I forget, I see and I remember, I do and I understand.' Most of us will need to practise a skill or process in order to fully understand it.

If you are planning to demonstrate something within your session, here are a few essential tips to ensure it goes well:

- Make sure you know how to do it properly yourself (practice first!).
- Make sure everyone can see and hear everything.
- Have enough of any materials to complete and repeat the demonstration several times.
- Have a Plan B – just in case it goes wrong... perhaps 'one I prepared earlier'.

 Activity 5.7

1 Think of a process that you know well – something at work, or an everyday day task like making a cup of tea.

2 Imagine you need to demonstrate this to a group of people who have never seen it before.

3 How would you break it down?

Managing learning activities

A truly engaging L&D session will involve a range of effective and interesting learning activities: for example, practice exercises, discussions, work simulations, role-plays /try-outs, games, self-analysis and action-planning.

> 'One message rings out loud and clear from all the research that I have undertaken on how people learn. That is, to involve the learners. Get them interested, excited. Intrigue them. Tell them stories and get them to construct their own. Use colourful language – employ humour – bring your message to life. Only by capturing people's imaginations and engaging their emotions will we provide learning that really makes a difference.'
>
> *Jane Church, Learning Facilitator, Novus Professional Development Ltd*

Here are some practical tips for managing learner activities:

1 If the activity requires the group to divide into smaller groups, decide beforehand whether these should be specific groupings (different job roles, different levels of prior learning, a mix of experience, people who work together, people who do not, etc) or whether random groupings will be best. If it is to be random groups, then either leave learners to self-select or, to avoid the awkwardness sometimes caused by this, have some fun ways of deciding groups. For example, a bag of coloured counters (if you want three groups then you need three colours of counter), or black shoes vs brown shoes vs all other colour shoes, or allocating 123, 123, 123 going around the room, then all the 1s work together, and so on.

2 Provide a context for the activity, ie why has the activity been included in the session and how is it helpful to learning? Adults need a good reason to engage with learning.

3 Give clear instructions – these could be verbal, or written, or ideally, both. Make sure that your instructions include the process you want learners to follow, the amount of time they have, and the output that you are expecting at the end.

4 Make sure that you have provided all the resources that they will need – space, equipment, materials, enough copies of the instructions.

5 Check in with the groups after a couple of minutes to make sure that they are underway and that they have understood the instructions. Clarify anything that is confusing them.

6 Monitor progress from a distance. Although you need to keep an eye on the groups and check occasionally that all is well, it is usually best to leave them to function if they seem to be progressing satisfactorily. On the whole you should trust the activity, trust the groups and leave them to get on with it.

7 If they do not appear to be progressing you may need to intervene – to clarify goals or processes or perhaps to remind the group of time constraints. If the group is completely off-track you may need to re-direct them, and if they are struggling offer some hints or advice.

8 After the activity, ask the groups to report back and share their outputs. Thank them for their efforts and praise the results.

9 Debrief the activity, giving any 'official' answers and discussing any differences with or between group responses. Make sure that a correct solution is agreed before moving on.

10 To conclude the activity, ask groups to consider the learning process, as opposed to the 'technical answers' referred to in point 9 above. For example, you could ask learners:
   - how their group functioned?
   - what they have learned from the activity?
   - what they will do differently as a result of the learning?

Giving feedback to learners

Receiving feedback is a crucial step in the learning process. It is especially useful for learners after they have taken part in an activity such as a role-play, skill demonstration or case study, as it helps them to reflect on their performance and provides a better balance of information, ie not just their own perceptions, on which to reflect.

Some key guidelines for giving feedback are:

- Always deliver it in a positive way, and for the benefit of the receiver.
- Concentrate on things that are within the receiver's control.
- Feed back on what went well, as well as what could be done differently – if a learner knows what they did well they can choose to do it again.
- Make feedback as specific as possible. 'That was very good' might make your learner feel good for a few minutes, but it does not really help them to learn from the experience. 'That was very good because you gave a detailed explanation that was pitched just right for your customer, and if you had added this one extra point that would have shown added depth…' is much more useful.

For example, imagine that on a course for presentation skills, the first learner has just delivered their presentation. A useful format to follow for giving them feedback could be:

1 Ask them how they think it went – and specifically for one thing they think was particularly good and one they think was less good.

2 Tell them something you really liked about their presentation and why you liked it.
3 Tell them something you think they could change or do differently. Again, be clear about what they did and how they could change or improve it. Give reasons – the difference the change could make.
4 Give an overall assessment of their performance.
5 Ask the learner to summarise what they learned from the experience and what they will keep and what they will change next time.

Remember to get learners to feed back to one another. They could use particular approaches such as: 'I really liked X…', 'I am going to use/apply this bit…', 'If I was doing what you did I would…'.

Not only are the extra comments and suggestions likely to be useful to the recipient, but the practice will also help everyone to develop their feedback skills. Discuss the above guidelines for giving feedback with the group first and use your observation and listening skills to ensure that feedback is being given supportively.

> 'For me, the important factor about feedback is the need for balance. Even if someone has not done something very well, there is always something positive to say. For example, in a presentation situation, if the presenter is reading from notes it is not good presenting but it could be fair to praise the attention to detail. If the presenter is winging it and there is little content, it is not good presenting but it could be fair to praise the open and friendly style.'
>
> *Wendy Strohm, Wendy Strohm Associates Ltd*

Working with visual aids and resources

> 'Learn to read your learners, not your slides.'
>
> *Rosie Renold, Trainer*

Whether we are presenting, demonstrating or managing activities, we will usually want to enhance and reinforce verbal inputs with different visual aids and resources. We have made reference to some of these in the sections above and Table 5.1 summarises the most popular ones.

Facilitating learning in a group

Learning activities will only be effective if learners actually engage with them, rather than just 'being present'. To engage learners, we need to deliver content competently, effectively and enthusiastically using all the skills already discussed in this chapter. However, when working with groups, we also need to support a learning dynamic in which learners feel safe, confident and motivated to participate.

Table 5.1 Visual aids

Visual aid	Advantages	Tips
Flipcharts	• great for building up ideas and models as you go along • learners can contribute and write on them for themselves • ease and immediacy of use encourages spontaneity and creativity, for both learners and trainers • can be pre-prepared or instantaneous	– write legibly and use colours that can be seen (not yellow on white paper) – check, before the session, that your writing can be seen from the back of the training room – make small pencil notes on the flips to remind you of your key points or do outline drawings of diagrams in pencil, in advance – try flipcharts that stick directly on the wall and are wipeable and re-useable to increase portability and flexibility (and economy) of use – use a digital camera to capture the content of your completed flipcharts so that you can distribute them later
Slide-decks and presentation software	• easy to prepare with the appropriate software • lots of new exciting software packages and features available • once prepared can be used many times and adapted for different sessions • great for giving structure and consistency across sessions • can be easily printed out as handouts, etc	– don't overuse slides to avoid 'death by PowerPoint' (or any other software!) – use pictures, images and graphs to bring a subject to life (but don't overdo the decoration) – there is no need to have a slide/screen for every learning point; intermingle slides with other visuals and props – if using a projector, be aware that some are noisy or give off a lot of heat/light; turn off when not in use – spend a bit of time using the help menus and tutorials to learn how to use more features of and get the best out of your software. – beware of copyright issues when using images from search engines; try exploring royalty-free Creative Commons image sites instead

(*continued*)

Table 5.1 (Continued)

Visual aid	Advantages	Tips
Interactive smartboards and screens	• great for combining video, slides and written material • can allow dual use by the trainer and the learners • allows for structure and flexibility	– make sure that you know how all the equipment works; experiment and make best use of all the functions – do not over-rely on the technology; remember that you are still the trainer – let the smartboard support your session rather than become the session – consider some of the commercially available training on how to use more complex equipment fully and effectively
Wall imagery	• can be photos, images or flipcharts created during the day • can reinforce the theme of the session • adds interest to the learning environment	– putting the flipcharts created by learners on the wall shows that you value their contributions – material can be easily referred back to – use flipcharts from different stages of the day to show the learning 'build' – make sure to remove any left over from a previous event which will just distract learners and make the room look untidy!
Podcasts and video clips	• great way of recording interviews, presentations, key facts, etc in a format that is relatively cheap to create and easy to use during sessions • also easy for learners to access after the training at a time and place to suit them	– check out different software to find one that works best for your purposes (some good free podcast software available on the Internet) – remember that podcasts can be visual as well as audio; consider using different content: images, video, audio, music, sound files – beware of video copyright issues! – podcasts and videos can also be a method of learning (creating the podcast) and a vehicle for assessment of learning (ie a demonstration of knowledge or practice)

(*continued*)

Table 5.1 (Continued)

Visual aid	Advantages	Tips
Music and scents	• as well as visual aids, you might consider learners' other senses and make use of music or scents to enhance your oral delivery	– choose music carefully and match it to the energy you want to create, upbeat to get things moving, slow tempo to calm things down – music can be a way of putting people at ease at the beginning of the day – check with learners whether it is helpful, it may be more of a distraction than an aid for some – if using scents (eg some of the new sensory sprays on the market) to evoke a situation, be very careful to ensure that there is no potential danger or discomfort for learners in any of the products you choose
Polling apps and software	• range of apps, including some (limited) free ones, available • useful for interim assessment activities, such as quizzes or for gauging opinions • way of engaging learners in L&D activities and adding real time interest to sessions	– may require learners to use mobile devices in the session, and you may want to agree how these are used at other times – voting systems/equipment can be expensive, but increasingly less so – explore some of the software/apps which are free (up to a usage limit) to work out how you can make use of them, eg testing knowledge before or after a session, checking if learners agree with a particular answer, enabling learners to choose from alternative courses of action
Props	• easily available; almost anything can be a prop • entertaining for learners • can provide a lasting and memorable image to reinforce learning	– choose props that will represent, highlight or enhance your message: eg a superhero model if you are asking people to 'go beyond'; a pair of shoes if you are asking people to understand others' perspectives (walk a mile in their shoes) – be creative in identifying props, but stay appropriate; if learners consider the use of a prop 'silly', your message will also lose credibility

Supporting an inclusive group learning environment

In an ideal L&D world, learner groups would fall naturally into an open, lively and inclusive group dynamic. In reality though, particularly if learners do not know each other, they may need a bit of help and encouragement. How you, as the trainer, communicate with learners from the beginning can set the right tone and subtly model behaviour for the group.

You can help to set an open, relaxed and inclusive dynamic by:

- smiling and using gentle humour;
- using people's names and giving attention;
- asking for people's opinions and acknowledging their contributions;
- not 'talking over' people (or letting others do this);
- acknowledging others' ideas when you are repeating or building on them;
- not accepting/allowing any comments that might be derogatory or offensive;
- being aware early on of any potential areas of conflict or disagreement and not letting these escalate in a negative way ('let's keep it friendly');
- managing the group so that everyone gets a fair chance to participate and contribute, without being made to feel embarrassed or inadequate.

If it fits the culture of the group and may be useful, consider asking the group to set 'ground rules' for how they will work together.

Managing learner participation

There is no requirement for every learner to participate in learning in the same way. Some people are naturally more inclined to contribute comments than others, and there will be times when some individuals in the group simply do not have anything to say. Equally, some people might just be happier, and learn more, listening to other peoples' views than offering their own.

The important factor is that everyone feels an *equality of opportunity* to contribute. Some helpful ways of managing over-involvement and under-involvement are outlined in the box below.

HIGH CONTRIBUTORS

- While listening to individuals is important, there is also a responsibility to the wider group and to balance our attention across all group members. Try to avoid getting into a detailed conversation with one learner at the expense of the rest of the group.
- Thank them, but say that you would like to hear from someone else.
- Check your body language and rapport – are you encouraging them with your eye contact and reactions?

- Give them another role to use up some energy – observer, flipchart writer etc.
- Consider mixing the groups so that they cannot dominate so easily.
- Monitor the effect they are having on the rest of the group – maybe it is OK for them to dominate sometimes?
- Consider having a quiet word with them in a break. Thank them for their contribution but request that they let others have a say too.

Low contributors

- Some people just find it difficult to speak up in a group but may still have plenty to say and need to be 'invited in' or given a space to speak up. You can give this by gently asking some direct questions of individuals or asking questions of learners in turn, going around the room. To avoid this approach embarrassing anyone, make a point of saying beforehand that it is fine to say 'pass' if people do not have an answer.
- Notice if someone is trying to make a point, but not managing to make themselves heard for some reason (often a lack of confidence), and give them an 'in', eg 'What were you going to say there Michael?' or 'Did you want to contribute something Jay?'
- Give them a particular role – spokesperson, syndicate 'group leader'.
- Put people into small discussion groups. A shy person may be more likely to put themselves forward in a less dominating group.
- When they do speak, give full attention, eye contact, nods, etc. And acknowledge their contribution fully, so they are encouraged to contribute again.
- Monitor the engagement – if someone is really engaged and attentive, but simply not speaking much, that is usually OK.
- If it is a real problem, take the opportunity to have a quiet word in a break and check that they are 'OK' with the style and level.

Another technique to help manage participation levels is to use your space effectively. For example, get into the habit of picking a point to train from where you can be seen and from where you can see. Make this your 'training spot' and begin your inputs standing on your training spot. Every time you want to get the attention of the group, return to your spot, signalling that you want to input something to the group. Similarly, when you want to encourage discussion, sit down – putting yourself on the same level as your delegates – in a space somewhere amongst the group (not at the front), encouraging learners to speak to the whole group rather than to you.

Managing group energy levels

As a trainer you can use your position to monitor the group's energy levels. You may sense that levels are low when you start seeing tired body language, yawns or general disengagement. When energy levels are beginning to drop there are a number of things you can do, including:

- Consider how you are presenting the material. Are you sounding tired, quiet or talking at too slow a pace? Try mixing up the speed and volume of your speech a little to stimulate a stronger group response.
- Mix up the group(s) to break up cliques, refresh how people are interacting and generally re-energise everyone.
- Get people moving about: instead of groups responding to an activity verbally, get them to come up and write their answers on the flipchart or to feed back via a short presentation.
- Assess whether the level of input is causing the problem – too detailed or too simple – and then change the level.
- Ask some questions: questions tend to make people more attentive.
- Add some humour into your delivery: laughter is one of the best energisers.
- Suggest a quick comfort break.

Monitoring individual engagement within a group

When we are working one-to-one with a learner, it is fairly straightforward to monitor their engagement and adjust learning activities – we can ask questions, look at learners' work, discuss progress with them and then make the necessary adjustments. Within group sessions it is more difficult to monitor individual engagement, and make related adjustments, but it can and should still be done. We can ask individuals how they are feeling, we can notice how they participate and listen to their questions and comments, and we can observe how they perform in activities.

One easy way to approach individual monitoring and related adjustment of learning activity is to consider a classic training cycle, with the four stages of: identify needs, design learning, deliver learning and evaluate learning (Figure 5.3). When we are delivering learning sessions we are, of course, operating in the third stage of the cycle.

But, while we are delivering group based learning, particularly a longer activity, we can in a very subtle and informal way, *repeat the cycle for an individual learner*, as in Figure 5.4.

So, while we are delivering learning for the group we can also think about how the training is impacting on individuals. We can ask and observe how the activity is working for a particular learner? Are they engaged? Are they learning? (*evaluate*) What needs are not being met or are emerging that require the learning to be adjusted for that individual? (*identify*) What adjustments are needed? (*design*) We can then make the required adjustments (*deliver*), and the cycle begins again.

For example, while we are working with a group, we might see that one learner is not getting the best out of the learning because of the particular subgroup they are working in – maybe the group is too advanced for them or not advanced enough – and

Figure 5.3 Traditional training cycle

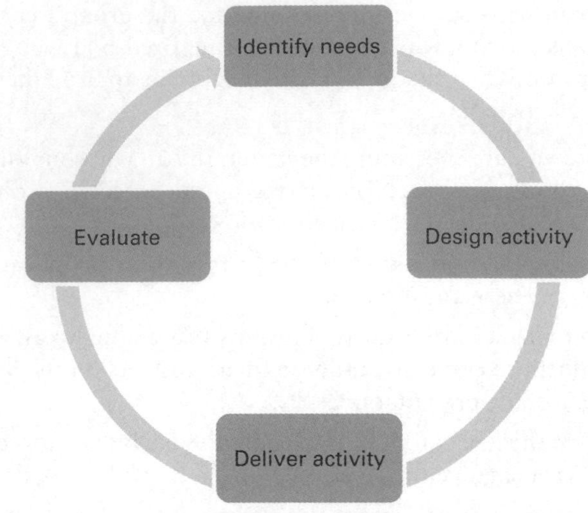

Figure 5.4 Embedded training cycle (Kathy Beevers)

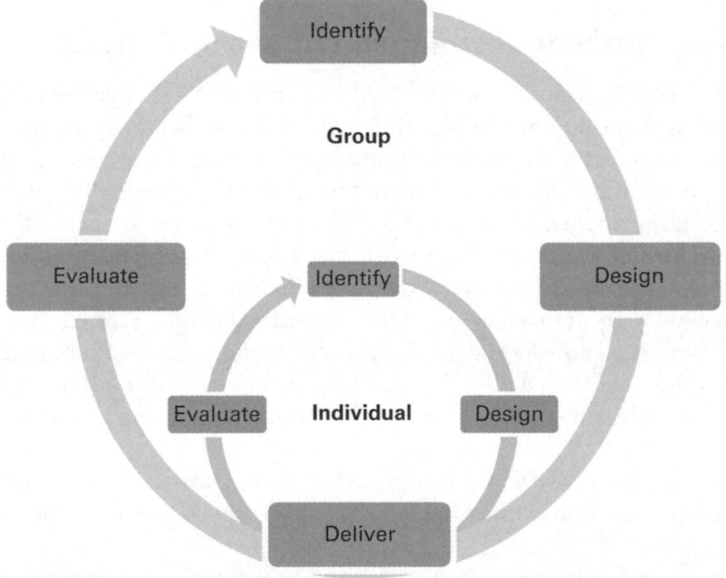

so for the next activity we can rearrange the groups to overcome this. Or we might recognise that a learner lacks confidence in relation to the learning and decide to focus on giving them more constructive and confirming feedback to help with this. The subtle individual needs you can identify and respond to through making small adjustments are endless, but your efforts to do this will help ensure a more engaging and inclusive experience for everyone.

> 'Always have extra learning activities to hand just in case the group or some individuals turn out to be extra smart. Also have parts of the training earmarked as non-essential in case some in the group are less quick on the uptake.'
>
> *Rosie Renold, Trainer*

Monitoring engagement – group reviews

As well as listening to the spontaneous comments made by learners and making our own observations of learner behaviours and performance, we can also hold some structured reviews with the whole group. These are useful for several reasons: the trainer gets information to help them manage the ongoing session; learners have an opportunity to reflect on their learning so far and identify how they may want to adjust the session or the way they are contributing; and the review provides a break, and a chance to refresh thinking, before the next chunk of learning.

A group review might just be a short (few minutes) group discussion, where everyone considers how they are progressing. Whether they are happy with the learning. Whether there is anything they want to add or change.

Reviews can also take a more creative form, engaging learners' different senses and helping to reinforce and embed learning. You can use your imagination here – as long as you follow the essential rule of 'keep it appropriate'. Here are a few examples:

- discussions in groups or pairs;
- creating a drawing that represents what has been learned;
- colouring in the bars on a graph to represent learning progress;
- creating a song, poem, mnemonic or performance that captures key learning points;
- creating a radio news report about the proceedings of the day;
- forming a human chain continuum, ordered to represent different levels of individual understanding of the topic, within the group;
- finding an object in the room that is a metaphor for what has been learned.

It is usually a good idea to have reviews just before a break – giving you time to make small adjustments before the group returns.

Bringing learning sessions to a close

Assisting transfer of learning to the workplace

The major point of most workplace L&D is to have a positive impact on some aspect of work performance, both individual and organisational. Ensuring that learning is effectively transferred back into the workplace is therefore a crucial part of any trainer's role. At all stages of the cycle, identifying needs, designing learning, delivering and evaluating learning, our mind should be firmly fixed on how we will support this transfer.

As well as ensuring that learners are fully engaged during training activities, we might also provide content, materials or guidance mechanisms for use after the main activities. We might also establish ongoing, work-based, support partnerships between learners and their managers or learners and their peers. We might also arrange L&D activities so that they are delivered in ongoing chunks interspersed with periods of application, enabling the continuation and consolidation of learning.

One of the most accessible and often effective means of achieving learning transfer is spending focused time on the development of meaningful team or individual action plans. Example questions that might be used for this, include:

- What are you going to do differently as a result of this learning?
- What specific actions do you need to take for this?
- When will you do them?
- What support will you need and from whom?
- What could stop you from being successful?
- How could you prevent this?
- How will you know that you have achieved your plan?
- What are the specific results you expect to see?

Remember that action-planning is a very separate activity to evaluation and recorded separately, so that ownership remains firmly with the learner. We have seen examples where delegates are asked to devise an action plan as part of completing a (paper-based) session evaluation sheet, which they then leave with the trainer. This might help the trainer to assess how successful their delivery has been ('look at all these learner action plans – haven't I done well') but it skews ownership of the plan and ultimately reduces the impact of the training.

Sufficient time should be allowed at the end of the session for learners to complete their action plan – and their ownership of the plan should be firmly established. Depending on the nature of the training, learners might share their action plans with their line manager after the event, so that managers can help them to monitor and measure their change in knowledge, skill or behaviour.

Closedown and evaluation

Before declaring the learning session closed it is important to check that people are ready for this. Ask people how they are feeling and if there are any outstanding issues to address. If these are group issues and the issues can be dealt with there and then, then it is best to do so. If there is not time for this, or further information is needed, then at least agree how they will be addressed. If there are individual issues or questions, where it is not appropriate to delay the whole group, you might offer to stay behind and deal with these.

It is also important to ensure that learners understand the 'next step' in their learning. What happens after the session – are there follow-on sessions, are they required to do anything other than their learning transfer activities?

If everyone is happy that the session has reached the end then it may well be time for some final evaluation. Typically, the trainer would introduce an activity aimed at measuring learner reaction to the learning session (Level 1 evaluation) and the extent to which learning has taken place (Level 2 evaluation). While this so often involves questionnaires, it doesn't have to. Consider, instead, creating a take-away menu or a learning map of the day or photos showing examples of what has been learned. And, along with Level 1 and Level 2 evaluation activities, now is the time to confirm arrangements for longer-term evaluation activities. (We have covered evaluation in depth in Chapter 10, where there are lots more examples of evaluation activities at all levels.)

Closedown is similar to session opening in many ways, as learners now move on from the activity. As discussed in the 'Opening Sessions' section above, you may want to display new visuals or play relevant music, possibly to calm down the group energy. It may also be appropriate to speak individually with people as they leave. Finally – don't forget to thank your learners for their time, participation and contributions. And hopefully they will return the thanks to you!

A final note about you

At the end of a long and intense training day or programme, you are likely to feel a mixture of euphoria, relief, and sometimes, drained of your energy – and just being left to clear the training room can be a bit of an anti-climax. If something didn't go as well as you would have liked, don't worry too much; remember you are never completely responsible for the success of an event; learners and managers, have a responsibility also. If possible, find someone to discuss things with as soon as you can, and learn from any mistakes you have made. If everything did go well, you might still want to review the day and feed back to someone who is familiar with the learning context. Either way, make sure you take time to reflect on things soon after the activity (what went well, what went less well, and what you might do differently next time). Above all – allow yourself time after the event to relax, enjoy your achievements and re-energise, before it all starts again.

Activity 5.8

Below are eight scenarios an L&D professional/trainer could face. Have a look at the scenarios – and imagine that they have happened to you.

Then consider the following questions:

1 What, if anything, could you have done to avoid the situation happening?

2 How would you manage the situation when it happened?

Scenario 1

You are delivering a one-day programme on 'Communication Skills'. During the introductions, one delegate mentions that he is attending the day because his manager is 'always complaining about my spelling' and he is hoping that today might help him improve this. Spelling is definitely not covered in your planned session, nor was it mentioned in any of the session information.

Scenario 2

Two delegates arrive at an event together and sit next to each other. The first session is a mixture of input from you and contributions from the group. The pair keep whispering to each other throughout this session. In the next activity, you ask people to work in pairs with someone they have not met before. The two delegates announce that they will work together and ignore any attempts from other delegates to pair up with them.

Scenario 3

You arrive at a venue some distance from your work-base where you are due to deliver a half-day training session. On arrival you discover there has been a mix-up with the booking, and that there is no screen, projector or laptop available for you to use. All you have with you is the memory stick containing your slide deck. You had planned to organise the whole session around the slides and some of them show diagrams of processes that are quite complex and essential to the delegates' learning.

Scenario 4

It becomes apparent from the introductory sessions that the delegates in your learner group have very different levels of prior knowledge. You had been led to believe that everyone had some basic knowledge, but no more than that. In fact, a few of the delegates seem to have a high level of knowledge and experience, while others are completely new to the subject.

Scenario 5

One of your delegates makes no contribution to the group at all. You have tried gently asking him a few questions but he has only responded with a shake of the head or a shrug. In the small group activities he has left everything to the others. Group members have also tried to involve him in things but are now tending to leave him alone. You are unsure if he is gaining anything from the session and are concerned that he is becoming quite isolated from the group.

Scenario 6

You are introducing a number of important changes that have been made to some key organisational systems. Every time you introduce something, one of your delegates comments along the lines that they have 'been there, done it and it didn't work'. Their negativity is starting to impact on the rest of the learners – some are irritated but some find the commentator humorous, and the more they snigger, the more the commentator is encouraged to keep on being negative. You can see that the session is rapidly losing credibility and impact because of all this.

Scenario 7

You have just finished delivering an enjoyable session about a new product and are reading the evaluation sheets. They are all very positive, until you come to one which says… 'the trainer should not have allowed delegates to make racist comments'. You have no idea what the delegate is referring to. The evaluation sheet is not named, but from the hand-writing you have a good idea who it was.

Scenario 8

You are coordinating a management development programme which includes managers getting feedback from their teams. When you pass the feedback on to one manager, you mention that one of her team thinks she is 'rather poor at giving her staff constructive feedback on their work'. The manager does not take this very well – and you later find out she has interviewed every team member and 'interrogated them' in an attempt to find out who made the comment – and will no doubt see them 'punished' for it. Feelings within the team are not good.

What next?

The activities below will help consolidate your knowledge from this chapter.

1 Ask a colleague to observe you delivering an L&D activity and to give you feedback. Ask them to pick some things that they particularly liked and some things that they think you could improve on.

2 Sit in on an L&D activity delivered by a colleague and give them feedback. You could follow the same structure as at 1 above. (If there is nothing available soon enough, find an online video of a session delivered by another professional trainer.)

3 Decide on one thing you will do differently when you next deliver an L&D activity and how you will make this change. Share your thoughts on Twitter using the hashtag #LDPintheW and copy in the account @ LDPintheW.

References

Cuddy, A (2015) *Presence: Bringing your boldest self to your biggest challenges* [update due January 2020] Orion, London

McGonigal, K (2015) *The Upside of Stress: Why stress is good for you (and how to get good at it),* Vermillion, London

Roche, J (2018) Face-to-face learning: Old hat or the future? Opinion, *Trainingjournal.com.* www.trainingjournal.com/articles/opinion/face-face-learning-old-hat-or-future (archived at https://perma.cc/6WEW-5BW6)

Explore further

Karia, A (2015) How to design TED-worthy presentation slides: Presentation design principles from the best TED talks, CreateSpace Independent Publishing Platform, South Carolina

Medina, J (2014) *Brain Rules (Updated and Expanded): 12 principles for surviving and thriving at work, home, and school*, Pear Press, London

Phillips, DJP (2014) How to avoid death by PowerPoint, TEDxStockholmSalon, www.youtube.com/watch?v=Iwpi1Lm6dFo (archived at https://perma.cc/8PDP-756U)

Tizzard, P and Evans, A (2003) *The Ice-Breakers Pocketbook*, Management Pocketbooks, Alresford

Wiseman, R (2013) *The As If Principle: The radically new approach to changing your life,* Free Press, London

Useful resources

Websites

www.cipd.co.uk/subjects/lrnanddev (archived at https://perma.cc/3JZA-QWZB)

www.cipd.co.uk/subjects/health/general (archived at https://perma.cc/NU2Y-58RG)

www.ted.com/talks (archived at https://perma.cc/4P5C-345V

www.businessballs.com (archived at https://perma.cc/UW7U-5HS8)

www.mindtools.com (archived at https://perma.cc/KU9K-TBA5)

www.trainingzone.co.uk (archived at https://perma.cc/PQQ4-K6N5)

06 Delivery

Using technology

Introduction

In Chapter 5 we looked at the concept of delivery in a face-to-face environment, and recognised that many of the skills required in that environment are surprisingly transferable to the delivery of learning interventions online. However, technology allows us some unique and interesting ways to deliver L&D which bring a range of benefits and perhaps one or two challenges. This chapter explores some of the opportunities and benefits technology can offer L&D and considers how we might address the challenges.

Key areas of content covered in this chapter are:

- different learning technologies and associated advantages and disadvantages;
- the timeline of technology in L&D;
- software and processes involved in providing a live online learning activity;
- the key skills involved in delivering an online learning session;
- different types of digital learning content;
- how to create engaging an effective digital learning content.

The technological context

Technology has become an accepted part of our everyday lives. Many of us couldn't imagine life without our mobile phones, tablets and the many apps stored on them. Technological advances allow us to keep in touch with family, friends and work 24/7, to access news or monitor our fitness at any time, and to give and receive information in ways that could not have been dreamed of a generation ago.

Technology also enables us to provide much more flexible ways of learning. We no longer have to rely on getting a group of people together in one room, or produce dull paper-based distance-learning manuals. Now we can harness the power of technology to facilitate learning in efficient and effective ways, at times and in locations that suit learners, and often within budgets that will please the employer.

That said, L&D have a reputation of sometimes going after 'the next shiny thing': a criticism targeted at some practitioners (but also sometimes applied unfairly to the whole profession) who introduce a technology without really thinking about the needs of the organisation or users.

In his blog (Ed Techie), Martin Weller, a prolific blogger on all things concerning technology and learning, reflects on 25 years of technology in education. He considers a raft of advances and their impact and discusses the resistance to change in some quarters and the caution that some people have with 'here today – gone tomorrow' types of technology. Finding the right balance in this is something we all need to be mindful of as it can involve a heavy (and occasionally wasted) investment for organisations.

Activity 6.1

1. What learning technologies have you experienced?
2. How has your experience of these changed over the years?
3. Have you experienced any investment issues with 'here today – gone tomorrow' ties to technology (for example, MySpace or MemoWriter)?

Whilst technologies such as e-learning, or online learning, can be economical and easy to access, they do provide L&D professionals with a number of challenges. Choosing the right hardware and software, creating engaging content, and making sure that learning objectives are met are all part of the challenge. The 2019 report *The Transformation Journey* (Towards Maturity, 2019) shows that there has been a slight reduction in practitioner skills across all the areas of technology design and delivery since the 2016 report, suggesting that practitioners still have work to do on this area of their own development.

Technology and learning

The Cegos Asia Pacific Workplace Learning Trends Survey (Blaine, 2015) states that, across Australia, China, India, Indonesia, Malaysia and Singapore 'technology is being used like never before', with more people now accessing learning electronically than via the classroom. Tablet-based learning is fuelling this growth, with desktop learning also seeing a growth.

In January 2019, *National Geographic* reported that Kenyan women are both teaching and learning through the use of tablets allowing for access to learning and increasing the value of education to them and their children (Petri, 2018).

There is an ever-growing range of technologies available to help us facilitate learning. Some, such as e-learning, have been around for a long time whilst others such as training apps on mobile phones are still in their relative infancy and part of an emerging market for adaptable learning methods.

The following section looks in detail at some of the most popular ways of using (and describing the use of) technology to facilitate learning. For each learning technology, we have provided a definition, given some examples of how it can be used, and explored some of the advantages and disadvantages involved in its usage.

E-learning

In pure terms, e-learning can refer to any sort of learning method that is accessed via a computer or electronic device In that sense, therefore, it could be said that many of the technologies that we are discussing in this chapter such as podcasts and virtual classrooms are 'e-learning'. An e-learning programme might therefore consist of a range of methods by which learners access different parts of the programme.

The term 'online learning' has replaced 'e-learning' for some, and for others 'e-learning' refers specifically to a discrete learning package. However, here we will use it as a generic term, as defined in the paragraph above.

E-learning has many critics, mainly centred around the design of the learning and how it relates to the users 'reality' (see Table 6.1). However, the Good Practice report *Learning Technologies: What managers really think* (Good Practice, 2017) showed that 86 per cent of managers in organisations of over 500 employees said that e-learning was useful in helping them do their job, suggesting that done well, e-learning can be impactful.

Table 6.1 Advantages and disadvantages of e-learning

	Advantages	Disadvantages
Learning effectiveness	Well-designed e-learning using a range of technologies can be a highly effective way of delivering learning.	There can be challenges around engaging some people, and it might be too easy for some learners to drop out or slip through the net. Learners' IT skills may also be an issue.
Flexibility	Well-designed e-learning is flexible enough to cope with many changes in need and demand.	The systems and content need constant review and updating to make sure they are relevant and covering all the key needs.

(continued)

Table 6.1 (Continued)

	Advantages	Disadvantages
Accessibility	In theory, e-learning should increase accessibility to learning by making it available in a range of formats to suit all needs.	There are potential issues about access to IT equipment and consideration needs to be given to staff who might have specific needs when accessing IT equipment (large screen, audio translation etc). Access to an Internet connection can also be an issue.
Scalability	A well-designed e-learning system should be adaptable enough to scale to any size of operation.	More investment may be needed if the system becomes very successful and capacity is reached sooner than expected.
Time efficiency	Long-term time savings should be worth any short-term time investment.	Initial set-up will take time, especially if building a bespoke system.
Cost efficiency	Can be much more cost effective than traditional face-to-face learning and can encompass many more people.	Initial investment in equipment and software may be high.

Activity 6.2

1. How is e-learning regarded in your organisation – positively, negatively or not widely used?
2. What reasons are there for the view taken?
3. Are there different views across different users?
4. What advantages does (or would) e-learning have for your organisation?

Case Example 6.1

Ensuring access to e-learning

A local authority commissioned an extensive e-learning programme for staff, believing that it would deliver cost savings and achieve higher levels of learner engagement. They were surprised to realise, however, that over one-third of their workforce (nearly 500 staff) did not have regular access to IT equipment at work. This included roles such as care assistants, gardeners, street wardens and lifeguards. Further investigation also revealed that a proportion of these (about 50 staff) either did not have access to a personal PC, smartphone or tablet, or were not confident about anything other than basic use of them.

Case study questions

1 What course of action do you think the authority should take?

2 What would you need to do in your organisation to make sure that every staff member was ready for e-learning?

Virtual classrooms

A virtual classroom can be defined as an online learning environment, usually accessed via the Internet. Just as in a 'real-world' training room, the trainer and the learners are logged into the virtual classroom at the same time, and are taking part in synchronous learning. In effect, the virtual classroom enables interactive learning to take place in a similar way to how it happens in the real-world training room.

A small-scale virtual classroom could be set up very easily using web-based conferencing tools such as Skype or Facetime, and these free tools work well for interactive meetings with a relatively small group of people. However, organisations that want to use virtual classrooms as a real alternative or addition to their real-world training rooms are likely to acquire more sophisticated platforms which suit their specific overall design and delivery needs (see Table 6.2).

Typically, the trainer will deliver their training session 'live' from a specialist training facility or, depending on the software, just from their desk. Everything that the trainer needs to control the session will be available onscreen. Learners will also be online, either participating from their workplace, home or on the move.

The technology behind these packages gets increasingly sophisticated, with updates and improved versions being released on a regular basis. Amongst the tools often included in virtual training room packages are:

- **Interactive whiteboards.** The trainer can prepare presentations which can be displayed, updated and discussed live online. Many packages allow multiple presentations, so learners could also share their presentations, or view presentations from multiple sources.
- **Multi-point video.** Some packages will detect who is talking and show their video more prominently on the screen. The clarity of picture and audio is improving all the time, along with the number of active participants that the programme will allow.
- **Moderator tools.** The trainer will have a suite of tools to help them stay in charge of the virtual space. They can view the work of learners, allow them to ask questions in private or open forum, allow or view private conversations etc.
- **Break-out rooms.** The trainer can set up and maintain break-out rooms for trainees to hold smaller conversations or carry out allocated tasks in smaller groups.
- **Integration with LMS.** If the virtual classroom is integrated with the organisation's learning management system (LMS) it can automatically keep a register of attendance, store test results and collect evaluation data etc.

Table 6.2 Advantages and disadvantages of virtual classrooms

	Advantage	Disadvantage
Learning effectiveness	Can provide a varied and engaging learning environment that appeals to different learner preferences. Used well, it closely replicates the traditional training room.	If not moderated well, it could be too dull or distractingly 'gimmicky' for some learners. Not always easy for the trainer to judge the level of learner engagement.
Flexibility	There is enormous flexibility in the design and delivery of programmes using virtual classrooms.	The main limit on flexibility lies in the skill and imagination of the trainer.
Accessibility	Good virtual classroom software will allow accessibility to all, including those using specialist programmes to help with sight, hearing or other disabilities. In theory, learners can access the classroom from any location.	Learners need to be using compatible hardware, with appropriate software to participate. They also need a reliable connection to the Internet which can potentially limit accessibility to some locations.
Scalability	Ideal for groups of between 6 and 20.	Once a group becomes too large you may lose flexibility and some engagement.
Time efficiency	Very efficient as it saves participants having to travel to a training location.	Can cause logistical difficulties if participants are in different time-zones.
Cost efficiency	Cost effective if used regularly and replaces physical classrooms.	Initial set-up costs may be high.

Webinars

'Webinar' is short for web-based seminar, and is a presentation, lecture, workshop or seminar that is delivered live over the Internet. It differs from a webcast in that the communication is two-way, with the audience being able to interact with the presenter in some way, perhaps through features such as polling or questions. A webinar is also different from a virtual classroom in that it is often broadcast to wider range of people and is not so focused on group learning. Webinars can be recorded and watched at a later stage by people who could not watch the original broadcast.

Webinars are usually 'visual' using slides and a video camera and will be watched remotely on PCs, tablets or phones. It is worth considering how the webinar looks and sounds on these different formats, and how the interactive elements of the webinar can be accessed. The control panel for adding text by the learner will be in different places if the learner is using a PC or a smartphone (see Table 6.3).

How the tools are used within a webinar is also important to consider. Polls can be straightforward across all different formats (phone, tablet and PC). However, interactive whiteboards may have very different functionality.

Table 6.3 Advantages and disadvantages of webinars

	Advantage	Disadvantage
Learning effectiveness	Good for transfer of knowledge or key messages.	Difficult to test the level of engagement.
Flexibility	They can be used for a whole variety of purposes and are, in that respect, flexible.	It's easy to get stuck in the same format using limited online tools, and be seen as stale or repetitive.
Accessibility	Highly accessible.	Needs a stable Internet connection.
Scalability	Suitable for small or large audiences.	The larger the audience, the less interaction there can be.
Usability	There are a range of polling, drawing and texting tools that can be accessed across PCs, smartphones and tablets	Some functions may be limited on some platforms. Interactive whiteboards could get very messy (think about dividing the space up on a whiteboard so people only use a certain space). Some learners can get very carried away with the function tools!
Time efficiency	Highly time efficient.	They need to be scheduled at convenient times of the day and not impinge on other important work tasks.
Cost efficiency	Highly cost efficient if reaching the right target audience.	May become over-used and not add any real value.

Online discussion forums

An online discussion forum is a form of message board, where people hold 'conversations' by posting messages. This is usually an asynchronous activity with people browsing and commenting at different times. Unlike a live chat-room, the messages can be fairly long and will be archived so that users who log in later can still see them.

Discussion forum software usually allows for the appointment of moderators who decide which posts to allow. There will often be several strands of discussion under different headings.

One of the early uses for online discussion forums was for pre- and post-course discussion of traditional training events or for distance-learning students of colleges and universities to be able to converse. Today this approach is still effective, but now forums are also being used as a primary development method through online peer discussions and sharing of practice (Table 6.4).

Table 6.4 Advantages and disadvantages of discussion forums

	Advantage	Disadvantage
Learning effectiveness	Good if the learner can get questions answered correctly.	The 'staggered' effect of asynchronous discussions can be frustrating to some learners.
Flexibility	Very flexible.	If the moderator is too flexible or inflexible it may inhibit the effectiveness of the forum.
Accessibility	Highly accessible	Usually voluntary so some users will never/seldom use the forum.
Scalability	Suitable for small or large numbers.	Large number of contributors can be difficult to moderate.
Time efficiency	Potentially a good way of engaging with learners, especially as they can access the forum in their own time.	You may have to wait for replies or comments about a post.
Cost efficiency	Highly cost efficient.	May disrupt more valuable work if accessed in the workplace.

Smartphones and learning-related apps

The smartphone is an ever-more powerful tool in the world of L&D; providing useful apps (applications) for trainers and for learners (see Table 6.5).

Table 6.5 Advantages and disadvantages of smartphones and learning apps

	Advantage	Disadvantage
Learning effectiveness	Highly effective for 'just-in-time' learning and for learners who are comfortable with the technology.	Phones in the training room can be seen as distracting and not everyone likes interacting with a small screen.
Flexibility	Highly flexible, especially for training on the move.	Might intrude into personal time. Not everyone has a smartphone, or may not want to use their personal phone for learning.
Accessibility	Potentially accessible to all.	Interacting with a small screen is not suitable for some learners. Dependent upon a strong mobile connection and good storage and memory on the device.

(*continued*)

Table 6.5 (Continued)

	Advantage	Disadvantage
Scalability	Suitable for a large community of learners.	Limited only by cost of phones and connections.
Time efficiency	Ability to learn in your own time can be very attractive.	May intrude into the work/life balance.
Cost efficiency	Many apps are free or very reasonably priced.	Providing smartphones for all learners could be expensive.

From a design and delivery point of view, there are a multitude of apps available for everything from defining outcomes to evaluation tools. Smartphones also enable us to facilitate mobile learning (m-learning) where learners can get short-burst sessions on the move. M-learning can also be described as 'pull learning', where learners 'pull' the learning they want, when they want it, rather than having learning 'pushed' at them by the L&D department.

There are also many apps for learners, allowing them to use their phones to take notes, share ideas, vote on content, etc. Some apps are free to use and take seconds to create content, others are more complex and some come with licensing requirements to use. Smartphones are really useful to create and share learning resources using video or audio.

Social media

As explored in Chapter 8 (Delivery: Social and collaborative learning) social media is playing a growing role in the lives of many of our learners, and L&D professionals can exploit this openness to sharing to enhance learning (Table 6.6).

Table 6.6 Advantages and disadvantages of social media

	Advantage	Disadvantage
Learning effectiveness	Can provide an effective platform for delivering learning. Perhaps most useful for 'informal' learning.	Not all learners and trainers are comfortable using public platforms for their learning, or may not be familiar with social media. Can be difficult to evaluate the level of learning taking place.
Flexibility	Highly flexible platforms allow learning at many different levels.	The trainer may not have much control over discussions, so learning and discussions can go down paths that the trainer hadn't anticipated.
Accessibility	Platforms already used by many people so highly accessible.	Requires mobile devices and good connectivity. There may be reluctance from some learners to combine their social sites with ones related to work or learning.

(continued)

Table 6.6 (Continued)

	Advantage	Disadvantage
Scalability	Suitable for very large audiences and learning communities.	Content can become too bland or generic when designed to reach a large diverse audience.
Time efficiency	Potentially very efficient, especially for 'just-in-time' learning and messages.	Can increase the time that people spend on social media and could conflict with workplace protocols about use of mobile devices.
Cost efficiency	Makes use of free or reasonably priced platforms.	Often relies on people being willing to use their own smartphone, and has resourcing costs if equipment needs to be provided.

Social media was first used as a means of supporting wider learning, ie as part of blended approach, but many trainers are now developing approaches that use platforms such as Facebook or Twitter to deliver short learning interventions.

File-sharing sites like Flickr and YouTube provide easy access to tutorials and 'how to' videos, whilst networking sites like LinkedIn, Facebook and WhatsApp allow discussion and idea generation in both open and closed spaces.

Every Friday morning at 8am UK time a group of people with an interest in L&D and OD get together to respond to a question on Twitter. The question is set by the team behind @LnDConnect (a group of volunteers who have the aim of growing the capabilities, thinking and development of the profession). For the next hour various people respond to the question using the hashtag #LDInsight. The responses are collated and shared (currently via the app Wakelet) so that anyone unable to join, or stay for the full hour, can catch up on people's views and comments.

Learning management systems

A learning management system (LMS) is a software application for the administration, documentation, tracking, reporting and delivery of e-learning or all L&D programmes. A well-designed LMS brings all the functions of the L&D team under one programme and becomes the 'hub' for information within the team (see Table 6.7). Nowadays it would be fairly unusual to find an L&D function in a large or medium-sized organisation operating without an LMS to help them to collect, monitor, store and share L&D information.

Table 6.7 Advantages and disadvantages of learning management systems

	Advantage	Disadvantage
Learning effectiveness	A good LMS will enable the L&D team to monitor the effectiveness of the learning.	There is a danger that an overly bureaucratic system could inhibit learning effectiveness or fail to measure the right data.
Flexibility	A good system will have sufficient flexibility to meet the changing needs of the L&D function.	An inflexible system can end up inhibiting the L&D team and result in missed opportunities for further developing the workforce.
Accessibility	Access permissions should be given to everyone who needs them.	There may be problems accessing the LMS remotely.
Scalability	A good system should be able to grow and change to meet the needs of the organisation.	A poorly designed system might need replacing if the organisation expands beyond its maximum capacity.
Time efficiency	By collecting all L&D data in one place, an LMS should provide considerable time savings.	Some generic systems could be incompatible with other L&D protocols thereby causing duplication or additional work.
Cost efficiency	After initial outlay the business should plan to see a return on its investment brought about by cost savings and increased efficiency.	An LMS could prove to be a poor investment if there hasn't been a properly researched business case to select the right system for the organisation.

E-portfolios

An e-portfolio is a platform for storing material put together by a learner to demonstrate their learning and development, and possibly competence. E-portfolios allow learners to upload their work, 'evidence', and information in appropriate formats, which can then be checked, assessed or critiqued by a trainer, assessor or mentor. Having received feedback, the learner can amend, edit or add to their work until it reaches the standard required.

Although primarily used in the context of professional qualifications, e-portfolios are increasingly being used to good effect in the wider L&D field, for example for logging and accessing CPD. When linked to a learning management system (LMS) or performance planning system, an e-portfolio can be a useful means for a learner, and their manager, to track a learner's progress towards various learning and development goals (see Table 6.8). Evidence captured in an e-portfolio can include almost anything 'uploadable', for example, documents, audio files, video clips, podcasts and references to external sources such as other websites or blogs.

Table 6.8 Advantages and disadvantages of e-portfolios

	Advantage	Disadvantage
Learning effectiveness	The dynamic nature of an e-portfolio and the ability to receive continuing feedback makes it an effective learning tool.	Requires commitment from both the learner and the trainer. If that commitment is lacking, the value of the tool is diminished.
Flexibility	E-portfolios can be used in a variety of flexible ways, driven by the L&D needs of the organisation or the individual.	Flexibility needs to come from users and managers – finding best and creative ways to use them within L&D initiatives.
Accessibility	Should be easily accessible.	Remote access could be an issue to some users. Some systems are overly complex and unfriendly.
Scalability	Suitable for any number of users.	Limited only by the availability of assessors or mentors to give feedback.
Time efficiency	It is an 'investment' of time by the learner. The return on that investment comes in the form of increased learning and good quality feedback.	If learners are required to create evidence just for uploading to a portfolio, this could be seen as a waste of time.
Cost efficiency	After initial set-up costs it should be a cost-effective tool to operate. (Some (limited) free systems are available.)	Initial set-up costs could be high, especially if additional access has to be provided for learners.

Activity 6.3

Thinking about the assessment criteria that we have used above (learning effectiveness, flexibility, accessibility, scalability, time efficiency and cost efficiency) how do other forms of training compare?

(Try selecting and comparing one of the following: traditional classroom training, 1:1 coaching, or workbook-style distance learning.)

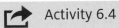

Activity 6.4

Think of an L&D or performance outcome that your organisation might need to achieve. It could be some sales training, a health and safety issue, or the launch of a new policy.

How could you use one or two of the technologies listed above to help you achieve that outcome?

Every one of the technological tools discussed above has a valuable role to play in L&D. But perhaps the biggest benefits are gained when they are used to provide a coordinated and blended solution which takes advantage of the cost savings and universal access of technology, whilst also harnessing the natural desire of a workforce to learn and progress.

Case Example 6.2

Selecting the best L&D option

Consider the example of a national freight company that has introduced a new disciplinary system across its 20 national distribution sites. The new process includes changes to paperwork and reporting, along with more emphasis on the performance improvement conversations that managers need to have with workers whose performance is of concern. The disciplinary process has been changed in the light of complaints that some managers were 'too soft' on underperformance, whilst others had failed to follow the right processes, resulting in successful claims of unfair dismissal or harassment by some employees.

It has been agreed that line managers at 20 sites will need training on the new system in order to understand the process and develop their skills.

There are a number of options under consideration:

A. Traditional training
A training officer from Head Office visiting each site to run group sessions on the new process, including practice sessions for the managers.

B. Cascade training
The training officer or HR rep trains the four regional managers in the new process and instructs them to cascade the training out to the managers at their sites.

C. Online learning
E-learning would consist of a variety of different methods, including:

- self-learn packages for managers to work through individually online;
- a discussion forum for questions or concerns;
- a video demonstration of an interview;
- a short reminder/follow-up which could be sent to managers just before they use the new disciplinary process for the first time.

Case study questions

1 What are the main advantages and disadvantages of each option in this case?
2 Which option would you recommend? Why?

Technology in the training room

Whilst this chapter is mainly about using technology to enable learning outside of a traditional training room, we should not forget the whole host of technology that can be used by trainers to enhance the quality of the training delivered face-to-face:

- presentation software, such as PowerPoint, Prezi and Sway;
- videos and video clips to bring content to life;

- video cameras to record skill-building sessions and provide feedback to learners;
- use of video recording by learners to capture key take-aways in face-to-face sessions;
- Internet connections to allow learners to use their own phones or tablets to research topics;
- voting and polling software to enable learners to interact using their mobile devices;
- using social media hashtags to gather immediate feedback and comment;
- note-taking apps so that participants can use their mobile devices to make sense of their learning.

 Activity 6.5

1 What technology do you use within face-to-face L&D activities?

2 What piece of technology would you love to invent that would really help you to deliver your L&D objectives?

The timeline of technology in L&D

Innovations in technology have been changing the face of training for many years, right back to the introduction of the chalk board.

Table 6.9 describes some of the key developments over the years.

The Centre for Learning and Performance undertake an annual survey inviting people across the learning profession to rate their preferred technology (CLP, 2018). Respondents to the survey are practitioners across the globe and the results are filtered to show the top tools in education, personal learning and professional learning categories. There is also a combined overall category. Some of the technologies are familiar to most (like YouTube and PowerPoint, rated no. 1 across the four categories in 2018) whilst others may be new or unfamiliar to many (like Pocket and Udemy, ranked nos. 35 and 36 in the combined category).

Delivering live online learning sessions

One of the aspects of emerging technologies that first excited the L&D profession, was the possibility of delivering live learning sessions in an online environment or 'virtual classroom'. When designed and delivered well, this sort of session can have many of the learning benefits of a physical classroom session, with the cost and logistical benefits that technology can offer. In this section we shall look at the skills needed (technical and delivery skills) when designing and delivering an online learning session.

Table 6.9 Timeline of technological developments in training

1890	Chalk boards move out of the school classroom and into the corporate training room.
1910	Correspondence courses become the forerunner of 'distance learning'.
1925	Trainers first start using film (movie) reels to show examples of processes in action.
1960	The first overhead projectors introduced, allowing trainers to pre-prepare visual presentations that can also be annotated and changed in the live training room.
1970	Audio-visual training crosses over from language laboratories in schools, enabling training that requires very little, if any, input from a trainer in the room.
1976	Computer-based training (CBT) allows mass training and testing, involving learners following a module through a computer terminal.
1980	The heyday of the corporate training video, often humorous and starring well-known actors from film and TV.
1985	Video technology enables trainers to video learners in action and give video-supported feedback.
1990	Microsoft launches PowerPoint as part of Windows 3.0. A growing range of commercially available LCD projectors soon make PowerPoint a training room staple.
1992	Video-conferencing technology allows delegates to contribute to live meetings and training sessions from different locations.
1993	AI (artificial intelligence) used in learning scenarios as teaching aids.
1996	The Internet opens up access to information in ways not known before.
1999	Interactive whiteboards bring together the flexibility of the flipchart and the professionalism of the projector.
2000	Virtual classrooms become a reality.
2004	YouTube brings video clips to the masses.
2006	Twitter is launched
2008	Smartphones and tablets make remote access and multiple communication strands an affordable reality. MOOCs (massive open online courses) are launched.
2012	Readily available learning apps bring mobile learning to life.
2015	The conversation around digital badging gains momentum.
2017	The conversation around virtual reality and its use in 'mainstream' L&D gathers pace.
2019 onwards	Many of the learning technologies of the past began their commercial lives in schools and colleges. Currently schools are making great use of tablet technology to enable teachers and students to share programmes which the students can annotate, alter and store in ways which most suit their learning preferences. Businesses meanwhile are excited about the growth of mobile learning, allowing staff to access 'short burst' learning or reminders whenever and wherever they need it.

What makes a good online learning session?

Whilst good online learning sessions can produce outstanding results, bad online sessions, just like poor sessions in a physical classroom, have the capability of missing the point, sending the participants to sleep and completely undermining the credibility of the training profession.

The best online learning sessions will be:

- well planned – with clear, realistic and measurable objectives that meet the needs of the organisation and the learners;
- timely – delivered at the right time for the learners and lasting an appropriate amount of time;
- interactive – allowing learners to engage with the trainer, and possibly with other learners, rather than simply being passive recipients;
- interesting – attention grabbing and appealing to learners' different senses;
- delivered on an appropriate platform – accessible to learners and using reliable hardware and software;
- programmed – part of a range of targeted L&D activities with appropriate pre- and post-event activities and contact.

We shall be discussing some of these characteristics later in this section.

Part of the planning for an online learning session involves preparing the learners for the event, especially if they are new to the world of the online classroom. When training takes place in a physical environment, we send out an invitation telling participants where and when to attend and a little about the training. Equally, when introducing participants to a live online learning session we need to tell them what to expect – but we may also need to do a bit more, in terms of preparation, with them.

For example, some of the protocols of being in a virtual classroom might be covered in advance, and, ideally, a demonstration of the programme could be available for participants to experience before they log in to the live event. Some preliminary preparation such as this will help to ensure that learners log in to your session ready to learn, rather than apprehensive of the technology or the process and unsure of what to expect.

> 'When doing a web session, I always state on the invite for people who have not used the system before or want a refresher, they can log on 15 minutes before the session starts to go through the practicalities. Then when everyone else joins we can start the content learning rather than discussing the system.'
>
> *Learning and Development Consultant*

Choosing your hardware and software

Notwithstanding content and trainer skills, the success of an online learning session will depend considerably on the right hardware and software being used. On the assumption that you will not want to invest vast sums of money in new devices just so that learners can access your session, you will need to ask yourself what equipment the participants in your session will need to have. Will they be on desktop PCs at their workplace, or on a tablet at home, or even on a mobile phone on the move?

It would be advisable that, wherever they are taking part, they have headsets. They will also need a reliable broadband connection that is fast enough to stream live video and audio.

If possible, it is also advisable for you to experience both the hardware and software before the session, not only as a trainer but as a learner as well. What does the invite look like, are all the features available if someone dials in rather than logs in? How different do the features look on a mobile? Is there a difference in the screen between Android and Apple phones?

Similarly, as the designer or deliverer of an online session, you will need access to an Internet-connected PC (with, possibly, another one available for backup) which has sound and camera enabled. It is important that you have your camera switched on so the learners can see you and your enthusiasm for the topic

As for software, there are many options available including: free (or partially free) open-source programmes such as WebEx, GoToWebinar, Adobe Connect and Hangouts from Google (the latter being an example of a technology product changing name and title over the last few years); and off-the-shelf packages or custom-built designed and licensed options specifically for your organisation.

We have already mentioned some of the features available for delivering live online learning. The list below includes those that many online facilitators consider to be most useful:

Application Sharing: Ideal for IT or process training – the trainer can share their screen with the group and demonstrate key features, skills etc.

Document Sharing: The tutor can open a document which individual learners can save, amend or annotate.

Multimedia: Allows the tutor to include slide decks, video, audio clips, etc to enhance the learning.

Chat: Allowing participants ask questions or respond to the trainer. Also allows them to communicate with each other (usually via instant messaging) which can be private or visible to all.

Break-out groups: Just as in a physical learning environment, learners can work in separate syndicate groups.

Whiteboard: A live whiteboard facility, enabling the tutor (and selected participants) to draw or write onto a blank screen, or annotate onto the pre-prepared graphics.

Status indicators: These allow learners to indicate their current 'status' to the tutor and/or the rest of the group. Examples of status could include:

- 'agree' or 'disagree' for group answers to questions;
- 'hands up' – either to respond to, or to ask, a question;
- 'away' – to indicate that the student is not currently looking at the screen.

Polling: The ability to take real-time surveys of the learners that require more than a 'hands up'. This could be used to test knowledge, collect feedback or aid evaluation.

Session record: Allowing the session to recorded and archived so that other learners can watch it later.

Live register: A means of capturing who joins and leaves the group.

Classroom control: All of the features of the programme should be easy for the trainer to navigate via an onscreen dashboard, making the running of the session as smooth and seamless as possible and allowing maximum flexibility in the amount of control required.

Community forum: A space for the learners to carry on the conversation after the session.

Activity 6.6

1 What software do you have available for online learning?
2 How thoroughly do you understand it? Could you, for example, teach a newcomer to your team how to use it?
3 What would you need to do to make yourself more knowledgeable or confident in using the software?

Designing the session

We have discussed the key principles of session design in depth in Chapter 4 (Designing L&D activities). The essential elements of agreeing objectives and outcomes, choosing the most appropriate activities, designing engaging materials and selecting how to assess the learning, are just as important when designing online sessions.

Agree the objectives

The overall objectives for your session will depend upon a number of factors:

- the needs of the organisation and the learners;
- the current level of knowledge of your participants;
- the current level of confidence and skill that your participants have in using an online classroom;
- the time available to you for the session;
- the technology available to you within your online classroom.

As always, well-defined objectives will help you to design the right content and help you to evaluate the success of your intervention, both during and after the running of the event.

Design the learning activities

One of the key challenges of an online training session is the need to keep your participants engaged. In her book *The Virtual Training Guidebook: How to design, deliver and implement live online learning* (2013), Cindy Huggett suggests that online learners need to be 'engaged' at least once every four minutes in order to achieve maximum attention. Engagement could come in the form of a question, poll, discussion or annotated graphic.

Your design should take account of the features and restrictions of the technology you are using – there is no point designing elaborate activities that will not be supported by your software, but equally, you should make the most of the opportunities the technology gives you to create an engaging session.

Table 6.10 Keeping online learners engaged

Tool	Example Activity
Application sharing	Facilitator shares their screen with the group as they demonstrate how to register a holiday request on the HR booking system. IT facilitator shares their PowerPoint screen as they talk the learners through how to embed video clips into a slide.
Document sharing	Customer care facilitator opens a list of the ten most common complaints and asks participants to use the annotation tool to highlight what they think are the top three for their part of the business. Health and safety facilitator shows a list of activities and asks participants to highlight which ones they think are safe or unsafe.
Multimedia	Safeguarding facilitator shows a short video of a care worker interacting with a vulnerable adult, having asked the group to watch out for five things that the worker did well. Sales facilitator plays a recording of a call from a customer, having asked the participants to listen for opportunities for a sale that the agent missed.
Chat	Technical facilitator poses a problem to the group and asks for suggestions of possible solutions. Induction facilitator asks for examples of experience from the learners.
Break-out groups	Sales facilitator puts participants into triads (groups of three) for role-play practice where one person plays the sales agent, one is the customer, and the third in an observer who gives feedback at the end. Equalities facilitator shares a scenario with the group and asks break-out groups to discuss and report back on the legal and ethical implications of the situation.
Whiteboard	HR/recruitment facilitator asks participants to write their 'what if...?' questions on the whiteboard to open up further discussion (eg what if the applicant a friend of mine?) Technical facilitator asks participant to map a process in the order that it should happen.
Status indicator	Compliance facilitator presents a short scenario and asks for 'hands up' if you think this is legal. Customer care facilitator asks for 'hands up' if you agree with the feedback that one of the break-out groups have just delivered.
Polls	Facilitator shows a list of the objectives that this session was designed to achieve, and asks participants to assess, on a scale of 0–5, how they feel we have done. Facilitator asks some multiple-choice questions that test the knowledge of the group to help evaluate how successful the objectives of the session have been. Learners select their responses.

Thinking about the common tools, described above, which are available in most virtual classroom software, Table 6.10 presents some ideas of how each could be used to engage learners.

You will also need to think about the optimum time that the session should take up. All-day training might still be an option in the world of the physical training room, but one of the advantages of the virtual classroom is that it allows for much shorter sessions. It is also true that it is more difficult to hold the attention of the learner for long periods online, compared with the traditional training room. If your session is two hours or more, it is advisable to build in a short ten-minute break half-way through.

Most live online learning sessions last between 30 minutes and two hours, and many businesses would not expect their staff to have to 'attend' sessions that were going to take them away from their day-to-day work for any longer than that. You may, therefore, be looking at designing a programme of sessions held over a period of time, rather than a long one-off session. A benefit of this is that you can build in reflection and practice activities between the sessions, allowing for the group to share their experiences at the start of the next session

Even if you are converting material from an existing course to use online, it is essential that you think about the online session design, otherwise it might just be a poor imitation of the original and you will have missed the opportunity to gain the advantages of going online.

Facilitating the session

As trainers, many of us are quite used to working 'alone' in the physical training room. In fact, it is difficult to convince most budget-holders that they need to employ a co-trainer, whatever the size of the cohort or whatever the subject matter.

In the world of virtual classrooms, however, it is more commonly accepted that there is a need for two staff – often referred to as the 'facilitator' and the 'producer':

- the facilitator – the main 'host' of the event, the person that the learners will see most of onscreen;
- the producer – operates most of the technology on the day and also deals with one-to-one queries or concerns (technical or subject-related) from the participants whilst the facilitator is dealing with the main group.

Delivering a webinar can be daunting at first. Depending on the software being used there may be a number of 'boxes' on the screen; for example, a chat box, a video screen, a poll, the slide deck and the whiteboard – all requiring facilitator attention. However, a face-to-face environment also has lots of things going on, just in a different way.

If you are using video, which is highly recommended, think about your positioning on the screen. If you facilitate in a face-to-face environment standing up, do this for online sessions too. Also, consider your background: are there things that could detract from your message or distract your audience.

Remember to use people's names as they put things in the chat box and think about some of the main challenges for people – can they see and can they hear?

You may also want to consider having a rolling welcome slide for your audience to see rather than a static one. This can have a number of benefits: it shows the audience that the technology is working for them, it allows you to share some of the insights for the session, and you could put a picture of yourself to help build rapport for the audience. Having 3–5 slides on rotation can be really useful: a welcome slide; a slide with your contact details and picture; a slide with the session objectives; a slide sharing what interactive tools will be used; and a slide that says 'we start at (time) – so grab a coffee and think about what you want to gain from this session'.

Cindy Huggett (Huggett, 2013) identifies nine core skills that the facilitator or producer needs to have in order to fully engage participants:

1. Build rapport. This could even start before the session has begun. Invitations and pre-course discussions play their part, as do welcoming individuals to the session, using names and acknowledging contributions.
2. Create community. Good use of chat and share facilities, both in public by the facilitator and in private by the producer help to create a sense of being part of a group – even if the participants are geographically far apart.
3. Read 'body language'. Even though you can't physically see your participants, it is important to read the signs that give you a clue as to their level of engagement. Are they joining in discussions? Are they answering polls? Are they shown as 'attentive' on the monitoring programme? Noticing these things gives you the opportunity to investigate and bring potential non-engaged participants back into the group.
4. Set expectations. This can include ground rules, discussing how/when to use facilities, the role of the producer etc.
5. Use platform tools. Knowing what your programme can do for you and having the skill to use each of the tools to their full effect.
6. Share only relevant examples. A big skill for the facilitator is to stay focused on the objectives and be respectful of the group by sharing only those examples that are most relevant to them.
7. Use voice. Tone, pace, volume, energy, sincerity and clarity – these are all vocal tools that people will engage with.
8. Multitask effectively. Facilitators and producers are constantly doing more than one thing at once – reading onscreen responses whilst talking though a slideshow for example. Multitasking relies on a high level of preparation, in-depth knowledge of the content and the technology, and application of the trainers' mantra 'practice, practice, practice'.
9. Manage technology. Be prepared for anything to happen and know how to troubleshoot and put things right.

As with any learning activity, the trainer needs to be prepared for the session and think about their role, the learners and their needs, and be able to confidently address any technical issues as they occur.

 Activity 6.7

This section has concentrated on the role of the L&D professional in designing and delivering live online learning events. But what about the role of the learner:

1 What are their responsibilities as participants in a live online session?
2 What would you include on a 'protocol' for participants?

Creating digital learning content

In his book *Digital Learning Content: A designer's guide*, Clive Shepherd defines digital learning content as:

> 'material stored on a network server, local drive or some form of removal storage, which is accessed through a browser, media player or some other application, whether that's on a personal computer, tablet, mobile device or any other piece of computing equipment, however disguised.'
>
> *Clive Shepherd, 2012*

In the previous section we looked specifically at creating and running a live online session. If that session was recorded and stored, to be accessed later by other learners, it would become 'digital learning content'. In this part of the chapter we'll take a look at other forms of digital content: thinking about what they are, some of the key design issues, and how to get the best from them as a learning tool.

Text and interactive text

The simplest form of digital learning content is text – a document onscreen for the learner to read. 'Simple' because it is easy to create (or indeed may already exist), easy to upload and easy for the learner to access.

It is also, therefore, potentially the dullest of digital formats – simply the equivalent of being sent a paper memo or article to read. Having said that, if the content is well written with plenty of relevant examples and opportunities for the learner to reflect and plan, it can be an effective form of learning. Have a think about the structure of this book, which could be all 'straight text'. But by speaking directly to the reader, offering case studies to review and reflective activities, a work of static text becomes much more 'dynamic'.

With the use of programmes that allow the learner to navigate and respond to the text on the screen, we can make text content even more interactive. This interactivity can take the form of: answering questions by inputting or selecting a multiple-choice option; placing content in order (for example, sorting a list of activities into the order that they should be done); navigating around the text document, or out of the document by clicking on hyperlinks to other media.

The questions or activities mentioned above can also be used to monitor the progress of the learner or to test the acquisition of knowledge before moving on or leaving the session.

Video

Creating training videos was once the domain of large production companies, often using well-known stars, producing slick generic videos to sell to corporate training departments. The advent of digital technology, however, means that video content can now be made 'in-house' fairly professionally and at a very reasonable cost. Many people even have the software to make and edit videos on their smartphone. Video gives us the opportunity to engage all the senses of the learner and to bring to life subjects that might be quite 'dry' if they were simply written about in text.

Some uses of video for online learning and development are:

- A demonstration of a task that the learner may need to carry out themselves, for example, using a fire extinguisher.
- A scripted scenario in which learners watch how someone deals with a situation, for example, a customer complaint.
- A case study for reflection. Videos aren't by nature interactive, but they can be used interactively if the learner is presented with a situation and then invited to analyse or critique what happened.
- A 'piece to camera' – the trainer or subject expert talking to the audience via the camera.
- An interview – for example, the subject expert answering questions put to them by the online tutor.
- A presentation – for example, a presentation at a conference or meeting that is videoed for transmission to a wider audience.
- Learner-generated content to provide information about a business context or skill improvement.

We've probably all seen amateur videos taken on people's phones – perhaps at a wedding, conference or social event, where the images are indistinct, the camera is shaking and we can barely hear what is being said because of background noise. If you are creating video for online learning, you will need to plan it in advance, rehearse it where possible, edit it after recording and make sure that microphones and cameras are placed in such a way as to capture the moment in the most professional way.

Slideshows

Slideshows are a useful way of putting across information in a somewhat more dynamic way than simple text. The most important thing for curators of online resources to remember is that slideshows should be more than just a series of static slides scrolling across a screen – thereby creating 'death by PowerPoint' for a mass audience.

The best slideshows will have been specially created for use online and will often combine a series of images and limited amounts of text, perhaps enhanced with spoken word, music or clips of video. Presentation software such as Prezi, PowerPoint, Sway and many others (try a simple Internet search) allow designers to make slideshows much more dynamic with the ability to zoom in and out, highlight and annotate slides, and have much more professional animations and transitions.

Screencasts

A screencast is the recording or broadcasting of the screen on a PC, so that others can learn from it using one of a number of widely available specialist software apps. It is a great way, for example, to show someone how to operate a software programme. As you go through the various stages the learner sees what will actually be happening on their screen. Screencasts are usually annotated with text or accompanied by a spoken soundtrack.

More sophisticated programmes may allow the learner to pause, rewind or operate a split screen where they can follow the instructions from one screen whilst operating the programme on another screen.

When preparing screencasts it is essential to make sure you are competent in the use of the software and are explaining things in a language, and at a level, that the viewers of your screencast will understand (ie not too technical or too basic).

Podcasts

A podcast is an audio recording, usually predominantly of speech, often listened to via mobile device such as phone or MP3/4 player. Many businesses already use podcasts for the distribution of key information – a weekly update from the chief executive, for example, or a regular motivating message from the sales director.

Many organisations are also now seeing podcasts as a useful and cost-effective way of delivering learning content: you will find many on the CIPD website, for example, covering a range of topics for people working across HR and Learning and Development. A podcast, or more likely a series of podcasts, might include hints and tips from experts, interviews with decision-makers or the live experiences of people in the field. As with all types of digital learning content, they work best when they are planned and, at least partially, scripted.

Although it's perfectly possible to record a podcast using the built-in microphone on a PC, tablet or smartphone via an app, the more professional the equipment used, the more professional the finished product will sound, especially after it has been rehearsed and edited. There are applications to support the recording of podcasts, especially if the participants are at different locations.

Learning tutorials

A digital learning tutorial is, in many ways, a sophisticated online version of a training manual. It uses a variety of media to take the learner step by step through the process that they need to learn.

The best tutorials will often combine text, slides, video and audio in order to engage the learner into the process.

As with any technical subject, the best person to teach it in an engaging way might not be the technical subject expert. Learning tutorials work best when they are structured in way that replicates the way people learn – so a subject expert guided by an L&D expert and created by an IT expert is often the best team to have on board.

Learning scenarios

A learning scenario is a specially created situation which allows the learner to consider a range of options for successfully dealing with that situation. It can be used very effectively in fields such as customer care, health and safety, safeguarding and many more.

The scenario could be presented in the form of a text description, images, audio or video (or a combination of all of them). Having been presented with the scenario, the learner is then offered options as to the approach to be taken and, depending on the option they choose, they get feedback on their choice. Some scenarios might involve a simple single situation, whilst other may take on a 'branching' format, where the choice made in the first part of the scenario will lead the learner into the next part of the scenario where a further range of choices will be offered.

Although this all sounds fairly simple, the actual design of the scenario can be complicated, especially if it is the branching style where the number of options and outcomes may become quite cumbersome. The most important thing to bear in mind at your design stage it to decide first on the principles that you want to be learned, *then* design the story that will help the learner discover those principles. This type of content should also be tested on 'real' learners before being widely published, to make sure that all the possible angles and options have been covered.

Infographics

Infographics allow for imagery to support complex topics. When launching a report, the CIPD now also create an infographic that covers some of the salient points of the report. Infographics can be made either from free open-sourced sites, or licensed ones. They can be designed to be 'static' or interactive.

In summary, there are some *overriding principles* that underpin the design of all online/digital learning content:

- be very clear about the objectives and outcomes of the learning;
- create short modules that keep the attention of the learner;
- choose the best medium to achieve your outcomes;
- engage the learner by appealing to all the senses;
- make each session as interactive as possible;
- consider and plan how you will monitor and assess the learning.

Key roles in creating digital content

In the section about 'facilitating the (online learning) session' above, we mentioned how there were often two people involved in this: the facilitator and the producer. In the world of creating digital content there is often a need for even more professionals to be involved. The roles spoken about most are:

- Content curator – the person responsible for collecting and selecting suitable content. This could mean converting existing material or commissioning new and original content.
- Subject matter expert – the person who knows the most about the subject that is being trained. They will provide vital insight into the content.
- IT expert – when working in new media it is crucial to have an expert on board who can help us to use the hardware or software as effectively as possible.
- Programmer – someone who plans in and manages the logistics of digital content.

Summary

Whatever technology is selected for the design and delivery of learning interventions it is paramount that it is the right technology for the purpose/objective and that it fits the organisation's needs. To help L&D to get this right, the CIPD report *The Future of Technology and Learning* (2017) offers a checklist of the five factors which should influence the implementation of technology. The five factors (explained in more depth in the report) are:

- organisational context;
- learner needs;
- purpose of technology;
- learning principles and evidence;
- technology trends.

We have also asked an expert in learning technologies, Clive Shepherd, to give us his views.

AN EXPERT OPINION ON USING TECHNOLOGY IN L&D

We asked Clive Shepherd, partner at The More Than Blended Learning Company and author, some key questions about the use of technology in learning. Here are his responses.

1. In a nutshell, what are the key things to bear in mind when designing and delivering online learning?

It is important to remember that technology is no more than a medium through which teaching and learning happens. No one learns from a computer – they learn from a teacher. The same principles that govern teaching and learning on the job or in the classroom govern online communication too. So whatever you deliver online needs to be as welcoming, engaging, relevant and pedagogically sound as anything you would have done in more traditional ways. What you will gain by delivering online is in flexibility, accessibility, scalability and cost efficiencies. But it will only be effective if you design it well.

2. What would be a good starting point for an organisation that is just considering using more technology to facilitate learning?

Think about how you use technology in your personal lives and bring that into the workplace. At home we are constantly learning online through YouTube, Wikipedia, mobile phone apps, forums and social networks. All of these are as relevant at work. And remember that humans are essentially social creatures. We want to learn from and with others, so too much self-directed learning is not going to work. Savvy organisations are mixing self-study, one-to-one and group learning, both face-to-face and online, to create rich, blended solutions that take advantage of how we learn best at each stage on our journey.

3. What does the future hold? What do you think will be the next big trend in technology and learning?

The way we use the Internet has already changed enormously into a much more social experience and one that is primarily carried out on mobile devices. That is not going to change. What you should expect is to see more intelligent software that personalises our learning experience and incentivises us using game techniques. But whatever technology has to offer in the future will not diminish the role of the teacher and the importance of a real human experience, often face-to-face.

Clive Shepherd, Partner,
The More Than Blended Learning Company

 Case Example 6.3

Effective use of e-learning to support business objectives

East Midlands Collaborative Human Resources Service – Learning and Development (EMCHRS L&D) covers four police forces in the East Midlands for all learning and development requirements to include design, delivery, evaluation and quality assurance. One of the teams is Digital Design who work together to create a range of digital learning solutions such as e-learning, videos and websites.

The e-learning courses are hosted on a learning management system which does have limitations. For all mandatory packages, completion rates are monitored to ensure compliance and by nature are often predictable, many learners see these packages as a tick-box exercise without understanding the learning behind it. It then comes as no surprise that learners do not find the packages particularly engaging or helpful. Mostly the training gets completed but does it really succeed in the understanding of why they should comply or any change needed? Recent evaluation and feedback show us not really.

EMCHRS L&D design team was requested to create an e-learning mandatory package to be rolled out through a force-wide campaign. Due to the nature of the learning, we decided to think outside the box to design an engaging course. This work was allocated to me and I was keen to avoid this 'tick-box exercise'.

The aim of this training was to raise awareness and refresh existing knowledge around a particular topic. The team had a very clear goal of how this package would support their objective and how it would promote culture change within the organisation. The solution would also tie into the work the corporate communications team was completing alongside L&D.

Good design and an understanding of the learners are essential when creating any digital learning solution. Involving stakeholders and using their skills and experience to manage the content and storyboarding process was important, to ensure learners were to be invested into the package. Visual images were used which related to the text and audio narration and this information was presented in small, bite-size chunks to reduce cognitive overload.

Due to the nature of this package, which is being completed at any time of the day or night, it is essential to think about the end user when designing any digital learning solution. In order to capture and retain attention, this was achieved by mixing images with occasional animation and sound effects.

As the stakeholders did not require a course assessment at the end, I used a variety of interactive activities which aimed to promote thinking and provide the learner with an opportunity to take ownership for their journey by making mistakes without the fear of not passing a test. When questions were asked, if the learner answered correctly the information was summarized; if the incorrect answer was selected then the information was presented in further detail.

Before the e-learning package went live, a small group of users was identified and asked to complete the training. This pilot group provided feedback in relation to the content, activities, length of the course and design. Their feedback enabled us to empathize with their needs further and amend certain elements of the course.

To date, Level 1 evaluation has been carried out and the innovative design has received positive feedback with a positive impact on how people perceive e-learning. One learner remarked: 'This was one of the best courses to date. Concise and well read. Very good. Can they all run like this one?'

Linking with the force-wide campaign and using a similar design to keep 'on brand' supported the business objective and positively enhanced the overall learning experience.

Niki Hobson, Digital Learning Designer, EMCHRS L&D – East Midlands Collaborative Human Resources Service (Learning & Development)

Case study questions

1. What do you think worked for Niki here to get the feedback she did?
2. What implications are there here for supporting the delivery of learning through a digital platform?
3. Would you have done anything differently?

What next?

The activities below will help consolidate your learning from this chapter.

1 Look at the range of digital content available to you from organisations such as CIPD. Critically assess that content in terms of its accessibility, engagement and content.
2 Think of an area of learning content that you currently deliver face-to-face, plan how you could convert it to digital material. You will need to identify:
   - the most appropriate form of digital learning material;
   - how you would re-design your content, ensuring that it remained engaging;
   - the help you would need to convert it to the new format;
   - how you would test the material and measure its success.
3 Read the CIPD report on the *Future of Technology and Learning* and the five factors that impact on the use of technology. Share your main insight regarding implementing learning technologies on Twitter using the hashtag #LDPintheW and copy in the account @LDPintheW.

References

Blain, J (2015) *Cegos Asia Pacific Workplace Learning Trends Survey 2015*, LinkedIn Leadership and Management, www.slideshare.net/JeremyBlain/2015-asia-pacific-worplace-learnign-trends-report (archived at https://perma.cc/AUZ5-ZRDS)

CLP (2018) *Top Tools for Learning 2018*, Centre for Learning and Performance, www.toptools4learning.com (archived at https://perma.cc/KMC9-GMUJ)

CIPD (2015) *Learning and Development Survey*, www.cipd.co.uk/knowledge/strategy/development/surveys (archived at https://perma.cc/83NF-8K9A)

CIPD (2017) *The Future of Technology and Learning*, www.cipd.co.uk/Images/the-future-of-technology-and-learning_2017_tcm18-29348.pdf (archived at https://perma.cc/5F79-SY83)

CIPD (2019) *Factsheet: Digital Learning*, www.cipd.co.uk/knowledge/fundamentals/people/development/digital-learning-factsheet (archived at https://perma.cc/FYP9-9YS8)

Good Practice (2016) *Learning Technologies: What managers really think*, www.goodpractice.com/ld-resources/learning-technologies-what-managers-really-think/ (archived at https://perma.cc/ABP3-E5CL)

Huggett, C (2013) *The Virtual Training Guidebook: How to design, deliver and implement live online learning*, ASTD Press, USA

Petri, AE (2018) In rural Africa, tablets revolutionize the classroom, *National Geographic*, www.nationalgeographic.com/photography/proof/2018/01/africa-technology-samburu-kenya-education/ (archived at https://perma.cc/2XTH-SZ7H)

Shepherd, C (2012) *Digital Learning Content: A designer's guide*, Lulu.com, London

Towards Maturity (2015) *Embracing Change: Improving performance for business, individuals and the L&D team*, https://towardsmaturity.org/2015/11/05/embracing-change-improving-performance-benchmark/ (archived at https://perma.cc/ZA5S-KF86)

(continued)

(Continued)

Towards Maturity (2016) *Unlocking Potential: Releasing the potential of the business and its people through learning*, https://towardsmaturity.org/2016/11/19/unlocking-potential-business-learning-benchmark/ (archived at https://perma.cc/PP28-KUSN)

Towards Maturity (2018) *The Transformation Curve: The L&D journey to lasting business impact*, https://towardsmaturity.org/2018/01/31/transformation/ (archived at https://perma.cc/W9PJ-58V3)

Towards Maturity (2019) *The Transformation Journey – 2019 Annual Research Report*, https://towardsmaturity.org/2019/02/14/the-transformation-journey-2019-annual-research-report/?mc_cid=c18ffac425&mc_eid=4e32f5c66a (archived at https://perma.cc/3QRY-29HW)

Weller, M (nd) The Ed Techie [blog] http://blog.edtechie.net/ (archived at https://perma.cc/4RDA-NZ6T)

Explore further

Collins, S and Lancaster, A (2015) *Webinars Pocketbook*, Management Pocketbooks, UK

Hubbard, R (2013) *The Really Useful eLearning Instruction Manual*, Wiley, Chichester, UK

Shepherd, C (2015) *More Than Blended Learning: Creating world-class learning interventions*, Lulu, UK

Useful resources

Websites

www.elearningindustry.com (archived at https://perma.cc/GGP6-ZFB9)

www.goodpractice.com (archived at https://perma.cc/V4NL-W3DE) [podcasts and reports]

07
Delivery
Coaching and mentoring

Introduction

In this chapter we explore the skills and processes of coaching and mentoring, with particular reference to coaching and mentoring in the workplace. As the chapter posits, coaching and mentoring have become an integral part of many organisations' L&D offer and a combined skill-set that is often expected of L&D professionals.

Whilst there is much cross-over between coaching and mentoring, and this is discussed, we will look at each approach separately and provide processes and tools for putting each into practice.

Key areas of content covered in this chapter are:

- the concept of coaching, including different types and styles;
- directive and non-directive approaches;
- the stages of a coaching process and the roles of the coach and coachee;
- the concept of mentoring and the activities involved in a typical mentoring relationship;
- the potential benefits of both coaching and mentoring;
- different models and techniques used in coaching and mentoring;
- if, and how, to capture coaching and mentoring activity, and examples for use.

Coaching

Coaching has enjoyed huge popularity over the last 20 years or so, with the CIPD 2008 *Learning and Development Survey* referring to coaching as 'the shining star of the L&D portfolio' and the CIPD 2019 *Professionalising L&D* report stating that 'organisations that are using coaching and mentoring as a development approach are 35 per cent more likely than the average learning organisation to build a learning culture, by integrating learning into the flow of work'.

> Most organisations offer coaching and/or mentoring. In similar findings to last year, just over three-quarters of organisations offer coaching or mentoring to employees, although this rose to 89 per cent of the public sector and is also more common in larger organisations.
>
> 65 per cent of all respondents believe that the use of coaching by line managers or peers will continue to increase over the next few years.
>
> CIPD *Annual L&D Survey*, 2015

Whilst some of the excitement around coaching may now have settled, this seems to be mostly because coaching has become 'business as usual' for many organisations. Its focus on the individual and on performance, along with its proven effectiveness, has made coaching one of the most established and popular options in the L&D portfolio.

The profile of coaching has been further consolidated by the growth of professional bodies for coaches, such as the European Mentoring and Coaching Council (EMCC), the Association for Coaching (AC) and the International Coach Federation (ICF). Most of these also have professional development and accreditation systems for practitioners. ICF for example, states that in 2019 it has over 25,000 'credential holders'.

Whilst many coaches operate exclusively as coaching specialists, perhaps the greatest area of growth has been the use of coaching methods and techniques by line managers, in and amongst their other functions, just as predicted in the CIPD surveys.

Defining coaching

Although the term 'coaching' is one of the most popular and widely used terms in the world of L&D it can mean different things to different people.

In simple terms, coaching refers to an interaction between two people, a coach and coachee, aimed at developing the performance of the coachee in some aspect of their life:

> 'A process that enables learning and development to occur and thus performance to improve.'
>
> *Parsloe, 1999*

Of course, this definition could be applied to many L&D interventions – so what makes coaching different? There are several answers to this, still to be explored in this chapter, but, essentially, the difference is the emphasis coaching places on 'empowering' the coachee: enhancing their understanding of their own performance and building their confidence and ability to manage and develop this for themselves.

The box below provides other classic definitions which particularly capture this aspect of coaching.:

MORE COACHING DEFINITIONS

'Coaching is centred on unlocking a person's potential to maximise his or her own performance... improving the individual with regard to performance and the development of skills.'

Gallwey, 1986

'Coaching is unlocking people's potential to maximize their own performance. It is helping them to learn rather than teaching them.'

Whitmore, 1992

'The purpose of the coach is to raise awareness in the coachee.'

Downey, 1999

'... Coaching is... partnering with clients in a thought-provoking and creative process that inspires them to maximize their personal and professional potential.'

International Coach Federation, 2016

Types and styles of coaching

The act of defining coaching is made a little more complicated by the fact that there are a number of different types of coaching, for example:

- **Sports coaching:** the popular use of the term 'coaching' came initially from a sporting context in which a 'player' was helped to develop their skills in their particular sport by a 'coach', who used a range of skills and techniques to do this.
- **Executive coaching:** executive coaching is often provided for senior managers by professional coaches who are external to the organisation. The coach will often not have expertise in the executive's area of work, and will usually follow a non-directive approach.
- **Career coaching:** career coaches work with clients who want to improve their job satisfaction, change jobs or make a career change. They help to identify a coachee's skills and talents and help them to prepare for the job search, application and selection process.

- **Life coaching:** life coaching is usually provided by independent freelance coaches, for an agreed fee, in response to a personal application from the potential coachee. Like executive coaching, life coaching tends towards being non-directive and has a high focus on assisting a coachee to define goals and maintain the motivation to achieve them.
- **Workplace coaching/performance coaching:** following the example of sport, and influenced by texts, particularly *The Inner Game of Tennis* by Timothy Gallwey (1972), and the various works of Sir John Whitmore, coaching was gradually taken up by the business world and moved into the workplace. Some writers and organisations refer to coaching in the workplace as 'performance coaching', a term generally attributed to John Whitmore, which emphasises how the focus of this type of coaching is very much on developing a coachee's work-related performance.

Coaching in the workplace often takes place between a team member and their line manager, but may also be between two team members or between a team member and an L&D professional. There are various debates around the role of the workplace coach and whether or not workplace coaches should have expertise in the coachee's area of work (more about this later). Workplace coaching is therefore generally less defined than some other types of coaching, and the particular model used within an organisation will depend on its structure, culture and general views on coaching, and is likely to differ from one organisation to another.

When we use the term 'coaching' in the remainder of this chapter we are primarily focusing on workplace coaching.

Directive and non-directive coaching styles

Above we have used the term 'non-directive' when comparing different types of coaching. Coaches can tend towards a directive or non-directive style or anywhere in between.

By directive, we mean how much the coach inputs their own view, expertise and advice into the process, as opposed to how much they stand back and resist inputting to the process, leaving the coachee to take responsibility for their own decisions and selection of activities.

We can consider 'directiveness' as a scale, from highly directive to non-directive:

If a key purpose of coaching is, as discussed above, to develop a coachee's ability to take responsibility for developing their own performance, then it is fair to say that all coaching activity has, or should have, a strong leaning towards being non-directive.

Figure 7.1 Coaching slide scale

Highly directive ⟵——————⟶ Non-directive

However, there will be occasions when more directive interaction may also be appropriate. Many workplace coaches consider it acceptable to provide occasional ideas and suggestions, providing this has been requested by the coachee and the coachee makes the decision about whether or not to make use of these (ie the coachee uses the coach as a resource but the coachee remains in control of their own decisions and actions). This can be a pragmatic workplace approach when the coach has the expertise or knowledge needed by the coachee to bring about an improvement in their performance. However, some organisations and coaches would not support this approach, feeling it may detract from building coachee 'ownership' and would resist inputting any of their own thoughts and suggestions.

This scale of 'directiveness' is well illustrated by Myles Downey (1999) who shows how the use of various coaching skills and techniques link to directive and non-directive approaches to coaching (Figure 7.2).

Figure 7.2 The spectrum of coaching skills

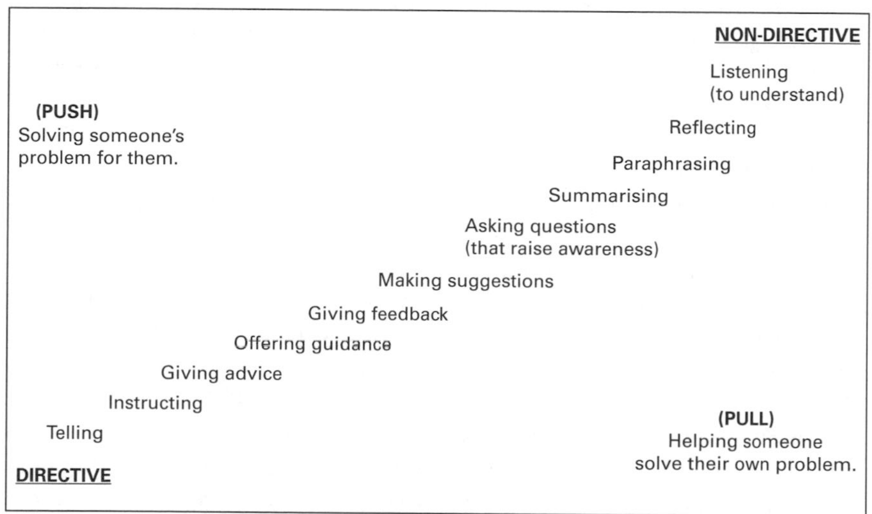

Downey, 1999

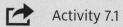

Activity 7.1

1 Do you think coaches should be directive or non-directive or both?
2 What do you think your natural coaching style would be: more directive or non-directive?
3 What kind of circumstances would make you adopt an approach further towards the other end of the scale?

Similar but different

The practice of coaching has lots of similarities with other developmental activities.

Activity 7.2

Can you think of at least one similarity and one difference between workplace coaching and each of the following: training, delegating, counselling and mentoring?

In the activity above you may have considered a number of factors, for example:

- **Training:** like coaching, training on a one-to-one basis involves two people working together with the aim of developing the trainee. It can involve a number of different communication techniques – such as questioning and giving feedback. Less like coaching, one-to-one training tends to be more directive than coaching and it is generally assumed that the trainer will have expertise in the subject that is being trained. There is usually an expectation that a trainer will provide information, whereas this is not typically the case with a coach.
- **Delegating:** like coaching, delegating generally gives responsibility for undertaking a task or activity to the person being delegated to, and it can be a developmental activity, if implemented in that way. However, unlike coaching there is a sense of greater detachment between delegator and person being delegated to, and may not include any element of support. Also, delegation is often used for reasons other than development, and there is often an assumption that the person being delegated to is already competent.
- **Counselling:** counselling focuses on personal issues, often where the person being counselled has undergone difficult experiences and seeks a therapeutic intervention or where they need help to cope with a current reality. To do this, counselling often tends to look backwards at personal experiences and issues. Workplace coaching tends to focus on specific performance issues, ie how something can be performed in a better way, and is forward looking. Although coaching can bring out emotions it does not seek to unravel deep emotional issues in the way that counselling does. The two disciplines are quite different in this aspect and it is important that coaches are very aware of this and do not stray into areas where a therapeutic solution, and professional counsellor, would be more appropriate. This essential consideration is a main theme of coaching ethics and most codes of practice.
- **Mentoring:** perhaps the activity which is considered to have most in common with coaching is mentoring – hence them both being included in this chapter. Indeed, many of the skills, and approaches used by a mentor in the mentoring process are the same as those used by coaches in a coaching process, and the two processes often generate similar benefits. However, there are also some significant differences, as highlighted in Table 7.1.

Table 7.1 Comparison of workplace coaching and mentoring

	Workplace coaching	Mentoring
Context/areas addressed	Work/task performance issues	Work issues Ongoing career issues Personal issues
Relationship between coach and coachee	Often coach is coachee's line manager, but could be peer or trainer	Usually a more experienced, senior work colleague, from outside the mentee's immediate work team or location
Coach expertise	Coach may or may not have experience in the area being coached	Mentor usually has general knowledge and experience of the mentee's work area and may even be an expert
Coach/mentor approach	Coaches are encouraged to, at least, limit the giving of advice and focus on assisting coachees to find their own solutions, ie to be non-directive	Greater acceptance of the mentor acting in an advisory capacity, and being more directive, allowing mentee to share and learn from mentor's experience
Typical nature of meetings	Focused, agreeing goals and reviewing progress towards them	General and informal discussion around work, personal and career issues
Frequency of meetings	Regular programme of meetings usually agreed in advance	May be more ad-hoc or called, when needed, by mentee
Duration of arrangement	Usually short term – until goals achieved (task-related)	Can last for a long period of time (career-related)

To suggest that all these differences make training, coaching, mentoring and counselling quite different activities would be wrong. There is much similarity between them and it can therefore be difficult to decide which intervention is most appropriate. Coaching is an effective and useful intervention for many occasions, but it may not always be the best for the circumstances. Other L&D approaches, or even performance management activities, will sometimes be more effective in improving work performance.

> 'Coaching is not a substitute for managing an individual's performance. A line manager who is also a coach needs to provide a clear boundary between when feedback is being given for performance correction and when support is provided for performance development.'
>
> *Wendy Strohm, WSA Ltd*

Activity 7.3

Consider the following four situations and whether coaching is likely to be the most effective intervention to enhance or improve work performance. If not, what might be? (We have added our thoughts in the text below, for you to compare your responses against.)

1. A new recruit to a job of which they have little or no prior experience.
2. A team member who is known to be competent but whose standard of performance has dropped significantly over the last few months.
3. A team member who knows and performs their job well, but who could undertake more complex tasks and contribute more to the team – and advance themselves within the team.
4. A very competent team member who is able to undertake all the tasks within the team and is seen as the most senior and expert by the rest of the team.

Whilst coaching might be effective in any of the scenarios above, a new recruit to a job is likely to need to build up some basic skills and knowledge before they can really benefit from coaching. A more directive approach to their early development might therefore be more efficient and effective.

A significant change in a team member's performance suggests that there are problems to explore – and it would be unwise for a manager to take any particular developmental approach without exploring what the problems might be. Ultimately, this is more likely to be about general management and support than a straightforward development intervention. An established relationship with a mentor could also prove very useful here.

Situation 3 above seems an ideal scenario for coaching to take place. The team member seems to have the basic skills and knowledge required but needs to build confidence and expertise in more complex tasks. Doing this in their own way and at their own pace, supported by a more experienced coach might be an ideal intervention here.

A very competent and experienced team member might find performance coaching unnecessary, even patronising, unless it was highly non-directive. A more appropriate development method here might be the full delegation of new responsibilities which will stretch and challenge them.

Another scenario to consider is when a coaching process starts to shift into other areas. Consider the example below.

Case Example 7.1

Coaching or counselling

A coach was working with a member of staff on aspects of managing a section of a small retail outlet. When exploring the coachee's difficulties in dealing with customer complaints (part of the team leader's job role), the coachee became emotional and began to relate her response to angry customers to a difficult relationship in her personal life. At further coaching meetings, the staff member brought up the personal situation more frequently and became very upset about it.

The coach, in this scenario, felt uneasy about some of this discussion and unable to keep the sessions to a work context. He suggested that they have a break in the coaching relationship and that the coachee may want to consider accessing the company counselling service.

Case study questions

1 Do you agree with the course of action taken by the coach here?

2 If you were the coach, how would you take this situation forward?

 Activity 7.4

When you have time, access the Global Code of Ethics for Coaches, Mentors and Supervisors (2018) via the website of either the European Mentoring and Coaching Council (EMCC – www.emccouncil.org) or the Association for Coaching (AC – www.associationforcoaching.com). Review how you could apply the code to your own role, or potential role, as a coach.

The coaching process

A typical coaching process has four main stages or phases: preparation and planning; contracting; coaching activity; and exit. Each stage requires certain actions from the coach and coachee, as in Table 7.2.

Table 7.2 The coaching process, with roles and responsibilities

Stage	When	Coach role/responsibilities	Coachee role/ responsibilities
Preparation and planning	Before coaching starts	Coach training and preparation Familiarisation with overall approach, parameters and procedures of coaching activity in the organisation Making initial contact with the coachee and agreeing the coaching relationship Arranging the initial coaching meeting General relationship/rapport building	Requesting coaching supportClarifying own thoughts around support needs Arranging the initial coaching meeting General relationship/ rapport building

(continued)

Table 7.2 (Continued)

Stage	When	Coach role/responsibilities	Coachee role/ responsibilities
Contracting	Initial meeting	Contracting with coachee. This will have differing degrees of formality depending on any existing coach–coachee relationship and the context of the coaching activity, but should include discussion and agreement of: • meeting timings • meeting locations • roles and responsibilities • 'ground rules' and risk factors • main areas or 'themes' to work on • general success measures The agreement would usually be recorded by the coach as a coaching contract or coaching agreement*	Contracting with the coach Being honest about own support needs Taking an active part in making realistic agreements, based on own situation, needs and preferences In some systems the coachee records the agreement, rather than the coach (as this is sometimes seen to increase the coachee's ownership of the process)
Coaching activity	Ongoing meetings	Ongoing relationship/rapport building and creation of a positive climate Ensuring coaching boundaries are maintained Using a range of coaching techniques and models to assist and motivate the coachee to: • determine and set goals • identify and complete courses of action • identify and fulfil learning needs • review progress towards goals • explore obstacles and set-backs • review, clarify, refine and re-set goals • take responsibility for their own development Again, key points of coaching meetings may be recorded by the coach (or coachee) to inform ongoing review*	Ongoing relationship/ rapport building and creation of a positive climate Taking responsibility for: • setting own goals • identifying and agreeing best options for improvement • implementing agreed options • identifying and undertaking development activities Completing agreed actions Requesting and accepting feedback Honestly reviewing progress, obstacles, etc and re-setting goals

(continued)

Table 7.2 (Continued)

Stage	When	Coach role/responsibilities	Coachee role/ responsibilities
Exit	Final meeting	Usually undertaken when objectives have been achieved, but may be appropriate at an earlier stage Reviewing and recognising the coachee's 'journey' and achievements Helping to identify any areas for the coaches ongoing development Reviewing the coaching process generally – to inform own coaching practice and areas for development	Reviewing and recognising own achievements Planning any further action to be taken after the coaching relationship Reviewing the coaching process and providing feedback to the coach, as requested

NOTE: *Example forms for contracting and recording coaching activities are provided later in this chapter

In many ways, and as with other L&D roles, we can think of the role of the coach as being to assist coachees to move around the Experiential Learning Cycle as presented by David Kolb (see Chapters 4 and 9 for more information on the learning cycle). This involves encouraging coachees to have experiences, reflect on these experiences, think about how they could do things differently, and then try out these new ideas (experiment) – and so on, moving round and round the cycle and so continuously developing.

> 'Coaching is helping someone to achieve their goals by themselves, though not on their own!'
>
> *Anon*

Similarly, we can consider the main role and responsibility of the coachee to actively participate in the coaching process, taking responsibility for their own decisions, completing agreed actions, reflecting and reviewing on their experiences, and managing, with support, their own ongoing development.

> 'I am always ready to learn. I am not always ready to be taught.'
>
> *Winston Churchill*

Mentoring

It is fair to say that mentoring has existed rather in the shadow of coaching in recent years. As we have discussed above, the popularity of coaching remains high and coaching continues to have a high profile in the learning and development media. This might be because coaching has previously developed a more 'exciting' image, or that the benefits of coaching have been more explicitly reported or even that the term 'coaching', in some contexts, implicitly includes mentoring.

However, just a small amount of research shows that mentoring is very much alive and well. A simple Internet search generates information about numerous organisation and sector based mentoring schemes, including CIPD's own mentoring schemes:

- Member-to-Member Mentoring (www.cipd.co.uk/learn/volunteer/mentoring/member-to-member); and
- Steps Ahead (www.cipd.co.uk/learn/volunteer/mentoring/steps-ahead).

Member-to-Member Mentoring enables CIPD members to support each other, whilst the Steps Ahead initiative involves HR/L&D professionals assisting new entrants to the labour market to build confidence and find work.

Defining mentoring

We have already touched on some aspects of mentoring in this chapter, but let's consider the approach in more detail.

> The original Mentor is a character in Homer's epic poem *The Odyssey*. When Odysseus, King of Ithaca, went to fight in the Trojan War, he entrusted the overseeing of his son, Telemachus, to Mentor.

So what do we mean by mentoring?

As with coaching, there are a number of variations of mentoring, and the term can mean different things to different people. In its simplest form, *mentoring is about two people coming together with a view to helping one of them progress more easily through work, life or whatever context the mentoring is taking place in.*

A mentor can be many different things to a mentee, for example:

- a role model – someone to whom a mentee can look up and on whom they can base their own behaviour;
- a sounding board – someone with whom the mentee can discuss ideas, problems and concerns within a safe environment;
- a source of advice – from someone who has already 'been there' and has real experience of the issues likely to be faced by the mentee;
- a source of work-related development – someone who can directly or indirectly help the mentee to develop their work-related skills and knowledge;
- an advocate – someone who can help support, represent and champion the mentee when needed;
- a referee – someone who can help make contacts and give access to opportunities or 'open doors' for the mentee (sometimes called 'sponsorship');
- a source of personal development – someone who can help the mentee to become more adept at managing themselves and their relationships and at achieving personal and career goals.

Activity 7.5

Many of us will be lucky enough to have people in our lives who fulfil some of these roles.

1 Who are the people who have provided these things in your life?

2 Have you thought of these people as your 'mentors'?

3 What have they done that has helped you most?

The mentoring relationship

Earlier in the chapter we explored the concept of a directive vs a non-directive style within a coaching context, and this can also be applied to mentoring. By directive we mean how much the coach/mentor inputs their own opinion, suggestions and advice into the process, in contrast to how much they stand back (non-directive) and desist from inputting to the process, leaving the coachee/mentee to take full responsibility for making decisions and selecting activities.

In very general terms, a mentor is much more likely to input ideas, suggestions and advice based on their own experiences and opinions than a coach. Indeed, if we were to look for the main difference between coaching and mentoring it is probably the fact that a coach will operate primarily at the right-hand side of Myles Downey's Spectrum of Coaching Skills (see Figure 7.2 on page 205) whilst a mentor might operate equally frequently at the left-hand as the right-hand side, and will generally move around the spectrum more readily.

In *Everyone Needs A Mentor* (Clutterbuck, 2014), David Clutterbuck refers to another dimension of mentor approach, a scale of 'stretching' through to 'nurturing'. On this scale mentoring can be geared towards stretching, ie stimulating greater learning through challenging and pushing the mentee, or towards nurturing, where the mentor takes a more comforting, confirming and reassuring approach.

So is there one correct approach? No. Ideally a mentor will move around the different styles finding the best way to support their mentees as they experience different challenges, performance results, emotions and, consequently, differing support needs.

> 'Learn from other people's mistakes; you don't have time to make all of them yourself.'
>
> *Source unknown*

Different types of mentoring

In the definitions of mentoring above, we referred to 'two people coming together…'. Whilst this arrangement remains the most popular, there are also various types of mentoring which involve more than two people, and increasingly where mentoring is undertaken remotely. Below are some of the types of mentoring happening in organisations.

Group mentoring

Where there are several potential mentees in an organisation and fewer potential mentors, it is possible for groups of mentees to work together with one or two mentors facilitating the group. The group might discuss a variety of issues from all mentees or concentrate on a particular issue at each meeting. This arrangement can allow a greater number of mentees to benefit from mentoring and, where available, different mentors may be asked to attend the meetings, enabling everyone to benefit from the different specialist experience of individual mentors.

Group peer mentoring

This is another type of group mentoring. Here, groups come together because they have a common interest, usually a similar work role; for example, new managers or owners of small businesses. Rather than have a lead mentor, the group operates in a self-directed way, in which all group members operate as both mentees and mentors.

A typical format for peer mentoring is for individuals to take it in turns, perhaps at successive meetings, to talk about challenges and aspects of their work, and for the rest of the group to focus on that person's situation, helping them to clarify issues, find new ideas – inspired by the suggestions and experiences of other group members – and determine potential solutions.

This type of mentoring arrangement, also referred to as Action Learning Sets and championed by Reg Revans (1971), brings forward a multitude of different experiences and allows all group members to learn from each other.

Online mentoring

The Internet has brought a new way for mentors and mentees to find each other and work together. An increasing number of sites (local, national and international) allow potential mentors to offer their services, and mentees to find and communicate with selected mentors. This is a voluntary arrangement in which mentors gain the satisfaction of passing on their wisdom to others and mentees have a safe and confidential (anonymous, if they choose) context in which to discuss their goals, concerns and uncertainties. Whilst many online mentoring schemes are positioned within specific contexts and professions, others are open to all. Certainly there may be safety considerations about use of some of these sites, but there is no doubt that the Internet has hugely widened access to mentoring, and to specialist mentors, for many more people.

One-to-one mentoring

Returning to the more traditional mentoring arrangement, of one mentor and one mentee, there are further variations possible in the type of relationship between the two. Typically, a mentor in the workplace is:

- a more experienced person in a senior position in the organisation, industry or sector;
- not connected to the mentee's management line (ie not the mentee's manager or their manager's manager);
- someone who may or may not have been trained as a mentor (although increasingly training is expected);
- someone who is motivated to assist the development of a 'junior' person in their organisation or industry.

Typical variations on this traditional arrangement are where the mentor is a mentee's peer or colleague, rather than being in a senior position, or where the mentor actually is the mentee's line manager. More recently mentoring relationships are also being reversed.

One-to-one peer mentoring

The term 'peer mentoring' has already been used above to refer to a form of group mentoring, but it can also refer to mentoring between two people, where the mentor is a peer, rather than someone of designated senior position in the organisation. In this arrangement mentoring may be one-way or two-way, with each of the pair taking mentor and mentee roles as required. This arrangement allows the two to learn from each other, share the challenges of the workplace and perhaps feel less isolated. It can also open up access to mentoring for a greater number of team members.

Line manager mentoring

This model no doubt happens informally all the time. However, discussing issues and uncertainties can be more sensitive within a management line relationship and could inhibit honest discussion and resolution of problems. On the positive side, managers may have greater insights into work situations and be able to facilitate more relevant and useful thinking, but the arrangement does require some careful and flexible shifting of roles by both manager and mentee.

Reverse mentoring

More recently we have also seen a new mentoring relationship emerge which turns mentoring 'on its head'. In reverse mentoring, a senior person is mentored by a younger inexperienced colleague. The idea here is that the younger person will see situations from a very different viewpoint to the mentee and be able to provide some new and fresh thinking for their more senior colleague.

Case Example 7.2

Group peer mentoring

The example here is of a group peer mentoring session or Action Learning Set, supported by a facilitator (whose role is not to act as a mentor but to facilitate the peer mentoring process). The six participants are all owners of small businesses who meet every four to six weeks as part of a 10-month peer mentoring programme. The number of meetings was determined to ensure that every participant could have a meeting devoted to their particular issues, plus an introductory meeting and a final review meeting. The facilitator, an L&D professional, explains about setting up the group.

When I started the peer mentoring group I couldn't decide if there ought to be two groups – one for very new businesses, and one for established businesses. The question I had was: 'What would start-ups have to contribute to the learning experience of more established businesses?' I could see the value that the established companies could potentially add to the new ones but was unsure how much value would be added in reverse. I wanted the sessions to be of equal benefit to everyone and I was concerned that the more experienced ones would do all the talking, limiting the participation of the newer ones – and also that the more experienced ones might feel that there was not much learning from the sessions for them.

Here's what I've found so far from the five sessions that have already run:

- The new owners are indeed keen to learn and ask lots of questions, and they listen. They have no previous experience so are very open to 'thinking differently' because everything *is* different. They respond well to anecdotal input and real examples, and the conversation flows easily with little input from me. The new owners leave the sessions with lots of new thinking, ideas and learning.
- However, the established business owners are also learning a lot from the sessions. Some of the established owners have been 'stuck and struggling', thinking the same thoughts and using the same ways of solving their problems even though the world has changed. The 'new guys' naive questioning has made them think about what they did in the past, what worked, what didn't and why. These questions cause them to relive past issues and so reflect on their own behaviour patterns, taking them to another level of learning.
- When the new ones ask completely open questions such as 'What do you *think* you could do about X?' it is because they have no idea themselves and are looking for suggestions, not because they are trying to be mentors and stimulate learning – but that is definitely the effect!

Christine James, Chris James Learning

Case study questions

1. Who could benefit from peer mentoring groups in your organisation?
2. Are you part of a peer mentoring group (formal or informal)?
3. What benefits do you get from that group?

The mentoring process

Most mentoring relationships are not governed by a highly prescribed process and will evolve as needed. However, all will have some variation of an introductory phase, a phase of mentoring activity, and an exit phase, each with typical activities. As you can see below, these phases and activities are not dissimilar to those in the coaching process, although there is usually less formality of meetings and therefore less emphasis on initial contracting and agreement.

STAGES OF THE MENTORING PROCESS

Introductory Stage – activities

- Making initial contact and arranging first meeting.
- Relationship/rapport building, introductions.
- Facilitation of initial meeting, to include:
  - exploring mentee's motivations and needs of process;
  - sharing and aligning expectations of process;
  - establishing a commitment to work together (or not);

- general agreement on how to work together, both in terms of guidelines and ground rules as well as logistics about where, when and how communication will take place.

Active Mentoring Stage – activities

- Assisting the mentee to reflect on, analyse and fully understand their challenges and issues, through:
  - clarifying goals and objectives;
  - actively listening;
  - using open questions to stimulate thorough reflection;
  - reflecting back, to clarify own and mentee's understanding;
  - challenging assumptions and perceptions;
  - providing different perspectives;
  - helping to identify and explore obstacles to progress;
  - giving honest and constructive feedback.
- Assisting the mentee to find appropriate solutions and best courses of actions, through:
  - drawing out mentees ideas;
  - encouraging mentees to find own solutions;
  - making suggestions and giving advice from own experience;
  - sharing technical knowledge;
  - sharing knowledge about the organisation;
  - providing 'nuggets' of direct training, coaching or teaching;
  - signposting mentees to useful resources or contacts;
  - helping convert thoughts into specific objectives for action;
  - arranging introductions or access to useful contacts.
- Assisting the mentee to become more self-aware, more self-directing and to develop personal effectiveness skills, through:
  - helping the mentee to recognise and understand their own behaviours, communication styles and learning styles;
  - summarising and reflecting back to aid self-awareness;
  - challenging assumptions and limitations to help develop greater self-responsibility;
  - providing encouragement and reassurance to help build confidence;
  - encouraging mentees to set the agenda for meetings and to 'drive' the mentoring process.
- Assisting the mentee to plan and progress their overall career, through:
  - reviewing career aspirations and goals;
  - developing a career plan;
  - exploring and identifying development needs and development opportunities;

- signposting or enabling access to opportunities.
- Assisting the mentee to build their professional networks, through:
  - role-modelling behaviour;
  - coaching in networking skills.

Exit Phase – activities

The mentoring relationship may come to a natural end when it is no longer useful or when situations change. Equally the relationship may change to a more distant one of friendship, based on the sharing of previous experiences, but no longer be a formal mentoring relationship.

There may be a set end to mentoring:

- a programme has come to an end (eg it may be a one-year programme)
- the context has come to an end (it may be linked to a particular phase of the mentee's work, such as the first year in the job, career progression or until a particular qualification is gained).

In these circumstances it is useful to formally close down the relationship.

Useful activities here are:

- reviewing progress and learning from the relationship;
- exploring how this can be taken forward into new aspects of work, and life generally;
- identifying further areas for and ways of developing;
- recognising and celebrating achievement.

The potential benefits of coaching and mentoring

Considering the many potential benefits attributed to coaching and mentoring, it is unsurprising that so many organisations continue to introduce and extend them. Reported benefits include the following.

For coachees/mentees:

- dedicated time to focus on own performance and development needs;
- support to clarify own thinking, set useful goals, reflect on events, challenge limiting assumptions, and plan further development and improvement actions;
- continuous learning;
- increased confidence, self-awareness and self-management skills which all transfer to other aspects of life;
- increased motivation from being encouraged and the desire to have 'achievements' to report back to the coach/ mentor;
- reduced stress as a result of being able to discuss challenges and frustrations in a non-judgemental context;

- greater understanding of own work role, the organisation and own contribution to the organisation;
- improved relationship with line manager (line manager-led coaching);
- links with a respected senior figure and their networks, and having a role model for success within the organisation (mentoring).

'I found the coaching process gave me a greater insight into the details of... (the task) ... and greatly increased my confidence.'

A coachee

'A lot of people have gone further than they thought they could because someone else (a mentor) thought they could.'

Zig Ziglar, author and motivational speaker

And for **coaches and mentors:**

- the satisfaction of helping someone else and seeing their development;
- own continued learning and development and enhancement of skills;
- insights into other areas and aspects of the organisation;
- an increased connection with team members and greater awareness of team strengths and learning needs (line manager-led coaching);
- an opportunity to pass on hard-earned knowledge and experience (mentoring).

'Although the agenda is the coachee's and the aim of our sessions is the coachee's development, I also get a real buzz from our coaching conversations and always come away with new ideas for my coaching practice.'

A coach

There are also significant benefits for **the organisation:**

- enhanced staff competence and greater individual ownership of development;
- enhanced transfer of learning to workplace making L&D more cost effective;
- increased involvement of managers in staff development;
- enhanced retention of knowledge within the organisation;
- better working relationships, with issues addressed in a safe context, before they grow in significance and related impact on staff welfare and staff retention rates;
- enhanced image of organisation both internally and externally – which can impact on, for example, recruitment and marketing;
- potential recognition of the organisation's efforts by staff and possibly others (eg external awards and accreditations).

'I never cease to be amazed at the power of the coaching process to draw out the skills or talent that was previously hidden within an individual, and which invariably finds a way to solve a problem previously thought unsolvable.'

John Russell, Managing Director, Harley-Davidson Europe Ltd

Coaching and mentoring practice – models

There is a vast range of different practice models available to coaches and mentors, each often having a related acronym title, representing a framework or guide to structuring a coaching or mentoring session. A search on the Internet will find several of these, some known and used generally, and others belonging to specific branded coaching programmes or individual coaches.

Some examples of coaching and mentoring models and their acronyms are given in Figure 7.3.

Figure 7.3 Some popular coaching models

GROW
- goals
- reality
- options
- will or wrap-up

(Alexander Graham & Sir John Whitmore)

CLEAR
- contracting
- listening
- exploring
- action
- review

(Dr Peter Hawkins, 1982)

COACH
- current competence (assessing)
- outcomes (setting)
- action (agreeing & taking)
- checking (feedback & review)

(Ian Fleming & Allan J D Taylor)

STAR
- situation
- task
- actions
- results

WINA
- where are we now
- investigate the options
- name the outcomes
- agree the action

Activity 7.6

1. Which of the above coaching models are you familiar with?
2. What other coaching models do you know?
3. Do you find any particular model immediately easier to understand and relate to than the others?

Using the GROW model

Probably the best known coaching model, GROW, was originally developed by Graham Alexander and later championed and made popular by Sir John Whitmore. In recent years, the model is often extended to TGROW, with 'T' standing for Topic to be discussed.

GROW stands for:

Goals: what does the coachee want to achieve and why; what does that mean in very specific terms and how will success be measured; by when do they want to achieve their goals; who else might be involved or have an influence on this; what would be the consequences of achieving these goals.

Reality: what is happening now, the current reality; what are the helpful factors, what are the unhelpful factors; what issues or barriers are there to overcome; who is involved; how did the current situation arise; what is real and what is opinion or assumption; what has already been tried; what have been the results.

Options: what possibilities are there for moving forward; what options are available; what other options might there be; what options could there be if there was more money, time, energy, resources, confidence, support available or if the context was somehow different or the situation seen through someone else's eyes (these questions being used to stimulate new ideas and thinking); what is possible; what really are the options.

Wrap up or Will (way forward): what is/are the best options and what specific action will be taken; what obstacles may be encountered and how will these be addressed; what support is needed to stay on track.

Being aware of GROW or similar coaching models can be very helpful for the coach in keeping the conversation flowing in a way that is productive and useful and results in some agreements to take forward.

Here is a simplified version of how a TGROW conversation might go:

Coach: What area would you like to discuss? (Topic)

Coachee: I'd like to get better at time management.

Coach: What, in particular, would you like to achieve? (Goal)

Coachee: I'd like to leave on time at least three times a week.

Coach: How often do you leave on time at the moment? (Reality)

Coachee: Only about once a week – I work over by at least 30 minutes most days.

Coach: What options could you consider to help you achieve that goal? (Options)

Coachee: I could cut down the time that my team meetings take. Or I could ask my deputy to do the end of day reporting. Or I could learn to say 'No' a bit more often.

Coach: And which of those options are you most committed to? (Narrowing options)

Coachee: Delegating the end of day reporting would be the easiest and might give me more time to draw up a plan for the other things.

Coach: OK, so what will you do between now and our next meeting? (Will)

Coachee: I'll arrange a meeting with my deputy to plan the handover and monitor how much time I can save.

In reality, the conversation is likely to be more complex with options taking longer to define and being explored in more depth, and goals and reality being revisited, before a final option is declared.

GROW does not need to be used in the order of the acronym. In practice, coaching conversations move backwards and forwards around goal setting, current reality and options, and may make several 'U-turns' before arriving at an agreed course of action. This is natural and how GROW should be used – ie it is not meant to create a strict four-stage conversation but to help guide the conversation and ensure that all important areas are covered.

Coaching and mentoring practice – communication techniques

The success of coaching and mentoring often depends on the effective use of a range of communication techniques. Here are some of the main ones and some tips on how to use them effectively.

Active listening

Active listening is the act of giving your full attention to the speaker, partly to ensure that you fully hear and understand what they are saying, but also to show, by the very act of giving your attention, that you place a value on hearing what they have to say.

Listening actively requires you to:

- try to eliminate other distractions and focus on the speaker;
- show your concentration physically (with body language) so the speaker knows and feels that they have your attention;
- avoid interrupting;
- summarise and reflect back to check your understanding.

Asking questions

Questions can open up or close down a conversation. They can be used to:

Draw out information (open questions):

- 'How are things going?'
- 'Tell me about X.'

Inspire deeper thinking:

- 'Why did you choose to do that particularly?'
- 'Can you say a bit more about what X involves?'

Clarify thinking:

- 'Where would that be on a scale of 1 – 10?'

Consider different viewpoints:

- 'Why do you think they might have responded in that way?'

Reflect back thinking:

- 'So, you feel that they did that intentionally?

Challenge assumptions:

- 'How do you know for sure that X feels that way?'

They can also be interesting, creative and engaging:

- 'Has this situation occurred before, and how was it resolved then?'
- 'If you could do anything you wanted in this situation, what would you do?'
- 'How would (celebrity, hero, person admired by the mentee) deal with this?'

Extend thinking (especially when 'stuck'):

- 'Can you think of just one more option?'
- 'If there were any other possibilities, what would they be?'
- 'If this didn't work what would be Plan B?'

QUESTIONS

I keep six honest serving-men
(They taught me all I knew);
Their names are What and Why and When
And How and Where and Who.

Rudyard Kipling

Using diagnostics

There are a number of diagnostic instruments available, freely or commercially, which can be used with or by coachees to help clarify their thinking. By 'diagnostic' we are referring to some form of self-analysis, personality test or assessment which provides the user with feedback on some aspect of their personality. For example, coachees might use a diagnostic to help identify their strengths and areas for development, or to help them understand how they approach certain things or maybe, how they operate within a team.

Diagnostics always come with a health warning. Some are simple and superficial and not intended to be taken too seriously, whilst others claim to be based on substantial social science and research. Current research is challenging the basis of some diagnostics, so be sure to read about any instruments you intend to use and check out their scientific validity. Also, make sure you know how they are meant to be used, and any requirements governing this. For example, some tests require the user (in this context, the coach or mentor) to be qualified or even licensed, whilst others are freely available, say on the Internet, for anyone to access.

There is a valid place for diagnostics in coaching and mentoring, providing they are used accurately and knowingly. Most of us enjoy finding out more about ourselves, and earlier in this chapter we defined one of the main purposes of coaching and mentoring as enhancing coachees' understanding of their own performance, and generally raising coachee awareness. Diagnostics, used appropriately, and regarded as providing insights rather than unassailable judgements, can be an enjoyable way of doing this.

Giving feedback

This is a skill already much discussed in this book, for example in Chapter 5, but here is a reminder of some of the key guidelines:

- be honest – (unless you have a very, very good reason not to be);
- be gentle – none of us take negative criticism well;
- be balanced – the good as well as the not so good;
- be specific – otherwise it may be general encouragement rather than feedback;
- be constructive – help the recipient to see ways of moving forward.

An acronym sometimes used to help in giving feedback effectively is BOOST.

BOOST FOR FEEDBACK

Balanced: include strengths as well as development points.

Observed: base it on what you personally have observed.

Objective: check for and avoid any bias or 'personal agenda'.

Specific: give specific examples.

Timely: give it as soon as possible after the event, when it is most useful – and likely to be most accurate..

Recording coaching and mentoring activity

There is some debate about whether coaching and mentoring activity should be recorded or not. Some feel that recording turns a voluntary and creative process into something overly formal and structured, whilst others find the recording of key points from a session to be a useful reminder and helpful to keeping the process 'on track'. Some coaches also find that taking a few notes enables them to catch key insights that can usefully be returned to later on.

Whether or not to record may be an organisational decision (some organisations may want records kept for tracking and evaluation purposes) or an individual decision. In our experience, some basic recording of activities and agreements is useful, but care should be taken not to overdo the requirements for this or to let things become bureaucratic. Figures 7.4 and 7.5 are two simple forms: the first for initial contracting of a process, and the second for recording meetings and agreements.

Figure 7.4 Simple coaching contract or agreement

Coaching Agreement

Between (1) Coachee and (2) Coach Date:
(1)
(2)

Background to meeting:

General goals & desired outcomes:

Agreed support arrangements:

Working together agreements:
We have both agreed to

- Honour meeting arrangements
- Fulfil undertakings between meetings
- Take responsibility for our own decisions, actions and development
- Honour confidentiality needs
- Discuss any concerns about the coaching process
-

Agreed -------------------------------- -------------------------------

Figure 7.5 Simple coaching (or mentoring) meeting record

Coaching Meeting Notes

Participants: Session No:
Date:

Key Notes from today:

Agreements for next time:

Agreed: ---------------------------- ---------------------------------

Case Example 7.3

One-to-one mentoring

This example is from a primary school, where an experienced teacher, Suzanne, acted as mentor to a newly qualified teacher, Rachael, during Rachael's probationary year of teaching. The purpose of the mentoring scheme was to ensure that Rachael met work standards and expectations whilst being supported with any difficulties or challenges that arose. Suzanne and Rachael describe how they worked together as follows.

We began with an initial discussion to understand Rachael's current experience and areas to focus on during the year. As our mentoring was part of a wider programme, we had specific documents to complete (an 'initial discussion record' and an ongoing checklist or 'calendar' showing completion of various required activities by Rachael, over the year). These standard documents ensured consistency of information and process for all mentees on the programme.

We met approximately every six weeks (half-termly) to reflect on progress made during that time and to find solutions to any problems encountered. We also discussed Rachael's development since the last meeting and updated her calendar.

A typical meeting took place at an appointed time and usually began with Suzanne asking how things had progressed since the last meeting, which then formed the basis of further discussion. Any minor problems were considered and solutions found together. For instance, when Rachael found that her PE skills needed developing, Suzanne referred her to a PE course with lots of hands-on experience. After the course, Suzanne was able to link Rachael to the local gymnastics coach, who then supported her in some lesson delivery. This proved to be very successful, with Rachael gaining increased confidence in developing more stimulating and interactive lessons for the children.

If Rachael has a problem that could not wait until the next planned meeting, she could always contact Suzanne and a suitable time found to discuss her concerns. It was times like these when a mentor's advice and support was most valuable. As an experienced teacher, Suzanne had a wealth of ideas and methods of dealing with behaviour and relationships in schools, which was of great help to Rachael. On one occasion, Rachael had issues that both she and Suzanne felt needed to be taken to a higher level and Suzanne was able to support Rachael in this and accompany her to a meeting to discuss the problem, where it was quickly resolved.

As the mentoring was part of a formal development scheme, Suzanne was required to give formal feedback on Rachael's progress, which contributed to Rachael's achievement of full teacher status. Both found the mentoring arrangement extremely helpful and satisfying and were thrilled with Rachael's success at the end of the year.

Suzanne Copley and Rachael Beech

What next?

1. Have a go. If you have not formally coached, now is the time. Identify a peer or colleague who would benefit from a coaching exercise, and on the basis that you are both experimenting, try out a coaching conversation.
2. Talk to colleagues from different organisations to find out how they are using coaching or mentoring within their businesses. What benefits has it brought? What works well? What would they like to change?
3. Explore the possibilities for your own development. Have a look online at some of the organisations that offer coaching or mentoring training. Could any of these be appropriate options for your professional development? If you are going to coach on a formal/regular basis then it's time to get trained. Share your ideas for this, and see what others recommend, on Twitter, using the hashtag #LDPintheW and copy in the account @LDPintheW.

References

CIPD (2015) *Annual Learning and Development Survey*, CIPD, London www.cipd.co.uk/knowledge/strategy/development/surveys (archived at https://perma.cc/VB2G-DQMM)

CIPD/Towards Maturity (2019) *Professionalising Learning and Development*, www.cipd.co.uk/knowledge/strategy/development/professionalising-learning-development-function (archived at https://perma.cc/43FG-KXSX)

Clutterbuck, D (2014) *Everyone Needs A Mentor*, CIPD, London

Downey, M (1999) *Effective Coaching: Lessons from the coach's coach*, 3rd edn, Texere Publishing, London

Gallwey, WT (1986) *The Inner Game of Tennis*, Pan Macmillan, London

ICF Survey (2016) *ICF Global Coaching Study 2016*, https://coachfederation.org/app/uploads/2017/12/2016ICFGlobalCoaching Study_ExecutiveSummary-2.pdf (archived at https://perma.cc/CF6P-MEE3)

Parsloe, E, Leedham, M and Newell, D (2016) *Coaching and Mentoring: Practical techniques for developing learning and performance*, Kogan Page, London

Revans, RW (1971) *Developing Effective Managers*, Prentice Hall New Jersey

Whitmore, J (1992) *Coaching for Performance: GROWing human potential and purpose – the principles and practice of coaching and leadership*, Nicholas Brealey Publishing, London

Explore Further

CIPD (2019) *Factsheet: Coaching and Mentoring*, https://www.cipd.co.uk/knowledge/fundamentals/people/development/coaching-mentoring-factsheet (archived at https://perma.cc/TGU2-GQWG)

Passmore, J (2010) *Excellence in Coaching: The industry guide*, Kogan Page, London

Starr, J (2010) *The Coaching Manual: The definitive guide to the process, principles and skills of personal coaching*, 3rd edn, Prentice Hall, New Jersey

Useful Resources

Websites

www.cipd.co.uk (archived at https://perma.cc/P3U6-SY6Z)

www.coaching-at-work.com (archived at https://perma.cc/7NEG-UV3V)

www.associationforcoaching.com (archived at https://perma.cc/5KHB-XSCM)

www.coachfederation.org.uk (archived at https://perma.cc/3EN4-Q446)

https://www.cipd.co.uk/podcasts/coaching-culture (archived at https://perma.cc/9A2U-A5J3)

https://www.peoplemanagement.co.uk/voices/comment/how-to-make-a-coaching-relationship-work

08 Delivery

Social and collaborative learning

Introduction

One of the real joys of facilitating L&D activities, face-to-face or online, is the way groups of learners can interact and share their views, thoughts and insights. This is not just a great experience for us but also an aspect that learners frequently cite when asked what they liked most about an activity. This kind of social and collaborative learning often happens naturally but it can also be encouraged, supported, and the benefits of it much enhanced, by a skilled facilitator. In this chapter, we will explore how we can apply our L&D skills, along with technology and particularly social media, to realise the full potential of social and collaborative learning.

Key areas of content covered in this chapter are:

- the concepts of social and collaborative learning and other associated terms;
- the impact of technology, particularly social media, on social and collaborative learning;
- different applications and platforms for social and collaborative learning;
- how to select and use social media to support social and collaborative learning;
- how to facilitate social and collaborative learning online;
- how to curate resources for social and collaborative learning.

What is social and collaborative learning?

Human beings have always learned by, and from, interacting with each other. Cave paintings were one of the earliest forms of sharing knowledge socially over 35,000 years ago. In fact, one of the things that define us as humans is our desire to seek out new knowledge and skills, question and challenge existing thinking, work with others to discover new things, and then share our wisdom through different channels. As new technologies, from the printing press onwards, have expanded the reach and frequency of human interaction, so the opportunities for us to share and collaborate in our learning, have increased.

There are a number of associated concepts and terms which underpin or overlap the umbrella term 'social and collaborative learning' and so it is worth spending some time considering these, in order to get a deeper understanding of the subject.

Social learning

The phrase 'social learning' was coined by Albert Bandura, a psychologist and professor of social sciences at Stanford University (Bandura, 2005). Bandura's social learning theory purports that people learn and modify their behaviour through observation of others and through making decisions about what they observe. Learning is therefore derived from a combination of cognitive processes (eg decision-making) and a social context where the opportunity for observation and interaction exists.

In everyday use, social learning has come to mean learning with and through others, be it small or large groups, online or face-to-face.

Collaborative learning

Collaborative learning can be defined as any situation in which two or more people learn, or attempt to learn something together. This might, in a workplace setting for example, be project led, with employees from different parts of the organisation working together on a particular issue, or it could be much more informal, where a student invites a friend to work with them on an assignment in order to pool their knowledge and resources.

Cooperative learning

Cooperative learning also involves people working together, but this time the work or study groups are purposely constructed to contain people of differing and diverse abilities (be that knowledge, skill or experience). 'Reward' is based on the success of the group, rather than on individual contribution. Depending on your point of view you may see this as inherently fair as it rewards the efforts of all participants regardless of their ability, or as inherently unfair as individual input or progress is not recognised.

Group or team learning

Whilst collaborative and cooperative learning have their origins in classroom education, team learning is more rooted in the context of learning at work. It may be defined as 'learning that takes place through the interaction of working together, learning from each other as well as from the task in hand'. In that respect, the development and sustainability of the team is often seen as being equal in importance to the achievement of the task or project the team are working on.

70:20:10 model

In recent years many researchers, including Charles Jennings, have written about 70:20:10 (Jennings, nd). This theory or model proposes that 70 per cent of learning in the workplace comes from experience – ie doing something (this can be naturally occurring or through structured support on the job) – 20 per cent comes from social interaction – ie sharing and discussing with others – and 10 per cent comes from structured courses and programmes.

Activity 8.1

Thinking about the four types of shared learning mentioned above (social learning, collaborative learning, cooperative learning and group or team learning):

1 What examples of your own learning fit into these definitions?
2 How have you made use of any of these ways of learning in the L&D activities you provide?

The growth of social and collaborative learning

Although social learning has been around throughout history, its relevance to workplace training or learning and development has really only been exploited from the latter part of the 20th century. Certainly, trainers have used group or syndicate working within training sessions, but the full potential value of collaboration in learning was only really recognised with the growth of Action Learning from the 1940s onwards.

Action learning

Developed by Reg Revans, action learning is a process in which managers in organisations help each other to solve real/live issues while, at the same time, developing their own capability for problem-solving (Revans, 1982).

Typically, an Action Learning Set will consist of around six members, each with an issue to solve, who will meet regularly over a set period, often with a trained facilitator. Time is allocated to allow each participant to present their issue to the group, be questioned about it and reflect on possible causes and solutions. This might be likened to a group coaching process.

Where Action Learning Sets have worked effectively people tend to stay in touch, continuing to learn and share with each other beyond the formal aspect of the learning set being formed.

The learning organisation

The next big development of note was the concept of the Learning Organisation that was first written about by Peter Senge and his colleagues in 1990 (Senge, 2006).

A learning organisation is generally defined as a business that facilitates the learning of its members and continually transforms itself. Peter Senge identifies five features prevalent in learning organisations:

- Systems Thinking: processes and structures that encourage and allow 'joined-up' thinking.
- Personal Mastery: having people who want, and know how, to learn.
- Mental Models: or, rather the ability and willingness to challenge conventional models and create a culture for learning.
- Shared Vision: all staff buy into the vision and goals of the business and are motivated to learn more about how to achieve them.
- Team Learning: by learning together, or by sharing individual learning, the business will learn more and grow more.

Within each of these areas there is a degree of both social and collaborative elements to the way learning is encouraged and developed.

The 2017 report *Driving the New Learning Organisation* reports that, in the top performing organisations, managers make time for social and informal learning (Towards Maturity, 2017, p 26).

The impact of technology on social and collaborative learning

The growth of the Internet, together with an explosion in the different ways in which people are able to access it (phones, tablets, laptops, etc) has enabled social learning to take on a new dimension, with many of our social networks now being virtual ones. Technology has allowed people to connect with others who share common interests wherever they are located in the world.

These advances have helped to make learning much more varied and offer a dynamic way of designing and delivering training, that can be highly social as well as economical. Some examples of how technology has enhanced social and collaborative learning are:

- Colleges and universities providing qualification and degree courses online. This allows for establishments to connect their learners wherever they are in the world, and enable them to share their experiences, creating a richer diverse group culture than a traditional approach might offer.
- The expansion of online qualification courses has also led to the emergence of MOOCs – massive open online courses. This is where an established provider such as a university makes an online course open for anyone to study: all the

materials, recorded lectures, resources, etc are freely available. MOOCs make learning easily accessible to anyone who wants to access it.

- Many businesses and employers now provide training packages online for employees to access from the workplace or elsewhere. This allows learning content to be distributed quickly and effectively to large numbers of employees in a cost-effective manner. As well as bringing high levels of consistency, packages that have community forums allow employees to make connections with peers across different functions and in different locations.
- Social media has provided an incredible platform for social learning, enabling groups of users with a common interest to 'meet up' or 'hang out', and share their opinions, resources and learning.

 Activity 8.2

What forms of technology have you used for learning that include social and collaborative elements:

1 At work?

2 In your professional studies?

3 In other areas of your life?

Which of these have worked best for you? Why?

Social networks

The way technology has encouraged people with a common interest to connect and share ideas has led to our social networks becoming more diverse. Networks are no longer limited by location and can include anyone with an Internet connection. Social networks can help with our personal learning and development, and consist of more than just our online friends (Figure 8.1).

A number of people on Twitter will use the hashtag #PLN meaning Personal Learning Network. This is an expansion of the concept of a Social Learning Network.

> 'My PLN has been essential to my career and personal development to date. The ability to nurture and tap into a professional network has helped me pursue career opportunities I may never have known about. Making better use of technology and the myriad of media available has allowed me to learn anywhere and anytime. Whether relaxing with a podcast whilst driving, reading a white paper on a tablet on a train, or watching an educational video on YouTube at home – these have all offered me the chance to learn flexibly, in different ways and at near zero cost.'

Giles O'Halloran, Strategist and Consultant, go2

Figure 8.1 A typical social network (eg of a CIPD student)

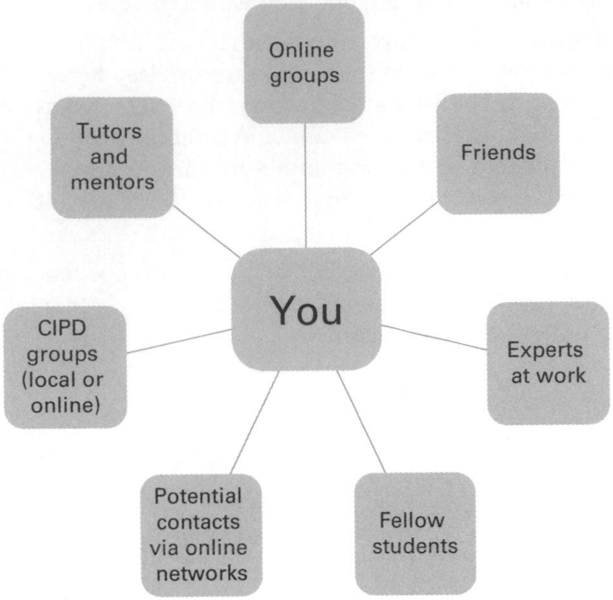

You
Online groups
Friends
Experts at work
Fellow students
Potential contacts via online networks
CIPD groups (local or online)
Tutors and mentors

Activity 8.3

Think about the network that you have available to help you with your work and professional studies:

1. Who do you interact with and learn from on a regular basis?

Then have a go at mapping out your own social network:

2. Which parts do you use well?
3. Which parts of your network are underdeveloped?
4. Which elements are virtual and which are face-to-face?

Social media apps and platforms

We have discussed how the rise in social and collaborative learning has been hugely enabled by the rapid growth of social media. Unlike some of the early attempts at setting up in-house systems for sharing information and discussion, the vast majority of new social media sites are free, open access and come ready to use – making them very user-friendly both for learners and for L&D professionals.

There are of course many different platforms and apps available, but as history shows, these can 'come and go' quite quickly. A decade or so ago, for example, some of the most popular sites might have been Friends Re-united, BeBo and MySpace. Google Hangouts is another one that has recently gone through some changes.

Some of the most popular social media platforms, currently used for social and collaborative learning, are described very informally in Table 8.1 and then followed up in more detail in Table 8.2.

As well as these (mostly) free social networking sites, there are also a growing number of professionally produced packages which allow an L&D team to tailor social collaborative learning to suit the needs of the organisation, the type of learners taking part, and the particular L&D initiative being undertaken. These platforms include the following.

Yammer

Owned by Microsoft and now part of the Office 365 package, Yammer is described as a 'private social network' helping teams to organise themselves, have conversations and work in collaborative groups within an organisation. It also has the facility for people outside the organisation to be invited into the group.

Moodle

Moodle is the largest free open-source learning management system (LMS) and is used in universities and schools as well as in business. As well as hosting online learning and virtual classrooms, Moodle also allows for collaborative learning, wikis, discussion forums, etc.

As an open-source platform, there are always new plug-ins being developed to help organisations tailor it to suit their needs.

Table 8.1 A humorous look at social media

Facebook	I'm on a customer care training course today
YouTube	Here's a video clip from the course I've been on
Twitter	Enjoying my customer training course today #heartofourbusiness
LinkedIn	I've added customer care to my list of skills
Google Hangout	Let's have a Hangout and chat about what we've learned.
Wordpress	Here is my blog all about customer care and how I implemented the learning from a course I went on
Skype	Let's chat next week about customer care
Dropbox	Here is some interesting background stuff I found about customer care in the 1980s
WhatsApp	Who knows anything about customers?
Pinterest	Anyone want to add more pictures of customers?
Instagram	Here's a photo of biscuits they served with the coffee on our customer care course

Table 8.2 Social media (description, useful for, pros and cons)

Platform		
Facebook	**Description** The world's largest social networking site with over one billion users.	**Useful for** Setting up groups for discussion and sharing of thoughts and experiences. Promoting and marketing L&D events. Reaching learners on a platform that they already use. Q&A discussions. Pre-course introductions and networking.
	Pros Familiar to many people as they already use it socially. Easy to use for new subscribers. Easy to adapt for social learning, as the platform is already designed for sharing comment and discussion. Can use closed groups where the conversation can be seen only by members.	**Cons** Some people may not want to mix their social network with their work or learning activity. Easy for users to be distracted into other non-learning discussions. Not a secure place for confidential discussions. No built-in method for feedback or evaluation.
YouTube	**Description** A platform for posting, viewing and sharing videos.	**Useful for** Researching topics and watching content created by experts. Creating content specifically for your target audience. Sharing video that it would not be practical to make in-house.
	Pros Enables the use of professionally made videos without the expense of making them in-house. Appeals to visual, auditory and kinaesthetic learners, allowing a richer learning experience. Can use contrasting videos to show different points of view.	**Cons** Producing bespoke professional video content can be expensive, whilst homemade video can look unprofessional. Good broadband speed is needed for uninterrupted viewing.

(*continued*)

Table 8.2 (Continued)

Platform		
Twitter	**Description** A microblogging service which allows messages containing up to 280 characters, pictures, links or short videos to be shared with online followers.	**Useful for** Short pithy messages. Promoting L&D events. Generating discussion and instant reaction. Signposting links to more in-depth resources. Researching or following experts, or people with alternative views. Sharing and monitoring ideas using hashtags and lists.
	Pros Allows instant comment and reaction. Very easy to use. Familiar to many people who already use it. Using the hashtag allows for interaction with users beyond own network	**Cons** May be seen as 'trivial' by some learners. The limit of 280 characters may prove difficult for some users and uses. Other apps are often needed in order to make the best use of Twitter (eg Tweet Deck).
LinkedIn	**Description** A social network programme aimed at professionals and businesspeople. Content and profiles tend to be 'professional' rather than 'personal'.	**Useful for** Setting up discussion groups which might be open to all, or restricted to certain members only. Networking with other similar professionals. Canvassing ideas and opinions from within or outside of your usual networks.
	Pros Recognised as a professional network and not as frivolous as some of the other networking sites. Provides learners with an opportunity to network with similar people or subject experts.	**Cons** Setting up a profile takes time and skill. Care is needed over confidentiality of information posted if used for learning or discussion.
Google Hangouts	**Description** A wide-ranging social networking site that uses a live online video chat facility.	**Useful for** Setting up discussion groups. Live chat rooms. Formal and informal opportunities to share information and questions.

(*continued*)

Table 8.2 (Continued)

Platform		
	Pros Offers a vast range of elements. Can be used for almost all social learning needs. Google products are very familiar to many users. Hangouts can integrate with other Google products.	**Cons** A single Google product usually comes as part of a much bigger suite of products, all of which have to be downloaded. Some people consider Google products to be invasive.
Wordpress	**Description** An open-source blogging site which makes it easy to create and share professional-looking blogs and websites.	**Useful for** Creating and sharing blogs. Promoting discussion and feedback.
	Pros Basic facilities are free to use. Provides a website address for your blog, making it easy to find from search engines. Blogs allow longer and more detailed posts than many other social networking sites. Readers of the blog can comment on, and recommend your blogs.	**Cons** May be seen as more formal or 'corporate' than some other sites. Not as instant or two-way as some other sites.
Skype	**Description** An application which enables voice and video calls between multiple users from computers, tablets and mobile devices.	**Useful for** Small group video meetings and discussions. Sharing of files, short demonstrations etc. Bringing guest speakers into a network.
	Pros Cost effective (free) way of hosting conference calls. Being able to see the people you are talking to adds richness to the conversation.	**Cons** People talking over one another can break up the quality of the sound. Poor connections or people dropping in and out of a call can be frustrating.

(*continued*)

Table 8.2 (Continued)

Platform		
Dropbox	**Description** A cloud-based file-sharing system which makes files available to selected users without the need for e-mails or downloads.	**Useful for** Instant file sharing. Collaborative working opportunities. Sharing additional or background information.
	Pros A very quick way of sharing files. Allows access to files from any registered location or device. Files are encrypted and password-protected for security.	**Cons** Can become expensive if large amounts of data are stored.
Whatsapp	**Description** A messenger app for smartphones, which uses the Internet to send messages, images, audio and video.	**Useful for** Group chatting for up to 50 people. Select groups of up to 100 members. Sending group messages to selected lists.
	Pros Often free to use if usage is within the account-holder's limit. Easy to install and use. Works on almost smartphone or network. Very popular in India, Malaysia and Singapore.	**Cons** Users can feel overwhelmed by messages, especially on their personal phones. Some concerns over the privacy of data that is transferred.
Pinterest	**Description** A web and mobile app for sharing and commenting on photographs and short videos.	**Useful for** Sharing information from a learning event. Learners sharing their own visual input. Collecting informal feedback on visuals.
	Pros Ideal for people with a strong preference for visual learning. Good for sorting and organising visual resources. Good for collaborative working.	**Cons** May not appeal to people who are not strongly visual in their preferences. It is reported to be more difficult to protect copyright on Pinterest than on some other social networks.

(*continued*)

Table 8.2 (Continued)

Platform		
Instagram	**Description** An online and mobile photo and video-sharing and networking service which allows the user to upload and annotate photos to a variety of different social media platforms, including Facebook and Twitter.	**Useful for** Sharing personal experiences and reflections in photo, or short video, format. Promoting L&D events.
	Pros Posts to many different platforms for maximum coverage. Saves time posting to different sites. Good privacy settings.	**Cons** Limited space for text or explanations. Instagram carries a vast amount of material so users can easily become distracted.

Noddlepod

Noddlepod is an example of an online community tool, described by them as 'a communication tool for groups that need to share knowledge, explore ideas and learn from each other'. Members of a learning community (a project team, training cohort, like-minded people from a network, etc) can share and organise content, information and discussion and store it in ways that make sense to individual learners.

Trello

Trello is a tool that is both collaborative and useful to use solo. It is based on some of the principles seen in lean engineering and uses a system of boards, lists and cards that allows users to keep track of project work.

Slack

Slack is another collaborative tool that allows people to interact and brings together a number of different message boards and applications. It allows users to share information in real time without the need to meet face-to-face. It follows a number of project management principles.

Selecting social media

When considering the use of any technology to enhance the L&D offering, there are a number of essential factors that we need to weigh up. The CIPD report *The Future of Technology and Learning* (2017) offers five lenses through which we can consider which technology to select. These lenses are:

1 Organisational content: will the technology and approach be supported by the organisation, is it in line with its needs, culture and policies?
2 Learner needs: what is level of 'digital literacy' within the workforce, how much time will need to be invested in the learner learning the platform as well as the content within the platform?
3 Purpose of technology: is the technology adding value or will it be seen as a 'shiny new thing L&D have brought in?'
4 Learning principles and evidence: is the technology in line with what we know about how people learn, does it allow easy interaction?
5 Technology trends: is L&D able to critically evaluate the effectiveness and relevance of the system or platform?

From our own experience we would also recommend the following set of considerations.

Ease of use

Social and collaborative learning is meant to be simple – the online equivalent of having a chat at the coffee machine. So, ideally, the platform or app that you select for your project needs to reflect this.

Key questions:

- Is the programme/platform easy to understand, regardless of technical ability?
- Does the usual operating mode of this platform work well for your purposes, or do users have to adapt the way that use it?

Access to technology

It is easy to assume that everyone has access to the technology that they need in order to use social media. But you need to be wary of making such assumptions. Not everyone sits at a desk with an Internet-connected device on it, and not everyone owns the latest smartphone.

Key questions:

- Do you need a form of social media that is available across a range of technologies (PC, tablet, smartphone etc)?
- Does everyone have access to the technology needed?
- Is the programme or app that you are considering easy to download and compatible with the equipment that people have?
- Do the devices that people will be using have the most up-to-date operating system to support the media being considered?
- If being used at work, will your firewalls allow the use of the programme?

User preference

Most people these days are used to some form or another of social media. Some may be big fans of Facebook, but not at all interested in Twitter. Others might love

WhatsApp, but think that some similar platform is simply a poor alternative. Certain platforms are more popular in different parts of the world, so understanding the preferences of your users is a useful thing to bear in mind.

Key questions:

- Who do I want, or expect, to be using this learning programme?
- What social media sites are they already using?
- Which social media sites are the most popular amongst my target audience?
- Would my users be more comfortable discussing and sharing their learning on an in-house (LMS) system, or on a public platform?

User engagement

Some of your workforce or target audience will be very familiar with using social media, and quite open to the idea of using it to enhance their learning and development. Others will need more convincing of the benefits. Also, some people who use social media for purely family or personal purposes might be very reluctant to use the same sites for more formal learning – people might post information on their personal profiles that they wouldn't want to share with their boss or the HR team.

Key questions:

- How much of a culture change will it be for my learners to start using an online platform?
- What will convince them that it is worthwhile?
- What sort of promotional campaign will I need?
- Will line managers and other stakeholders support the initiative?
- Will learners see being able to access learning resources in their own time as an invasion of their work/life balance, or as a positively flexible arrangement for learning?

Ability to monitor efforts and progress

Elsewhere in this book we have discussed the importance of monitoring and evaluating learning at key points along the way. Even the most basic of classroom courses will have an attendance register so that the L&D or HR team know who attended. Purpose-designed online learning or learning management systems have monitoring protocols built into them, but social media platforms that are being adapted for social collaborative learning might not be so easy to control.

Key questions:

- Do you need to be able to monitor effort and/or progress for this programme of learning?
- Do you need a platform that allows you (or someone else) to regulate, control or moderate activity?

- Does the system that you choose have a feedback or evaluation option, or will you need to invent one (or use a different medium for that part of the process)?

Cost

Most of the social media products referred to in this chapter are free to download and use. They may, however, require a certain level of equipment or operating system in order to perform.

Key questions:

- Are the programmes I am considering free to download and use?
- If users need to upgrade their equipment or software/operating systems, is the organisation prepared to cover the costs?
- Are there additional costs involved in buying software to help us manage or evaluate the planned learning project?

Confidentiality and privacy

The use of mobile devices and social networks for learning raises some issues about the confidentiality of the content being used.

Key questions:

- Do I need to issue guidelines about the use of devices in public places (including making sure screens cannot be overlooked, headphones are worn etc)?
- Are there some elements of our business that can absolutely only be discussed on in-house forums?
- Can I be sure that the copyright of any material posted is protected?
- Might my learners be subjected to spam, unwanted friend requests or advertising as a result of signing up to a public site?
- Does the site I am considering allow inappropriate material to be posted by other users (porn or offensive humour, for example)?

Examples of using social media

Facebook

A UK-based insurance company with overseas subsidiaries had traditionally brought newly promoted team leaders to its Manchester-based head office for their 'Introduction to Management' programme: three two-day modules covering the role and key skills of the new manager. In order to reduce training costs and time away from the workplace, the business transferred this programme to an online format, using a mixture of self-learning, webinars and a moderated discussion forum.

Although this new format achieved the time and cost savings that were planned, the training team was worried that new team leaders were missing the opportunities for informal learning and networking that used to occur in the training centre, when the learners were chatting casually at lunch breaks, overnight in the hotel and so on.

Although the new online programme had elements of social learning, these were always managed and moderated by course tutors.

One of the trainers happened to notice that some of the delegates were connecting with each other on Facebook and elements of the course were being discussed in their posts to one another. She suggested, therefore, that they set up a dedicated group within Facebook and invite all of the members of their learning cohort to join so that these discussions could be enjoyed by more of the trainees.

FACEBOOK TIP

Use groups so that people don't have to share their profiles or become friends with other users in order to join the discussion.

Twitter

The L&D team of a global manufacturing business were given a slot at their international sales conference to announce a new approach to ongoing sales training.

Whilst the general outline of the new online programme was already agreed (online content, webinars, discussion forums, etc) the L&D team still wanted to check and collect ideas from the conference delegates as to their learning needs. It had been six months since they had carried out their learning needs analysis and they knew that the sales teams operated in fast-changing and dynamic marketplaces.

They decided to set up a hashtag on Twitter to collect the information they needed from the delegates. By using the hashtag #tellusyourneeds they could ensure that all the posts were easy to find. Twitter also proved to be a good tool as all the sales executives had Twitter accounts, and it encouraged all their suggestions to be kept brief. They also found that, by keeping the hashtag active for seven days after the conference, it encouraged the more reflective delegates to carry on posting ideas.

TWITTER TIP

Decide whether to reply to tweets to the individual poster, or to include others in the conversation by use of the @tool.

Skype

Three independent training consultants from different parts of the UK were working together on the design and roll-out of a training programme for a national chain of garden centres.

After a couple of initial face-to-face meetings they soon realised that video calls were going to be a much more time- and cost-effective way of collaborating on the project. They tried Skype and, after agreeing a 'one person talking at a time' protocol, found that it worked well for them.

Initially the Skype calls were just used by the three consultants to communicate about the project, but they soon discovered that Skype was quite widely used within their client's business, so they started using it for joint planning calls between themselves and some of the key stakeholders within the garden centre chain.

Despite all the preparation, there were some unexpected difficulties in the first phase of the roll-out, and the consultants found that Skype was a very useful tool for conference calling about the difficulties, discussing the possible causes and options, and supporting one another with quick changes to the programme. In that sense, it supported the collaborative learning of the consultants and their client.

SKYPE TIP

Have a clear protocol for location and privacy when using Skype on mobile or non-workplace devices.

WhatsApp

A group of Singapore-based training professionals were travelling to London for a work project and planning to meet up with a number of contacts they had made in the UK through LinkedIn and other networks.

Individual texts, e-mails and phone calls would have been a cumbersome and possible expensive way of making all the arrangements, so it was suggested that they set up a group in WhatsApp. This proved to be much more convenient and, as WhatsApp works across all smartphones and networks, it suited everyone. Once in London they continued to use WhatsApp as their main means of contact.

Although it had only been intended to use WhatsApp for the ease of logistics, it soon became the group's preferred means of communication, with a wide range of discussions taking place. This allowed everyone to make the most of the visit and to continue networking long after the trip was over.

WHATSAPP TIP

Agree guidelines about posts and reposts to avoid people being swamped with messages that will not be of interest to them.

Pinterest

A specialist consultant in customer care was looking for the 'right social media' for him. Although he had a strong presence on LinkedIn and a well-visited website, he hadn't found any other network which suited his style. As a strongly visual person he decided to give Pinterest a go, and found that he enjoyed using it very much.

He has boards that represent different aspects of his work and he regularly pins new items to each board. These 'pins' include pictures, articles from across the Internet, or links that people from his network have sent him. His original intention in using Pinterest was to promote his business in a way that represented his style, and to show potential clients that he has a depth and range of interest in his subject which he keeps continually updated.

As time has passed, however, he has found more and more of his Pinterest followers are commenting on his pins – adding their own wisdom or experience, and generally expanding the discussion and learning.

PINTEREST TIP

Use a Pinterest board as a virtual brainstorm, so that people from different locations can pin ideas and resources to the board and discuss or comment on the contributions of others.

 Activity 8.4

Think of an L&D programme that is delivered by your organisation or a programme that you are familiar with.

1 What elements of social and collaborative learning are included in that programme?

2 What else could be done to encourage the learners on that programme to engage in and benefit from social collaborative learning?

Social and collaborative learning within an online programme

Pre-2000, any technology-based learning (or computer-based learning) was often about self-learning, with very little planned collaborative learning, other than, perhaps sometimes, students or employees coming together for a formal tutorial or practice session. Any social learning that occurred almost happened by accident; with colleagues or students arranging to keep up to date with one another, or schedule in meetings or phone calls to share their questions and learning.

The growth of technology and the advent of Web 2.0 in the early 2000s meant that these social collaborative opportunities could be written into the programme so that more learners could take advantage of collaborative learning. Some of the main social collaborative learning elements of a typical e-learning programme are listed below.

Live chat-rooms

Live 'virtual' classrooms can be used for tutor-led sessions as part of the formal learning element of an e-learning programme. Chat-rooms, however, are much more informal and very much aimed at facilitating social learning, where learners chat amongst themselves about their experiences and their learning.

The 'chat' might be by text or audio/video chat, depending on the platform being used. The extent to which the chat is facilitated or moderated by the course tutor will depend upon the subject matter, the level of 'maturity' of the learners, and the culture of the organisation.

Discussion forums

Discussion forums are an online facility in which topics or 'threads' are posted and replied to. Unlike the 'live' or synchronous discussions that take place in a live chat-room, discussion boards and forums are usually asynchronous – ie the posting and replies take place over a period of time. Discussion forums also offer the opportunity to look back over the history of a thread and see what previous contributions have been made.

Discussion forums are usually topic-led with any forum member being able to start or add to a thread, although, in some cases, a moderator may approve posts before they are published or may decide how long to keep a board or thread open.

Wikis

A wiki is 'a web application which allows collaborative modification, extension or deletion of its content or structure'. This definition comes from Wikipedia, which is the world's largest example of a 'wiki'. The content is entirely created and edited by members of the community, without any defined leader or owner, and with little implicit structure, allowing the structure to emerge according to the needs of the users.

Wikis are a great tool for collaborative learning, allowing group-authoring of projects, and for creating and sharing a knowledge base.

Blogs

Although a blog is usually written by one individual, it is shared with anyone who follows or subscribes to that blog. The blogger often has the choice to allow comments or feedback on the blog, and those comments will be displayed for other subscribers to see. In this sense, a blog is a useful reflective tool, allowing the author to air their views, opinions and experiences and collect reaction and feedback to their posts.

Designing for social and collaborative learning

In Chapter 4 (Designing L&D activities) and Chapter 5 (Delivery: Face-to-face training and facilitation) we laid out the key principles of design and delivery for all L&D interventions. These fundamental theories and practices, which underpin successful L&D, are just as important when thinking about how to manage the social and collaborative learning elements of an online programme. In this section we will consider other aspects of design and delivery particularly relevant to social and collaborative learning within online learning programmes.

Context

Thinking seriously about the organisational context at the design stage will help to ensure that we are considering the business need for the programme and taking account of organisational and learner factors. It will also help us to promote and describe the programme in ways that are appealing and engaging, especially if part of our challenge it to get learners to engage remotely. Learners may have specific views on the use of Twitter for instance and may need to be convinced of its relevance to learning in the workplace; providing context will help overcome barriers to learning.

Challenge

All online learning needs to provide a suitable level of challenge for the participants. That might include activities that move the learner on from their current level of skill or knowledge, or it could mean challenging an existing concept, culture or way of thinking. Learning without challenge will be boring and unlikely to produce any sort of lasting or sustainable results. On the other hand, programmes that are too challenging will move participants into their stress zone, which is not conducive to good learning either. One challenge may well be the use of applications and familiarity around social media platforms; therefore it is just as important to think about the time it takes any learner to be familiar with the functionality as well as the content the platform or app brings (Figure 8.2).

Figure 8.2 The challenge zone

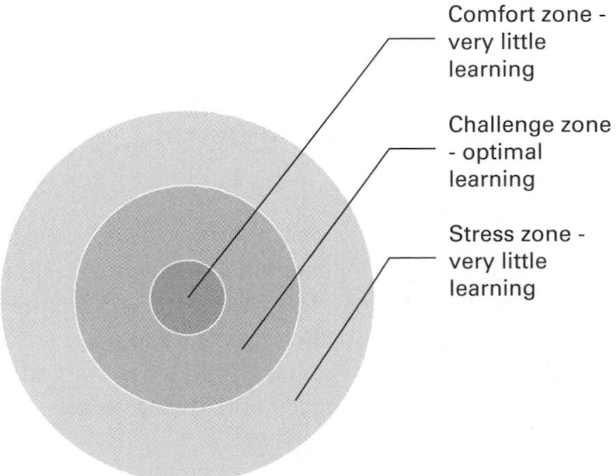

Activity

Online does not need to be a passive, one-way transfer of knowledge; indeed the beauty of using social media apps and platforms is that there is an ingrained social connection aspect to them. Activities can be designed which help participants to test their knowledge, develop their skills and see the effects of applying their learning in things such as case studies and simulations. Interaction is a vital way of learning and the inclusion of suitable activities needs to reflect this.

Feedback

Learners need feedback to help them recognise that they are learning and that participation in the programme has been worthwhile. This could include tests and self-analysis, seeing the results of case studies, or taking part in polls and evaluation activities at different levels. Again, the very nature of social media platforms and apps allows for ease of communication between users.

Facilitating online discussions

The online discussion forum is an important part of many online programmes. In Table 8.3 we look at the skills involved in facilitating useful discussion forums, whether they are synchronous or asynchronous.

Table 8.3 Skills required to facilitate discussion forums

Skills relevant to all online discussions	• Consider and plan the learning outcomes or objectives of the discussion. What do you want your learners to get out of participating in the discussion, and how does that fit into and complement the overall aims of your programme? • Use the software of your discussion app to know who has registered and attended each discussion. • Set the tone. Right from the start, your participants will take your lead on the tone of the discussion. You can model how formal or informal you expect the discussion to be, what level of discussion is expected etc. • You might want to consider creating ground rules or 'netiquette' for using the forum. This could come from you, it might follow your corporate guidelines, or, for more experienced groups, you could ask the participants what they would want to see included. • Address any breach of the ground rules, inappropriate language etc as soon as it happens. • Prepare and ask really good questions to get the discussion going.

(*continued*)

Table 8.3 (Continued)

Skills relevant to synchronous (live or chat-room) discussions	• Decide whether attending the discussion is a mandatory or voluntary part of the programme. • Consider the ideal size of group. Would it be better to run two discussion sessions, each with 6 people in, rather than try and facilitate 12 participants all at once? • Consider assigning different roles – eg someone to formulate and ask questions, someone to answer, and someone to summarise and comment. These roles could be rotated throughout the discussion, or over a series of discussions. • Allow the participants to do most of the 'talking'. If you are constantly interjecting it could inhibit contribution from the others. • Encourage participants to ask questions of each other, rather than just asking you. And, when asked a direct question, consider putting back to the group 'what does anyone else think?' • Ask probing questions to get to the bottom of issues: 'I'm wondering what's behind that question?', 'What else could we consider?' • Watch out for silent participants. Consider asking them a direct question or checking for their understanding (whilst respecting that more reflective learners can get more out of observing or listening to a discussion rather than actively contributing to it). • Control over-contribution. It can be dangerous for one person to dominate the discussion, as it may deter other learners from participating. • Summarise at the end of the discussion and ensure that all threads have been dealt with. Be prepared to bring some topics back into the discussion the next time. • Build in some time for introductions, especially if your group consists of people who have not previously met. • Intervene if discussion is veering off-track and help to move it back in the intended direction. • Decide whether a transcript or recoding of the discussion is going to be made available. • Use people's names to help them feel part of the community. Introduce guest speakers or subject specialists.
Skills relevant to asynchronous discussions or discussion boards	• Design effective questions or pieces of input that will promote and provoke useful discussion. • Build in and communicate deadlines for contribution to help create a sense of urgency. • Watch for threads or questions that go unanswered. Prompt responses or draw attention to them so that the person who posted that thread feels connected and supported. • Make decisions about when a thread is finished and be ready to archive threads that have run their course.

 Activity 8.5

Think about the last time you participated in a live online discussion:

1 What was your overall experience of it?

2 Which aspects worked well for you? What didn't work so well?

3 If you had been the person running that discussion, what would you have done differently?

Curation

The concept of curation within a learning and development context has captured the imagination of many in the profession. Essentially, curation (a term historically associated with museums and art galleries) refers to the act of collecting, filtering, organising and sharing resources, usually for a particular purpose.

There is a whole host of free resources already online that individuals and organisations have created for the use of others – which can make redundant the need for us to create yet more content. In theory, curation can be a great time saver and even greater cost saver. L&D teams with limited budgets or limited content creation skills now have a quick and effective alternative. Curated material can be provided relatively cheaply and at the time of need rather than learners having to wait for a formal course.

However, curation is not just about 'throwing every bit of available information on a subject at learners'; rather it requires careful focusing, selecting and sifting to ensure that information is relevant and credible and truly meets the (organisational and individual) learning need. There is a clear need to take care when searching for information online, to ensure the credibility and accuracy of any information you select. When curating we need to apply the same rigour as in any other walk of life. Just because it is online doesn't make it true! And the rise of 'fake news' is well documented. Getting into the habit of checking and cross-checking information with others in your network, and establishing the source of information is vital for your own credibility, as well as that of the resource itself.

Martin Couzins, a recognised practitioner and award winner in this field, talks about 'reducing the noise' for learners, meaning that there is a vast amount of information available online in a wealth of different formats and that it is our role, as L&D practitioners, to make it easier for employees/learners to find what will be most relevant and valuable for them (Couzins, nd).

Harold Jarche also has advice to offer in this area, recommending a 3-step 'Seek, Sense and Share' approach to curation (Jarche, 2014).

Seek, sense and share (Harold Jarche)

Firstly, Jarche advises that we are pro-active in *SEEKing* out information. For example, you may want to find information on something you are working on, your organisational challenges, events you are designing or may just be interested in finding out more about a particular topic. Doing online searches, linking into personal learning networks or checking in with forums is a good start for this.

Secondly, he asks us to make *SENSE* of that information, to internalise it, to consider how we can apply it to our world, or maybe why it may not apply in our world. This encourages us to work out what we agree with or disagree with, what we have found out and why we think as we do, and whether or not the new information fits with our existing knowledge and experience.

Finally, Jarche says we need to *SHARE* our insights. Sharing can be within our network or community forums or within our organisation. This allows the conversation to grow and allows a build-up of insights and, ultimately, a diverse range of views and insights.

One of the most common ways we can see Seek, Sense and Share in action is Twitter, where users will retweet a post or article, adding a comment or insight on the original posting. This idea links in with Stephen Covey's approach (Covey, 1992) when he tells readers: 'If you share the habits you learn the habits on a deeper level.' Jarche might say in a similar way: 'If you share information, you will learn about that information on a deeper level.'

Using curation in your L&D practice

You can curate information and materials to meet almost any purpose, and a number of examples are described below.

For new starters you could create an interactive PDF containing links to targeted curated material from both within and outside your organisation. This might include promotional material, customer case studies, and videos (*seek*), along with welcome messages from the wider team and some top tips on why this information is important (*sense*). This could be sent prior to starting in the organisation to give a warm welcome (*share*).

To support a company-wide change project, you could check out the wealth of 'how to' material that is online and send out specific related material. This could be anything from 'how to embed video in a slide deck' or 'how to create a pivot table in a spreadsheet' to 'how to add images to a text report'.

Curation can bring expensive conference speakers to a much wider audience. TED Talks and Learning Technologies both have extensive back catalogues that the L&D practitioner can sift through to provide a tailored conference package for employees. Again, using the seek/sense/share approach, we should not just send out an e-mail with a link saying 'watch this TED talk', but should take time to find the most relevant resource, work out why it is relevant to the target audience and how it will help meet their learning need, and then provide some guidance on the relevance of the material and how best to use it. We could even add some reflective questions so that the learner can make some deeper connections from the resource to their need or context.

Curated resources can be used as part of a wider blended approach of using a range of different materials in a learning programme. For example, prior to a face-to-face workshop on customer service skills, to set the scene for the learners you could send out a video link, housed on a video-sharing platform such as YouTube, about why customer service matters.

Curated resources can also be a means of further learning after a face-to-face or online activity. No one learning event will cover everything so providing a list of curated further resources is one way of tapping into learners' ongoing curiosity about a topic. Resources might include videos, podcasts or reports and should clearly link to the subject matter covered.

Curated resources may also be a standalone activity in itself. When budgets are tight this is a particularly cost-effective way of providing L&D at low or no outlay cost. Providing tailored e-mails containing interactive PDFs or lists of materials to different teams within the organisation is a good way of signposting learning resources without the expense of creating new content or delivering formal L&D events. Team meetings can then be used to check in on the learning acquired.

When identifying materials to address a particular need, Martin Couzins advocates asking 'customers' about their challenges rather than simply what content they would like. According to Couzins, knowing more about peoples' challenges will allow you to take a wider view on the information that is available and tailor it in a more relevant and efficient way for the recipients.

Providing and justifying access to curated materials

One of the biggest challenges to L&D teams setting up a curated system is how to 'contain' the materials to be held. As we have discussed there are many platforms and systems for this, but there may also be a need to involve the IT department and to rework the organisation's access or social media policies.

Another challenge is how to measure the effectiveness of any curated material. This can be undertaken by checking in with a sample of those who have undertaken their learning through curated resources and discussing (along with more specific evaluation) the impact of this on their knowledge, skill or behaviour. Being aware of, and able to articulate, the cost–benefit analysis of a system of curated materials will aid our case to gain acceptance of curation as part of the organisation's everyday L&D offering.

Activity 8.6

1 Have you ever curated content for your learners? How did it work?

2 Are there areas where you know you could already supply curated content to your learners which would help them develop?

Case Example 8.1

Setting up an online community forum

Jonathan is an L&D adviser for a global pharmaceuticals company. In the recent past there had been feedback that the national sales teams in each country rarely communicated with each other, were reluctant to share their success stories, and would not seek help from other more successful teams. On the whole, it seemed that these teams viewed each other as rivals rather than colleagues in the same business.

Jonathan decided that an online discussion forum could be a good solution. He was able to utilise a forum programme that was already available on the business's intranet. This was well used by the IT and product development teams across the world, but hadn't really ever taken off amongst the sales teams. He knew that he needed to get the national sales managers on board to encourage their teams to use the discussion forum, so he e-mailed them all asking them to promote the use of the forum.

To get things started, Jonathan posted several topics that he hoped would be of interest. There were some responses from a few of the national teams, and Jonathan always made a point of responding to every new post. Within a few weeks, however, he noticed that the number of posts had reduced to practically zero, only one person other than him had started a topic, and most of the teams around the world hadn't made a single contribution.

Case study questions

1. What has Jonathan done that you think was right for the time?
2. What could he have done differently to get a better result?
3. What could he do now to ensure the success of the online forum?

 Activity 8.7

1. Imagine that your organisation was recruiting someone to be responsible for facilitating social collaborative learning with your organisation's online learning programmes.
2. What do you think the 'person specification' part of the job description would list as essential knowledge, skills and experience' for the role?

EXPERT VIEWS ON FACILITATING SOCIAL COLLABORATIVE EVENTS

Julie Drybrough and Rachel Burnham, who co-host the Manchester @LnDCoWork group, explain the power of social and collaborative learning in both face-to-face environments and online – and some of the demands these make of L&D.

Face-to-face time

In work, carving out face-to-face time together to plan, puzzle and collectively collaborate is essential. This can require more from L&D than delivering prepped content or pre-thought learning outcomes to participants. It requires Learning Professionals who can make the case for the importance of allowing non-structured time together.

Facilitation in these spaces requires building trust, a belief in the power of collective intelligence for better outcomes and creating an environment where people feel able to explore, share and take action with good intent. It then requires good curation skills to pull everyone's ideas together.

I've worked a lot with methods for convening conversations that encourage collaboration and shared learning – open space sessions, unconferences with the @LnDConnect community, Action Learning Sets – these sessions provoke insights and give people permission to co-create, often coming up with things way beyond what specific learning outcomes could ever allow.

The added bonus is there is real joy in this work – people participate, they question and connect and see possibility. Social and collaborative learning is lively; it can produce unexpected outcomes; it can be tough to evaluate and sell. But in my view, its value is not to be underestimated.

Julie Drybrough, Director fuchsia blue ltd
@fuchsia_blue

Online discussions

Here are some of the things I have learned:

- The start is really important – whilst many people are comfortable sharing ideas and having discussions online as a result of their experience with social media, many people don't have this experience or have had bad previous experiences. It is good to begin by building relationships and making sure everyone is comfortable with using the technology. Start with introductions and relatively easy questions or tasks for people to get involved with.
- Be present and role-model – particularly in the early stages, it is helpful if you are quite visible and responsive to participant's contributions. It helps people to feel that someone is listening and paying attention.
- Nudges can be useful to build the habit of contributing – this can be done through e-mail or in person, if a face-to-face element is involved and can prompt people to get involved and keep contributing.
- Encourage stretch – it is great to start with simple, small ways for people to contribute, but as people get more comfortable and confident, build in more stretching ways to contribute. Resources can be shared to stimulate discussion; participants can be invited to share their experiences, present alternative ideas, resources they have found or created themselves; and they can also be challenged to share ideas about how they are going to apply their learning.

Rachel Burnham, L&D Consultant,
Burnham L&D
@BurnhamLandD

 Case Example 8.2 (1)

Developing a global social and collaborative approach to learning

Alice works as an L&D adviser for a large global retailer. She is based at their headquarters in London and the organisation she works for is a group that manages eight different retail brands (predominantly selling DIY and home improvement products). The group is large – across its eight different companies it employs around 80,000 people located in six different countries (UK, France, Turkey, Germany, China and Russia).

Although there are some great L&D initiatives running within each of the companies, Alice's director Anna is aware that as a group, the L&D function has very little global presence and impact. The L&D teams from each organisation rarely communicate with each other and work predominantly in silo. This, in the past, has led to issues such as:

- unnecessary duplication of work and lack of consistency;
- inequality of access to L&D opportunities across the group;
- budgetary implications and a dilution of buyer power when negotiating with training suppliers;
- very little knowledge management structures in place (and they only operate at organisation rather than group level).

Anna wants Alice to start tackling these issues by developing a more collective and social learning approach to learning within these organisations. She envisages an organisation where content is easily created and shared, not only by the L&D teams, but by individuals within each of the organisations.

This will not be an easy feat. The range of people that the group employs is very diverse; they speak different languages (although English and French are predominant) and they have varied levels of expertise and engagement with technology.

Case study questions

1. Identify what factors Alice should consider in order to successfully implement collective and social learning programmes across the group.
2. Identify who the key stakeholders would be.
3. Design a short social learning strategy outlining:
   a. which (if any) products/platforms Alice would use;
   b. ways in which this strategy will help learners create and share content;
   c. some of the expected challenges and ways how Alice can overcome these.

Joseph Grech, Smarter Learning Ltd

NOTE Joseph, who kindly provided this case study, has also provided his own thoughts on the case study questions – and these can be found at the end of this chapter.

Social and collaborative learning across this book

It might be tempting to think of social and collaborative learning as being a small and exclusive part of learning and development – some sort of new phenomenon that sits by itself, slightly unconnected from the rest of the L&D story. This would not be an accurate way of looking at it, however, as the principles and platforms of social learning permeate and play an increasingly essential role in all aspects of L&D. Remember the opening comments of this chapter, that we have been learning through social interaction from the day we were born, and generations of people have been doing this before us.

If we consider the other nine chapters in this book, we can see how managing and manipulating the power of social collaborative learning can greatly increase the breadth, depth and effectiveness of the L&D function. The chapters are:

Chapter 1 – The L&D professional

Our own effectiveness will be built and enhanced by our professional network. In-house experts at work, interesting co-learners on our qualification programme and industry role-models from across the profession are all out there using social learning platforms that we can be part of. Plus, there are untold numbers of learning opportunities on those networks, just waiting for us to access, engage with and learn from.

Chapter 2 – The organisational context

Collaborative earning takes place naturally within any organisation. If the L&D function can understand these existing channels of learning, create new channels and then exploit them, they will really establish themselves as being a vital and dynamic part of the structure.

Chapter 3 – Identifying L&D needs

Listening to, and utilising the information that comes out of collaborative learning channels can help us to research, identify and clarify learning needs in the organisation. Because social platforms are so quick and far-reaching, we can use them to foresee and collate needs from the farthest reaches of any business.

Chapter 4 – Designing L&D activities

L&D activities cover a whole range of activities, from formal classroom training through to self-study. Well-designed activities that encourage and use the power of collaborative learning will always have a valuable place in the toolkit of the L&D team, especially as social and collaborative learning can reach more people at a fraction of the cost of classroom events.

Chapter 5 – Delivery: Face-to-face training and facilitation

L&D activities executed in face-to-face sessions that allow for interaction and collaboration between learners are powerful ways to share existing knowledge and gain insights and deeper understanding of the topic. The role of the trainer or facilitator to engage the group to make the most of this opportunity is key.

Chapter 6 – Delivery: Using technology

The growth in technology has fuelled the expansion of collaborative and social learning opportunities, and the L&D practitioner should be exploiting these channels for the good of the profession and for the benefit of the business. Online delivery via discussion forums, mobile learning etc can reach to all corners of the organisation, and is particularly useful for those workers who are on shifts, work in remote locations, work from home or are in different parts of the world or different time zones from the L&D team.

Chapter 7 – Delivery: Coaching and mentoring

Whilst formal coaching is usually one-to-one, the use of social networking technology can facilitate long-distance coaching opportunities and new ways of sharing ideas and results. Social media networks are also an excellent way for learners to encounter subject experts, colleagues from other fields and mentors who may have a different view of the world than their own.

Chapter 9 – Engaging learners

As we know, people learn in a variety of different ways, and today's generation of tech-savvy learners are ready to embrace learning which uses convenient and accessible methodologies. Get your collaborative and social learning policy right, and you'll create good levels of learner engagement.

Chapter 10 – Evaluating impact

Most of the time we need to collect evaluation data from individuals and avoid the potential contamination of 'group-think'. However, using social channels to find out informally what people thought of our events, or formally to encourage to ongoing feedback and evaluation, gives us another strand of information to collate and analyse.

Case Example 8.2 (2)

Thoughts in response to case study questions

1 **Identify what factors Alice should consider in order to successfully implement collective and social learning programmes across the group:**
- Budget – is there a budget that has been provided for this project?
- Language barriers – decide whether English should be used as a common language. No point in trying to share content in own language otherwise you will not break the silo across the organisations.
- Senior management support – has this project/idea already been run past them?
- Technology available – what current L&D technologies are used within each organisation. What is their uptake? Can a technologies survey be launched?
- Social tools – which social tools would be used? Would a bespoke product be developed or something like Moodle/Yammer used (depends on budget).
- Marketing – how will this initiative be launched? Viral launch? Pilot?

2 **Identify who the key stakeholders would be:**
- L&D directors across the eight organisations;
- L&D teams;
- global HR;
- senior management;
- individual users/employees;
- suppliers (social learning tools).

3 **Design a short social learning strategy outlining:**

a. Which (if any) products/platforms Alice should use.

'Typically there are two ways – either an in-house bespoke developed product which would be ideal in this situation. However, if there are budgetary constraints a solution such as Yammer could be appropriate'.

b. Ways in which this strategy will help learners create and share content.

'It allows employees to upload and store comments. As an L&D adviser you can curate information and upload it accordingly'.

c. Some of the expected challenges and ways how Alice can overcome these.

'As well as the factors mentioned in Q1, Alice will need to consider:

- getting engagement and buy-in from learners;
- finding 'champions' who would use the system;
- how participation will be rewarded;
- technology issues: eg firewalls, support, bring your own devices, confidentiality;
- training on how to use the social platforms;
- language – how is she going to control (or not) language issues'.

Joseph Grech

What next?

The activities below will help consolidate your learning from this chapter:

1 Use your network to see how other people and organisations are using social and collaborative learning: are there any ideas that inspire you and that you can make use of in your work as an L&D practitioner?

2 Review your personal use of social media:

- what sites do you currently use and are they working well for you?
- do your profiles say what they need to, or could you do more to encourage more interaction by changing your approach?
- how pro-active are you in seeking out opportunities for social or collaborative learning?

3 Search online for a piece of information that would be relevant and developmental for your learners or for employees in a particular organisation. Apply the 'seek, sense and share model', and repost the material on Twitter using the hashtag #LDPintheW copying in the account @LDPintheW.

References

Bandura, A (2005) The evolution of social cognitive theory, in *Great Minds in Management,* eds G Smith and MA Hitt, pp 9–35, Oxford University Press, Oxford, www.professoralbertbandura.com (archived at https://perma.cc/LS4H-QD9F)

CIPD (2017) *The Future of Technology and Learning,* www.cipd.co.uk/knowledge/work/technology/future-technology-learning (archived at https://perma.cc/KLC5-PNHN)

Couzins, M (nd) LearnPatch, www.learnpatch.com/about (archived at https://perma.cc/E6A9-FU39)

Covey, S R (1992) *The 7 Habits of Highly Effective People: Powerful lessons in personal change*, Simon & Schuster Ltd, New York

Jarche, H (2014) The Seek-Sense-Share Framework, https://jarche.com/2014/02/the-seek-sense-share-framework/ (archived at https://perma.cc/XEH3-4KDQ)

Jennings, C (nd) What is the 70:20:10 model?, https://702010institute.com/702010-model/ (archived at https://perma.cc/VSJ8-5VCC)

Revans, R W (1982) *The Origin and Growth of Action Learning,* Chartwell-Bratt, Brickley, UK

Senge, P (2006) *The Fifth Discipline: The art and practice of the learning organization,* 2nd edn, Random House, New York

Towards Maturity (2017) *Driving The New Learning Organisation,* https://towardsmaturity.org/2017/09/07/driving-new-learning-organisation/ (archived at https://perma.cc/N27M-7LCV)

Explore further

Bingham, T and Conner, M (2015) *The New Social Learning: Connect, collaborate, work,* ATD Press, USA

Collins, S and Lancaster, A (2015) *Webinars Pocketbook*, Management Pocketbooks, UK

Hart, J (2014) *Social Learning Handbook 2014*, Lulu, UK

Matthews, P (2013) *Informal Learning at Work: How to boost performance in tough times*, Three Faces, Milton Keynes

Quinn, C (2014) *Revolutionize Learning and Development: Performance and innovation strategy for the information Age*, Wiley, UK

Useful resources

Websites

www.cipd.co.uk (archived at https://perma.cc/C7JJ-UE7P)

www.linkedin.com (archived at https://perma.cc/B6TN-YWD7)

http://www.c4lpt.co.uk/blog/ (archived at https://perma.cc/R3BJ-W548)

www.learningtechnologies.co.uk/welcome/resources (archived at https://perma.cc/QFX6-H9XC)

Twitter

@cipd.co.uk
@hjarche
@LnDConnect
@LnDCoWork
@LDPintheW
#LDInsight
#HRHour
#LDPintheW

09 Engaging learners

Introduction

This chapter looks in detail at the important concept of 'engagement' within learning. All the chapters in this book are concerned, in one way or another, with engaging learners and if you apply the relevant guidance in identifying needs, design, delivery and evaluation of L&D you should have every chance of success in this area. However, because learner engagement is so crucial to the effectiveness of L&D and its impact on organisational performance, this chapter delves further into the concept and offers practical advice and tips for you to follow.

Key areas of content covered in this chapter are:

- the concept of learner engagement and why it is desirable;
- factors that can affect learner engagement;
- aspects of psychology which have informed and influenced L&D approaches to engaging learners;
- aspects of neuroscience which are influencing L&D approaches to engaging learners;
- ethical factors in relation to the use of psychology and neuroscience in L&D;
- practical strategies for enhancing learner engagement at different stages of the training cycle.

Learner engagement

Definitions

'Education is not the filling of a pail – but the lighting of a fire.'

WB Yeats

The term 'engagement' is used in all kinds of contexts and usually refers to making a commitment to something or someone or involving ourselves in particular activities. We might engage someone to do some work for example, or we might be 'engaged to be married'; we might be engaged in conflict or we might more happily be engaged in a watching a film or playing a game.

Equally, when we use the term 'learner engagement' we are referring to a learner's commitment to and involvement in learning and learning activities.

DEFINITION

'...engagement refers to the degree of attention, curiosity, interest, optimism and passion that students show when they are learning or being taught, which extends to the level of motivation they have to learn and progress in their education.'

The Glossary of Education Reform

A number of academic studies, particularly in the USA, have attempted to deepen our understanding of learner engagement by exploring the different ways a learner may or may not be engaged. For example, education psychologist Jennifer Fredericks provides a three-dimensional view of learner engagement, where the three dimensions or aspects of engagement are:

Behavioural engagement: referring to how the student actually behaves in the learning: Do they participate? Do they do what is asked of them? Do they demonstrate good conduct? (But if yes – how deep does this go?)

Emotional engagement: the extent to which the student enjoys the learning? For example, do they feel happy, comfortable and included?

Cognitive engagement: how much does the student actually apply themselves to the learning and exert the mental effort required to learn?

An alternative framework is provided by Phil Schlechty (Schlechty, 2009) who describes five levels or positions of engagement (or disengagement) based on two main factors: attention, ie how much attention the learner gives to the activity; and commitment, ie how much genuine commitment the learner really has to the learning. In the context of workplace or professional learning, these positions can be expressed as in Table 9.1.

Table 9.1 Quality of engagement in professional learning

1. Engagement *(high attention – high commitment)*	I was very involved in this learning experience most of the time. The activities were designed in ways that appealed to the various ways that I best learn such content. The content will be valuable to me and to my department.
2. Strategic Compliance *(high attention – low commitment)*	I participated in this learning experience throughout the time allotted. I attended because I believe attendance at this seminar/workshop/course is part of what others expect of me.
3. Ritual Compliance *(low attention – low commitment)*	I was in attendance throughout the session(s). I made some contributions, but nothing significant.
4. Retreatism *(no attention – no commitment)*	Although I was present during the learning experience, I did not always clearly focus on the content, presentations or discussions. Most of the time, my attention was on other matters.
5. Rebellion *(diverted attention – no commitment)*	Throughout this learning experience I found ways, other than the planned activities, to occupy my time and attention. I chose to derail some of the work during the seminar/workshop/course.

SOURCE: Adapted with permission from the Schlechty Center

Activity 9.1

Consider the Schlechty Center's five levels of engagement described in Table 9.1.

1 Can you relate personally to any of these positions within your own history of learning?

2 Can you think of learners you have worked with who you can link to these positions?

3 What might be the reasons for positions 2–5?

Why is learner engagement desirable?

The 2017 report *Driving the New Learning Organisation* (Towards Maturity/CIPD) discusses the importance of employee/learner engagement to both business leaders and the L&D teams within organisations. They see this as pivotal to organisational success.

For workplace L&D teams, there is less likelihood of our learners being fully disengaged. The workplace context and the fact that we are dealing with adult learners should mean that we are mostly working with engaged learners who are motivated to participate in learning activities and who want to learn. Unfortunately, the reality is that in many organisations we still hear learners say 'I have to do this piece of e-learning' or 'I have been told to go on a course'.

As we have seen above, engagement is not an absolute factor, where learners are either engaged or not, but rather a scale or spectrum with high engagement at one end and low (or no) engagement at the other. Most L&D professionals are instinctively driven to wanting learners to be at the high engagement end of the spectrum – but what are our reasons for this?

Again, there is a significant body of research about the benefits of school and college student engagement in education, which to some extent translate to an L&D context, but when it comes specifically to workplace learning we are partly dependent on our own informal research and experience. From this, we can say that the main benefits of high learner engagement in workplace L&D are:

For learners:

- more effective achievement of learning objectives and therefore continuous improvement in skills and knowledge;
- more enjoyable learning;
- ongoing development of learning skills.

For organisations:

- more capable and adaptable workforce through effective L&D;
- maximised benefits of spend on L&D;
- development of a learning culture (where staff are willing and enthusiastic about L&D and ready to undertake it as needed).

For L&D professionals:

- reputation (more likely achievement of learning and business objectives, and therefore seen to be making a valuable contribution to the organisation);
- validation of ability to design and deliver effective, enjoyable L&D;
- pleasure of working with motivated and participating learners.

Activity 9.2

1. Do you agree that you want learners to be highly engaged in the learning activities you support?
2. If so – what are your reasons for this?
3. Why does it matter to you?

Factors affecting learner engagement

We asked some learners if they had any experience of NOT being fully engaged in learning activities. Here are a few of the (anonymous) responses:

> 'Every year we all have to do a series of e-learning modules, health and safety and similar things. It is such a waste of time. At first you could just skip through it, but now you have to answer questions after each section before you can move on. It doesn't make much difference as the answers are fairly obvious or we just tell each other. I just try to get through it as quickly as possible so they can say that I have done it. It is several wasted hours of my life I will never get back.'

> 'We were all put on a project management programme. The course itself wasn't bad but it was really stressful to take time out for this when we are so busy – I couldn't concentrate and I don't know if or when I will ever use what I learned. Plus it probably cost a fortune which could have paid for something more relevant to me.'

> 'It's a long while ago, right at the beginning of secondary school… but it had a big impact. Without any preparation or warning, we were told we each had to stand up and sing solo (in front of the rest of the class), so that our singing ability could be assessed. I was shy and mortified by the idea. When my turn came I squeaked out my verse, and heard the tutor say "very poor". It was the last time I sang in public. Following the assessment I decided music wasn't for me anyway and although I had to keep attending music lessons for years, I have no memory of any learning from them and contributed nothing. Uncharacteristically, I also became a bit disruptive in those classes, nothing serious, just talking mainly, but enough to get me 'sent out' several times.'

We also asked some trainers for examples of when learners are likely to be disengaged and why:

> 'I have found that people who don't engage on a training programme are often angry at a situation at work or have not been very well informed as to the work situation and the relationship between work and the training programme.'
>
> *Ian Favell, Accredited Training International*

> 'When the workplace culture does not welcome and include everyone, particularly those from diverse backgrounds, employees don't feel accepted and so don't feel they belong in the organisation's development processes. Also, if employees believe it is too late for them to develop and that learning will be hard for them, they lose confidence in workplace learning.'
>
> *Ali Alaradi, Trainer and Writer, Bahrain*

Case Example 9.1

Expert insights into engaging learners

Steve George, HR Portfolio Manager at the CIPD, who has researched this topic, explains his views on why learner engagement is desirable and reasons why leaners may not be engaged.

Advantages

Learner engagement is arguably the foundation for all the good outcomes that result from the content you create. Engagement is the psychological investment made by a learner… aspects such as the level of curiosity they show, their attention and reflection on the learning, the extent to which they are an active participant in the learning experience and not just a passive observer. Engagement is considered by some to be divisible into emotional, cognitive and behavioural aspects, and thinking of it this way perhaps makes it easier to consider how to approach it, particularly on occasions where that engagement has to be earned or won, and once you have this engagement the learning you create can have a transformative impact.

On the other hand, without engagement you can have the best content in the world and still fail to meet your objectives because disengaged learners may not have the motivation or the understanding for why completing a course is necessary, or how they can apply what they've learned to any benefit. There are occasions where gaining engagement requires stealth not persuasion or data, and understanding our audience needs to be a key part of our practice in this. I've worked with senior leadership teams who wouldn't engage with learning but *would* engage with 'executive briefings'. The content was the same, the presentation and title was all that changed.

Amongst school students, those who are more engaged have often been shown to achieve higher scores in standardised tests than those who are disengaged, but this isn't only about making learning more effective; it's also about creating a positive experience for the learner. Learning effectiveness and a positive learning experience are two sides of the same coin; both of them are created by engagement, and neither should be thought of in isolation of the other.

Reasons for non-engagement

There are many reasons why learners might not engage with L&D, and principle to understanding this is first of all knowing your audience and assuming nothing. Ask first: Why *should* someone engage with learning and development? Not just on a compliance level, but on a personal level. Consider why might someone not engage, and also what their barriers are to engagement.

For example, those who travel a lot for work might not engage with your learning if it's only available in a format that requires viewing on a screen so they can't take part while driving, or which isn't downloadable to be stored locally so can't be completed on a train. Do they have to remember login information that's completely different to any other system they use or is it seamless? Many in your organisation will likely be time-poor and trying to manage their L&D around competing and more immediately pressing priorities, and some will consider themselves as not needing any L&D at all to perform their role. Others might really want to take part but have a manager who views L&D as a luxury or discretionary effort to be completed out of core hours. Knowing your audience is key. A vital question we as L&D practitioners need to ask is: 'What problem are we trying to solve?'. Once we understand what the problem is we can approach it on a human level, not just an organisational level, and through doing so understand more deeply how to create engagement.

Many organisations attempt to solve the engagement puzzle by just making all learning mandatory, either through punitive measures (I've worked with organisations where logins stop working if training isn't completed in a set time) or through setting it into work objectives. However, this is far from a fix and only disengages people further – it makes learning a box-ticking exercise, one more thing to do, a hassle and something which is done under sufferance, and none of those are conducive to effectiveness. A 100 per cent completion rate – even 100 per cent assessment scores – don't show effectiveness, or recall after time, or performance in role and they definitely don't show engagement. The converse is also true: requiring training to be enforced and mandatory *does* show disengagement. Your job is to find out why.

Steve George
@Steveinlearning

Whether learners are engaged, or not, will always depend to a great extent on factors about each individual learner, but there are other forces which can also have a significant impact. In the four-box model shown in Table 9.2, we have identified factors which are likely to impact negatively on learner engagement, across four different areas:

- factors concerning the learner;
- factors concerning the learning;
- factors concerning the trainer/facilitator;
- factors concerning the wider organisational context and/or logistics of the activity.

Table 9.2 Factors affecting learning engagement

Learner Factors	Learning Activity Factors
Lack of time Lack of energy Lack of confidence Failure or fear of failure Previous bad experience Unable to see relevance Rebellion (told to do it – but not going to comply) More 'important' things to do (priorities)) Prejudices – in relation to the training or the trainer Domestic/personal issues Not feeling part of the group	Not well designed, ie: - not realistic/appropriate in relation to objective - not relevant to work - technology issues - dull, boring, lack of variety Technology overly complex or unfamiliar or needs extra learning in order to access Poor group mix or group dynamics Training content or message conflicts with learner values, beliefs or prior knowledge No adequate debriefing of why the activity was in the session

(*continued*)

Table 9.2 (Continued)

Trainer/Facilitator Factors	Context and Logistic Factors
Insufficient subject knowledge Inappropriate delivery style Lack of variety in methods used Lack of credibility No understanding of the learners' context of the topic Lack of interest (passion) for subject Lack of training/facilitation skills Physical factors, characteristics, training style (off-putting for some learners?)	Lack of management support for L&D Impact on workloads Difficulties caused by extra travel or venue access Distracting or unattractive learning environment

PAUSE FOR THOUGHT

Based on your context, would you add any factors to any of the four boxes?

Adult learners

The CIPD Profession Map (2018) emphasises the need for L&D professionals, at all levels, to understand 'adult learning and motivation theories' and to be able to apply these in different contexts.

Some of the most influential work on adult learning, and barriers to learning, is that of educationalist Malcolm Knowles, sometimes referred to as the 'father of andragogy' (Knowles, 1984). Andragogy can be defined as the science and art of helping adults learn, as opposed to pedagogy which refers to the science and art of helping children to learn.

Knowles put forward six key assumptions or principles about adult learners:

1. Adults are self-directing and capable of making their own decisions about learning (Self-Concept).
2. Adults bring a range of prior learning and experience to learning which forms a basis for, and affects, new learning (Foundation).
3. Adults are most interested in learning which has immediate relevance to their work or personal life (Readiness).
4. Adults are most interested in learning which helps them perform tasks or solve problems (Orientation).
5. Intrinsic (internal) motivation may play a bigger part in motivating adult learners than extrinsic (external) motivators (Motivation).
6. Adults need to know and understand the reason for learning something (Need to Know).

According to Knowles, and most L&D professionals now, learning which does not take account of the particular nature of adult learners and attempts to treat them like school children is highly unlikely to be successful and may create immediate barriers to effective learning.

Hase and Kenyon (2013) build on the work of Knowles. They comment that Knowles was describing 'self-directed' learning and introduce the concept of 'self-determined learning' or 'heutagogy'. Hase and Kenyon say self-determined learning is a natural adult progression: if adults are motivated to learn, then they will actively seek out opportunities to learn regardless of the learning offered by the organisation. Hase and Kenyon advise that L&D teams should provide resources and a series of signposts for a particular topic, leaving the learner to decide their own approach to the materials offered. They argue that the real measure of success for L&D teams is the ability for employees to be great learners, not whether they successfully learn something led by the L&D team.

Despite our theoretical understanding of adult learning principles, we are often guilty of not applying them. For example, we tend to replicate terminology from our school days, calling our rooms 'classrooms' or 'lecture rooms'. We have titles like 'tutor' and say things like 'today I am going to teach you' and we might set our rooms and equipment out in ways that look like schoolrooms. So, it is not surprising that sometimes our learners think that the experience we are offering will be just like the experience they had at school. This may be a positive one or it may not!

Recent research further confirms our ongoing tendency to offer L&D in a pedagogic style and to find it difficult to embrace the concepts promoted by Knowles and Hase and Kenyon. This may be because of our own resistance or it may be resistance from those around us. The 2019 report *Professionalising L&D* (CIPD/Towards Maturity, 2019)) states that 78 per cent of the L&D practitioners surveyed 'struggle with leaders having traditional expectations of L&D that are difficult to challenge'.

Activity 9.3

1. As an adult learner yourself, how much do you relate to each of Knowles' principles?
2. If these principles were ignored or 'contravened' within your own workplace/professional learning, would it affect your level of engagement with the learning?
3. What about Hase and Kenyon's view?
4. To what extent do you think L&D already embraces this idea?
5. How would (or does) their approach work in your organisation?

Psychology and learning

Because the concept of learning is so central to human behaviour and development, it has understandably been a key theme within the main branches of psychology. Consequently L&D has long looked across to psychology for new information and ideas which might improve the learning experience and help us to enhance learner engagement.

The discipline we refer to as 'psychology' actually embraces many different fields, branches and areas of cross-over with other disciplines such as sociology, education and the sciences. It is a vast and complex subject which we can only touch on in this chapter. However, our aim is to present you with an overview of psychology's main influence on learning, along with plenty of names, concepts and references for you to follow up.

As well as the CIPD's Profession Map (CIPD, 2018) emphasising the need for L&D practitioners to understand adult learning principles and motivation theories, their 2017 report *The Future of Technology and Learning* lists 'an understanding of learning theory' as a prerequisite for implementing learning technology.

To help us manage and understand the vast amounts of psychological thinking and theory relating to learning, we will focus on the three schools of thought that have dominated learning theory over the last century. These are Behaviourism, Cognitivism and Constructivism.

Behaviourist learning theory

Behaviourism was the predominant theory of learning in the early to mid-20th century and is associated particularly with the work of Ivan Pavlov, Edward Thorndike, John B Watson and BF Skinner.

As the name suggests, behaviourism was concerned with how humans behave and how they could 'learn' to change that behaviour or develop new behaviours. To build their understanding of how people learn, the behaviourists took a highly scientific approach, of systematically observing and measuring human, and often animal, behaviour and experimenting with different ways of affecting it. Some of the most famous and occasionally notorious psychological experiments such as Pavlov's Dogs, Cat in the Box, Little Albert, and numerous experiments with rats and pigeons are associated with the behaviourists. (It was a reaction to these experiments that motivated Malcolm Knowles to explore how adults learn differently to children and animals.)

In simple terms, the behaviourist psychologists viewed learning as requiring some kind of initial trigger or need for learning – this could be an internal desire or some kind of external stimulus – which then required some form of response (behaviour) from the learner. The responding behaviour could then be shaped through positive or negative 'reinforcement' or even 'punishment', although it should be emphasised that most behaviourists did not recommend the use of punishment to either encourage desired behaviours or reduce/eliminate unhelpful ones. The process of shaping learner behaviour in this way is known as 'operant conditioning'.

For the behaviourists, knowledge was something external to the learner but which could be acquired through the appropriate processes. The trainer/instructor's role was to help the learner acquire the desired learning or behaviours, through clearly identifying what was required and then making appropriate use of positive and negative reinforcement to bring about the desired behaviour. Along the way, behaviours should be repeatedly measured and adjustments made to the learning/conditioning process.

Despite its success in progressing our understanding of human behaviour, behaviourism was criticised for being overly objective, not taking account of human emotions and intellectual capabilities, and for seeing the learner as primarily a passive recipient of external shaping by others. Also, there was obvious evidence of learning taking place without the use of any reinforcement or punishment. Learning theory has now mostly moved on, but behaviourism continues to have a voice in psychology and to inform some current approaches to learning, particularly in relation to skills development. Behaviourist thinking is also a key influence on some modern therapeutic approaches which focus on changing unhelpful behaviours. Some would also say that some of the current approaches in brain science have clear links to behaviourist practice and approaches.

The influence of behaviourism on L&D is easy to see. The systematic approaches taken by the behaviourists can still be seen in how we often approach L&D in organisations; seeking a clear and systematic understanding of what needs to be achieved (or changed), directing our efforts and resources at bringing about the change, measuring our effectiveness on an ongoing basis, and making adjustments to achieve the desired results. Most L&D professionals will also relate strongly to the concept of 'reinforcement', and how we use our attention, feedback and rewards such as prizes/treats, certificates, marks or grades or even favourable reporting back to managers, in order to influence learners' engagement in learning.

Cognitivist learning theory

Cognitivism came into prominence in the mid-1950s onwards, partly as a reaction to the behaviourist focus on factors external to the learner (ie behaviour) rather than on learners' internal processes. Some key names are Jean Piaget, Robert Gagne, Noam Chomsky, Jerome Bruner, Howard Gardner, George Miller and John Sweller.

Like behaviourist learning theory, cognitivist learning theory positions knowledge or learning as something external to the learner but which can be internalised (learned) through the appropriate processes and support. However, the cognitivist focus is on the processes that take place 'inside the learner'; the complex internal mental processes that result in learning – rather than 'external behaviour' which was the key focus of the behaviourists.

These internal mental processes can be very generally summarized as perception, processing and storage (memory), and the main aim of cognitivist psychology has therefore been to understand how these processes work and determine how their effective operation can best be supported and learners assisted to learn as efficiently as possible.

Cognitivist learning theorists, and their vast range of experiments, have provided us with much information about how (they believe) people learn. For example, the cognitivists recognized that in order for us to take in data (perceive something) we need to give it our attention, either consciously or subconsciously, and we have a range of ever-changing 'filters' at work which influence how our attention is given. Data might be received via any of our senses: hearing, sight, taste, touch, smell.

Once we have perceived some data we then need to analyse and evaluate it (process it) in order to determine how best to use or store it. The cognitivists, particularly Piaget, demonstrated that learners find it easier to store information that relates to similar concepts they have already stored (schema) (Piaget, 1973). Piaget called this 'assimilation'. Where information is new to us and does not fit into existing schema then more complex and slower processes are involved in order to adapt and develop new schema, a process Piaget calls 'accommodation'. A third response, 'rejection', occurs where the new information is so new or incongruous with existing schema that we choose not to accept it all.

Storage processes (basically memory), are particularly crucial to learning if the data we receive is to be of any long-term use. We need to be able to retrieve data when we need it. Apparently, our memory problems have much more to do with problems in retrieving stored information than in actually storing it. There is much more 'in there' than we know – we just can't always locate it!

Cognitivist learning theory continues to have a big impact on L&D. Amongst many things, it has helped us understand that there may be different types of learning which involve different cognitive processes, that learners need time to process and effectively store information, and that we may be able to assist these processes by thinking carefully about how we organise and present information and making links to concepts that learners are already familiar with.

There are several examples of learning-related theory which reflect cognitivist thinking, which have had a big impact on both education and L&D. For example, there is the significant work of educational psychologist Benjamin Bloom (discussed in Chapter 4), whose Taxonomy of Learning Domains has given us a comprehensive framework for designing and assessing learning (Bloom, 1956). We could also cite Howard Gardner's Theory of Multiple Intelligences (MI) which has made us consider the possibility that there may be different types of 'intelligence' and to value 'intelligences' other than just academic or intellectual, and also the (often called) VARK Theory of Learning which has encouraged L&D practitioners to appeal to different senses (or modalities) when designing and delivering learning activities (Fleming, 1995).

Learning-related theories, such as those mentioned in the last paragraph, continue to inform L&D practice although some are now being challenged, replaced or updated by new ideas, particularly from the neuroscientists (see later section on the 'Criticism of learning styles').

As L&D practitioners we must make sure that we understand any theory we use in our practice and keep up to date with new thinking. If you make use of models or theories in your L&D work, make sure that you regularly review how you use them and check out any critical thinking and updates which may impact on this.

Constructivist learning theory

Constructivism is sometimes presented as a separate school of thought to cognitivism and sometimes as a subdivision of cognitivism (cognitive-constructivism). Either way it can be seen as an evolution of cognitivist thinking, in that it is equally concerned with the mental processes of learning; although it takes a significantly different view of what these actual processes might be. Some of the leading thinkers in this area are Jean Piaget (again), Lev Vygotsky and John Dewey. Constructivist learning theory is probably the most dominant learning theory of current times.

Whereas behaviourist and cognitivist learning theories differ in many ways, they both include a generalised view of knowledge as 'something that exists independently of and separately from a learner', but which a learner can seek to acquire. Supporting learning therefore is about finding the most effective ways for learners to access and internalize this external knowledge. Constructivist learning theory takes a very different view to this, ie that knowledge does not exist independently of or separate from a learner, but only exists when it is 'constructed' by the learner from their own experiences and interactions with their world and other people.

Helping people learn is therefore no longer about breaking down learning and organizing it in ways that might help it to be internalised. Nor is about finding best ways to 'pass on' knowledge. Knowledge is not acquired from others (a teacher or learning materials) but is constructed, as concepts and ideas, through experience. Learning is therefore a highly individualised process.

In order to support learning then, L&D needs to focus on providing an environment in which learners can explore and find out for themselves, test out new ideas, share their thinking with others and reflect on learning in order to make their own sense of it. Learners come up with their own ideas which are to be respected rather than simply judged. In pure terms, there is no 'right answer', although learners can be guided towards thinking in ways that are most useful to them, and in this context the L&D professional is very much a facilitator of learning.

Many of these principles are already in place in our L&D practice, particularly as we shift towards more technology-based and learner-curated learning, where learners have greater choice about what, where, when and how they learn. Constructivist principles can also be seen in L&D's use of coaching and mentoring, on-job learning and different types of collaborative learning. Constructivist leaning theory also sits well with some of the key principles of adult learning, ie that learners are generally self-directing beings, who need to have an internal motivation for learning and be actively involved in planning and managing their own learning activities.

A popular model often used and cited in L&D, which reflects cognitivist-constructivist learning theory, is David Kolb's Experiential Learning Cycle.

Kolb's experiential learning theory

David Kolb has been a highly regarded influence on modern thinking about how people learn, and indeed has been quoted in various other chapters of this book. Two connected ideas from Kolb that have had a big influence are the Experiential Learning Cycle and the related model of different learning styles, the Learning Styles Inventory or LSI (see next section).

The Experiential Learning Cycle has four stages (see Figure 9.1). Starting from the top and moving clockwise, these are: concrete experience, reflective observation, abstract conceptualization and active experimentation.

Kolb proposes that for most effective learning to take place, learners need to move around the full cycle, touching on all of the four stages. For L&D this has meant acknowledging how much learning takes place outside the classroom or training room but it has also encouraged us to provide learning opportunities that will support and assist learners to move around the cycle.

Figure 9.1 Kolb's Experiential Learning Cycle

Concrete experience
Feeling

ACCOMMODATING

DIVERGING

Active experimentation
Doing

Reflective observation
Watching

CONVERGING

Abstract conceptualisation
Thinking

ASSIMILATING

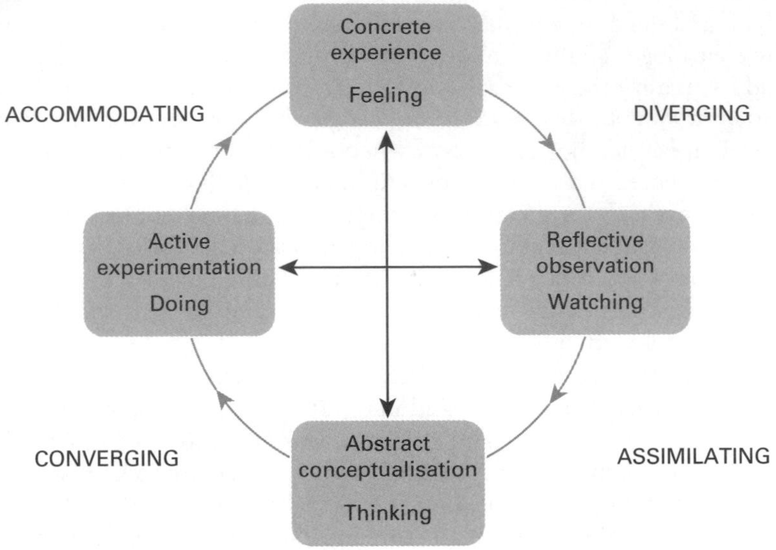

For example, we have been:

- facilitating learning 'experiences' (or these may be brought forward from learners' prior experience);
- supporting learners to reflect on their experiences;
- introducing (or facilitating the generation of) new ideas and concepts about how things could be done differently or further developed;
- and providing safe opportunities and encouragement for learners to experiment with these new ideas.

Think about some learning programmes you have experienced and you are likely to see some evidence of how the programme was informed by this thinking.

The learning cycle is not presented as a 'one-off' cycle, but as a loop, so the cycle, and therefore learning, continues indefinitely.

Learning styles

One of the most popular learning concepts of recent decades has been learning styles. However, the concept has also been the subject of debate and criticism. We explore this below.

Kolb's learning style inventory

Going back to Kolb's Experiential Learning Cycle above, Kolb also posed that we do not all move around the cycle in the same way and that learners, particularly young learners (Kolb suggested we may become more effective learners as we mature and our leaning processes and preferences become more integrated), usually have a dominant style of learning based on how they tend to perceive the world around them and how they process the information perceived. This could be plotted on two axes, as shown in the centre of Figure 9.1 above:

Figure 9.2 Perception and processing axes

Therefore, as also shown in Figure 9.1, someone with a feeling/watching (CE/RO) preference is said to have a Diverging learning style; someone with a watching and thinking preference (AC/RO) is said to have an Assimilating style; whilst a doing and thinking preference (AC/AE) is described as Converging; and a doing and feeling preference (CE/AE) as an Accommodating style.

Honey and Mumford's learning styles

The psychologists Peter Honey and Alan Mumford built on the work of David Kolb, to develop a more simplified classification of learning styles and a related Learning Styles Questionnaire (LSQ). Possibly because of its simplicity, the model quickly became one of the most popular and well-known learning models, in both adult learning and child education, across the world (Honey and Mumford, 1982).

Honey and Mumford's four learning styles, described as 'descriptions of the attitudes and behaviours that determine an individual's preferred way of learning' have the labels Activists, Reflectors, Theorists and Pragmatists. The basic premise of the theory is that an individual learner who is aware of their preferred learning style, through completing the questionnaire, can then identify learning methods and approaches that will be most effective for their style of learning.

Criticism of learning styles theories

As mentioned above, some of the psychological theories and models that have informed our L&D approaches in the past are now being challenged, both on the basis of the original research undertaken and by the science that has followed them. In terms of overall human learning this is no bad thing as each new idea and theory helps lead us to the next.

Learning styles theories in general (not just the ones mentioned above) have been under particular scrutiny and debate since the 1990s, as neuroscience has challenged the idea that human learning can be classified in this way. A report by Frank Coffield and colleagues is one of the seminal critiques of learning styles as a concept (Coffield *et al*, 2004). Building on this, Carole Wilson wrote in an article for *Training Journal* that included the following insight:

> 'There are tens if not hundreds of different variants on the theme of learning style. Thirteen of the most popular models were subjected to intense scrutiny by a team of researchers led by Frank Coffield (then of the Institute of Education, University of London). Their report was published in 2004 and attracted a good deal of attention from academics and practitioners: for example, in a piece in the *Times Educational Supplement*, Baroness Susan Greenfield was quoted as saying that "from a neuro-scientific point of view [the learning styles approach] is nonsense".'
>
> *Wilson, 2010*

Whilst many trainers continue to use learning style questionnaires and learners enjoy self-analysis techniques, recent research opinion often challenges the validity of using this type of personal diagnostic. However, the general concept, that learning and engagement is enhanced by a range of design and delivery approaches, remains valid.

As L&D professionals, we do have a responsibility to stay abreast of these debates and ensure that we choose and use any profiling tools knowingly and wisely. And perhaps, what the debates are telling us most of all is that we need to keep reviewing and updating our 'L&D toolbox'.

I have had conversations with a number of people in L&D about the criticism of learning styles, and typically find three responses:

1 Oh – never thought of that – I will do more research.
2 I agree – this echoes my view and my own research on the topic.
3 I find the criticism hard to accept – learning styles are an integral part of what I do and how I do it, so I will carry on regardless.

The first and second responses demonstrate how practitioners are reflecting and developing their professional practice, but I worry about the third response – it is hardly role-modelling professional development.

For me, whilst people may have a preference in how they learn (eg read a book, watch a video) it does not categorise them and cannot determine their whole approach to learning. As one colleague said to me: 'If our job is to be a lifeguard, then the only sure way of delivering training is to get in the water. No amount of reading books or watching videos will substitute the practical experience of being in the water, regardless of people's preference.'

L&D Consultant

Neuroscience and learning

So how can neuroscience help us update our L&D practices and enhance learner engagement?

The 2014 CIPD research report, *Neuroscience in Action: Applying insight to L&D practice* (CIPD, 2014a), explains neuroscience as follows:

> 'Neuroscience is the scientific study of the brain and nervous system. In the last 20 years there have been significant advances in the field because of technological developments, such as functional magnetic resonance imagining (fMRI) technology. This enables scientists to accurately depict brain activity through changes in blood flow. Many neuroscientists and practitioners have now started to explore how the key findings from cognitive and behavioural neuroscience translate to individual behaviour and learning within the workplace. This is an emerging, but rapidly growing, field.'

Whilst the vast amounts of information coming from neuroscience can feel overwhelming and occasionally cause us to retreat to the safety of the models and theories we have used for many years, various CIPD surveys indicate that both neuroscience and adult learning principles are increasingly recognised themes in L&D.

'New insights on learning and development are being developed from areas such as neuroscience, social psychology, economics, computing and the natural sciences. Many professionals are unaware of these developments and they are rarely incorporated into learning and development practice.'

CIPD *Annual Survey Report: Learning and Development* (2012)

'Awareness and use of all the methods listed has increased since 2012. Overall, more than half of respondents (55 per cent) had integrated one or more of the new insights listed into practice compared with 36 per cent in 2012.'

CIPD *Annual Survey Report: Learning and Development* (2014)

'Most respondents are aware of the relevance of other disciplines such as social/behavioural neuroscience and cognitive psychology for L&D, although not all fully understand them. Nevertheless, a quarter and a fifth, respectively, report they are conversant with and integrate findings from these disciplines into practice, representing growing awareness of these disciplines.'

CIPD *Annual Survey Report: Learning and Development* (2015)

'Adult learning theories and principles explore how adults effectively learn. There has been a move to underpin learning design through andragogy, in which learners are encouraged to be self-directed and heutagogy, where learners develop skills to be fully autonomous. In addition, behavioural science and neuroscience are providing insights into how to design effective learning interventions.'

CIPD *Professionalising Learning and Development* (2019)

In some ways, much of the emerging information doesn't seem new – but seems to be about proving or disproving some of the concepts that are already in the L&D domain. This is very useful; the fact that our ideas and concepts about cognitive processes can now be scientifically checked out is giving us a sound evidence base for making decisions about L&D. But, also, we are gradually seeing ideas emerge which we can use to develop our practice and enhance the opportunities we provide for learners.

We will now consider three broad categories of neuroscience research, relevant to L&D: brain health; the brain and learning; and motivation.

Brain health

One of the big benefits of neuroscience is that we are all gradually gaining a better understanding of our incredible brains (and the more we learn about our brains the more impossible it is to refer to them without using words such as 'incredible' or 'amazing'. Our brains are that and more!)

As we learn to understand our brains better – what they are made up of and how they work – we should be increasingly better able to look after them and support their effective function. Equally, passing this information on to learners could help them to be more effective at learning and to find more enjoyment in learning, which in turn will make them more engaged learners. Some of the key ideas we are learning about brain health include the following.

Brain hydration

Several studies, including on school children, adults and the elderly, have identified that dehydration has a negative impact on the brain: impairing memory, causing 'foggy thinking' and generally reducing the effectiveness of our cognitive processes. This has been particularly noticed in elderly people who may tend to restrict their liquid intake, and so display symptoms not unlike early symptoms of dementia, and has led to some simple but interesting approaches in care homes to counteract this problem. Some commentators suggest a little dramatically that even moderate dehydration, if prolonged, can cause considerable 'brain shrinkage'. Whilst, this last point is debatable (the brain may well shrink but only when levels of dehydration are unusually severe) and the general advice to drink something like two litres of water a day is contested by some of the experts, it makes sense for us to encourage learners to maintain good levels of hydration.

The 'jury is out' on how much water humans need to maintain good levels of hydration, but as L&D professionals we can encourage learners to recognize and respond when they are feeling thirsty and, within training spaces etc, ensure that water is easily available for when learners want it.

Exercise

One area that all the neuroscience and neuroscientists seem to agree on is the positive impact of exercise on the brain. Exercise causes blood to flow to the brain, bringing with it essential oxygen and glucose for cell maintenance, and 'washing away' unhelpful waste material. Exercise also stimulates the production of a range of helpful hormones, which impact positively on our mood and emotional state.

The idea that exercise can impact positively on our cognitive processes is not new; we have long thought that a short walk can help clarify our thinking or free-up our thinking when it seems 'blocked'. In L&D we have instinctively found ways of getting learners to move around in order to refresh a learning activity, and neuroscience has now given us a scientific base on which to build this practice. Going forward, we can help learners perform better by emphasizing the importance of building exercise into their own personal routines, encouraging them to make exercise a habit, and where we have the facility – build exercise (or at least plenty of movement) into learning activities. How about an occasional 'walk and talk' rather than a seated group discussion, for example?

Stress

Another area on which most of the science agrees is that whilst small amounts of stress may be helpful to learning processes and to the brain's development, too much stress is definitely not a good thing. Studies, albeit mainly on children and students, have shown direct and strong correlation between (particularly long-term) stress and impaired cognitive processes. As well as releasing a number of potentially damaging hormones, stress can reduce the flow of blood to the brain affecting the brain's ability to process and store data.

Encouraging and helping learners to manage stress – and being careful not to create too much stress for them ourselves – can be a big factor in helping learners enjoy and engage with learning. We can do this by sharing information about how the brain works so that learners are more open to managing stress and by signposting them to methods that will help with this, eg exercise, mindfulness and relaxation techniques, and better self-management approaches. We can also seek to create comfortable, pleasing and joyful training environments where learners feel listened to and included, and are stimulated without being made to feel inadequate or failing. In Chapter 8 we considered a 'challenge zone' which is also very relevant here (see Figure 9.3).

Sleep

It will come as no surprise to anyone reading this that good sleep habits are essential for brain health and effective cognitive processes. It is whilst we sleep that some of the most crucial processes for learning take place: learning is consolidated in memory, waste 'matter' is removed from the brain and our brain cells are prepared for new learning.

Figure 9.3 The challenge zone

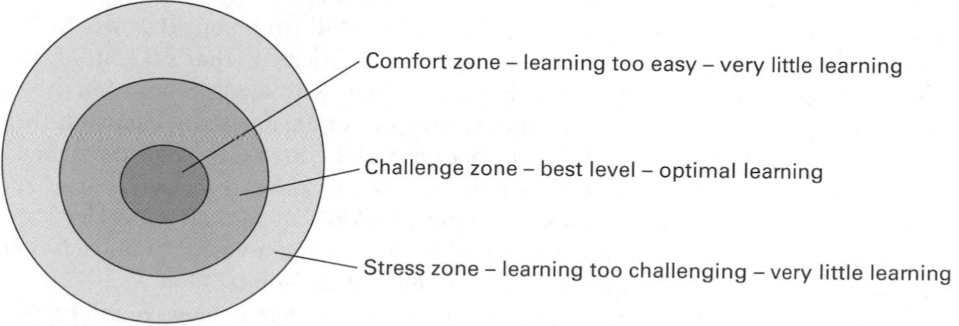

So how do we help learners with this? Well, our influence here is not huge (telling someone to 'get more sleep' is unlikely to be successful) – but as in the areas above we can help learners to understand their brains and raise their awareness about the links between brain health and effective learning. Armed with this knowledge learners may make better choices about their lifestyle, particularly when they are facing demanding learning challenges.

RAD: THE NEUROSCIENCE OF JOYFUL EDUCATION

Judy Willis writes about the importance of making learning a stress-free and joyful experience and how neuroscience can help us to do this. She uses the acronym RAD to help educators remember three important neuroscience concepts which should inform education/L&D. RAD stands for:

- Novelty promotes information transmission through the **R**eticular activating system.
- Stress-free classrooms propel data through the **A**mygdala's affective filter.
- Pleasurable associations linked with learning are more likely to release more **D**opamine.

Judy Willis, 2007

You can read more about this work at: www.psychologytoday.com/files/attachments/4141/the-neuroscience-joyful-education-judy-willis-md.pdf

The brain and learning

Neuroplasticity

One of the most optimistic concepts emerging from neuroscience is neuroplasticity or brain plasticity, ie the ability of the brain to keep on growing, developing and changing. This goes against some of the previous demotivating thinking for adults that as far as our brains are concerned, 'it is all downhill from your twenties'!

One of the most quoted illustrations of brain plasticity is that of London taxi drivers, whose intense learning of London routes ('The Knowledge') has been shown to have caused obvious extra development in their brains, actually changing their brain structure (Maguire *et al*, 2000). Other examples concern the particular developments in the brains of professional musicians and other subject experts, and joyful stories of elderly adults, who as a result of taking up gaming (Gazzaley Lab's 'Neuroracer') have strengthened connective paths between areas of brain cells, and significantly improved their overall cognitive functioning (Anguera *et al*, 2013).

The wonderful thing about neuroplasticity is the message it sends to all learners that, if they persist, they can keep on developing new knowledge and improving their skills providing they are willing to work at it. This can be a highly motivating idea, particularly for learners who feel they are not good at something or are 'never going to get it'. So, whilst many of these concepts do not seem new, perhaps neuroscience is now giving us an evidence base for some of the traditional words of encouragement we use, such as 'practice makes perfect', 'genius is 1 per cent inspiration and 99 per cent perspiration' and 'you are never too old to learn'.

Attention

Attention is essential for us to receive information and sensation (perception) and therefore for us to learn, and yet our ability to pay attention is not as great as we might expect. We are highly susceptible to becoming bored and are easily distracted. Recent studies have found that children and young adults will only pay attention to the same thing for about 10 minutes, and that even older adults will not last much longer than this. Other studies have challenged this finding but most agree that the brain has a high tendency to 'wander'.

However, there are strategies we can take to influence attention. For example, when we introduce something new and novel to a presentation or discussion our learner's 'attention cycle' may be re-started. Appealing simultaneously to learners' different senses (an image, smell, sound or touch to support oral information) will increase our opportunities to grab learners' attention, as well as providing a stronger and more likely remembered 'message'.

Also, studies have shown that learners are more likely to pay attention (and have significantly better recall) when their emotions are aroused as well as their intellect, and so introducing 'stories' or showing images or sounds that stimulate relevant emotions will all help gain and hold learners attention. (It should be said here that there are lots of arguments against stimulating particularly negative emotions in learners, and so as ethical L&D practitioners we should focus on supporting positive emotions.)

Memory

Studies in how 'data' passes from immediate and short-term memory into long-term memory are revealing some interesting findings for L&D. It would seem that specific pieces of information or memories are not held, as once thought, holistically in specific places in the brain, but are spread across the brain's grey matter (cells etc) and connected by a web of neural connections, referred to as 'white matter'. The more a web of neural connections is revisited and extended, the stronger it becomes (a process known as myelination) and the more established is the memory or learning. This is a major argument for revisiting knowledge and practising skills, and exploring them in different ways to build strong and extensive connections and consolidate learning.

Spacing

Spacing is an emerging concept about the optimal 'size' and frequency of learning activity in order for learning to be most effective. For some commentators, 'spaced learning' is a very exact way of providing learning, involving a set number of minutes of learning, followed by a set number of minutes of other (non-learning) activity, followed by a further set number of minutes of learning. For others the concept is more generally about ensuring that learning is not overloaded (we are told that humans can only process between three and seven 'chunks' of information at a time) and that learners have enough time to digest new learning, review and reflect on it, and transfer it effectively to long-term memory before the next 'chunk' of learning is undertaken. However, there is now a generally agreed understanding that learning is most effective when it is accessed through several smaller and well spaced-out activities, where learning can be revisited, reviewed and applied, over a period of time.

AGES

Four key areas of neuroscience findings, which relate to learning, have been positioned together by Dr Lila Davachi, Dr Tobias Kiefer, Dr David Rock and Lisa Rock to form the four-part model AGES.

AGES is an acronym for the concepts: Attention, Generation, Emotion and Spacing. You can read more about the AGES model at: https://davidrock.net/portfolio-items/the-science-of-making-learning-stick-an-update-to-the-ages-model-vol-5/

Motivation

Another major focus of neuroscience studies is human motivation – what makes us respond to life's choices and challenges in the particular way we do? An influential piece of work that brings together some of the recent research results, and referred to previously in Chapter 1 of this book, is Dr David Rock's SCARF model (Rock, 2009). SCARF is described by Rock as a 'brain-based model for collaborating with and influencing others'.

SCARF is based on two key concepts, firstly that human behaviour is essentially driven by two basic needs or desires, ie to *minimise threat* and to *maximise reward*. Secondly, and as brain studies have shown, these drivers can operate as much within a social context, where human beings interact and collaborate, as they might within a basic survival context.

To explain how these two essential drivers can impact on our social behaviour, Rock positions them within five 'domains of human social experience': Status, Certainty, Autonomy, Relatedness and Fairness (S-C-A-R-F). Understanding how we might perceive threat and reward within these domains, and how we might act as a result, can help us to both manage our own behaviour more effectively, and as L&D practitioners create more engaging (more rewarding and less threatening) learning environments for our learners.

Rock points out how our natural response to threat, based on our primal need to survive, is to cognitively label it as 'bad' and seek to avoid it (*avoid response*), whilst our natural response to something we perceive as reward, is to label it as 'good' and seek to engage with it (*approach response*).

Therefore if we perceive something as a threat to our STATUS (for example, we are to undertake a learning activity where we do not expect to do well, or we are treated in a way within a learning activity which makes us feel undermined) this may cause us to disengage ourselves (*avoid response*), in one way or another, from the activity. Equally if we consider that something is unfair ('why is our team having to take on this new work area, we already do more than the others?'; ' why is X getting more positive feedback than me when I am contributing more?') this will also affect our level of engagement in a learning activity.

Conversely, where a learner can see potential reward, say to their status ('this learning will raise my profile in the organisation') or we feel validated (relatedness) within a learning session, we are more likely to engage with the learning.

For L&D practitioners, SCARF (or similar models) can give us a comprehensive framework for thinking about the factors that might affect learner motivation and engagement, and find strategies for interacting with these. It can also help us to understand and manage our own social behaviour.

SCARF is a popular model in management, business and L&D, particularly in the United States, and we have provided a number of follow-up references at the end of this chapter, if you want to find out more about it.

AN EXPERT VIEW ON NEUROSCIENCE FROM GARY LUFFMAN

Any type of learning and development is a cognitive process and not just a podcast, session, programme etc. This may sound a little abstract at first, but I would promote this as the first and central concept of any L&D practitioner and L&D event. Using this as our guiding philosophy will help to plan, deliver and embed the learning with individuals and ultimately change something in their brains in some way and for the change to remain.

More often than not, insights from neuroscience should match insights we have gained through experience. Rather than this being an undesirable situation I see it as positive as it helps bring greater focus and understanding to our knowledge or difficult to articulate thoughts/concepts. It also means the brain has less 'work' to do in order to conceptualise and store this information, which aids retrieval and application. It can also help us adhere to 'best practice' or defend it when necessary.

I see increased understanding of our brains in the learning environment as having relevance for practitioners and learners. Practitioners can inform their consideration of the Architecture – Design – Delivery – Embedding stages of an L&D occurrence. Learners can understand what they have to actively bring to the L&D event in order for things to leave a trace in their brains and adjust their perception, thinking and behaviour.

Many aspects of the world of work are developing extremely fast and look set to continue in this vein in the future. However, our brains do not evolve at such speed. Luckily our understanding of humans at work is gathering pace through behavioural science and particularly neuroscience. This understanding affords us opportunity to understand key limitations and mitigate them and build on our strengths in the learning environment. Our understanding of the brain can help us with getting attention, holding on to it and embedding learning through adjusting habits.

Garry Luffman, Director,
Think Change Consulting

Psychology and neuroscience summary

In the sections above we have provided some key theories from psychology and insights from neuroscience. There is so much happening in these areas we could fill another book with them, but there are already many books and articles to explore.

Theories we have not yet mentioned include, for example, Paivio's Dual Coding, which explores how combining both verbal and visual images can assist learning, and Reigluth's Elaboration Theory which promotes how learning concepts need to be built up from simplistic foundations with greater complexity added in stages. These, along with many others, may be relevant areas for further research and we have provided a range of further references at the end of the chapter.

We would always recommend that you critically evaluate any research or theory before applying it to your work and that you seek underpinning evidence of an idea before using it to inform important decisions. (One of CIPD's key values for the L&D profession is evidence-based decision-making.) As new ideas emerge, they lead to further ideas which can either confirm or overturn what has gone before. We therefore encourage you to explore for yourself, find areas of interest, think critically, experiment and draw your own conclusions about how to use science in your L&D practice.

'There is a new field of enterprise and enquiry emerging at the interface of neuroscience and education. It has been called a variety of different names including "neuro-education", "educational neuroscience" and "brain, mind and education". These names may reflect some diversity in approach, but all the research is inspired by one common idea: burgeoning scientific insights about the brain can inform the ways in which we teach and learn.'

Dr Paul Howard-Jones, CIPD
Research Insight, 2014 (CIPD, 2014b)

Case Example 9.2

Engaging 'hard to reach' learners

Our learners typically have multiple social, emotional and physical issues, and individual needs including dyslexia, partially sighted, learning difficulties, severe depression and English as a second language – as well as a range of educational levels.

We take a positive approach to engaging learners, based on accepting them as they are and trying to gain the most benefit for them. We find it really important to give lots of praise and positive energy to help learners feel comfortable in a learning context and build their confidence. Isolation and anxiety is a crippling factor for many and so it is important that we create a positive and supportive social environment and a relaxed forum for learning. At the beginning of each programme, we decide our ground rules as a group – and then we all stick to them.

We also try to build confidence and engagement by encouraging individuals and small groups to work independently on their own initiative, which builds their belief in their own abilities. In addition, we delegate responsibility for some set tasks to individuals. As soon as possible we establish learner (peer) mentoring, a two-way process, that gives them all someone to support and encourage, whilst at the same time being supported and encouraged themselves.

Within the group we make sure we have some 1:1 time with each learner to discuss progress and issues, make sure that the learners are meeting their objectives and check that they are still engaged with the programme – and tackle any problems. On a practical level we offer small 'freebies' such as vouchers for fruit and vegetables to encourage healthy living and, sometimes, travel expenses. The programme is very structured so that everyone knows where and when they should attend and learners can plan ahead (which helps reduce anxiety) – and attendance can become a habit.

Judith Crampton, Trainer

Strategies for enhancing engagement

In many ways this whole book is about enhancing learner engagement! If you follow the advice in each chapter you will:

- be an enthusiastic self-developer;
- fully understand the relationship between L&D and organisational objectives;
- know how to determine accurate learning objectives;
- devise and deliver L&D activities which address them, and evaluate outcomes to inform further activity;
- know how to use different skills and techniques to make learning rich and inclusive;
- know about emerging technologies, developments, theories and thinking in L&D to keep your practice edgy and up to date

You are therefore very likely to be effective in engaging learners in your programmes.

Perhaps most importantly, you will think of your learners as 'individuals' and take steps to ensure that in any learning activity, they all feel included, their contributions are valued and they are able to fulfil their learning objectives. Chapter 5 of this book (Delivery: Face-to-face training) looks particularly at how you can monitor individual learning within a group and support learner involvement, and you may find it useful to refer back to these sections.

Based on many of the insights throughout this book, and from this chapter particularly, we have summarised some strategies for enhancing learner engagement, at different stages of the training cycle, in Figures 9.4 and 9.5. Figure 9.4 considers the identification and design stages and Figure 9.5 explores delivery and evaluation.

We also asked some L&D experts for their thoughts on enhancing learner engagement; their responses are reported in the box below.

'In my experience, learners are more engaged when learning is active, collaborative and fosters learning relationships between peers. Utilising mobile devices and phones within learning also raises levels of learner involvement and increases engagement in a learning activity.'

Ali Alaradi, Trainer and Writer, Bahrain

'I find that learners always engage more when they are able to connect learning activity directly to their own working context.'

Jacqui Ruding, MOL

'Learning is an active process – people learn best when they feel involved, can ask and answer questions, discuss, debate, try things out, work in teams, and reflect on and apply ideas.'

JJ Lynch, Leading Edge Leadership Ltd

'I always find that humour helps to create a relaxed environment and so helps learners engage in L&D activities. Humour related to the context or situation is better than standard jokes as we are not comedians or entertainers.'

Professor Jim Stewart, Professor of Human Resource Development

'We find that learners are more engaged in online learning when the material is personalised, relevant and challenging. Encouraging the learners to view the course through the context of their own workplace, to incorporate the latest thinking and push themselves slightly beyond what is comfortable makes the learning experience more meaningful.'

Lead Instructional Designer, online learning provider

Figure 9.4 Strategies for engaging learners in identifying L&D needs and designing activities

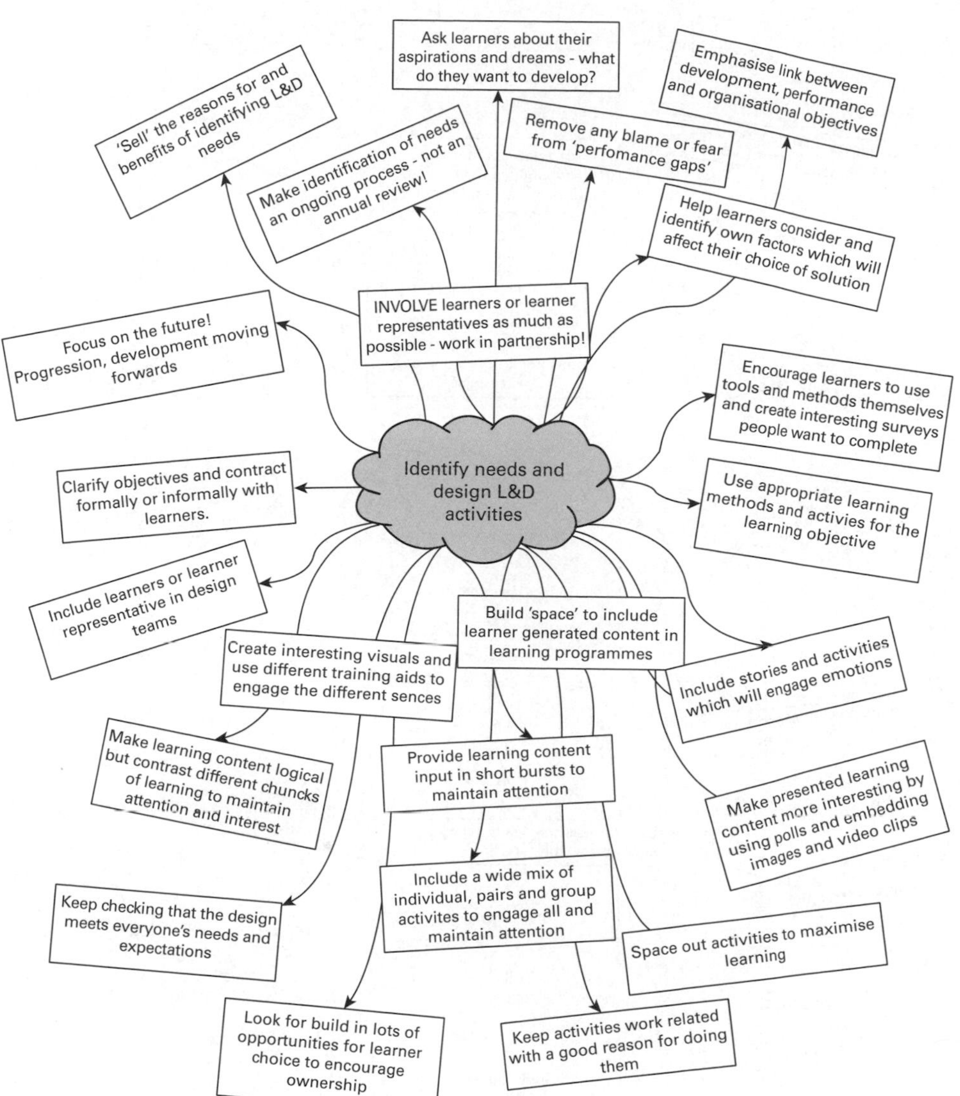

Figure 9.5 Strategies for engaging learners in L&D activities and evaluation

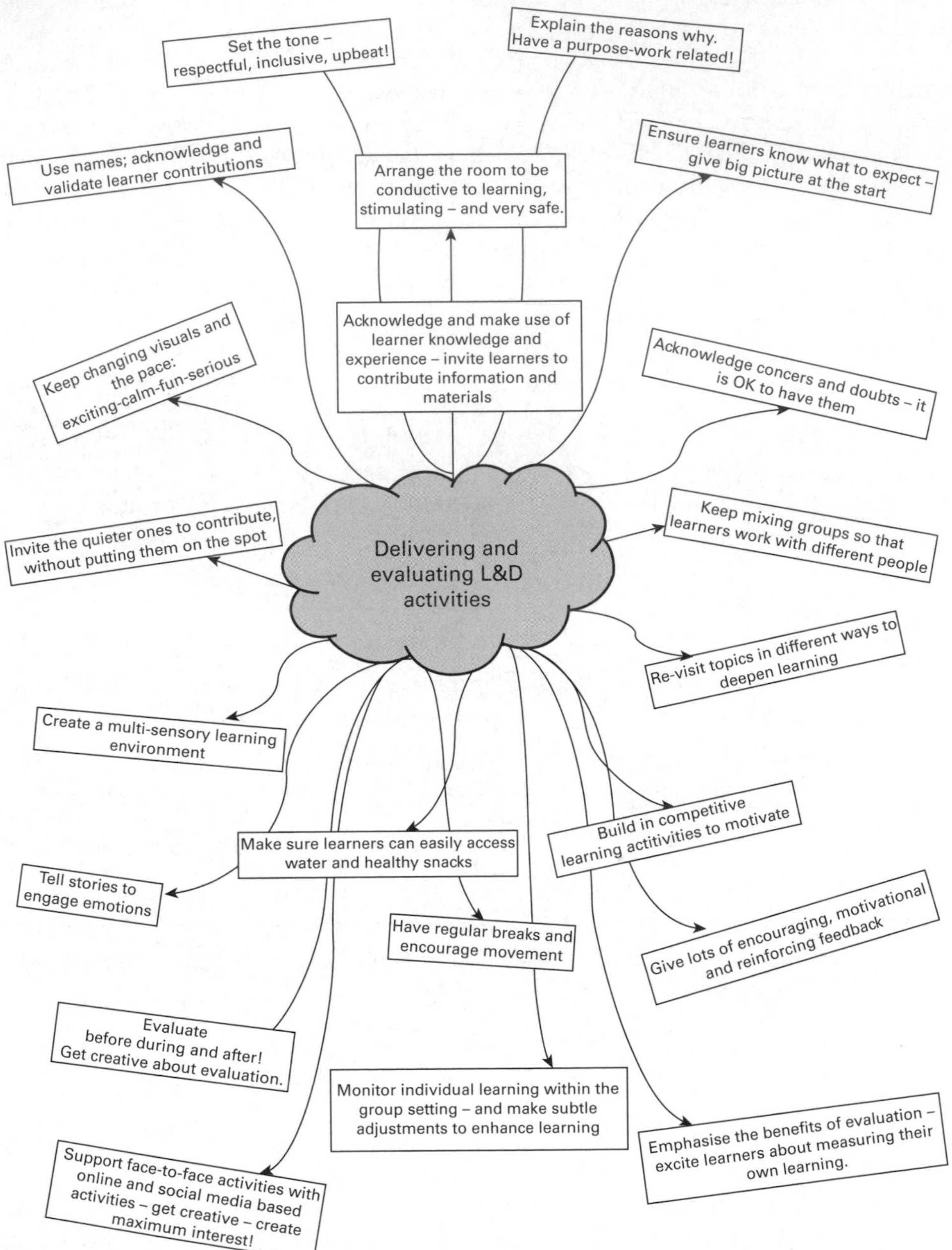

Case Example 9.3

Engaging managers in a leadership programme

Working in a very large organisation undergoing significant organisational change, our clear aim was to improve managers' leadership skills. The changes were 'political' and sensitive and it was crucial that managers developed strong leadership skills in order to lead the organisation through the changes.

The strategies we employed to engage learners in the (five-day residential) programme included:

- course leaders who were known to understand the work and the changes;
- making the programme intensive – long working days and evening work;
- extensive use of teamwork and building competition between teams;
- sharing experiences/practice – the knowledge and resource is within the team, it's for them to discover;
- clear course structure – complying with timetable is fundamental;
- range of stretching activities: knowledge-based, practical and physical;
- course based around six set group tasks/challenges with specific themes: communication, unlocking potential, decision-making, leading change, continuous improvement and customer perception. Each (of 6) team members lead on one task.
- tasks overlap, and start/finish at different times, simulating workplace pressures. Report re how management of (their theme) will be enhanced back in the workplace;
- reports presented back to the plenary within strictly timed three-minute slots – and assessed by a senior manager;
- invited external specialists (respected leaders from commerce and sport) provide inputs;
- all delegates must produce a personal action plan and answer challenging questions about it in a 'Making it Happen' session;
- course ends with formal celebratory dinner to acknowledge learning and successes;
- ongoing three-monthly follow-ups of personal action plan.

David Crosby, Former HR/L&D Director

Activity 9.4

1. Consider Case Examples 9.2 and 9.3.
2. What do you like about each of them?
3. What similarities and differences can you identify?
4. The two case studies involve quite different learner groups. What strategies would most engage the learners you work with?

What next?

The activities below will help consolidate your learning from this chapter.

1 Consider any theories, models or profiling tools which underpin, or you use within, your L&D activities. Undertake some research to ensure that your knowledge about them is up to date and adapt your practice accordingly.

2 Check out the CIPD video 'Why a learning philosophy is so important to an organisation'. (You can find this on the CIPD's YouTube channel.) The video sets out what 'a learning approach' is, who it is aimed at, why it is important and how to implement one. Consider if the video challenges any of your beliefs about learning and learners.

3 What strategies for enhancing learner engagement do you want to introduce into your L&D activities. Could you add any ideas to Figures 9.3 and 9.4? Tweet your ideas using the hashtag #LDPintheW and copy in the account @LDPintheW.

References

Anguera, JA, Boccanfuso, J, Rintoul, JL, Al-Hashimi, O, Faraji, F, Janowich, J, Kong, E, Larraburo, Y, Rolle, C, Johnston, E and Gazzaley, A (2013) Video game training enhances cognitive control in older adults, *Nature*, September, **501**, pp 97–101, www.nature.com/articles/nature12486 (archived at https://perma.cc/3W7A-F5XX)

Bloom, BS (1956, ed) *Taxonomy of Educational Objectives Handbook 1: Cognitive domain,* Longman, New York

CIPD (2014a) *Neuroscience in Action: Applying insight to L&D practice,* www.cipd.co.uk/Images/neuroscience-action_2014-applying-insight-LD-practice_tcm18-9714.pdf (archived at https://perma.cc/S3BT-Q4RY)

CIPD (2014b) *Research Insight: Fresh thinking in learning and development (Part 1 of 3), neuroscience and learning,* CIPD, www.cipd.co.uk/Images/fresh-thinking-in-learning-and-development_2014-part-1-neuroscience-learning_tcm18-15114.pdf (archived at https://perma.cc/9ZVG-SUEW)

CIPD (2015) *Annual Learning and Development Survey 2015,* www.cipd.co.uk/Images/learning-development_2015_tcm18-11298.pdf (archived at https://perma.cc/68J3-Z47J)

CIPD (2017) *The Future of Technology and Learning,* https:// www.cipd.co.uk/Images/the-future-of-technology-and-learning_2017-infographic_tcm18-29349.pdf (archived at https://perma.cc/Y9GE-MSHH)

CIPD (2018) *Profession Map,* www.cipd.co.uk/learn/career/profession-map (archived at https://perma.cc/GV96-GEAT)

CIPD/Towards Maturity (2019) *Professionalising Learning and Development,* www.cipd.co.uk/knowledge/strategy/development/professionalising-learning-development-function (archived at https://perma.cc/3MWS-8ZMC)

Coffield F, Moseley, D, Hall, E and Ecclestone, K (2004) *Learning Styles and Pedagogy in Post-16 Learning: A systematic and critical review,* Learning and Skills Network, London

Davis, J, Balda, M, Rock, D, Mcginniss, P and Davachi, L (2014) The Science of Making Learning Stick: An Update to the AGES Model, **5,** *Neuroleadership Institute,* https://davidrock.net/portfolio-items/

(*continued*)

(Continued)

the-science-of-making-learning-stick-an-update-to-the-ages-model-vol-5/ (archived at https://perma.cc/3F6A-7WWJ)

Fleming, ND (1995) I'm different; not dumb: Modes of presentation (VARK) in the tertiary classroom, in *Research and Development in Higher Education*, ed A Zelmer, Proceedings of the 1995 Annual Conference of the Higher Education and Research Development Society of Australasia, HERDSA, **18**, pp 308–13

Fredericks, JA, Christenson, SL and Reschly, L (2019) *Handbook of Student Engagement Interventions: Working with disengaged students*, Elsevier Science Publishing Co Inc San Diego, USA

Gardner, H (1983) *Frames of Mind: The theory of multiple intelligences*, Basic Books, New York

Glossary of Education Reform (nd) *www.edglossary.org/student-engagement/* (archived at https://perma.cc/FS5C-852S)

Hase, S and Kenyon, C (2013) *Self-Determined Learning: Heutagogy in action*, Bloomsbury, London

Honey, P and Mumford, A (1982) *The Manual of Learning Styles*, Peter Honey Publications, Maidenhead

Howard-Jones, P (2010) *Introducing Neuroeducational Research*, Routledge, London

Knowles, M (1984) *Andragogy in Action: Applying modern principles of adult learning*, Jossey Bass, USA

Kolb, DA (1984) *Experiential Learning: Experience as the source of learning and development*, Prentice Hall, New Jersey

Maguire, EA, Gadian, DG, Johnsrude, IS, Good, CD, Ashburner, J, Frackowiak, RSJ and Frith, CD (2000) Navigation-related structural change in the hippocampi of taxi drivers, University College London, www.fil.ion.ucl.ac.uk/Maguire/Maguire_CORE_2000.pdf (archived at https://perma.cc/A9LH-XN9N)

Piaget, J (1973) *Memory and Intelligence*, Basic Books, New York

Rock, D (2009) *Your Brain at Work: Strategies for overcoming distraction, regaining focus, and working smarter all day long*, HarperBusiness, USA

Schlechty, PS (2009) *Leading for Learning: How to transform schools into learning organizations*, Jossey Bass, USA

Towards Maturity (2017) *Driving the New Learning Organisation*, https://towardsmaturity.org/2017/09/07/driving-new-learning-organisation/ (archived at https://perma.cc/N27M-7LCV)

Willis, J (2019) RAD Teaching: www.radteach.com/page1/styled-5/index.html (archived at https://perma.cc/KN8J-BHSW)

Willis, J (2007) The Neuroscience of Joyful Education, *Educational Leadership*, **64,** www.psychologytoday.com/files/attachments/4141/the-neuroscience-joyful-education-judy-willis-md.pdf (archived at https://perma.cc/BYU6-LAB4)

Wilson C (2010) Tools of the trade, *Training Journal*, April, pp 61–6

Explore further

Brann, A (2013) *Make Your Brain Work: How to maximize your efficiency, productivity and effectiveness*, Kogan Page, London

Collins, S (2015) *Neuroscience for Learning and Development: How to apply neuroscience and psychology for improved learning and training*, Kogan Page, London

Lewis, J and Webster, A (2014) *Sort Your Brain Out: Boost your performance, manage stress and achieve more*, Capstone, USA

Medina, J (2014) *Brain Rules (Updated and Expanded): 12 principles for surviving and thriving at work, home, and school*, Pear Press, USA

Paivio, A (2006) *Mind and Its Evolution: A dual coding theoretical approach*, Routledge, Abingdon-on-Thames

Ratey, J and Hagerman, E (2013) *Spark: The revolutionary new science of exercise and the brain*, Little, Brown and Co, Boston, MA

Reigeluth, CM (1983) *Instructional Design Theories and Models: An overview of their current status*, Routledge, Abingdon-on-Thames

Useful resources

Websites

www.cipd.co.uk (archived at https://perma.cc/C7JJ-UE7P)

www.learningandteaching.info (archived at https://perma.cc/W2RE-NC6C)

www.simplypsychology.org (archived at https://perma.cc/GJF5-35TD)

www.educationalneuroscience.org.uk (archived at https://perma.cc/S6D8-6D3R)

www.cipd.co.uk/knowledge/work/technology/future-technology-learning (archived at https://perma.cc/KLC5-PNHN)

www.cipd.co.uk/knowledge/work/technology/future-technology-learning (archived at https://perma.cc/KLC5-PNHN)

https://en.wikipedia.org/wiki/Dual-coding_theory (archived at https://perma.cc/424Q-4RSK)

www.learning-theories.com/elaboration-theory-reigeluth.html (archived at https://perma.cc/6GL9-L7TY)

www.learningscientists.org/learning-scientists-podcast (archived at https://perma.cc/XCV9-VPEB)

CIPD Podcasts 139

Twitter

@NeuroscienceNew

@Neurophilosophy

Video

Suzuki, W (2018) *Exercise and the Brain*, TED Talk, https://www.youtube.com/watch?v=LdDnPYr6R0o (archived at https://perma.cc/YMN9-VTWJ)

Iliff, J (2014) *One more reason to get a good night's sleep,* TED Talk, www.ted.com/talks/jeff_iliff_one_more_reason_to_get_a_good_night_s_sleep (archived at https://perma.cc/2SBR-UZNA)

Rock, D (2013) *Learning About the Brain Changes Everything*, TED Talk, www.youtube.com/watch?v=uDIyxxayNig (archived at https://perma.cc/G525-WT6F)

Rock, D (2010) *SCARF Model – Influencing Others with Dr David Rock,* www.youtube.com/watch?v=isiSOeMVJQk&list=PLrFukCUmFYVgmlIkcI1OvYvLuUGTpASmV (archived at https://perma.cc/W32V-EGKL)

CIPD (2018) Learning Philosophy, www.youtube.com/watch?v=dH1HIZuA2vk (archived at https://perma.cc/6LYK-LJNR)

10 Evaluating impact

Introduction

When preparing this book, we deliberated a little about where to position the chapter about evaluation. Its natural place, in line with the training cycle, is to follow analysis, design and delivery, and evaluation does indeed complete the cycle, hence our final decision re chapter position. However, as stressed in all the previous chapters, evaluation really belongs at every stage of the cycle and, if we are fulfilling our role effectively, will inform our activities at each of them (Figure 10.1).

Figure 10.1 Evaluation at the heart of the training cycle

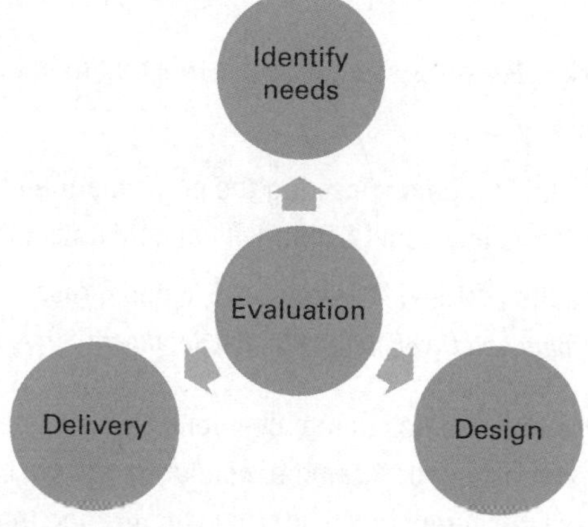

Key areas of content covered in this chapter are:

- the importance and the benefits of evaluating L&D activities;
- what we mean by evaluation and how it differs from related terms;
- key theories and thinking on evaluation;
- a straightforward plan for evaluation;
- how to decide what to evaluate and the information to collect;
- different methods for evaluating L&D activities;
- how to analyse evaluation information and ideas for presenting your findings.

Why evaluate?

The argument for evaluation and the desire to implement evaluation practice remains as strong as ever.

In the survey:

- 70 per cent of respondents expressed feeling pressure from leadership to measure the impact of learning, reflecting a 38 per cent increase on the previous year;
- 96 per cent of respondents stated that they 'wanted to measure the business impact of learning' and believed it possible to do so.

Measuring the Business Impact of Learning 2019 Survey,
Piers Lea, LEO Learning and Watershed

The survey (which asks L&D professionals 'what will be hot in L&D next year') found that:

- in 2018 'Showing value' (ie demonstrating the performance improvements and business benefits that arise from L&D activities) held its position at no. 6;
- previous years' results (2015-–17) were nos. 6, 8 and 6 respectively.

The Learning and Development Global Sentiment Survey 2018, Donald H Taylor

'Impact measurement's time has come. Everyone has long been predicting that on-the-job and post-learning programme measurement will revolutionize the sector. This year, we will begin to see learning integrating more cleverly with data diagnostic systems to create measurable, meaningful, learner-centric data. This can be used to assess the effectiveness and value of L&D activities on an individual learner basis, as well as on a strategic, organisational level.'

David Wells, What will 2019 bring for learning and development?
People Management, *21 January 2019*

However, when it comes to actual practice, the picture is a little less encouraging. The 2019 results of the *Learning & Development Global Sentiment Survey* show a slightly reduced position (10) for 'Showing value' and the *LEO Learning and Watershed Survey* found that only 50 per cent of respondents were evaluating L&D based on factors such as job performance, organisational impact and ROI, with the other 50 per cent either not evaluating or focusing only on learner satisfaction and content utilization. And to some extent this split between belief in the value of evaluation and the level of practice reflects our own informal findings from talking to L&D practitioners.

The LEO survey shows progress on the situation detailed in earlier reports, such as the reports, *Making an Impact: How L&D Leaders can demonstrate value* (Towards Maturity, 2016 and 2017) which found that only around one in four (2016) and one in five (2017) of the respondents were able to provide data on the impact of L&D on business indicators. Still, it is obvious from the surveys, as well as anecdotally, that we still have room to make our evaluation practice significantly more meaningful.

Without honest and useful evaluation, L&D risk delivering the same initiatives over and over again, whether or not they are known to be effective. If our prime purpose is to contribute to business or organisation effectiveness, then how, without evaluation, can we be sure that we are doing this?

So why don't we do more evaluation – and how can we increase our activity in this area? As the metrics show, evaluation is not always seen as the most critical or engaging process. It is sometimes considered too vague for information to be relied upon or useful only as a quick way of gauging learner satisfaction. It is considered overly time-consuming by some and too complex by others, but as our recognition of the absolute need for L&D to contribute to organisational performance and achievement of goals increases, and the potential ease and accuracy of evaluation is improved by technology, we really have no excuse not to take evaluation more seriously.

Thorough and accurate evaluation can bring all kinds of benefits, for organisations and learners, as well as for L&D practitioners. Some key benefits are:

- a measure of how learning has impacted on performance, skills and knowledge;
- a crucial source of information about what still needs to be done;
- clearer links and alignment between business objectives and L&D;
- more effective targeting of limited budgets and resources;
- continuously improved learning activities for learners;
- increased learner and line manager engagement in learning;
- greater confidence (ours and others') in our training delivery;
- an evidence base to demonstrate our contribution to the business.

> 'Most people like learning new things, but without accountability for improved performance back on the job, learning will always be vulnerable and its value questioned.'
>
> *Robert O Brinkerhoff and Susanna Brinkerhoff Zens*

Defining evaluation

So, what do we actually mean by the term 'evaluation'? According to the dictionaries...

> 'Evaluate... to ascertain or set the amount or value of; to judge or assess the worth of.'
>
> *Collins Concise Dictionary*
>
> 'Evaluation... the act or result of judging the worth or value of something.'
>
> *Roget's II: The New Thesaurus, 3rd edn*

In an L&D context, evaluation is about measuring and analysing various aspects of L&D provision, with a view to determining the effectiveness and value of that provision and informing decisions about how it can be improved.

The earlier chapters of this book have focused on the first three stages of the training cycle (see Figure 10.2). Evaluation is the final stage of the training cycle and so completes it. However, the nature of a cycle is that one flows into the next – hence much evaluation activity overlaps with learning needs identification, taking us into the next cycle. While evaluation essentially looks back at training that has already taken place and learning needs identification looks forwards at learning that is required, some of the same activities will inform both processes.

It is important that we see evaluation as part of a continuous cycle, something to be done on an ongoing basis, as an integral part of continuous improvement. If we view evaluation in this way, we make it easier to manage and less off-putting than the idea of big 'one-off', and probably more costly, evaluation initiatives.

Figure 10.2 The training cycle

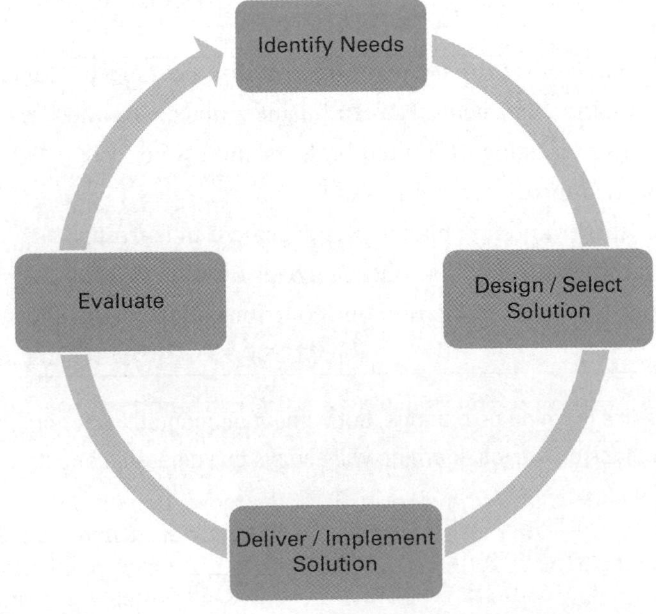

Related terms and processes

There are several similar terms and processes which are associated with evaluation but which have slightly different meanings. Some of the most widely used of these are explained in Table 10.1.

Table 10.1 Evaluation and links to similar terms and processes

Process	Definition	Links to evaluation
Validation	Validation – meaning to establish the truth of, confirm or corroborate – is about establishing whether learning activity achieved its stated objectives. Did the training activity do what it said it would do?	Evaluation (usually) includes validation, but may also include other factors or purposes, such as whether training activity was good value for money – or whether resources were used effectively. For example, a learning programme may achieve all its learning objectives and be deemed very successful. However, the programme may be expensive and the costs may not be worth paying for the level of organisational benefits gained from the programme.
Assessment	In a training context, generally applied to individual progress and achievement. The measuring, by a range of methods, of how well someone can perform an activity or demonstrate knowledge, usually against some pre-set criteria.	Assessment is frequently used to establish levels of individual learning and ability. It might be undertaken prior to, during or after (various duration) a learning activity to establish any impact of learning and/or to establish further learning requirements.
Testing	Very similar to assessment but often used to describe an assessment activity which is specifically set within a very controlled environment – such as an exam or observed practical activity.	Similar to assessment above. The format of testing will vary depending on what is being tested – for example, knowledge may require written or verbal tests, while skills may be best tested through observation.
Monitoring and review	A collection of activities to gauge learner progress towards goals.	Information collected for, and from, monitoring and review activities will often be useful to evaluation processes.

(*continued*)

Table 10.1 (Continued)

Process	Definition	Links to evaluation
Return on investment (ROI)	A measure of the financial impact of training/learning activities on an organisation.	Assessing ROI is about accurately calculating the financial impact of the training. ROI is usually considered to be the highest level of evaluation (and whether or not it can be done with complete accuracy is sometimes debated). Our understanding of this practice has been enhanced by the work of Jack Philips (see end of chapter reading list).
Return on expectation (ROE)	Whereas ROI explores quantitative factors and specifically financial return, ROE is more concerned with stakeholder satisfaction and whether learning activities have met the expectations of key stakeholder groups (learners, managers or customers).	Stakeholder satisfaction with learning initiatives should be a part of any evaluation. CIPD has championed this approach and captured its importance in the term ROE. An ROE approach to evaluation begins with an understanding of stakeholder expectations and then seeks to measure the extent to which these have been met. In assessing the contribution of learning to an organisation, equal consideration is given to intangible, long-term benefits as to more tangible and quantifiable outcomes.

VALIDATION 'IN THE ZOO' AND 'IN THE WILD'

Michael Privett, a training specialist at Lightspeed POS, explained how participants on his organisation's Train the Trainer programme are encouraged to approach evaluation.

The second of the programme modules is called Designing a Training Plan. In this, the participants explore learning objectives, the importance of relevance, what are KSAs (knowledge, skills and abilities) and why participation is important. They also look at validation techniques they can use during the actual training. We refer to this as 'validation in the zoo'.

The last module is called Observing Results in Action. In this module, we share validation techniques for participants to use to help them gauge the longer-term impact of their training events. We refer to this as 'validation in the wild' as it is about them validating that the new KSAs are being applied back on the job.

Evaluation theory and thinking

Without doubt, the person who has had most impact on our understanding and implementation of evaluation over the last 60 years is Donald Kirkpatrick. Kirkpatrick produced his Model of Evaluation – now thought to be a development of earlier work by Raymond Katzel (Thalheimer, 2018) – back in the 1950s, yet it remains the model most L&D practitioners would cite if asked to name one and it still underpins many modern evaluation systems and approaches.

The basis of the Kirkpatrick model is that evaluation should take place at four different levels, as below.

Kirkpatrick's four levels of evaluation

Level 1– Reaction: At Level 1, evaluation is primarily about how well the training activity is 'received' by the learners. Did learners enjoy it? Did they find it useful? Did they perceive it to be of value?

Level 2 – Learning: At Level 2, we are seeking to establish whether learners did actually learn as a result of the activity. It is quite possible that learners could have enjoyed the training activities while learning very little. Level 2 evaluation is concerned with testing and establishing whether learning has actually taken place.

Level 3 – Behaviour (transfer to workplace): Even though learning may have taken place, there is no guarantee that new learning will be applied and result in changed behaviour (improved performance). Level 3 evaluation is concerned with identifying the impact of training activity on learner behaviour, ie do learners do something extra, better, quicker, differently as a result of their learning?

Level 4 – Results: Level 4 evaluation considers the impact of any individual behaviour change on the organisation. Has changed behaviour had an impact on organisational results such as targets, production figures and sales figures? In other words, has the training initiative had a positive impact on organisational performance?

Whilst some aspects of Kirkpatrick's model have been debated (as with most models and theories), it continues to be a most popular and useful model helping many trainers to understand evaluation and providing them with a sound framework in which to carry it out. As you might expect, Kirkpatrick's model has not remained static, and his work has been continued by family members, for example, into the New World Kirkpatrick Model which further clarifies and extends the original.

Others have also sought to extend Kirkpatrick's work, most notably, Jack Phillips, who has published many books on this subject of evaluation since the 1980s (Phillips, 1991). As well as extending definitions of each of the four levels, Philips encourages 'evaluators' to move beyond Level 4, particularly when evaluating expensive programmes, to a 5th level of more quantitative financial evaluation. This 5th level is labelled Level 5: Return on Investment (ROI) and requires evaluators to isolate and quantify the costs and benefits of programmes in order to calculate the financial value of a programme to an organization (Philips, 2007). This is not an easy process, but Philips provides a methodology and formula, the Philips ROI Methodology, which enables organisations to calculate a reasonably accurate value of the return on their investment in L&D. (This is explained in detail in Philips' books.)

Another contributor who has helped our understanding of the purpose of evaluation is Mark Easterby-Smith, who within his wider writings describes four main underpinning purposes of evaluation – Proving, Controlling, Improving and Learning. These are explained in Table 10.2.

Table 10.2 Easterby-Smith's purposes of evaluation

Proving	Demonstrating that training has worked and has had the desired impact on learners.
Controlling	Checking and ensuring that learning is being delivered in the way it is required to be (eg trainers are following any required procedures and fulfilling any requirements).
Improving	Exploring and identifying how a learning programme can be adapted and improved.
Learning	Using evaluation activities (eg self-reflection) to aid and reinforce individual learning.

Whilst the four purposes are closely interlinked, controlling and improving generally relate to the L&D activity (process), whilst proving and learning are more about impact (outcome). Considering Easterby-Smith's four purposes can help us clarify what we actually want to achieve from an evaluation and remind us that evaluation is not just about improving L&D processes but about checking and ensuring L&D's impact on the organisation.

More recently, new ideas about evaluation have been brought forward by Robert O Brinkerhoff, who has introduced a different approach, The Success Case Method, to the evaluation arena (Brinkerhoff, 2003). This method differs from some of the aforementioned in that there is a little less emphasis on hard quantitative data and a greater use of qualitative data. In essence, the method involves identifying, via a survey, a sample of learners who have been most successful in transferring learning to the workplace and improving their performance as a result, and a small sample of those who haven't had this success. The evaluation then focuses on the more detailed individual 'stories' of people in these sample groups, highlighting the real factors that have enabled transfer of learning as well as some of the barriers that have prevented this. As well as generating very relevant and useful information, the focus on real 'stories' can help to make evaluation findings and recommendations more interesting and engaging to people in the organisation.

Case Example 10.1

An evaluation strategy (1)

An organisation describes its approach to evaluation of management programmes.

End of session evaluation

Our first stage of evaluation is to make sure that learners have met the session learning objectives. We do this by questioning throughout the session and asking learners to complete a test of learning at the end of the session. We then evaluate learner's initial reaction using an evaluation questionnaire, which focuses on three key areas: session effectiveness, materials and the trainer. A summary sheet is created for each course to identify trends.

Intermediate (learning) evaluation

To measure the extent to which learning has been applied back in the workplace, we undertake observation and interviews with delegates (and sometimes follow up with their line manager) after the learning.

This will normally be around two months after the course or activity, but for courses where learning will only be put into practice at certain points (eg recruitment and selection) intermediate evaluation is timed for after this.

Quarterly evaluation report

On a quarterly basis, evaluation information is collated into an Impact Evaluation Report, which summarises the overall impact and benefit the course has had in line with the organisation's objectives and to the organisation as a whole. This is then cascaded to senior management.

Evaluation – process and practice

'The organisations that really understand evaluation have few forms but do have:

- line managers that are actively involved in the development of their people;
- people who are involved in their own development and are very clear what any learning and development activity should achieve for them and their organisation;
- a learning and development function that constantly seeks information from managers and individuals as part of a much wider approach to evaluation and uses the information to bring about continuous improvement.'

Jane Elliott-Poxon, Elliott Partnership

Whilst not over-simplifying things, we believe that useful evaluation need not be a cumbersome or costly process. The box below details our 10-point plan to approaching evaluation in a logical and efficient way. Remember that evaluation must be planned in the earlier stages of the training cycle, when we are identifying needs and designing L&D activities, so that pre-learning metrics can be collected and evaluation is fully integrated in the L&D process.

Planning evaluation

1 Identify what learning activity is to be evaluated (the 'scope' of the evaluation).
2 Determine and clarify the purpose(s) of the evaluation – what you are trying to establish and why (ie your 'evaluation criteria').
3 Work out the information you need for each purpose/criteria and the source of that information.

4 Select appropriate methods and timing to obtain the information you need.
5 Design/obtain any evaluation 'tools' eg questionnaire, survey, observation checklist, video diary format.
6 You now have your evaluation plan – and should embed this in your training design or plan. You should also agree your plan with relevant stakeholders.

Implementing evaluation

1 Collect information as per your plan.
2 Analyse collected information in relation to each of your objectives.
3 Draw key conclusions and consider relevant improvement actions.
4 Present your findings and recommendations to relevant partners and stakeholders.

Now, let's consider each stage.

Identifying what is to be evaluated (scope)

Where evaluation is in relation to a single session, it might be relatively straightforward to state what you are evaluating. However, bigger or blended programmes may be more complex.

For example, a Team Leader Development Programme might include an initial self-analysis exercise, a one-to-one meeting with a line manager, a number of group workshops and some optional online learning modules. If you want to evaluate the programme fully then you will need to include all these aspects in your evaluation. On another occasion, however, you might just want to focus your evaluation on the online learning modules or the self-analysis exercise.

Clarifying the scope of your evaluation is important as it sets the boundaries for the evaluation activity to be undertaken and provides a clear context for when you are presenting your findings and recommendations.

Clarifying the purpose(s) of evaluation

The main purpose of our evaluation is almost always going to be to establish the extent to which the aims and objectives of the L&D activity have been met, and the longer-term impact of this in the workplace. There should be a clear follow-through from learning needs analysis, to learning aims and objectives, and to evaluation criteria. For example:

If the learning need is:

– managers need to be able to move from a traditional directive style with team members to more of a coaching style.

this should become the aim (or one of the aims) of an L&D activity aimed at addressing this need for the managers.

The learning objectives might then include:

- learners will be able to explain a simple coaching process;
- learners will be able to demonstrate effective coaching skills;
- learners will know when coaching is an appropriate approach to take with team members.

and the evaluation criteria should include:

- the extent to which learning objectives were met;
- the extent to which learners apply coaching skills in the workplace as a result of the training.

Most evaluation initiatives seek to establish a range of factors, as well as validating the training in terms of fulfilment of aims and objectives. For example, we might choose to carry out an evaluation which requires all of the following:

- the extent to which a learning activity has met its stated aims and objectives;
- the impact of training on learners' work performance;
- learners' reaction to the training and methods used;
- the overall costs of the learning activity.

A more complex and far-reaching evaluation might also add:

- the return on investment (ROI) in the learning.

One way of clarifying purpose and ensuring our evaluation is comprehensive and useful is to consider the different parties who may have an interest in the learning initiative and what their particular interest might be. In any evaluation there will usually be learner, organisation and trainer interests to consider and possibly those of other internal and external partners. For example:

- Managers (organisation) will be concerned with if and how training has impacted on learners' performance in the workplace.
- Learners need to be sure that the learning activities they are giving their time and effort to are effective and are providing an appropriate vehicle for their development.
- Leaders and L&D need to know that L&D initiatives are having the required impact on the business.
- The L&D team will also be interested in how immediate programme objectives have been met and how learners respond to different methods and approaches.
- The finance function (organisation) might be particularly interested in the costs and financial impact of the training.
- Awarding, accrediting and regulatory bodies may have an interest in the type of training and learning support provided, as well as aspects of learner achievement.

In fact, evaluation can answer many questions.

Activity 10.1

Thinking about a learning programme you have delivered or been involved in, consider the list of evaluation outcomes in Table 10.3 and who each outcome would benefit or be useful for:

1. the learners (L);
2. the organisation (O);
3. the trainer (T);
4. or any external partners (E), such as regulatory, funding or awarding bodies.

Table 10.3 Evaluation outcomes

	POTENTIAL PURPOSES (AND BENEFITS) OF EVALUATION	USEFUL TO*			
		L	O	T	E
1	Establish how L&D is contributing to the achievement of a particular business objective				
2	Establish whether (level 2) learning objectives have been met				
3	Establish learner achievement of qualification units or standards				
4	Establish whether learners enjoyed the learning				
5	Receive feedback on trainer performance				
6	Establish the costs of L&D activities				
7	Establish specific (quantitative) information about changes in skills and knowledge				
8	Establish whether learning has been transferred to the workplace and the extent of this				
9	Establish user response to a new mobile learning App				
10	Increase learner engagement in learning by asking them to reflect and give feedback				
11	Enable learners to influence future learning provision				
12	Check that L&D/trainers followed correct procedures				
13	Establish if any particular learning needs have not been effectively addressed				
14	Generate information to 'prove' and promote the value (or not) of L&D to the organisation				
15	Identify gaps in the current provision of L&D				

(continued)

Table 10.3 (Continued)

	POTENTIAL PURPOSES (AND BENEFITS) OF EVALUATION	USEFUL TO* L	O	T	E
16	Get new ideas on how L&D could/should be improved or extended				
17	Establish whether selected learning methods were effective				
18	Establish 'value for money' or return on investment of L&D activities				
19	Help learners to establish next steps in their learning				
20	Increase engagement of managers and other stakeholders in L&D provision				

Once we are clear about the scope and purpose of an evaluation, we have our general evaluation criteria. For example, to establish:

- the levels of learning achieved as a result of the activity;
- the extent to which skill X has been applied in the workplace;
- the impact of the learning on specific productivity metrics;
- workplace changes and improvements made as a result of the learning;
- the projected financial benefits of the initiative;
- the overall costs of the learning;
- how accessible and useful learners found different learning approaches and resources.

These direct us to the evaluation information we need to collect, the questions we need to ask and the most appropriate methods we should use for collecting required information.

Before moving on from 'purposes', we should emphasize that evaluation is not always an exact science, particularly when we are seeking to establish the impact of training on individual or organisational performance. Some commercial providers of ROI evaluation services could challenge this, and it is fair to say that as a profession we are getting much better at measuring impact. Generating accurate HR and L&D metrics is a huge theme of current practice. However, separating out the exact impact of training from the impact of all kinds of other factors such as the economic climate, organisational culture or personal behaviour and motivation issues can be difficult, and we should be aware of this when making claims about the impact of L&D. Providing we are aware of these constraints, there is a vast amount of information available to validate, inform and continuously improve our L&D activities.

Identifying information for evaluation

Types of information

Once we have identified the key purposes of our evaluation, we can more accurately identify the types of information we need, depending on the specific purpose.

Example 1

If the purpose of evaluation is to identify the extent to which a programme has met its learning objectives and impacted on work performance, then we will need to collect information relating to each of these objectives. Depending on the particular learning objectives, this will include information about:

- levels of learning before the programme;
- levels of learning after the programme;
- work performance before the programme;
- work performance after the programme.

In this example, the main sources of information might be pre- and post-learning tests, self-assessments, manager assessments and work result metrics. This clearly takes us back to the need for us to begin evaluation activity before a programme starts and for us to set very clear learning objectives for our learning programmes.

Example 2

If the purpose of an evaluation is to establish the effectiveness of a particular training/learning method or resource, then we may seek the following information:

- the trainer/facilitator/coach's reflections on how well the method worked, the level of participation generated, any constraints or problems encountered and the ease with which the method led to the desired result;
- the learners' feedback on how accessible the method was, how helpful and engaging it was and any problems or limitations caused by the particular method;
- we could also involve an independent evaluator or IT specialist to give objective feedback on the learning resource.

Example 3

A more complex evaluation, seeking to determine the financial impact of L&D activity on a business, through an overall cost–benefit analysis, would need information about:

- Costs:
  - trainer-team costs (including LNA and design costs, as well as delivery costs);
  - learner 'down-time' costs;

  - materials and equipment costs;
  - venue and any travel costs.
- Benefits:
  - positive impacts on performance (eg work results, behaviours);
  - positive impacts on the organisation (eg improved business results, reputation);
  - information about costs saved by the programme (eg resolved production or service delivery issues, reduced absenteeism);
  - information about potential losses or problems avoided by the programme (eg health and safety or compliance issues);
  - recognition of other factors that might have led to, or detracted from, benefits.

Sources of information

We can see in the types of information needed above that key sources of evaluation information are usually likely to be:

- learners: their opinions, their feedback and experience of the learning, their results in knowledge or skills tests, their demonstration of changed behaviours;
- line managers: the differences in knowledge, skills and attitudes they have observed in team members;
- trainers: what they observed, tested, recorded and experienced during the event;
- business information and metrics: business/KPI results, achievement of business and team targets, production records, wastage rates, sickness and absence records;
- customers and service users: feedback on service delivery, complaints, compliments, defections to other providers;
- staff (other than directly involved learners): feedback on colleagues, feedback on L&D processes, perceptions of the organisation, employee satisfaction, staff turnover;
- other stakeholder groups: monitoring of service level agreements, measured improvements in partner working, measured improvements in reputation;
- external partners: qualification results, awarding or inspection body feedback, compliance issues;
- key financial information and metrics: cost savings, increased profits, costs of training;
- ITC systems: system user information, VLE activity.

 Case Example 10.2

An evaluation strategy (2)

A large service organisation states on its L&D website:

'We evaluate every L&D event we provide by:

- sending a survey to learners three months after the course, checking how the learning has made a difference to their performance at work;
- sending a survey to learners' line managers six months after the course for their views on how the course has impacted on the learner's performance;
- checking service information for any improvements 12 months after the course.'

Selecting evaluation methods

There are many different ways of collecting information and evaluating learning and development, some of which we have touched on above. Here is a summary of key methods.

End of programme questionnaires

Often known as 'happy sheets', these are primarily useful for collecting learners' general comments and measuring their initial thoughts and feelings about the learning event: do learners consider their needs to have been met, was the training activity well organised and supported? These questionnaires provide a good and useful opportunity for learners to give their immediate feedback, but they are rarely sufficient to evaluate overall effectiveness.

Pre- and post-testing

Whilst testing is the norm in many sectors, particularly those that are highly regulated, the word 'test' can have negative, 'school-day' connotations for some people, so use with care. To show an improvement in learning, tests should be done before or at the beginning of learning, as well as at the end of learning activity. The test could also be repeated sometime after the event to assess how much of the knowledge has been retained and can be recalled.

Tests should always be appropriate for the learning outcomes being assessed, for example:

- **Tests for knowledge:** you might have a learning outcome that participants on a training course would be able to 'list at least 10 benefits to customers of buying our product X'. This learning outcome could be tested by written questions within a formal test or e-learning module, or by verbal questions within a training session.
- **More complex areas of knowledge and understanding:** this could perhaps be about why customers behave in a certain way or how learners would respond

to particular work situations, and are best assessed by discussions and scenario exercises/case studies, as well as real work performance.

- **Skills and behaviours:** a key method for assessing changes in skills and behaviours is observation. During the training event, you could observe and measure skills demonstrated by learners in a practice activity – for example, handling a customer complaint. The same skills could be formally observed and recorded in the workplace by learners' line managers, after the training.

Learner self-assessment

In this method the learner assesses their own level of skill or confidence, against a list of pre-set criteria, both before and after a learning event. Because this method is dependent on personal perception, however, it is possible that a learner's 'score' could actually decrease after training, as learners become more aware of 'what they do not know' or realise that they are not as skilled as they thought they were.

Line manager assessment

A useful evaluation method can be for line managers to assess team members against a list of pre-set criteria or competences before and after a learning event. The assessment form could be completed directly by the line manager or by an L&D representative in an interview with the line manager. (Here the assessment is about line managers' perceptions of team members' ability, based on their everyday observations and examination of work outputs – rather than a formal recorded observation as described above.)

If the assessment form is designed to include rating scales, then improvements in performance can be more easily quantified – providing useful evaluation information. This method can also help managers to see the impact of training for themselves and can help engage them in team members' development.

Learner action plans and records

Towards the end of the learning programme, participants complete a plan of how they will transfer their learning to the workplace. Learners then log their progress against their plan, identifying any problems or barriers along the way. Time points are set for L&D to collect and collate this information to feed into evaluation activities.

Surveys

Professional-looking surveys can be designed with relative ease, using online survey software (some of which is freely available) and sent to large numbers of participants and/or other stakeholders – eg line managers, customers, service users. Because online surveys are generally quick easy to respond to, participant response rates can be increased and information quickly collected. An added bonus of most survey programmes is that information can be analysed within the system and presented in a number of text and graphical formats. Surveys can be carried out before and after the training and are particularly useful if large numbers of learners are to be contacted. If you are new to designing surveys try a few 'dummy runs' using the tutorial programmes, in order to get the best out of your design. Don't forget to use them with learners' line managers, or other stakeholders, as well as with learners.

Focus or review groups

For large learning programmes it can be appropriate to establish a programme review group who will meet (actually or virtually) to review the progress of the programme (including post-programme application), identify any issues or emerging problems and make suggestions for improvements.

Typical representation within a review group would be: at least one L&D representative, a representative number of learners and at least one line manager, although for large-scale L&D initiatives it would make more sense for a review group to include learner and manager representatives from different areas of the business. There may also be some external representation if appropriate (an external provider or other stakeholder representative). Depending on the scale and duration of the programme the group might just connect at a few key points or at more frequent and regular intervals.

Desk research/organisation metrics

Remember that much of the information that is useful to evaluation is already available in the organisation – performance review information, customer comments, production and service statistics, financial and operational information, systems information, sales figures, etc. These can usually be accessed directly without having to take other people away from business activities in order to be involved in your evaluation.

> 'Learning professionals know that proving the value of L&D is essential to keeping and increasing the resources at their disposal. According to our survey of L&D departments in the UK, one of the key differentiators of top performing departments, regardless of industry or size, is their close relationship with senior executives and their commitment to measuring the ROI of corporate learning.'
>
> UK L&D Report: 2018 Benchmark Your Workplace Learning Strategy *(Findcourses, 2018)*

Social media

As well as creating our own surveys, accessed via phones and tablets, we can also use social media to assist in evaluation. Surveys can be promoted via social media and feedback can easily be given via Twitter or Facebook or by instant feedback Apps.

Case Example 10.3

An example of using social media for evaluation

Twitter can be used to evaluate a training/learning session, for example, by using a hashtag (#). People use hashtags to create conversations across Twitter that include people who don't necessarily 'follow' each other. Therefore, if you wanted to discuss a particular topic – say, CPD – you can compose a tweet which includes the hashtag #cpd. Then anyone interested in that subject can search for #cpd and so pick up your tweet – and ask a question or give feedback on a training session.

An example of how a trainer has used this is a company Reach Further who specialize in social media training. They had a course for people that lasted 12 days and was all covered on Twitter through tweeting links to handouts, feedback, blogs and website information. In managing their large group they used the hashtag #12dot which stands for 12 days of Twitter. This was very effective as all on the course including tutors could search for the topic and would be able to see and contribute to the conversations about that subject.

Karen Waite, Founder and Director, leaplikeasalmon.com

Some creative approaches to evaluation

You may encourage participation in evaluation by employing some quick, easy and engaging methods. While these will not be particularly scientific or give vast amounts of information, they can certainly generate useful feedback. For example:

1 At the beginning of the learning session, you could ask learners to take 'selfies' of themselves looking happy and of themselves looking sad. At the end of the session they can tweet (or upload to an LMS) the photo that most represents their response to the session. You can extend this – and make it more fun if appropriate – by having photos of them looking more 'clever' or knowledgeable, or looking more excited about their work, or whatever is most relevant to the session.

2 You could create a big two-axis graph on a wall, with one axis representing level of 'enjoyment' and the other level of 'learning'. Give learners a sticky post-it or sticky dot and ask them to plot their position on the graph. (This could also be done via presentation or polling software.) This provides you with a quick ready-made evaluation graphic (Figure 10.3).

Figure 10.3 Enjoyment–Learning grid

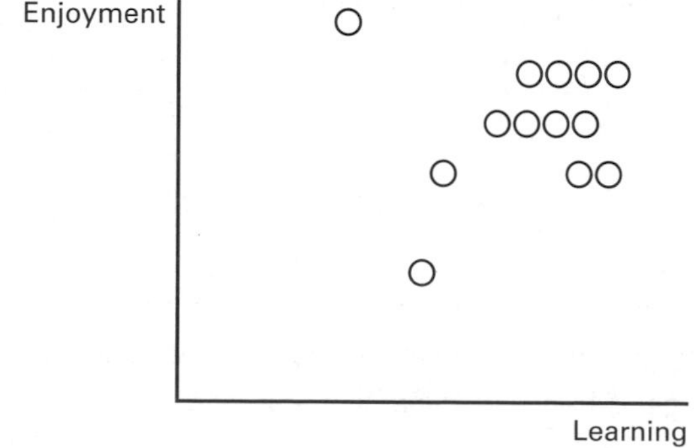

3. Set up two flipchart stands or designate areas of wall, and label them something similar to 'I liked X because Y' and 'I did not like X because Y'. X will equal an activity undertaken within the training. Give out sticky post-it notes and ask learners to complete and add at least one sentence to each wall.
4. Give out post-it notes, some shaped as 'hearts' and some as 'squares'. Ask learners to complete heart-shaped post-its for positive feedback and square shapes for 'suggestions for improvement' and stick them all on a flipchart or area of wall.
5. Have three buckets in the room – ideally a red, a green and a yellow one (traffic lights). Give each learner a ping-pong ball or small suitable item and ask them to put the ball in the green bucket if a session has met their objectives, in the yellow bucket if their objectives have only been partly met, and in the red bucket if their objectives have hardly been met at all. You could ask learners to do this after each main session, ideally as they leave the room for breaks so that you can do a quick summary. Hopefully – there will be more items in the green bucket by the end of the day!
6. Ask learners to describe to the group what they will tell their family about the learning event, when they get home that evening and what they will tell their manager about it when they return to work the next day.
7. Instead of issuing individual questionnaires, draw one big questionnaire on a flipchart or whiteboard and ask the group to work together to complete a joint evaluation. You might want to combine this with some individual verbal questions as well.
8. Hand out or show several pictures of faces, real or cartoon, showing different expressions (happy, confused, inspired, bored, excited, knowing, frustrated, confident, etc) and ask learners to say which they most relate to at this point in time. Another version of this is to have images of people climbing a tree or ladder (of knowledge) so learners can identify 'where they are' in terms of progress, as well as how they feel.
9. Invite learners to an 'evaluation café' one month after the training. This would just be a one-hour session, with sandwiches (at lunch or breakfast time) to share how they had started to apply their new knowledge in the workplace.
10. Invite learners' line managers to an evaluation café (as above), where they can share and compare their perceptions of how the L&D activity had impacted on team members and how they, as managers, have supported the transfer of learning into the workplace.

 Case Example 10.4

An informal approach to evaluation

Although we use formal evaluation forms, some of the best evaluation information we get is from the informal discussions after each training session where we all sit down to eat or drink something together.

We ask participants to tell us what they have learned, how the (overall) training is impacting on their skills and confidence, what they would like to include in further sessions, how we could improve things for them and for their general feedback on the training. Participants are usually more relaxed about this than completing the forms and give us really useful information.

Nadia Alonzi, Cooking and Budgeting Trainer, Edinburgh Cyrenians

Timing of evaluation

Along with determining best evaluation methods, you will also need to give some thought to the timing of evaluation activity and what is best done:

- prior to learning;
- at the beginning of the learning;
- during the learning;
- at the end of the learning;
- immediately after the learning;
- three months after, six months after, longer.

Again, this emphasizes the need for evaluation to be an ongoing process and not something to be left until the end of a learning programme.

Decisions about the timing of specific evaluation activities will depend on the purpose of your evaluation and the type of information you are collecting.

For example, to assess whether training has impacted on performance, it would make sense to leave this assessment until a reasonable time after the training. Showing an impact on performance one week after training may not be too impressive. However, proving an impact on performance six months after training suggests that the training has had long-lasting impact and that changes in performance are becoming entrenched.

Activity 10.2

Thinking back to Kirkpatrick's and Philips' levels of evaluation and the methods discussed above, or any others you can think of, complete the second and third columns in Table 10.4. Column 2 requires you to insert some methods that would be appropriate for the level of evaluation. Column 3 requires you to comment on the timing of each of your selected evaluation methods.

Table 10.4 Methods and timing of evaluation

Evaluation Level	Appropriate Methods	Timing
Level 1: Reaction		
Level 2: Learning		
Level 3: Behaviour (Application in workplace)		
Level 4: Results(Impact on organisation)		
Level 5: Return on Investment		

Case Example 10.5

An evaluation strategy (3)

We have a pre-course questionnaire five days before the learning event takes place. One of the questions asks the learner to measure their current understanding of the subject on a scale of 1–5. There is a similar measure on the immediate questionnaire, which is sent out up to two days after the L&D event. Again, it asks how far they would now measure their understanding. Six weeks later a post-course questionnaire is sent out and again the same measure is asked for.

We also ask the learners what has been in place to help them transfer their learning: it's felt that if particular departments are consistently showing that transfer is not being enabled, we can contact the relevant management team and explore how we can support this.

Linda George, Training Manager

Case study questions

1. What do you think about the three organisational approaches to evaluation, described in Case Examples 10.1, 10.2 and 10.5 above?
2. How do these case studies reflect any evaluation theories or models?
3. What do you like, or not like, about each approach?

Designing evaluation tools

There may be times in your evaluation activity when you need to design a specific tool, maybe a questionnaire or observation checklist in order to collect the required information.

Some simple rules to follow are:

- Begin by asking yourself: what is the specific purpose of the evaluation instrument? Identify the most appropriate type of instrument for the purpose – eg a questionnaire to use at the end of the session, a survey you can send out, a checklist to use for telephone interviews, an assessment activity for use by learners or their managers.
- Make sure your method is user-friendly. Put yourself in the shoes of the learner or manager it is aimed at – and check that your questions and instructions make sense. Is it easy and logical to follow? Will it be quick and straightforward to complete?
- Consider 'piloting' the instrument or questionnaire to check that your questions are understood as you intend them to be, that the instrument will generate the type of information you require, and that the information will be easy to analyse.

Asking the right questions

Just as in identifying learning needs, one of the most important aspects of evaluation is the questions that are asked. If the information that comes back is not very useful, then it is quite likely that the questions asked were too general, irrelevant or just not well considered.

For example, if you ask 'What did you enjoy most about the training day'? your respondents might well tell you about how good (or not) the sandwiches were or the fact that there was a car park near the venue. This is fine if it is the kind of information you want but if you really want to know about how much learners enjoyed the learning activities then you may need to be more specific, eg 'For each session please rate your enjoyment in relation to: 1) methods used, 2) learning content, and 3) the approach of the trainer.'

If you want to engage learners in transferring their learning and establish specific criteria for further evaluation, use specific questions which will hook into their (formal or informal) action plans, such as 'What three things will you take forward and implement in your workplace?'

Also when devising questions, consider what quantitative information and what qualitative information you want (see Table 10.5), and how these will be analysed. Quantitative information is usually easier to analyse than qualitative but qualitative will give you some of the detail you need to identify areas such as barriers and improvements.

Survey systems will allow you to set different types of questions – eg open, multiple-choice or rated questions, and you will need to consider the best style for the information you want to obtain. Once you have worked out the type of information you need, you can structure and word your questions accordingly.

Table 10.5 Qualitative and quantitative data

QUANTITATIVE INFORMATION	QUALITATIVE INFORMATION
Quantitative information is 'hard' data – eg statistics, definitions, and measurable responses to questions.	Qualitative information is 'soft' data – eg opinion, personal narrative and general comments.
Quantitative data is usually easy to measure and compare.	Quantitative data can be difficult to measure or compare.
Examples of quantitative data might be: attendance figures for a learning event, scores obtained in learning tests or outcomes of learning expressed on a ratings scale.	Examples of qualitative information might be: a learner's general comments about a learning programme and their suggestions for how it can be improved.

Activity 10.3

We have provided some (extracts of) evaluation questionnaires, in Figures 10.4, 10.5, 10.6 and 10.7.

1 Have a look at these and consider how they compare with the ones you use.
2 What do you consider to be the strengths and weaknesses of these examples?
3 Who is the information being requested for? And for what purposes?
4 Example 2 (Figure 10.5) requires a numerical response. What responses would you be happy with? Suppose the average for some of the questions was 6? Or 8.5? What would that mean and how would you respond to these scores?

Figure 10.4 Evaluation questionnaire – Example 1

Webinar Evaluation

Thank you for attending the session today and for sharing your feedback with us.

1. What were your key (up to 3) learning points from the session?

2. How will you make use of this learning?

3. Please tell us what you liked most about the event, and what you think should KEEP DOING?

4. And...anything you did not like about the event, or that you think we should STOP DOING?

5. Overall – would you rate the session as:

○ Excellent ○ Good ○ Just OK ○ Disappointing

6. Finally, please add any further feedback or comments.

Figure 10.5 Evaluation questionnaire – Example 2

The aim of this training is to ensure you are have the knowledge and skills required to conduct effective telephone interviews and that you feel confident to do this. For each of the areas below please indicate how confident you feel in your abilities–and indicate any areas where you need further information, support or practice.	
Topic Areas	**Comment re further needs**
1. Using the system Not at all 1 2 3 4 5 6 7 8 9 10 Fully	
2. Following the opening procedures Not at all 1 2 3 4 5 6 7 8 9 10 Fully	
3.Effective use of questioning to establish client needs Not at all 1 2 3 4 5 6 7 8 9 10 Fully	
4. Current range of customer option available (headlines) Not at all 1 2 3 4 5 6 7 8 9 10 Fully	
5. Option 1 – Full features and conditions Not at all 1 2 3 4 5 6 7 8 9 10 Fully	
6. Option 2 – Full features and conditions Not at all 1 2 3 4 5 6 7 8 9 10 Fully	
7. Option 3 – Full features and conditions Not at all 1 2 3 4 5 6 7 8 9 10 Fully	
8. Circumstances in which options can be varied Not at all 1 2 3 4 5 6 7 8 9 10 Fully	

Collecting evaluation information

Using samples

When applying evaluation methods, it may not always be feasible, necessary or good business practice to involve all learners. Instead, an appropriate sample of learners, managers, customers or work results can be determined and used to inform the evaluation.

Figure 10.6 Evaluation questionnaire – Example 3

LEARNING & DEVELOPMENT ACTIVITY EVALUATION

NAME:

PRE-ACTIVITY OBJECTIVES - Please complete the five questions below prior to the activity.

Your job demands a variety of skills and knowledge. Please list the ones you think are most important, indicating whether they are essential or developmental.
Which of the above do you plan to improve through completion of this learning and development activity?
What knowledge do you expect to gain, or what competencies do you expect to develop through completing this training?
Which aspects of your role do you expect to do differently on completion of the proposed learning and development activity?
Are there any specific directorate/corporate objectives that you aim to deliver/assist with on completion of the learning and development activity?

POST-ACTIVITY (EMPLOYEE) – To be completed within one month of the activity.

Just as it is important to think about your learning objectives before a training/development activity, it is equally important to evaluate what you have learned afterwards, in order for you to successfully transfer your learning into the workplace. Use the following template to review how useful the activity has been. You should then discuss this with your line manager. This discussion will ensure that you get maximum benefit from the activity and will help further your development.

Look back to the learning objectives that you identified before the activity. To what degree were these achieved? [Please circle the words that most accurately reflect your experience.]		
Fully achieved	Partially achieved	Not achieved
Please list any learning objectives that were not achieved.		
How will you apply newly acquired skills, knowledge or behaviour at work? Consider any relevant timescales.		

POST-ACTIVITY (MANAGER) – To be completed within four months of the activity

Has the employee been given appropriate support to enable him/her to implement the newly acquired knowledge, skills and/or behaviours developed through learning and development?
How has the employee applied the newly acquired skills, knowledge or behaviour at work?

HUMAN RESOURCES DIRECTORATE, JAMESTOWN, ISLAND OF ST HELENA, SOUTH ATLANTIC OCEAN, STHL 1ZZ

Provided by Jackie Moyce, HR Officer (Adapted, with permission, from original used by the HR Directorate, St Helena Government)

Figure 10.7 Evaluation questionnaire – Example 4

Name:		**Course Title:**		**Date:**	
Please rate your knowledge and or skill level AFTER attending the course					
1	None		Please explain your response a bit more here.		
2	Just aware				
3	I know a bit more				
4	I know a lot more				
5	I am confident in the subject area				
How often have you made use of the knowledge/skill?					
1	Not at all yet		Please explain your response a bit more here.		
2	Just once				
3	Occasionally				
4	Regularly				
5	Almost every day				
Please give an example of how you have applied your learning in the workplace					
Have you met with your line manager to discuss your learning from the course?					
1	Yes				
2	No				
What support have you been given to help apply your learning back at work?					
1	None		Please tick all that apply - and please explain your response a bit more here.		
2	Verbal encouragement				
3	Supported by experienced colleague				
4	Supported by my line manager				
5	Other				
What other support would have been useful for you?					
Thank you for completing this survey					

Samples should be large enough to be credible and to give a fair representation of different groups and types of learner but be small enough to avoid placing a burden on the business. You might decide, for example, to involve 'representative' learners from different departments, different grades or different levels of experience in your evaluation activity rather than every learner.

Handling information appropriately and in line with legislation

We should always remember that information collected for evaluation can include very personal and sensitive data – learners' performance results, learners' opinions of others, others' opinions of learners. What may just be interesting evaluation data to you may be someone else's individual work results or negative feedback on their performance. Therefore, it is crucial that you follow good practice when collecting, analysing, using and storing information.

Think carefully about whether information can be collected anonymously and always look for ways to validate information, such as finding different sources saying the same thing, or matching information against other types of data, before acting on it.

There should always be a good reason for collecting particular information, which should be explained to contributors, and it should be collected and stored in line with your country's data protection legislation. In the UK that is the 2018 Data Protection Act.

PAUSE FOR THOUGHT

Make a note to access your local data protection legislation and ensure you are familiar with its requirements, particularly in the context of collecting and storing evaluation data.

> 'While there is no silver bullet to define ROI, talent development is looking for ways to measure learning based on team metrics and retention. Executives and people managers agree that retention and team metrics are the best ways to demonstrate the success of learning programmes.'
>
> *Workplace Learning and Development Report, 2018*, LinkedIn Learning

Analysing information

The availability of survey and applications programmes for analysing, manipulating and presenting data has made data analysis an increasingly user-friendly and interesting activity to undertake.

Survey programmes and spreadsheets allow us to analyse, organise and view data in different ways, and to establish, for example:

- ratings relating to levels of learning or transfer of learning to the workplace;
- ratings relating to improvements in performance;
- ratings applied to different 'reaction factors' – the training approach, the venue, the learning experience.

Ratings and scores can be 'sliced', further analysed and compared to give us information such as:

- key learning outcomes in relation to different groups, contexts or training delivery factors (eg timing, trainer, methods, follow-up approach);
- percentage improvements in performance for an individual, for a group of learners, for learners who work to a particular manager or who used a particular learning transfer method;

- comparison of work results between trained groups and control groups (who have not had the training);
- areas of knowledge or skill where improvement levels are greatest or lowest;
- areas where learning is still required;
- areas where learning is high but has not been transferred to the workplace;
- a timeline of how skills have improved in a certain area over a particular period;
- patterns in learning or of learner satisfaction with training activities;
- unusual or inconsistent 'scores' requiring further investigation.

This kind of information enables us to draw important conclusions about the impact and effectiveness of learning approaches and learning events, most importantly, about their impact on business/organisational performance. The data can also reveal: further learning needs, potential skills or knowledge gaps and future requirements of the L&D function; the performance of individual trainers and the support provided by managers; the relative costs of different training initiatives; and the benefits of training in relation to costs incurred. Good data and data analysis is invaluable, giving us a sound evidence basis from which we can determine and justify improvement action and make our recommendations.

PAUSE FOR THOUGHT

Select any five items of information from the lists above and consider how each item of information could inform improvements to L&D activities.

Presenting findings and making recommendations

We can present our evaluation findings in the form of:

- a report;
- a presentation at a meeting;
- tables of statistics;
- diagrams, charts, graphs;
- images representing changes and improvements

A good structure to follow for an evaluation report or a presentation is the evaluation process described in this chapter, ie:

- what was evaluated (scope);
- purposes of the evaluation (evaluation criteria);
- how evaluation was undertaken (methods, participants, timing);

- findings (key conclusions from the analysis);
- recommendations.

If you are presenting information to different stakeholder groups, you might want to emphasise information relating to their particular area of interest and any improvement or ongoing actions that are required from them. For example:

For learning sponsors:

- the business benefits gained from their time/money/emotional investment;
- the case for continuing funding and support for the same training.

For line managers:

- improvements in knowledge, skills and performance;
- ways in which managers can support team members' ongoing learning.

For learners in the programme:

- clarification of learning achievements;
- performance improvements;
- how they may have influenced further developments.

For the training team:

- confirmation of 'successes';
- required changes and updates to the programme.

For course organisers:

- required changes to admin procedures;
- required changes to venue or 'hospitality' arrangements.

Using images/visual representations makes data more accessible and interesting, and makes patterns, trends and deviations more easily apparent. Simple visuals are easy to create within survey software or standard office applications, such as spreadsheets. (An Internet search will reveal a number of video tutorials relating to 'presenting data' or 'using tables, charts and graphs'.) Even a bar graph, or a bar graph with symbolic people (of different heights) rather than just columns, will make information more eye-catching. You could also consider 'talking heads' video clips where learners describe how their performance has changed as a result of the development programme.

Whilst we would encourage you to be creative in your communication, always remember who your audience is and the purpose of your communication. Presenting a professional, business-focused, credible message is ultimately more important than having lots of colourful graphics – but you can do both. For some ideas for good visuals to represent evaluation outcomes, have a look at the surveys mentioned in this and other chapters in this book and at some of the Figures, such as the infographic at Figure 1.5 in Chapter 1.

> 'As well as our formal evaluation report, we held a feedback session where we presented the key points from the evaluation. We used a visual timeline of where the

team started and key milestones along the way. We also did motivational exercises such as a quiz about the improvements and some physical exercises, such as getting the group to stand along a continuum based on before and after scores. In this way, everyone could see and 'own' the improvements brought about by the programme.'

Kieleigh Dixon, Talent and Leadership Development Manager

 Case Example 10.6

An exercise in evaluating online learning

Gordon Linford, a Risk Management Specialist and Trainer developed an online learning module for his client. The requirements of the presentation were that it would:

- be specific to their own H&S policies, regulations and processes;
- cover specific selected H&S/staff safety issues (eg staff whereabouts, driving for work);
- promote and develop staffs understanding of their personal welfare responsibilities;
- be developed in a way that made it engaging for staff (not just the usual presentation);
- be accessible to staff via their laptops, tablets, mobiles, etc 'wherever and whenever';
- allow staff members' 'completion' of the presentation to be monitored and logged (this was essential for the company's induction and compliance procedures).

Gordon developed a 30-minute presentation using a commercially available presentation tool which allows the main user to develop their own content and an explanatory voice-over. A built-in time-bar ensures that people viewing the session cannot fast-forward or skip (and have to view at least 90 per cent to access a completion certificate for the session).

The presentation worked well and has now been viewed over 275 times. As a result of this success, the client has commissioned, and Gordon has provided, two other presentations on different H&S themes.

Case study questions

1. How could Gordon evaluate the suite of three online learning presentations?
2. What should he seek to find out (ie his evaluation criteria)?
3. What evaluation methods would you recommend he use?
4. What timing of evaluation would you advise?

'Evaluating training-related performance improvement provides the most credible basis in the argument for more interventions.'

Peter J Mayes, Founder and Editor, www.trainerbase.co.uk

What next?

The activities below will help consolidate your learning from this chapter:

1 Research your organisation's approach to evaluation:
   - Is it done?
   - What level does the evaluation usually go to?
   - How is evaluation data collected?
   - How is the data used?
   - How could the approach be improved?

2 Devise an evaluation plan for a piece of learning that you are undertaking (for example, your CIPD programme). Consider:
   - What impact do you want it to have?
   - How will you measure that impact?
   - How will you know you have achieved?
   - How could you present your findings?

3 Tweet your ideas for fun/creative ways of evaluating learning activities using the hashtag #LDPintheW and copy in the account @ LDPintheW.

References

Brinkerhoff, RO (2003) *The Success Case Method: Find out quickly what's working and what's not,* Berrett-Koehler, San Francisco, CA

Easterby-Smith, M (1994) *Evaluating Management Development, Training and Education*, Gower, Aldershot, UK

Findcourses (2018) *UK L&D Report: 2018 Benchmark Your Workplace Learning Strategy*, https://www.findcourses.co.uk/inspiration/learning-report-2018-13279 (archived at https://perma.cc/9RUQ-2UVG)

Kirkpatrick, D (1994) *Evaluating Training Programmes,* Berrett-Koehler, San Francisco, CA

Lea, P (2019) *Measuring the Business Impact of Learning,* LEO Learning and Watershed, https://leolearning.com/2019/02/measuring-the-business-impact-of-learning-2019 (archived at https://perma.cc/DH37-P8VW)

LinkedIn Learning, *2018 Workplace Learning and Development Report*, https://learning.linkedin.com/resources/workplace-learning-report-2018 (archived at https://perma.cc/XBT2-PXXR)

Phillips, J and Phillips, PP (2007) *Show Me the Money: How to determine ROI in people, projects, and programs,* Berrett-Koehler, San Francisco, CA

Phillips, J (1991) *Handbook of Training Evaluation and Measurement Methods*, 2nd edn, Gulf Publishing, Houston, TX

Taylor, D (2018) *The Learning and Development Global Sentiment Survey*, http://donaldhtaylor.co.uk/wp-content/uploads/10_GSS-2018-mail.pdf (archived at https://perma.cc/X3B7-R78A)

Thalheimer, W (2018) *Donald Kirkpatrick was not the Originator of the Four Level Model of Learning Evaluation,* www.worklearning.com/2018/01/30/donald-kirkpatrick-was-not-the-originator-of-the-four-level-model-of-learning-evaluation/ (archived at https://perma.cc/CRZ2-G4FW)

Towards Maturity (2016) *Making an Impact: How L&D leaders can demonstrate value,* https://towardsmaturity.org/elements/uploads/In-Focus_2016_-_Making_an_Impact.pdf (archived at https://perma.cc/3486-5RVU)

Towards Maturity (2017) *Making an Impact: How L&D leaders can demonstrate value,*

(*continued*)

(*Continued*)

https://towardsmaturity.org/2017/7/17/in-focus-impact-how-demonstrate-value/ (archived at https://perma.cc/29TA-NLDF)

Wells, D (2019) What will 2019 bring for learning and development? *People Management*, **21** January 2019, https://www.peoplemanagement.co.uk/voices/comment/what-will-2009-bring-learning-and-development (archived at https://perma.cc/F5TT-KC4C)

Explore further

Anderson, V (2007) *The Value of Learning: From return on investment to return on expectation*, CIPD, London

Bee, R and Bee, F (2003) *Learning Needs Analysis and Evaluation*, 2nd edn, CIPD, London

Brinkerhoff, RO (2006) *Telling Training's Story: Evaluation made simple, credible and effective*, Berrett-Koehler, London

Griffin, R (2014) *Complete Training Evaluation: The comprehensive guide to measuring return on investment*, Kogan Page, London

CIPD *Factsheet: Evaluation*, www.cipd.co.uk/subjects/lrnanddev/evaluation/evatrain.htm (archived at https://perma.cc/6YJJ-BERJ)

CIPD *Factsheet, Data Protection*, www.cipd.co.uk/subjects/emplaw/dataprot/dataprotec.htm (archived at https://perma.cc/Z867-R9FU)

Useful resources

Websites

www.businessballs.com (archived at https://perma.cc/UW7U-5HS8)

www.freeonlinesurveys.com (archived at https://perma.cc/4FTN-ZHPP)

www.surveymonkey.com (archived at https://perma.cc/5H4T-TKWS)

www.smart-survey.co.uk (archived at https://perma.cc/BRS6-7CUS)

INDEX